Celluloid China

Celluloid China

Cinematic Encounters
with Culture and Society

Harry H. Kuoshu

Southern Illinois University Press
Carbondale and Edwardsville

05   04   03   02   4   3   2   1

Library of Congress Cataloging-in-Publication Data

Kuoshu, Harry H., date.
  Celluloid China : cinematic encounters with culture and
  society / Harry H. Kuoshu.
    p. cm.
  Includes bibliographical references and index.
    1. Film criticism—China. 2. Motion pictures—China. 1. Title.

PN1995 .K86 2002
791.43'75'0951—dc21
ISBN 0-8093-2455-5 (alk. paper)
ISBN 0-8093-2456-3 (pbk. : alk. paper)   2002018750

Printed on recycled paper. ♻

The paper used in this publication meets the minimum requirements of American
National Standard for Information Sciences—Permanence of Paper for Printed Library
Materials, ANSI Z39.48-1992. ∞

In memory of my father, **Xing Xu (1921–2001),** who was a mentor and friend.

Contents

Illustrations

Preface

The idea of writing and compiling an introductory book on Chinese film evolved during my years of teaching classes in this subject area at Reed College in Portland, Oregon, and at Northeastern University in Boston. The immediate and obvious benefit of this book for students and instructors in Chinese film is the availability of readings that they would otherwise have to seek from different books, anthologies, and journals. More importantly, this book was created with American college students in mind. It provides a teaching framework for the source materials and complements the academic and scholarly research essays with classroom activities, making all of them more accessible to college students.

In recent years, especially since the mid-1980s when Chinese Fifth Generation filmmaking began drawing increasing international attention, Chinese film studies have attracted a substantial amount of writing and translation. This body of literature makes teaching a Chinese film class both more feasible and more exciting. It enables such a class to broaden the cinematic analysis to include an investigation of cultural, cross-cultural, intellectual, social, ethnic, political, and artistic issues. This body of literature also illustrates how a film can provide distinctive samples of artistic fashion, social taste, ideological tension, cultural geography, and historical moments. In other words, Chinese film has become an ideal pedagogical subject for a cross-cultural and interdisciplinary class.

The films selected for this book were produced solely in the People's Republic of China (PRC) and do not include many important titles produced in other parts of today's Chinese-speaking world, such as Hong Kong or Taiwan. This exclusion is due by no means to prejudice but rather to a pedagogical choice to focus on films that reveal certain predominant ideological discourses, historical events, and cinematic trends that affect mostly mainland China, including the May 4th New Cultural Movement, leftist filmmaking in pre-PRC Shanghai, the cultural fad of Nora-like Chinese "new women," the war with Japan, the founding of the PRC, the anti-rightist campaign, the Cultural Revolution, a post-Mao cultural identity crisis ("roots-searching"), and postsocialist ideological or existential anxieties. This focus allows for a better understanding of both the genesis of a special kind of film art from the PRC

and the culture and society that can be learned from films. While this particular book is intended for use in a film class about PRC films, I hasten to note that
other kinds of Chinese film classes are increasingly in demand. Among them—
as influenced by recent scholarship—is a class on Chinese films more broadly
defined, including films from Hong Kong and Taiwan and even the Chinese cinema of diaspora in certain overseas Chinese communities. Such a class may offer
an opportunity to place these additional cinematic efforts in a global context for
comparative study.

In order to provide varying perspectives for an in-depth understanding of
representative films from the PRC, this book organizes fifteen films into five
topics: (1) History In and Out of Melodrama: Glory, Guilt, and Fantasy, (2)
Speaking for the *Other*: Changing Allegorical Roles for Women, (3) Cinema
Exotica: Ethnic Minorities as the PRC's "Internal *Other*," (4) The Chinese
Western: Roots Hidden in the Yellow Earth, and (5) New City Films: Beyond-
Yellow-Earth Experiences of Postsocialism. Whereas the first two sections offer
historical perspectives on the different periods of Chinese filmmaking, the last
three sections focus on a few important aspects of the post-Mao new cinema.
Each section begins with a brief introduction, explaining the topics and high-
lighting related issues. Although I have chosen more films produced since the
1980s, that is, films of the post-Mao new cinema, I have also made sure that students sample earlier films to get a sense of Chinese film history. For this purpose,
I selected one film from the 1930s, one from the 1940s, and one from the 1960s.
An overview of the generations of filmmaking in mainland China precedes the
film sections to enhance the students' sense of history. This overview uses the
careers of the film artists whose films are selected in this book to illustrate the
general characteristics of the history of filmmaking. The criteria for film selection have been shaped by current criticism and scholarship, by the central issues
in this book, by feedback from students at Reed College and Northeastern
University, and by the availability of films and videos with English subtitles.
This last factor is obviously crucial to the success of a film class. (Information
for purchasing Chinese film videos and for renting Chinese films is given at the
back of the book.)

For each film under discussion, I have written introductory notes designed
to enhance the students' comprehension of production and related cultural
issues. Whenever available, I have also selected a few passages from the director's own words about the film, found under "Director's Notes." While some
critics are dubious about the value of such words in contributing toward our
understanding of films (Foucault, for example, has long reduced the authors to

mouthpieces for certain discourses), I still believe in the individual's role in the discursive dynamics—here, an *auteur* film director focusing our attention on various ideological tensions in a particular artistic fashion. (Note: The sources of some of these texts are Chinese. Unless otherwise noted, the translations of all passages of Chinese sources in this book are mine.) Students will then find critical essays or book chapters about the film under discussion. To reduce the number of notes and to make the bibliographical information about the selected films more comprehensive, author/date references (for example, Berry 1988a) are used in these texts; all refer to a single bibliography found at the end of the book. Suggested reading for some films that have received more critical attention are given at the end of my introductory notes. In the bibliography, the full citation of these titles and the titles of some English-language books on Chinese cinema are marked with asterisks—they constitute a further reading list for a Chinese film class.

Discussion questions for these fifteen films are found in Appendix 1. In class, students should be required to read the texts of criticism before they consider the discussion questions. The purpose of these questions is to help in analyzing the films and to highlight key issues in each film. In addition, these questions should serve as a catalyst for more questions from students. Some of these discussion questions may also be easily turned into project assignments that may help students with cinematic analysis, for example, an examination of editing styles by focusing on some sequences from *Street Angel;* an investigation of the general color schemes used in *Black Cannon Incident, Sacrificed Youth,* or *Ju Dou;* a closer look at the composition and interplay of *mise-en-scènes* in *Good Morning, Beijing;* a character analysis for better understanding the drama of *Hibiscus Town;* an exploration of Chinese cinematic symbolism through watching *Old Well* carefully; and so on.

So many people have helped in the completion of this book. Among them, I would like especially to thank the following persons: Lucy and Momo, my wife and daughter, for allowing me to "disappear" to work in our study; Charles Wu, my mentor and three-year-colleague at Reed College, for his ideas and suggestions; Dennis Cokely for his support as my department chair at Northeastern University and for his constant computer help; Stephen Sadow for his editorial advice; Jill Kelly for her ideas and indispensable editorial assistance; and Sandra Maloney for manuscript preparation in the early stage of the project. Most important of all, I am indebted to the authors of the film criticism used in this book; they are my inspiration. A generous award by the Minority Faculty Development Fund from Northeastern University greatly facilitated my work.

Finally, I hope that teachers, students, and general readers will find this an interesting, stimulating introduction to Chinese film and will come away with not only a better sense of film art but also some sharpened insights into Chinese culture and society.

Celluloid China

Overview The Filmmaking Generations

The year 1905 saw the first Chinese film—an opera recorded by a photography shop in Beijing; 1921 saw the first feature-length film, *Yan ruisheng*, a screen adaptation of a popular stage play (a "civilized play," as it was then called); 1931 saw the first sound film, *Singsong Girl Red Peony*. Dates like these offer a quick sense of the history of the burgeoning Chinese film industry, and if one is familiar with the title mentioned or knows the director, the quick sense of history is substantiated by an understanding supported by textual details. This effect is what I hope to achieve in this overview: I use a broader concept of filmmaking "generations" to highlight some characteristics of almost a century of Chinese filmmaking, and I illustrate this historical outline with the careers of those directors whose films are included in this book, with the hope that the reader will feel better related to this history.

In the twentieth century, as critics commonly assert, Chinese filmmaking has generated five or six chronological groups, or generations, of filmmakers. The uncertainty of the total number of generations, as will be discussed later, is primarily due to a dispute about whether the most recent group of Chinese film directors should be labeled the Sixth Generation and whether this group of artists has actually and sufficiently challenged the conventional concept of filmmaking generations so that they should not be considered a generation any more. Before these younger directors broke onto the scene, film scholars had commonly divided Chinese filmmakers into five generations. The First Generation refers to China's film pioneers of the 1920s; the Second Generation, the leftist filmmakers of the 1930s and 1940s (mostly working for various private film studios in Shanghai); the Third Generation, mostly Yan'an-trained filmmakers who became important in the early PRC cinema of the 1950s (Yan'an, a rural town in northwest China, was the capital of the Communist revolution before the founding of the PRC); the Fourth Generation, those trained in the early 1960s but who had to wait until the post-Mao late 1970s to start making films; and the Fifth Generation, the first post-Mao graduating class from Beijing Film Academy and other young directors who joined them in the post-Mao cinematic new wave.

It is important to know that most film scholars use the five/six-generation concept with discomfort because of its oversimplification. Indeed, as with any

1

simplification, this minimal chronology of Chinese film history hardly accounts for the richness and diversity of the changing film culture. However, the simplicity of this chronology allows us to cut Chinese filmmaking history into a few easily remembered blocks through which we may identify changing social concerns, trace common discourses, contrast different artistic styles, and contextualize individual films. This simplification will be enriched and revised through our later viewing, reading, and studying of Chinese films.

The First and Second Generations

These two generations were making films in the 1920s, 1930s, and 1940s, the three decades prior to the founding of the PRC in 1949, and they were making them in major treaty-port cities with foreign concessions and foreign cultural presence. Just as with any national industry that had to compete with foreign companies in this semi-colonial nation with its forced-open sea ports since the Opium Wars, small Chinese film companies had to grow in the shadow of the foreign film industries. In these decades, most films shown in China were foreign-made. In 1929, whereas Chinese companies produced fewer than 50 films, 450 films were imported, 90 percent from America (Paul Clark 1987b, 7). To some extent, this was not a bad year in Chinese filmmaking; Chinese companies from 1921 to 1931 produced about 650 films (Cheng et al. 1963, 1:56). The registered number of Chinese film companies reached 141 in 1926, even though only about 40 among them actually produced films (Cheng et al. 1963, 1:53–54).

The artists of these two filmmaking generations are the direct descendants of the May 4th New Cultural Movement of 1919, a national culture critique and renovation in response to the mixed calls of social Darwinism, bourgeois individualism, and Marxism. Noted for their youthful idealism and sentimentality, these artists were strongly concerned with the social and cultural crisis that China faced as it entered the twentieth century. Most of them are referred to as leftist filmmakers, not because they were members of the Chinese Communist Party necessarily, but rather, as Leo Lee suggests, because of their common obsession with the socially oppressed and with social ills (1991, 7). This obsession has always reflected a strong sense of cultural crisis that occurred as Chinese national identity confronted Western colonialism; this obsession is cherished widely by intellectuals as a "social stance of discontent" (see Lee 1991, 7).

Many prominent scriptwriters, directors, and actors of Shanghai in the 1930s were eager to belong to the Film Group, a subdivision of the League of

Left-Wing Writers. To produce art films with social concerns, leftist filmmakers had to deal with government censorship (the Nationalist government's film censorship rules were introduced in 1929), to contend with the challenge of foreign films, and to resist the treaty-port cities' commercial thrust. *Street Angel* (*Malu tianshi*, 1937), selected in this book, illustrates all these features: it concerns the poor people living in the "lower depths" of metropolitan Shanghai; it resembles a classical Hollywood movie but actually has revised the Hollywood formula by introducing other cinematic elements like montage; it entertains as the market requires but delivers serious social and political messages with the entertainment; and it delivers its social and political messages subtly so that it may pass the censors.

Among the First and Second Generation artists, the scriptwriters were preeminent, receiving more critical attention than the directors. This preeminence of the writers indicated, on the one hand, how a theatrical play and a film were considered almost the same kind of art—to the Chinese, film was just a "shadow play"; on the other hand, it indicated how the literary elite of the New Cultural movement were trying to cast their influence on both arts. Leo Lee suggests that "the modern Chinese film grew into a mature art form by virtue of its closer interaction with modern Chinese literature" (1991, 6). Literary works were adapted into films, writers and playwrights were turned into scriptwriters, and films were considered the newest branch of literature. "The interaction between literature and film, which began in the early 30s and culminated in the late 40s," Lee believes, "produced a generic tradition of social realism, which in turn yields an aesthetic legacy of film style" (1991, 6). The general feeling produced by this filmmaking legacy is also identical with that of modern Chinese literature, showing, as Rey Chow sums up, "a profound unhappiness, and unabashed sentimentalism, and a deep longing for what is impossible" (1991, 121). Two film artists, whose films appear in this book, will help describe this period.

The director of *Street Angel*, Yuan Muzhi (1909–78), illustrates a certain continuity between various periods of Chinese filmmaking; his film career links Shanghai's leftist filmmaking to Yan'an filmmaking, the influence of the former Soviet Union, and the PRC's early cinema. Yuan had been a successful stage actor in Shanghai, known as "the man with a thousand faces," before he joined Diantong Film Studio, then the base of progressive filmmaking. There he successfully wrote and acted in his first film, *Plunder of Peach and Plum* (*Taoli jie*, 1934), the story of a young person's social disillusionment. From that point, Yuan displayed his diverse talents in scriptwriting, directing, and acting. Yuan's

Street Angel was one of over fifty leftist films produced prior to 1937 when Shanghai was occupied by Japanese troops and it became an "orphan island"; the Chinese film industry there was dispersed to Wuhan, Chongqing, Hong Kong, and Yan'an. Not until 1946 did progressive filmmakers return to Shanghai to create another brief golden age of leftist filmmaking for three years—before the founding of the People's Republic in 1949. When Shanghai was lost to the Japanese in 1938, Yuan traveled to Yan'an and founded the Red Army's Yan'an Film Troupe; en route, he had stopped in Hong Kong and purchased the necessary equipment and supplies. At Yan'an, he directed a documentary film about life there. In 1940, Yuan traveled to Russia to study, and there he finished postproduction work on his full-length documentary about Yan'an. Upon his return to China in October 1946, Yuan founded Dongbei Film Studio. Equipped with what had been left behind by the Japanese occupiers, Dongbei became the first of the PRC's state-owned film studios.

The second example is Tian Han (1898–1968), whose *Three Women* (*Liren xing*, 1949) was produced during the years when the leftist filmmakers returned to Shanghai after Japanese surrender and used "orphan-island" Shanghai as the setting for their stories. Tian himself has always been better known as a playwright than as a scriptwriter. *Three Women* is actually an adaptation of his stage play of the same title. Tian illustrates early Chinese filmmaking's close relationship with theater and its heavy reliance on script.

Tian Han returned from Japan in 1921 to start a literary career in Shanghai. His stay in Japan had exposed him to Western ideas, and he had been greatly inspired by the May 4th New Cultural Movement of 1919. In 1923, Tian established the Southern Society (Nanguo she) to promote experiments in a new kind of theater. Three years later, the society evolved into the Southern Movie-Theater Society (Nanguo dianying jushe) to justify its additional interest in writing for a new art form: theater on-screen. Tian's statement for the society reads: "Wine, music and film are the three greatest creations of human beings. Among them, film is the youngest and the most attractive since it can produce a dream in the daytime. Dream is freedom for the heart; any bitterness accumulated here from the oppression of the real world can be completely released. Nevertheless, one is not supposed to make a false dream" (qtd. in Cheng et al. 1963, 1:112). Tian's earlier film scripts were noted for their romantic defiance of the real world.

The harsh Chinese social reality, however, soon changed Tian's outlook. In the 1930s, Tian published a self-critique, believing that his romanticism had not been very helpful in fighting bourgeois vulgarity and imperialist cultural hegemony. Discarding romanticism for rationalism, he also turned more radically left-wing: he joined the left-wing writers association as well as the Communist Party and was even imprisoned briefly for his political affiliation. His scripts started to show more social concern; *Three Women* is a good example.

Shanghai was the site of Tian's literary career; here he wrote over twenty plays and about a dozen film scripts. After 1948, Tian left Shanghai to join the new regime. His writing became secondary as he assumed administrative duties as a cultural leader for the new China.

The Third Generation

If the geographical locus for the first two generations of filmmaking was Shanghai, that of the Third Generation was Yan'an, which was the birthplace of, and trademark for, Mao's theory that the arts should be both mass media and weapons in the revolutionary cause. This strong emphasis on the mass nature of the arts and their utility as weapons alienated the older generations of film directors. Although many of these directors continued to make films during the early years of the PRC, they found it hard to adapt to the new ideological mode of these now highly didactic arts. Enter the Third Generation, a new group of directors either trained at Yan'an or quickly trained during the beginning years of the PRC. As private film companies soon merged into state-owned studios in the 1950s, the Third Generation directors became the new blood who built up a nationwide studio system closely monitored by the Communist Party.

Social realism, the legacy of leftist filmmaking from the earlier period, was redefined. First known as "socialist realism," it included the Yan'an formula of arts as mass media plus weapons for revolutionary causes; then, after China broke with the Soviet Union, as a result of the Chinese Communist Party's resistance to "Soviet revisionism" by not joining in the repudiation of Stalin, it turned into "socialist realism and revolutionary romanticism" in order to distance itself from Russian influences. With the newly added romanticism, this artistic convention could maintain revolutionary ideals and its representational hyperbole.

In this book, Xie Jin (b. 1923) represents the Third Generation, illustrating not just its years of growth in the 1950s and the 1960s but also how it became an obstacle to the post-Mao new cinema—the younger generations, for instance, had to denounce the "Xie Jin model" to find their breakthroughs. "Xie Jin's model," as Zhu Dake, a Chinese film critic, defines it, is a "magnificent moral fairy tale in which all social contradictions are resolved." He goes on to explain that the model "consists of a variety of both superficial and profound cultural codes. All follow some kind of common structure, function, and characteristics. An outstanding example is the magnification of emotions: the moral enthusiasm tactically centered around the protagonist and ingeniously extended to others evokes profuse tears from performers and audience alike, manipulating the audience to accept the conventional morality of the artist" (Semsel et al. 1990, 144–45). Reflecting a post-Mao disgust with propaganda, Zhu Dake compares this manipulation of emotions to the dissemination of religion in the Middle Ages. More interestingly, he also notices how Xie Jin appropriates the classical Hollywood model by following the pattern in which good is wronged, value is discovered, morality changes through persuasion, and good conquers evil.

The two Xie Jin films here serve as good examples. *Two Stage Sisters* (*Wutai jiemei*, 1965), which depicts how women are drawn to the Chinese Communist revolution, illustrates Third Generation filmmaking toward the end of its years of growth. It presents a mature aesthetic with didactic inspiration, melodramatic tension, and warring spirit. The other film, *Hibiscus Town* (*Furong zhen*, 1986), shows the Third Generation as political critics in the post-Mao era. This film too has a female lead. This time, however, she is not drawn to the revolution but becomes the target of it; her misery shows how the revolution has erred. The film is the call of the believer for the revolution to correct its mistakes, and it implies a confidence that the revolution has the ability to do so.

Xie Jin had a theater background. He started his film career in Shanghai in 1948, working as assistant to various directors. With the founding of the PRC, he enrolled in Revolutionary University in northern China for two years. After graduation, he was assigned to work at Changjiang Studio, which was later merged into the state-owned Shanghai Film Studio. In 1954, Xie became one of the first group of film directors appointed in the PRC. His fame was soon established with *Woman Basketball Player No. 5* (*Nülan wuhao*, 1957) and *The Red Detachment of Women* (*Hongse niangzijun*, 1961)—now PRC classics. *Two Stage Sisters,* however, was banned during a prelude to the Cultural Revolution. The ban was lifted fifteen years later when the film won the British Film Association's annual award at the London Film Festival.

After being attacked as a bourgeois artist at the start of the Cultural Revolution, Xie was assigned in 1970 to shoot "revolutionary films." The real "revolution" for him, however, came a decade later when he pioneered a bold criticism on-screen of the Party's bureaucratism and abuse of power, shown in such films as *The Legend of Tianyun Mountain* (*Tianyunshan chuanqi*, 1980) and *Hibiscus Town*. During the decades prior to and after the Cultural Revolution, Xie had a profound influence on Chinese filmmaking.

The Fourth Generation

Although most Fourth Generation directors were trained in the 1960s, their chance in filmmaking came after post-Mao 1979 when the whole nation was licking its cultural and social wounds through political, intellectual, and artistic means, such as the democracy movement, traumatic literature, misty poetry, expressionist theater, and modernist painting. The Fourth Generation filmmakers joined this trend by proposing a Bazinian *documentary aesthetics (jishi meixue)*, a documentary realism based on the translation of French film theorist André Bazin's writings on cinematic realism. This stylistic breakthrough emphasized a humanist prose style versus revolutionary melodrama, distinctive cinematic expressions versus the traditional mode of theatricality, and the individual styles of the auteur director versus the political monopoly. A groundbreaking article by Li Tuo and Zhang Nuanxin, "On the Modernization of Film Language," is often hailed as the proclamation of Fourth Generation filmmaking.

Rehumanization (renxing de fugui) came hand in hand with the documentary aesthetics to emancipate human beings from the yoke of a political dominance that had very much simplified and even denied any human nature other than that based on social class affiliation. To undermine that characters had been stereotyped according to social-class typology, rehumanization in films presented socially ambivalent characters exposed to a much wider spectrum of influences: cultural, ethical, social, historical, physical, and psychological. An ambivalence associated with the complexity of human nature became the index of this much-desired artistic sophistication. Sharing the "culture fervor" (a broad cultural retrospection and reevaluation begun in the mid-1980s) of those involved in roots-searching, film critics quickly realized that the artistic sophistication achieved by rehumanization could be described as a replacement of social-class logic by cultural logic. Critics generally believed that these cultural concerns were making Chinese films and their receptions more sophisticated and thus more artistic.

The fading away of dramatic intensity and the increasing ambivalence in human characterization helped form a new Chinese cinema alienated from the class struggle ideology of Maoist China. The change here, again, is better understood through the appeal of Bazin's ideas. Ever since 1979, Bazin's ideas had appeared repeatedly in nationwide discussions that featured such themes as "film's divorce from drama" and "an effort to find film's own language." This fascination with Bazin was later seen by Chinese film critic Dai Jinhua as both "a historical misreading" and "a historical strategy" that helped Chinese film-makers subvert their assigned social and political roles as tools for propaganda (Dai Jinhua 1989, 4). Just as Bazin tried to distance film art from the dominant bourgeois ideology in the West, Chinese filmmakers tried to distance it from the dominant ideology of the Communist Party in China. Although dealing with different kinds of dominance, the same distancing effort produced this histori-cal coincidence. The Chinese filmmakers, with aspirations to restore the status of the individual on humanist terms, certainly made good use of many Bazinian arguments (such as his antagonism to the priesthood of film) that were backed up by Bazin's belief in personalism and in existentialism, the belief in the indi-vidual's salvation through his or her own choices.

In this book, the following directors belong to the Fourth Generation: Wu Tianming of *Old Well*; Huang Shuqin of *Woman, Demon, Human*; Xie Fei of *Girl from Hunan*; and Zhang Nuanxin of *Sacrificed Youth* and *Good Morning, Beijing*. We'll focus here on the representative careers of Wu Tianming and Zhang Nuanxin.

Wu Tianming (b. 1939) has been known for his crucial role in promoting a special genre in post-Mao new cinema, that is, the Chinese Western *(Zhongguo xibu pian),* and in encouraging the young directors of the Fifth Generation after he became head of Xi'an Film Studio in 1983. Wu changed the title of the studio journal to *Chinese Western (Zhongguo xibu dianying)* and used it as a marketing strategy to emphasize the studio's specialty. Featuring films set in the rural northwest of China, the genre became an important cine-matic response to the nationwide intellectual and artistic craze known as roots-searching *(xungen).* In his role of encouraging young directors in an industry where seniority had been the criterion, Wu made his Xi'an Film Studio, along with a few provincial studios, the cradle for Fifth Generation filmmaking. Under Wu's leadership, Fifth Generation directors produced important titles at Xi'an: *Horse Thief, Black Cannon Incident, King of the Children, Red Sorghum.*

Wu's own film career started in the 1960s, when he worked as an actor, director's assistant, codirector, and, eventually in the post-Mao era, independ-ent director. The two titles from this last phase of his career, *River Without Buoys (Meiyou hangbiao de heliu,* 1983) and *Life (Rensheng,* 1984), left film viewers with unforgettable impressions of the films' emphases on psychologi-cal complexity and the ambiguity of human characters—a filmic testimony of the contemporary rehumanization culture. His *Old Well (Lao jing,* 1987) is selected in this book; his more recent film, *King of Masks (Bianlian,* 1995), has been commercially released to the American market.

Zhang Nuanxin (1940–95) taught Fifth Generation directors at Beijing Film Academy and gave them her best gift, "On Modernization of Film Languages," a ground-breaking essay written with her film critic husband, Li Tuo, in 1979. Zhang herself studied in the directing department at the academy from 1958 to 1962 and stayed on to teach. She started directing in the post-Mao era whenever she could get a break from her teaching. Her films *The Drive to Win* (*Sha'ou,* 1981), *Sacrificed Youth* (*Qingchun ji,* 1985), *Tears of the Bridal Sedan* (*Huajiao lei,* 1988), and *Good Morning, Beijing* (*Beijing, nizao,* 1990) led the way for such filmmaking trends as documentary aesthetics, fading dramatic intensity *(danhua),* and the emphasis on auteurism.

Although she made films mostly about women, Zhang was not very interested in the idea of women's cinema; she emphasized individuality as the way to break the filmmaking conventions, as she said in an interview: "I think art is basically about expressing yourself. Being a woman is part of that, but I don't think it should come before everything. From my first days in filmmaking, I've been very interested in auteurism. I feel that for me film is like an author's pen. I want to use it to write the things I want to write, and not as a means of propaganda for official policy" (Berry 1988b, 21).

The Fifth Generation

In 1982, with the decade-long break of the Cultural Revolution, the first renewed class of film directors, cinematographers, and art designers graduated from Beijing Film Academy, China's only film school and the one that had trained the Fourth Generation. The conventional career pattern available to these graduates was to work for ten to twenty years in apprentice-like jobs before they were sufficiently indoctrinated, experienced, and senior to make their own films. History, however, smiled on these newcomers and allowed them to make their own films within two years of graduation. The reasons for this luck, as summed up by film critic Tony Rayns, were many: "One was that many of them were assigned to small, regional studios, which didn't have hordes of directors on their books already. Another was that the rapidly burgeoning TV industry offered a lot of work to underemployed directors at all film studios. Yet another was the election of the middle-aged director Wu Tianming as head of Xi'an Film Studio at the end of 1983. Wu made it a matter of studio policy to give opportunities to young directors, with excellent (if controversial) results" (1991, 107). The remote regional studios of Guangxi became the cradle for the Fifth Generation. It was there that director Zhang Junzhao, cinematographer

Zhang Yimou, and designer He Qun teamed up to make *One and Eight* (*Yige he bage,* 1984), and then director Chen Kaige, with Zhang Yimou and He Qun, made *Yellow Earth* (*Huang tudi,* 1984). These two films proclaimed the arrival of the Fifth Generation.

Yellow Earth, included here, radically changed a conventional subject assigned by the studio for these young people to shoot. They had being given a conventional script because of what had happened with *One and Eight,* of which Tony Rayns writes:

> Faithful to its source, the film *[One and Eight]* depicts an episode in the anti-Japanese war: the chain-gang of prisoners, who include a falsely accused officer from the Communist army, demand their freedom so that they can protect themselves—and get it, in the process discovering unexpected reserves of patriotic feeling. The film neither looked nor sounded like any Chinese film before. Brutal behavior and brutal language were matched by Zhang Yimou's brutally grimy and unsentimental images, and the film had a conspicuously unreverential attitude to the role of the Communist army. Inevitably, the Film Bureau in Beijing objected, particularly to the representation of the wronged Communist officer. Many changes were demanded before the film was cleared for release; some were simply cuts, but others involved reshooting entire scenes. The revised version (which preserves the original "look" of the film but crucially alters much of the meaning) was released in China with fair commercial success, but banned from export until 1987. Its major impact was in critical circles: it demonstrated that a Chinese film could break the usual mould. (1991, 107–8)

Films that followed by other newcomers soon further confirmed that the usual mold could be broken. Although early-stage Fifth Generation filmmaking displayed an impressive diversity of auteur individuality and formalistic experiments, it also developed some era commonalities. It sought out subjects ignored by or excluded from earlier PRC films, it shunned melodramatic theatricality and didacticism, it minimized dialogue in order to emphasize a consciousness of other cinematic means, it valued ambiguity, and it presented unconventional anti-heroes.

Since that initial breakthrough with *One and Eight,* the Fifth Generation filmmaking has come a long way on different paths of development. The careers of Chen Kaige and Zhang Yimou highlight certain characteristics of this development. Chen and Zhang were both born in 1952, the Year of the Dragon. The association with the dragon, however, was rediscovered much later—very likely after the post-Mao roots-searching when such ancient symbols were revived. Before that, both were told that they were born under the red flag of the PRC and were the sons of the new Communist republic. Their childhood memories, however, differed, partly because Chen was from a film director's family in Beijing and grew up among the cultural elite, whereas Zhang felt alienated in a provincial town near Xi'an because his father had once been an officer in the counter-revolutionary (Nationalist KMT) army before the Communist takeover in 1949. The Cultural Revolution temporarily erased the difference between their family backgrounds, and they were both sent to the countryside as part of the nationwide exile of educated youth. Later, the two men met and became friends when both enrolled at Beijing Film Academy, Chen as a student of directing and Zhang as a student of cinematography.

The two had a chance to explore their dragon affiliation in 1984 on the Loess Plateau in northwest China. After graduation, they were anxious to change Chinese cinema. The small studio in the remote Guangxi province where Zhang had been assigned offered them this chance. Upon Zhang's invitation as chief cinematographer, Chen took over the directing of *Yellow Earth*. The film had such an impact on Chinese filmmaking that ever since it has been acclaimed as the Fifth Generation's declaration of their version of cinema: an artistic filmmaking that relies less on melodrama, dialogue, and didacticism and more on profound uses of image and sound and their concealed subtleties. In this film, the dragon's yellow earth and yellow river, the ancient and enduring collective roots that the two explored, are mysteriously enticing and, at the same time, repellent.

After *Yellow Earth,* their collaboration continued with *The Big Parade* (*Da yuebing,* 1985, released 1987), an examination of the relationship between the individual and the collective from another perspective, that is, how individuals have to abide by tough collective rules. In the film, an air force unit arduously rehearses for the National Day parade in Tiananmen Square.

With the Fifth Generation's rise to fame, Zhang Yimou temporarily overshadowed Chen Kaige. While Chen continued with his exploration in art films, producing the striking but poorly received *King of the Children* (*Haizi wang,* 1987) and *Life on a String* (*Bianzou bianchang,* 1991), Zhang successfully engaged public—and even international—attention with his impact on cinematography, acting, and directing in what critics have referred to as the "Zhang Yimou phenomenon." Zhang had, by chance, gotten a leading role in Wu Tianming's *Old Well* and was named Best Actor at the Tokyo Film Festival for his performance. He had also begun directing his own films; his first directorial effort, *Red Sorghum (Hong gaoliang, 1987)*, won a Golden Bear at the Berlin Film Festival in 1988. Other prizes followed, such as the two Oscar nominations for Best Foreign Film for *Ju Dou* (1990) and *Raise the Red Lantern (Da hong denglong gaogao gua, 1991)*. Critics in the PRC worried that Zhang was single-handedly burying the cinematic new wave as well as the cultural movement of Fifth Generation filmmaking. Although Zhang's films retained a strong critical edge toward the culture, these critics believed that his films had not only surrendered to melodrama and star appeal but had also abandoned the needs of the Chinese audience for the demands of the international film markets.

Chen soon caught up with his friend. In 1993, his three-hour epic *Farewell My Concubine (Bawang bie ji, 1993)* won the top prize, the Palme d'Or, at Cannes. During a short stay in America, Chen saw this film open there to warm acclaim from the media: the *New York Times* found it "one of those very rare film spectacles that delivers just about everything"; *Newsweek* hailed it as "a cinematic grand slam" with "the lushness of Bertolucci and the sweeping narrative confidence of an old Hollywood epic"; and the *San Francisco Chronicle* described it as an "intricately beautiful film" comparable with *Doctor Zhivago* (qtd. in Zha 1995, 79). Specialists in Chinese film in this country and other Western countries, however, also began to worry about the price Chen was paying for his success. Chris Berry, for example, observed how this impressive film "is an entirely conventional piece of filmmaking with none of the daring innovation that characterized his [Chen's] earlier career" (1993, 20).

Chen and Zhang have continued their filmmaking with the help of international investments and have won more international prizes and recognition. Many fellow Fifth Generation directors have followed suit. Critics are now beginning to explore the implications of these specially packaged Chinese films primarily aimed at the international film market. This special branch in Chinese filmmaking, many believe, offers an interesting case of postcolonial cultural exchange. In fact, many critics of the PRC, seeing that the Fifth Generation was losing its innovative edge, eagerly tried to promote the even younger Sixth Generation, a group of young urbanites shooting not allegories of ancient China but a living China as they found it, often with disgust. While critics were busy assessing these often nihilist and decadent younger film directors, Zhang also "returned to the city"—producing a film for Guangxi Studio, which was once the cradle of his cinema career. This popular urban film was hard to sell to the foreign market: *Keep Cool (Youhua haohao shuo, 1997)* is a bizarre comedy about the unlikely friendship between two comic anti-heroes, a dead-serious bookworm and a hooligan bookseller. Zhang's cinematic style has also turned further and further away from cinematic allegories. His *Not One Less* (Yige dou buneng shao, 1998), for example, has a documentary style. In this film about a substitute teacher in a village school, the substitute teacher and her students perform their own story directed by Zhang. Showing great resourcefulness in cinematic styles, Zhang may have once again moved one step ahead of his friend Chen Kaige. Chen, in the meantime, decided not to move his career to Hollywood. Instead, he stayed on in China and directed *The Emperor and the Assassin* (*Jin Ke ci qinwang*, 1999), another grand epic with lush cinematography and panoramic frames. Costing upward of $20 million, it is the most expensive Asian film ever produced.

The Sixth Generation

Contemporary filmmaking in the PRC has undergone a tremendous transformation in recent years. Faced with the post-1989 (Tiananmen Square massacre) political control, the changed situation of film production financing, and renewed competition from Hollywood, a group of younger filmmakers has quietly begun to make films that are attracting increasing critical attention at home and abroad. When this new cinema first appeared, critics in the PRC eagerly referred to it as Sixth Generation filmmaking, making the younger film directors the successors to the commonly held chronology.

Representing the start of the Sixth Generation filmmaking are titles of the early and mid-1990s such as *Beijing Bastard* (*Beijing zazhong*, dir. Zhang Yuan), *Weekend Lovers* (*Zhoumo qingren*, dir. Lou Ye), *Red Beads* (*Xuanlian*, dir. He Jianjun), *Days* (*Dongchun de rizi*, dir. Wang Xiaoshuai), *Lost Youth* (*Yanmo de qingchun*, dir. Hu Xueyang), *Yellow Goldfish* (*Huang jinyu*, dir. Wu Di), *Dirt* (*Toufa luanle*, dir. Guan Hu), and *Rainclouds over Wushan/In Expectation* (*Wushan yunyu*, dir. Zhang Ming). In subject, these films engage the youth culture and urban life; stylistically, they turn their back on elaborate allegories. *Beijing Bastard*, for instance, uses amateur actors and hand-held cameras; it prefers less artificial *mise-en-scènes* and avoids dramatic intensity. In a way, this group of films returns to a style similar to the mid-1980s documentary aesthetics, which had been hastily given up by Fourth and Fifth Generation directors in order to build cultural allegories on-screen. Financially, these Sixth Generation films attracted private Chinese investment instead of the overseas funding used by the established Fifth Generation directors and the government funding used by mainstream films. However, in the early stage, Sixth Generation filmmaking also seemed a disgrace, according to some PRC critics. Although these young artists had taken the trouble to produce art films, their nameless sense of pain, self-indulgence, and lack of social concern offended many. These young film artists disappointed the critics who once endorsed the Fifth Generation but now looked anxiously for worthy successors to the first five filmmaking generations.

The contrast between the baby boomers and Generation X in the United States may better help readers understand the disappointment here. We know that while the X-ers believe that they "are a culture, a demographic, an outlook, a style, an economy, a scene, a political ideology, an aesthetic, an age, a decade, and a literature" (Rushkoff 1994, 3), their elders' attitude is reflected in such titles given them: "the Doofus Generation," "the Tuned-Out Generation," "a generation of animals," "the Blank Generation," and so on (Holtz 1995, 1). The age difference between the Fifth and Sixth Generations roughly corresponds to that between boomers and X-ers: whereas those of the Fifth were born in the late 1940s and 1950s, those of the Sixth were born in the late 1960s and 1970s. Differences in group identities also roughly correspond. The X-ers realize that while the boomers had the civil rights movement and Vietnam War as powerful touchstones for their group identity, they have nothing as exciting. In the same way, members of the Sixth Generation also believe that they are overshadowed by the Fifth, who have such touchstones of group identity as the Cultural Revolution, the Red Guards, the enforced migration to the countryside, and the post-Mao economic reformation as well as cultural critique. While the Fifth Generation's coming of age is accompanied by all these highly idealistic (though often painful, in retrospect) big events, the Sixth's coming of age appears rather insipid. The decade of the Sixth Generation filmmakers' growth, especially the latter half of the 1980s, was an age of vagueness, what a film critic describes as having "gray ideological syndrome of *fin de siècle*" *(yishixingtai shijimo huise zonghezheng):* "Following 'the death of God,' the [established] altruism-based moral code . . . has collapsed. A new, self-principled moral code has yet to be developed. A value vacuum exists while all conventions are lost" (Huang Shixian 1989, 41).

In such a vacuum, those of the Sixth Generation grew up with no heroes, no ideals, no government-sponsored jobs, and no hope for the country's future. Most of the success stories of self-made *dakuan* (big money) also belong to their elders, while they themselves seem to experience only the impact of money worshiping and the depreciation of the humanities. It was an age of de-politicization; people were disgusted by government corruption and would fashion an aloofness from the Party. Yet, it was the politics that gave the Sixth Generation its defining moment: the Tiananmen Square demonstration and massacre, an event that still is so politically sensitive and so brutal that those of the Sixth Generation can rarely revisit it in their art as those of the Fifth had done with the Cultural Revolution.

The discomfort that critics experienced with the newcomers, however, also challenged the use of film generation labels. The diversified artistic outpouring of this group of artists represents either an era with no commanding social concerns or a group of self-indulgent artists who resist using social concerns to mark their group identity. For this reason, a film critic in the PRC declared the end of the Chinese filmmaking generations, believing that post–Fifth Generation filmmaking has entered a nongenerational, individualistic, and urban-realist era (Han Xiaolei 1995). The noted self-pity, isolation, and self-indulgence at the onset of this post–Fifth Generation cinematic movement also seem to have passed. Now at the beginning of a new century, more and more such hard-to-define young directors are producing films "outside" the state-owned studio system in various ways. They are unleashing an explosive energy that has created a high tide of films on urban subjects. Although it is still too soon to include some of these films in this book, due to the lack of adequate critical access and video availability, it is important to acknowledge the development of this new cinema. The urban concerns of this new cinema develop the issues discussed in the last section of this book.

One of the better known directors of this group is Zhang Yuan, whose films are more easily accessible. For example, Zhang Yuan was the visiting director at the Harvard Film Archive in November 1999, where four of his films were shown.

Born in 1963, Zhang Yuan graduated from the Beijing Film Academy in 1989 with a Bachelor of Arts degree in cinematography. Not pleased by his job assignment to a military film studio, he chose not to report to work but rather to focus on directing and producing his first feature-length film, *Mother* (*Mama,* 1990). This film involves a woman's frustration at looking after her retarded son without social help or sympathy. Shot in black and white and interspersed with color footage of interviews with other mothers of mentally disabled children, the film has a documentary scope and raw emotional effect.

With this first film based on the real-life experiences of actress Qing Yan, who plays the title role, Zhang Yuan established his cinematic style of minute emotional exploration through real-life characters and experiences. He enjoyed mixing his subjective lyricism with the objective documentary approaches. In most of his later films, there is a purposeful blurring of the line between docu-

mentary and feature film and the line between real life and its performed representation. I would suggest that Zhang Yuan's cinematic style has at least two
implications. First, his films reconfirm the documentary aesthetics advocated
by the Fourth Generation directors about a decade before. The earlier style, in
the hands of such directors as Zheng Dongtian and Zhang Nuanxin, served to
separate them from the dominant ideological discourse and melodramatic representation. Now, in the hands of Zhang Yuan, this style helps draw our attention to the less represented margins of a culture that has become more and more
plural as central control has relaxed. The candid camera is actually the rebels'
camera, using what is real (what is less represented) to challenge what is artificial (what is overrepresented).

Second, in discussing Zhang Yuan's staging of gay life in *East Palace, West
Palace* (*Dong gong, xi gong*, 1996), Chris Berry notes one of the focal points of
contemporary cultural and queer studies, that is, how one's identity is constructed through the performance that is true to both stage/screen and real life
(1998, 85). Berry moves from there to emphasize how Zhang Yuan's films draw
our attention not so much to Western theories of perversion but to the Chinese
cultural minorities' access to public discourse and to their right to be represented
on-screen. In this light, the second implication of Zhang Yuan's style points to
the awkward status of those on the cultural and social margins both in real life
and in any kind of representation. Since there are neither norms of behavior nor
conventions of representation for these margins, both the objective documentary approaches and the subjective lyricism by the director are harder to achieve,
are difficult to be accepted, and are even more difficult to be well coordinated
with each other. On this point, the differences between Zhang Yuan's documentary realism and that of the Fourth Generation also surface. Whereas the
Fourth Generation could win over the audience with a familiar reality, Zhang
Yuan's awkward reality of the cultural margins causes them discomfort.

The documentary realism of Zhang Yuan's first feature film on an ignored
aspect of Chinese urban life was not well received initially in China. After being
banned, *Mother* was smuggled out of China and won a Special Jury Prize at the
1991 Nantes Film Festival in France. As with many other Chinese films, foreign
recognition led to attention at home; *Mother* was eventually broadcast on
Beijing cable television in 1997. In between, Zhang Yuan's international recognition was accumulating, due to his unique cinematic perspectives, his efforts
toward independent filmmaking, and his career in music video production. In
1994, Zhang Yuan was selected by *Time* magazine as one of the 100 young
leading figures of the world for the twenty-first century.

Beijing Bastard (1992), Zhang Yuan's second feature, became China's first genuinely independent film and broke the monopoly of the PRC state-run studio system established since 1949. The film follows a rock and roll band while it rehearses and performs its music. It also offers glimpses of the lives of some of the musicians and their friends. Watching *Beijing Bastard* is to experience the boredom of these characters and to understand the exhilaration at their concerts. The concert sequences are usually shot in warm colors, lit by fire or strong lamps; they proceed rhythmically with songs and cheering, and they feature frequent close-ups of agitated faces. The nonconcert or "life" sequences are usually in colder gray tones with low-key lighting and few close-ups; there are a lot of medium and long takes of the characters' slow-motion lives.

A young musician's search for his girlfriend, Maomao, provides a narrative frame for the film. Not wanting to terminate her premarital pregnancy, Maomao hides away to give birth to the baby, who presumably gives the film its title. Through the young man's frustrated search for Maomao—his talk with the musicians, his pursuit of other women, and his introduction to us of other characters such as painters, writers, jobless young urbanites, and college students—we realize the meaning of "bastard" has been broadened in this film to refer to a decadent aspect of urban youth culture. A decade ago, John Minford used the broad term "*liumang* generation" to describe this subculture: "Rapist, whore, black-marketeer, unemployed youth, alienated intellectual, frustrated artist or poet—the spectrum has its dark satanic end, its long middle band of relentless gray, and shining at the other end, a patch of visionary light. It is an embryonic alternative culture" (1985, 30). *Liumang,* as Minford explains, is an untranslatable term loosely meaning loafer, hoodlum, hobo, bum, or punk. Today, *Beijing Bastard* suggests that this embryo has grown, further demonstrating its heterogeneous nature and asserting its impact on such young film artists as Zhang Yuan.

Sons (Erzi, 1995), Zhang Yuan's next film, illustrates how alcoholism and insanity tear apart an ordinary Chinese family and how the two twenty-something sons experience it. The parents are retired professional dancers. Their boredom with life and their constant bickering, which leads to divorce, contrasts with the youthful ideals they once had. The father not only indulges in liquor but also displays symptoms of schizophrenia. The two unemployed sons indulge equally in alcohol, not only because of their own boredom with life but also because of the constant embarrassment they feel at their neurotic father's behavior both inside and outside their apartment. *Sons* can be considered a sequel to *Beijing Bastard;* it explores the real family life of the young man searching for his girlfriend-in-hiding. As Zhang Yuan's downstairs neighbor, this young man urged the budding director to do a film about his family. When Zhang Yuan eventually worked out a script and "borrowed" the father back from the mental hospital, the four members of the family, playing themselves in the film, reenacted the family's troubles, loosely following Zhang Yuan's script and direction.

East Palace, West Palace is about the infatuation of a young gay writer, Ah Lan, with his persecutor, a policeman whose job is to keep homosexuals out of his park. Among Zhang Yuan's films, *East Palace, West Palace* is the most lyrical; it repeatedly uses an ancient opera scene about the impossible love of a female prisoner for her persecutor to help represent this present-day equally impossible gay love. While there is a tradition of same-sex love in ancient China (Hinsch 1992), modern representation has turned the subject into a major taboo and created a sense of discontinuity. Homosexuality on-screen is rarely seen in light of the ancient Chinese tradition; rather, it is depicted as an import of a decadent Western life-style. "Although there are many stories recorded about gays in Chinese culture," Zhang Yuan comments about this film, "after the Liberation of 1949 and especially during the Cultural Revolution (1966–76), the very word 'homosexual' disappeared from all newspapers, books, and even public discussion" (Berry 1998, 88). Today, channels to public representation of homosexuality are closed, and the homosexuals are hounded in everyday life as "hooligans" *(liumang),* the same name given to the decadent youth. Owing to this cultural reality, any representation of homosexuality in China cannot interact with other realms of life on an equal footing as, for example, in Ang Lee's *Wedding Banquet (Xiyan,* 1993), a comic depiction of cultural differences, generation gaps, and lighthearted interactions of gay persons with heterosexual persons in the United States. On the contrary, the representation of this taboo gay culture in China is more about persecution and protest.

Seventeen Years (Guonian huijia, 1999), Zhang Yuan's more recent film, is about the first visit between a female inmate, Tao Lan, and her mother and step-father after Tao Lan's seventeen years in prison. The film conveys a sad overtone of how humans are overcome by their surroundings, here, a young inmate who has been brainwashed by prison life. Part of the film was shot at Tianjin First Prison, a female prison in China; it was the first film production to receive government permission to show the actual interior of a Chinese prison. The real impact of the film, however, rests not on the few moments in the prison interior but on its reference to an absence—the seventeen years of jailed life. The gap of time and the part of prison life in this gap that is not shown is what this film is actually about. What this gap has constituted in this woman prisoner is a psychological wasteland that has transformed an earlier free-spirited tomboy into a docile inmate who has learned the virtue of confession, even the confession to a crime that the audience knows for certain that she has not committed. Interestingly enough, the older cityscape in rubble, awaiting reconstruction, becomes the symbolic *mise-en-scène* that comments on this woman's psychological wasteland. The most memorable frame in *Seventeen Years* shows Tao Lan walking across the rubble of the older buildings in a vain search for her lost youth and the memories of her past. Her earlier timid gaping at a much changed city life—busier, noisier, with more diversified people and demonstrating more energy—helps, too, to comment on this vain search. Ironically, the virtue this inmate has acquired throughout her prison life is exactly what the outside world has started to discard.

Zhang Yuan started a trend among the younger film directors of making films outside the state studio system. Not including those producing independent documentary videos, a few of Zhang Yuan's peers also ventured into independent filmmaking. Examples include Wang Xiaoshuai's *Days* (1993) and *Frozen* (*Jidu hanleng*, 1995) as well as He Jianjun's *Red Beads* (1993) and *Postman* (*You chai*, 1995). Although this trend met with a setback in 1996 when a film law made film production outside the studio system illegal, Zhang Yuan, and directors like him, soon found ways of going around this roadblock. Many films that were virtually independently produced bear state-studio logos because the directors paid a fee and went through the censors enforced by those studios. Such films as Wang Quan'an's *Lunar Eclipse* (*Yue shi*, 1999) and Ah Nian's *Call Me* (*Hu wo*, 2000) are examples of state-issued independent films. More radical films, such as Liu Bingjian's *Men Men Women Women* (*Nan nan nü nü*, 1999), which depicts the gay culture in a Chinese metropolis, have not been able to circumvent the roadblock and have had to be smuggled out of China for viewing.

As indicated at the beginning of this overview, this outline of filmmaking generations in China is sketchy and can serve only minimally as a backdrop for an enriching process of watching, discussing, reading about, and writing on individual films. It is my hope that the fifteen films of this volume will help start this process.

Part One

History in and out of Melodrama
Glory, Guilt, and Fantasy

Chunhua and Yuehong in *Two Stage Sisters (Wutai jiemei)*, directed by Xie Jin, 1965.
Courtesy of China Film Archive, Beijing.

To understand recent Chinese history through film, we must be aware of the artistic modes through which that history is represented. In other words, we need to know that we are dealing with both history and historiography, that is, particular ways of representing history, of retrieving history in relationship to a present time. Time always leaves its mark on our ways of retrieving history; different times write history in different manners. In this respect, melodrama, the most dominant artistic mode in some important periods of Chinese cinema, offers us a point of entry into a cluster of issues that will make an initial engagement with Chinese film enlightening. In Chinese cinema, melodrama has been an inclusive mode used for numerous subjects. We will explore some of these subjects—and melodrama—by examining selected films through which recent Chinese history has been represented.

Melodrama is well known for exhibiting strong emotions, exaggerated action and rhetoric, stereotypical characters and situations, and clear-cut confrontations between Good and Evil. There is a long tradition of melodrama in the West; etymologically, *melos* means a song, and it helps us trace the origin of this mode to the chorus in Greek theater. In this light, melodrama is best understood as a dramatic mode of lyrical overstatement. Melodrama, literally "song drama," was also once used interchangeably with the term "opera." In the eighteenth century, Handel called some of his works "opera" and some "melodrama." A major reference to the more recent characteristics of melodrama as a distinctive genre in Western (French) literature is Peter Brooks's *The Melodramatic Imagination* (1976). Brooks emphasizes "the cultural specificity of the genre" (xi) and qualifies melodrama as "the principal mode for uncovering, demonstrating, and making operative the essential moral university in a post-sacred universe" (15). In other words, this artistic mode of lyrical overstatement was favored by the rising European bourgeoisie in representing history, in denouncing enemies, and in building up its own universe of values. Showing a similar train of thought in his study of "family melodrama," Thomas Elsaesser specifies the social implication of melodrama as representing the subjectivity of the European bourgeoisie in the struggle against the authority of a declining feudal system (1985). These scholars, in specifying the historical roles of melodrama, also reserve the term as a particular European artistic mode for that particular time.

In his discussion of *Hibiscus Town* included in this book, Nick Browne (1994) appropriates the Western melodramatic mode to an analysis of Chinese films by seeking similar sociohistorical tensions as defined by Brooks and Elsaesser. This search leads Browne to focus on *Hibiscus Town*'s "relation among the self, the family, the workplace and the state" and how this relation "embodies the negotiation between the traditional ethical system and the new state ideology" (40). Here, the traditional ethical system is best exemplified by the misery of the Party's totalitarian rule of a rural town, and the new state ideology represents the hope of China's open-door policy inspired by bourgeois individualism and a capitalist market economy. In appropriating melodrama sociohistorically, Browne also questions other kinds of loose appropriation of the mode of melodrama that pay more attention to artistic similarities but ignore sociohistorical comparison.

However, some other scholars prefer an expanded definition of melodrama that can apply to any historical period and that will enrich our understanding of any cultural tradition. In *Melodrama and Asian Cinema*, Wimal Dissanayake writes, "In most Asian societies melodrama has a distinguished history considerably different from its history in the West and is intimately linked to myth, ritual, religious practices, and ceremonies. Although there is no term for melodrama in the classical vocabularies, Asian scholars and critics of cinema are increasingly using this Western term to effect finer discriminations" (1993, 3). In Chinese cultural tradition, for example, some scholars have noticed the melodramatic nature of Chinese ancient theater with its characterization in types. "In traditional Chinese theatre," Jerome Silbergeld writes, "drama *is* melodrama. In further support of this, the character *ju* [means 'drama'] itself has a second reading that means 'acute, severe, intense', and that is certainly an apt description of most Chinese drama. . . . This leads to the questions not only of how Chinese melodrama (if that is what we agree to call it) relates to modern Western form, but also of how contemporary Chinese film melodrama relates to traditional Chinese theatrics" (1999, 191).

Interestingly enough, melodrama has proven to be a meaningful concept with different approaches and for different contexts. Here I would like to point out one particularly meaningful aspect of the concept that will further our understanding of recent Chinese history and films. Melodrama, it is important to note, has been widely adopted and further defined by recent Chinese social revolutions initiated by Marxism. Referring to Marxist theories of social revolution, Wylie Sypher sees melodrama as a feature of Marxist ideology that is "pressed away from the neutrality of the world toward overstatement" (1965, 259). In other words, melodrama is the mode through which social contradictions and class antagonism will be magnified for the purpose of a revolution. In recent Chinese history, as the Chinese Communist Party obtained political power over the country and during the Party's reign of totalitarian politics, melodrama became both a forceful weapon of propaganda and part of the everyday Chinese reality. Melodrama has helped the Party create a society driven by constant campaigns: each time there is a campaign, a certain over-statement is circulated for targeting the enemies, for affirming certain myths, for creating new heroes, and for mobilizing the mass involvement.

The melodramatic nature of China's Party-promoted political life, however, does not necessarily mean that melodrama is the dominant Party-engineered genre in Chinese cinema. In the history of Chinese filmmaking, as Paul Pickowicz has shown in his excellent article "Melodramatic Representation and the 'May Fourth' Tradition of Chinese Cinema" (1993), melodrama reigned in Chinese leftist filmmaking in the 1930s and 1940s before the Party had any direct control of the film industry, and melodrama resurfaced in the post–Cultural Revolution decade (the 1980s), right after the bankruptcy of the Party's campaign politics. During the decades in between, the 1950s and the 1960s, melodrama became much less important and was often measured, when used, for its extreme expressions. Film scholars and artists would often call for a revision of melodramatic representation: they would not dispute class antag-onism but whether this antagonism was represented complexly and appropri-ately enough, and they would caution against "vulgar sociology"—the stereotypical equivalence of characters with their class affiliations (compare Kuoshu 1999b, 67). In the PRC's early cinema, melodrama might still be used to denounce the pre-PRC "old society." However, "socialist society itself," Pickowicz reminds us, "could not be subjected to the direct and highly exag-gerated critical reviews typical of the melodramatic genre" (1993, 314–15). Melodrama thus became secondary in importance.

The first high tide of the Chinese cinematic melodrama came with leftist filmmaking. Leftism, Leo Lee writes, "was basically a social stance of discon-tent. In both fiction and film one finds an overriding obsession with the ills of contemporary society" (1991, 7). In denouncing the social ills, film, as a more public form of representation, seems to resort much more to the mode of melo-drama than does contemporary left-wing literature. According to Pickowicz (1993), a few issues of this period need to be noted. (1) It was no coincidence that melodrama, which had been a popular cultural response to the anxieties and moral confusion caused by the 1789 revolution in France, became popular in China before and after the 1911 revolution that overthrew the last emperor. (2) Influenced by Hollywood and catering to the popular taste of urban cul-ture, the fledgling Chinese film industry from around 1910 through the 1920s had allowed melodrama to flourish. (3) Leftist filmmaking led to a marriage of

classic melodrama and the elementary Marxism of class struggle, and it attributed the crisis of contemporary China to a spectacular moral struggle between
the forces of darkness and light. (4) The war with Japan, which divided leftist
filmmaking into two periods, encouraged the dominance of melodrama; leftist
filmmaking wanted to use melodrama in response to the national crisis. (5)
Leftists failed to bring a proper understanding of Marxism to China through
cinema—Marxist ideas were swallowed up by the melodramatic genre and
reduced to stereotypes and caricatures.

The second time that melodrama reigned in Chinese filmmaking, it was in
dominant cinematic response to the nationwide reflection on the catastrophe
of the Cultural Revolution. As illustrated by Xie Jin's *Hibiscus Town,* melodrama offered an emotional way of licking the wounds left by the Party's mistakes in a series of political campaigns that culminated in the Cultural
Revolution. In cinema, Pickowicz writes, "it was finally possible not only to
talk about socialist society in terms of darkness and light, but to identify the
Party as the agent of darkness" (1993, 325). This second high tide of cinematic
melodrama was very short-lived. The post-Mao film scholars and artists soon
identified this mode of representation with the melodramatic nature of China's
Party-engineered political life, and starting in the mid-1980s, Chinese cinema
made a conscious effort to separate itself from melodrama. The call to end the
dominant "Xie Jin model" (a melodramatic formula), the proposal to reduce
dramatic intensity in films, the suggestion that cinema should divorce itself from
theater (for example, with less dialogue and fewer stereotypical characters), the
rise of cinematic documentism (literally "documentary aesthetics"), and many
other broader cultural endeavors emphasizing the representation of social ambiguity all bore testimony to this effort to move beyond melodrama.

The three films in this section cover significant parts of recent Chinese history. Whereas the founding of the PRC in 1949 separates the first two films,
Two Stage Sisters and *Hibiscus Town,* the third film, *Farewell My Concubine,*
covers a sweeping range of Chinese history from the 1920s and 1930s to the
Cultural Revolution of the 1960s and beyond. The three production dates—
1965, 1986, and 1993—dictate why these historical periods are represented in
these films in their specific fashions.

Let's contrast the first two dates and films first. In 1965, Mao Zedong was
tightening his control of the Party by enforcing rigid totalitarian rules and by
removing any liberal forces within the Party's leadership. In Chinese terminol-
ogy, simplified for our purposes here, the supporters of the totalitarian rules
based on class struggle and a planned economy are known as "leftists," and

those who advocate for democracy and a market economy are labeled "right-ists." A few years earlier, in 1957, Mao had led an anti-rightist campaign that denied the intellectual diversity of the nation. And in 1966, he would start the Cultural Revolution and further lead the leftists' onslaught on those rightists hidden in the leadership of the Party. With the enforcement of more rigid requirements that the arts serve as weapons of revolution, *Two Stage Sisters* sought the glory of the earlier Communist revolution in order to justify—although this might not have been the director's intention—the removal of the rightists and any bourgeois tendencies from the Party. The film has a militant spirit about class struggles. In contrast, 1986 was the early stage of the ideo-logical re-orientation of the post-Mao era. Reflecting a nationwide fatigue with class struggle and a bad economy in the wake of the Cultural Revolution, *Hibiscus Town* helped to rehabilitate the rightists and sought to lay the blame for a revolution that had gotten out of control.

Although they retrieve history from different historical perspectives, these two films by the same director, Xie Jin, share similar features of melodrama. *Two Stage Sisters,* as Marchetti observes, "deals with crystal-clear conflicts between masters and servants, lords and peasants, powerful men and helpless women, in which traditional power relations are overturned [by revolution]" (1997, 69). In a word, it is a melodrama. Yet it is an example of the *measured* melodrama of the time. In the hands of the master Xie Jin, this melodrama resourcefully blends elements of Chinese traditional opera (characterization and epic scope), naturalistic details characteristic of May 4th literature, Western critical realism, Hollywood backstage melodrama, Soviet socialist realism, and Brechtian epic theater. The film is a typical Third Generation art film, produced prior to the Cultural Revolution and confirming the Party's historical role in revolution. *Hibiscus Town* is a believer's critique of the guilt of the revolution with a weapon from the post–Cultural Revolution intellectual arsenal: human-ism, or rehumanization, as it was more precisely known in Chinese, suggesting that the revolution had distorted or ignored human nature and now it was time to restore it. Humanism offered this film a new way of organizing its melodra-matic confrontation of Good (human) and Evil (anti-human).

In *Farewell My Concubine,* the younger director Chen Kaige clearly sets himself apart from the melodramatic tradition. "I don't feel comfortable with melodrama because I don't like emotional excess," he says. "I could never make a film like Xie Jin's *Hibiscus Town,* which says that there are good people and bad people and that everything will be fine if we can just get rid of the bad peo-ple! It seems to me that all of us have positive and negative sides, and the same capacities to love and hate" (Rayns 1994, 52). *Farewell My Concubine,* produced in 1993, leads us into a de-politicized postsocialist era that features a mass nonparticipation, or boycott, of Party politics. With the end of the Cold War as the global backdrop and China's opening of its markets (including the filmmaking market) to international investment as everyday reality, this film puts a different spin on recent Chinese history. Although the history it deals with is as tumultuous as in the first two films, *Farewell My Concubine* moves far from political melodrama into what Max Tessier terms "aesthetic realism" (1993, 16). *"Farewell My Concubine,"* Tessier observes, "is a powerful metaphor for the eternal supremacy of art over destructive politics and the recurring perils of History: regimes go by, art lives on, says Chen" (17). Here the fantasy of an aloofness from a destructive historical past reflects a general cultural desire of the post-Mao China.

One
Two Stage Sisters
(*Wutai jiemei,* dir. Xie Jin, 1965)

Screenplay Lin Gu et al.
Cinematography Zhou Daming, Chen Zhenxiang
Producer Tianma
Cast Xie Fang, as Chunhua
Cao Yindi, as Yuehong
Li Wei, as Manager Tang

Xie Jin's *Two Stage Sisters* forms an interesting contrast to Chen Kaige's *Farewell My Concubine,* the third film in this section. They both trace the lives and friendship of two fellow actors/actresses, and both use the characters' stage performances to comment on history. Since these histories end at different times—*Two Stage Sisters* in the highly idealized early decade of the PRC and *Farewell My Concubine* in the much more somber post-Mao era—they represent the celebration and disillusionment of the Communist revolution respectively.

The contrast in the gender concerns of the two films is most interesting to note. *Two Stage Sisters* reflects the transvestism of Shaoxing Opera's "female playing male" (the female perspective) and *Farewell My Concubine,* the Peking Opera's "male playing female" (the male perspective). Reflecting the common practice of single-gendered theater troupes from different gender angles, the two films also, in an allegorical sense, illustrate the gender politics of the times of their production.

The female perspective of *Two Stage Sisters* was produced in the spirit of "socialist feminism," that is, to use women in representation to promote various broader issues of social revolution. Two plays are performed within this film. The first is *Xianglin's Wife (Xianglin sao).* It is based on *The New Year's Sacrifice (Zhufu)* by Lu Xun, an important cultural critic of the early twentieth century. Deviating from the original story's self-reflective tone of cultural scrutiny, the play elaborates a tragic pathos. The central female character is

29

known only in relation to her first husband, as Xianglin's wife, and her story starts upon his death. She runs away from her tyrannical mother-in-law to work as a servant in town. She is happy with her job, and her extreme industriousness, evident in her single-handed preparation of the host family's New Year's sacrifice, wins her their respect. All, however, ends abruptly when her mother-in-law discovers her whereabouts, takes her away, and forces her into another marriage to a man in a remote mountain village. After her second husband dies and their small son is eaten by a wolf, she returns to her host family in town. Seeing her misfortune as Heaven's displeasure with her, the townspeople start to scorn her. Her host family forbids her to prepare for the New Year's sacrifice. Even the donation of all her income to the town's temple does not remove this pollution. Her mental disintegration follows. She is kicked out of the host family, becomes a beggar in the town for a few years, and dies one cold New Year's Eve. Her frozen corpse becomes the New Year's sacrifice of the town.

The second play within *Two Stage Sisters* is *The White-Haired Girl (Baimao nü)*, a typical melodrama of class antagonism engineered in Yan'an, China's capital of Communist revolution prior to 1949. A vicious landlord, Huang Shiren, has his eye on Xi'er, the daughter of his tenant, Yang Bailao, who is heavily in debt to him. Huang Shiren forces the tenant to sell the daughter to his family as a maid, which causes the tenant to commit suicide, and the landlord eventually rapes the girl. Xi'er escapes the landlord's family, hides in a mountain cave where she gives birth to a baby, and is determined to have her revenge. Her hair turns white from years of hiding in the mountain, and a few glimpses of her by the local people turn her into a legendary "White-Haired Immortal" with a wrathful spirit. Even the landlord uses this legend to scare his tenants from joining the land reform organized by the Red Army. Eventually the girl is located by the Red Army; her identity is clarified, her story told (mobilizing the tenants to overthrow the landlord), and her revenge secured by a death sentence for the landlord.

The performance of these two plays in *Two Stage Sisters* emphasizes women as victims of old social orders desperately waiting to be rescued and as joining revolution to avoid being victims anymore. (For a detailed study of the plays, refer to Kuoshu 1999b, 51–83.) The story of one actress, Chunhua, echoes those of Xianglin's wife and Xi'er, demonstrating that women can change their fate by joining the revolution. The story of the other actress, Yuehong, demonstrates the danger women face of becoming again the victim of a male-dominated social order if they choose not to join the revolution.

The play the two male characters perform in *Farewell My Concubine* reflects a post-Mao cultural retrospect from the male angle and in the figures of the "damaged male" or the "feminized male." (For a discussion of the roles of performance within performance in *Farewell My Concubine,* refer to the introductory notes of the film in this book.) "Given the prior phallic order, and given classical Oedipal rivalry with the Father," men in the gender representation in recent China, as Ann Kaplan observes, "may be harmed even more than women. State communism, in demanding male submission to the Law of the Father with little possibility for obtaining at least some parity with the Father position (as in free-enterprise capitalism), may produce men psychically damaged in deeper ways even than women" (1991, 153). In this light of gender representation, we notice alienation—men who find it difficult to identify with the prevailing cultural order or who find that the opposite gender is being elevated (as in "socialist feminism") to further ensure that they, the male, would conform as the male had always been asked to in history, for example, in the numerous role models of the Confucian conformist scholars.

To this point, Xie Jin's major films had all been about women or a kind of "sisterhood" showing a need for political consciousness and Party leadership. *Woman Basketball Player No. 5* emphasized the importance of the collective over the individual, and *The Red Detachment of Women* delivered a similar message by diverting a woman slave's will for personal revenge to one of sacrificing for a revolutionary cause. Now, *Two Stage Sisters* showed how an actress bears hardship and resists the corruption of a rotten society, coming to understand that her performance on the small stage is related to changing the bigger stage, that of society itself.

Suggested readings for *Two Stage Sisters* are as follows:

Da 1989
Semsel 1987
Tung 1987

Director's Notes

The script [of *Two Stage Sisters*] has a distinctive local flavor; it depicts China as a semi-feudal, semi-colonial society as represented by villages in Zhejiang and the world-renowned city of Shanghai. [Our] *mise-en-scènes* need to be typical of that.

We need to have strong emotions about social classes. The script is a testimony of an old society that devours human lives. Therefore, we have to make clear social distinctions in our execution of each single scene. Take the first performance scene at the temple, for example. If we are not careful, we may well create the wrong impression of "a peaceful life with songs and dances," misleading the audience to feel that "the old society seems to be fun."

The film is Chunhua's ceaseless exploration of the meaning of life. . . . [W]hat she asks in the film needs to inspire the viewers, resonating with them, and inducing them to think.

The general tone of the film should be of human vitality and optimism defying an overall sadness. (Xie Jin 1982, 276–77)

Two Stage Sisters: The Blossoming of a Revolutionary Aesthetic
Gina Marchetti

On the eve of the Great Proletarian Cultural Revolution in 1964, Xie Jin brought to the screen a story about the changing lives of women in twentieth-century China set against the backdrop of the Shaoxing opera world. Although rooted in the intimate story of two actresses and the vicissitudes of their relationship, Xie gave the film, *Two Stage Sisters (Wutai jiemei)*, an epic scope by showing these women's lives buffeted by tremendous social and political upheavals.[1] The film covers the years from 1935 to 1950, the expanses of the Zhejiang countryside as well as Shanghai under Japanese, Guomindang, and Communist rule.

Chunhua (Xie Fang), a young widow about to be sold by her in-laws, escapes and becomes an apprentice in a traveling Shaoxing folk opera troupe. Yuehong (Cao Yindi), who plays the male roles in the all-female opera company, befriends Chunhua. After the death of Yuehong's father, Chunhua and Yuehong find themselves sold to a Shanghai opera theater to replace the fading star, Shang Shuihua (Shangguan Yunzhu). Eventually, Yuehong falls in love with their manipulative stage manager, Tang (Li Wei), and the sisters quarrel and separate.

Inspired by the radical woman journalist, Jiang Bo (Gao Yuansheng), Chunhua continues her career, giving a political flavor to her performances. After an attempt to blind and ruin Chunhua by using Yuehong's testimony to trick her in court Tang goes off to Taiwan to escape the revolution. Although unable to harm her stage sister in court, Yuehong has been publicly humiliated. Abandoned by Tang, she disappears into the countryside. After Shanghai's liberation by the Communists, however, Chunhua manages to track down Yuehong, and the two reconcile.

Two Stage Sisters uses the theatrical world of Shaoxing as a metaphor for political and social change. The film also represents a search for a Chinese cinema aesthetic based on these traditions as well as on Hollywood and socialist realist forms. This analysis will explore the intermingling of these aesthetic currents and the ways in which art and politics intertwine in *Two Stage Sisters*. By placing the film within the context of the political and cultural movements that spawned it, the drama of the development of Chinese cinema aesthetics since 1949 can be understood more clearly.

The Place of *Two Stage Sisters* in Xie Jin's Career

Xie Jin's own background made him particularly well-qualified to direct this tale of Shaoxing opera and Shanghai's theatrical world. Xie was born in Shaoxing (Zhejiang province) in 1923. At the age of eight, he and his family moved to Shanghai. From an early age, Xie was fascinated by the theater and cinema. While growing up in the 1930s, he had the opportunity to see the work of directors like Cai Chusheng, Sun Yu, and Yuan Muzhi, the cream of Shanghai film's "golden era." Also, he began a life-long enthusiasm for the Shaoxing opera of the region.

During the Japanese occupation, Xie moved to Sichuan province in the interior and studied theater at the Jiangen Drama Academy. There, he worked with noted theatrical personalities like Huang Zuolin and Zhang Junxiang. In Shanghai and Sichuan, Xie encountered both Chinese folk traditions and Western dramatic and cinematographic forms. This blending of these two traditions came to characterize his mature work.

When Zhang Junxiang accepted work at the Datong Film Studio in Shanghai in 1948, Xie went along as his assistant director. After 1949, Xie continued on in Shanghai, codirecting *A Wave of Unrest (Yichang fengbo;* also translated as *An Incident)* with Lin Nong in 1954. His first solo effort was *Spring Days in Water Village (Shuxiang de chuntian;* also translated as *Spring Over the Irrigated Land)* in 1955. From the mid-1950s to the mid-1960s, Xie's style matured in an aesthetic crucible that ground together Hollywood classicism, Soviet socialist realism, Shanghai dramatic traditions, and indigenous Chinese folk opera forms.

Many of Xie's films focus on the lives of women, workers, artists, or students. *Woman Basketball Player No. 5 (Nülan wuhao,* 1957) explores the problems that a young female athlete faces in coming to grips with her ambitions in the field of sports. *The Red Detachment of Women (Hongse niangzijun,* 1961) deals with the heroism of women who go from peasant life to guerrilla warfare in the 1930s. *Two Stage Sisters* explores the lives of women working on the Chinese stage. In all these films, women's lives represent both hardship and oppression as well as the potential for revolutionary change. In fact, throughout most of his career, Xie Jin has been at the forefront of the exploration of different representations of women within socialist cinema.

With the condemnation of Xie's comedy, *Big Li, Little Li, and Old Li (Da Li, Xiao Li, he Lao Li,* 1962), and *Two Stage Sisters* (1964) soon after, followed by the complete shutdown of the Shanghai studios, Xie's output dwindled to next to nothing during the Cultural Revolution. During that period, however, Xie did work on two films based on model operas—*The Port (Haigang,* 1972; also translated as *On the Docks)* and *Panshiwan* (1975). Since 1976, Xie has made several films, including *Youth (Qingchun,* 1977), *Ah, Cradle (A! Yaolan,* 1979), *The Legend of Tianyun Mountain (Tianyunshan chuanqi,* 1980), *The Herdsman (Muma ren,* 1982), *Qiu Jin* (1983), *Garlands at the Foot of the Mountain (Gaoshan xia de huahuan,* 1984), *Hibiscus Town (Furong zhen,* 1986), and *The Last Aristocrats (Zuihou de guizu,* 1989).

These films made after the Cultural Revolution show a marked change in Xie's oeuvre. Diverging from his earlier films that deal with and ostensibly support socialist revolution, the later works seem to be more nationalistic than revolutionary in character. Several explicitly criticize past party policies.

The Theatrical World of *Two Stage Sisters*

Two Stage Sisters is one of the few films made at that time in the People's Republic of China (PRC) to be based on an original screenplay rather than a script adapted from a well-known and accepted literary or dramatic work. However, the film still remains deeply indebted to the literary and theatrical world of modern China. In fact, the entire film revolves around the theater and uses the stage to underscore the changes in its protagonists' lives as well as the dramatic political changes that occurred between 1935 and 1950.

The first third of *Two Stage Sisters* deals with the itinerant opera theater of Zhejiang province. Shaoxing opera differs considerably from the Beijing style opera better known outside of China. Although Beijing opera has set a certain standard of performance that has influenced regional styles considerably, other non-Mandarin-language opera styles have existed and continue to flourish in most regions of China. According to Colin Mackerras' account of Chinese opera (1975), Shaoxing opera originated in the later days of the Qing dynasty and is, therefore, a rather recent addition to the history of Chinese regional theater. Arising out of folk music traditions in the countryside, Shaoxing eventually became popular in urban areas, where it began to be performed in permanent theaters as well as tea houses and open-air market pavilions.

The prevalence of all-female troupes makes Shaoxing stand out among other Chinese regional opera forms. Records show that in 1923 an all-female company performed in Shanghai. Eventually, schools were started in the countryside for actresses, and many troupes either added women to their companies or performed with exclusively female casts.

Because of its elegant costumes, complex gestures, and often intricate plot lines, many may be under the mistaken impression that Chinese opera is an art form exclusively for aristocrats, intellectuals, and the wealthy. Although performed at court and patronized by powerful landlords and businessmen, Chinese opera has always remained a folk form enjoyed by a broad range of people in Chinese society. In fact, the opening sequence of *Two Stage Sisters* delineates the differences between the glittering fantasy of the stage performance and the poverty of both the players and their audience. Performed in marketplaces and financed by the passing of a hat, opera could be listened to and enjoyed by everyone regardless of social station or gender. The volume and exaggerated articulation of the singing, the use of stylized gestures in pantomimes, and the elaborate costumes attracted the attention of passersby, who may have had no intention of watching the opera but who were drawn in by the commotion.

If nothing else, Chinese opera is loud, and its extensive use of percussion instruments like the ban (clapper) not only emphasizes important actions for dramatic effect but also reminds an audience preoccupied with gambling, bartering, snoozing, or chitchat that something important is happening on stage. Thus, as Chunhua's escape from her in-laws causes a tremendous ruckus in an already cacophonous marketplace, Yuehong, playing the young gentleman, and Xiao Xing, another actress playing a comic servant, as indicated by the white band of makeup across her nose, barely bat an eye and continue singing.

Although many urban intellectuals were attracted to and wrote for the opera stage and although a select few opera performers such as the noted female impersonator of Beijing opera, Mei Lanfang, achieved super-stardom, most opera singers and musicians were of peasant stock and as poor as their audiences. Most of these itinerant performers, much like the theater artists of the Elizabethan stage, were treated like thieves and prostitutes and considered the lowest rung of society. Despite this stigma, however, desperate women, trying to escape the harshness of the feudal peasant family in an overpopulated countryside bled dry by greedy landlords, continuously fueled the Shaoxing opera ranks.

In many ways, the life story of the Shaoxing actress Fan Ruijuan parallels that of the fictitious Chunhua in *Two Stage Sisters*. Fan's account of her life on the Shaoxing stage reflects the same sense of desperation and determination evident in the film. As Fan Ruijuan states in her memoir, hers was not an uncommon life:

> I was only 11 when I joined a Shaoxing opera theater in 1935. At that time, more than 20,000 of the 400,000 people living in Chengxian County, my native place in Zhejiang Province and the birthplace of Shaoxing Opera, had left their homes to become opera singers. Life was hard. My family was living on bran cakes, sweet potatoes and clover, which were all we could afford on father's meager income as an odd job man. To me, opera singing seemed to be the only alternative to the miserable life of a childbride. (1983, 158)

Ironically, for Fan as well as for Chunhua in *Two Stage Sisters,* joining the Shaoxing opera meant jumping from the frying pan into the fire. Early opera training for these young girls consisted of beatings, starvation, humiliation, and long hours of hard labor. Virtually enslaved to the troupe's manager, opera performers often worked for room and board alone in order to pay for their training. Underfed and often lice-ridden or tubercular, they were forced to travel miles on foot through winter storms and still perform flawlessly the moment the troupe arrived at its destination.

Aside from being indentured to a theatrical manager, opera performers were also looked upon as sexually available to customers. Throughout the history of Chinese opera, stories abound about young boys taken into opera companies to play female roles and act as homosexual prostitutes. Traveling female performers also were known to serve as prostitutes. When the opera troupe in *Two Stage Sisters* performs an all-night engagement, expectations extend beyond the singing of opera tunes. Lord Ni, a wealthy land owner, hopes to enjoy more than an evening of opera from Yuehong and Chunhua as an unspoken part of his agreement.

This incident not only underscores opera performers' lack of power over their lives, but it also brings out the ironic contrast between the fantasies performed on stage and the actual lives of the Shaoxing actresses. Yuehong as the young gentleman scholar and Chunhua as the innocent ingenue sing operas about romantic love. Yet, this type of romance was completely beyond the expectations of young women born into a brutally patriarchal society of arranged marriages, child brides, concubines, prostitution, and child slavery.

Many operas feature dynamic female generals, swordswomen, and female fairy spirits with martial talents supported by a will to exercise them. In contrast, the lives of the actresses in Shaoxing opera only testify to the powerlessness of women in the Chinese countryside. In one scene, for example, the local policeman, sent by Lord Ni after Yuehong refused the lord's advances, drags off and pillories a defiant Chunhua, still wearing the opera costume associated with a female warrior role. Chunhua resists, but to no avail. Romance and martial victory for women on stage contrast sharply with oppression, humiliation, and total impotence off stage.

The theatrical world Yuehong and Chunhua enter in the Shanghai of 1941 is, in many ways, as harsh and demanding as the one left behind it, the countryside. However, they also enter an urban environment very different from rural life. Shanghai was a thriving port filled with Western concessions not allowed in other parts of China during the late Qing and early Republican periods. It had a reputation as a wide-open port and city of intrigue, which continued through the Japanese occupation and civil war periods depicted in *Two Stage Sisters*. Shanghai was a center of progressive ideas and innovative theatrical forms, as well as a haven for those drawn to its seamier side of money, power, and corruption. Notorious for harboring revolutionists, the Shanghai theater district was home to many actors-turned-activists from the turn of the century.

When a demonstration in Beijing on May 4, 1919, led to China's refusal to sign the Treaty of Versailles because it favored Japanese interests in Asia, the Shanghai intellectual community also helped to usher in a new movement begun with the demonstration and called the May 4th or New Culture Movement. Trying to bring China into the modern world, artists, politicians, literary and theatrical figures, young scholars, and students in all disciplines looked to both Western culture and a new sense of Chinese nationalism for inspiration.

Although many artists involved with the May 4th Movement tried to survive in Shanghai under the Japanese occupation, most involved in radical politics fled either to the Communist Party strongholds around Yan'an or the Guomindang-controlled areas in the south. Traditional opera and the world of light entertainment, however, managed business as usual under the Japanese.

After World War II, Shanghai once again fell under the control of the Guomindang. In *Two Stage Sisters*, the bitter political struggles that ensued between the Communists and the Nationalists are metaphorically represented by the turmoil within the theatrical world. Jiang Bo, who represents the spirit of May 4th and its hope for the emancipation of women, and Chunhua go to battle with the Guomindang-backed theatrical producer Tang over their right to produce socially conscious operas and compete with Tang's more commercial productions.

In 1946, Jiang Bo takes Chunhua to an exhibition commemorating the tenth anniversary of the death of Lu Xun. A principal motive force behind the May 4th Movement, Lu Xun stands as a symbol of the interconnection between revolutionary politics and the arts. Born in Shaoxing, Lu Xun was associated throughout his life with the literary and theatrical world of Shanghai, and Zhejiang province. Always a champion of the rights of women, Lu Xun wrote essays on Ibsen's *A Doll's House* and against enforced chastity for women and the sexual double standard, as well as several essays commemorating the deaths of young female student activists.

Lu Xun also dealt with poverty and women's issues in his fiction. His terse prose and use of keenly observed detail became the model for a type of critical realism still favored by many writers today. His novella, *The New Year's Sacrifice (Zhufu)*, for example, deals with the plight of a poor widow in China known simply as "Xianglin's Wife." When Chunhua sees an etching of this character, a superimposition of her face with the print shows Chunhua's identification with Lu Xun's creation.

On stage, in an opera based on the novella, Chunhua appears as the doomed peasant widow, singing an aria in torn rags with whitened hair. This brief excerpt from the opera acts as a shorthand reference to the quantum changes going on within the Chinese theater at that time and, by extension, Chinese society. Western influences have been absorbed and come full circle, so that the plight of a downtrodden peasant widow can become fit subject matter for an art form that had entertained the imperial courts and the landed gentry. The opera world had changed significantly.

At this point, the onstage world of *Two Stage Sisters* parallels rather than contrasts with the backstage drama of the film. Instead of a world of light comedy and romance, *The New Year's Sacrifice* points to the possibility of a socially and politically committed theater. This theater takes the plight of the average woman in China as a metaphor for the oppressive aspect of the society generally.

After the revolution, Chunhua resumes her life as an itinerant opera performer—with a difference. Now, she performs revolutionary opera and travels from village to village as a theatrical cadre to educate the peasantry about revolution. She performs a type of opera stylistically closer to traditional Shaoxing than the socially committed *New Year's Sacrifice*, but with a clear political message.

In Hangzhou, where Chunhua had been pilloried, the troupe stages an opera version of *The White-Haired Girl (Baimao nü)*. Written in Yan'an in 1943, this play became the standard for all sorts of revolutionary drama to follow after 1949. Originally a play, *The White-Haired Girl* has been produced as an opera, filmed, danced as a ballet, and has inspired revolutionary graphic art.

The White-Haired Girl tells the story of Xi'er, a young peasant woman brutalized by feudal landlords and their minions. After all sorts of violations and humiliations, she takes refuge in a cave, living like a wild animal. Because of this adversity, her hair turns completely white, and she acquires a reputation for fierceness. The local population considers her mad. When the Red Army liberates the area, she is reunited with her fiancé and joins the revolution. As Raphael Bassan has pointed out, *The White-Haired Girl* (here referring to the earliest film version of the play) contains all the elements necessary to insure it a lasting place of influence on all revolutionary film and theater to follow in the PRC:

> It serves as a model, particularly at the level of the presentation of the conflicts of the people in opposition to the landlords, for all revolutionary realism to come. All is, in fact, judiciously coded: the unfailing will of the heroine, the courage and abnegation of the disinherited, the always 100% negative profile of the oppressors, and, finally, the idealistic portrait of the Communist soldiers (who are also party cadres), new guides of the Chinese nation.[2]

The spirit of Yan'an drama as well as the theater that followed the revolution can be traced to Mao's personal interest in art and cultural affairs. In his famous "Talks at the Yenan Forum on Literature and Art," Mao took time out from the arduous tasks of fighting the war against the Japanese and dealing with the daily difficulties of running the Yan'an soviet to discuss the importance of China's "cultural army" in the country's battle against both foreign enemies and domestic oppressors. He calls for committed artists to draw on a variety of forms, including traditional ones, to both appeal to and educate the Chinese masses:

> We should take over the rich legacy and the good traditions in literature and art that have been handed down from past ages in China and foreign countries, but the aim must still be serve the masses of the people. Nor do we refuse to utilize the literary and artistic forms of the past, but in our hands these old forms, remolded and infused with new content, also become something revolutionary in the service of the people. (Mao 1971, 259)

Not surprisingly, Mao's talks at Yan'an led to the type of revolutionary drama exemplified by *The White-Haired Girl*. Firmly rooted in traditional theater and folklore, the play presents a clear moral universe with peasants replacing noble lords and generals as heroes and heroines. Its mythic elements, magical transformations, and stock character types place it squarely within folk theater traditions. Later, Yan'an theater became the basis for Mao's "revolutionary romanticism" as well as the Cultural Revolution's model operas.

In *Two Stage Sisters,* Chunhua's performance of *The White-Haired Girl* bears as much resemblance to *The New Year's Sacrifice* as it does to traditional Shaoxing opera. Within the film, *The White-Haired Girl* functions as a synthesis of the old and the new, China and the West, spoken and opera forms, and as the culmination of all the other, often contradictory, aesthetic currents to which the film refers. Although it relies on the stylization of traditional opera for its effect, it also deals with contemporary life, with actual change, and with current political and social concerns. Performing in the public square of Hangzhou, Chunhua comes full circle. Her performance melds a May 4th, urban critical realism with the fantastical nature of folk opera.

Taken as a whole, *Two Stage Sisters* transcends the insular world of Shaoxing opera to make some far-reaching statements about the nature of oppression and the power of change in twentieth-century China. Shaoxing serves as a metaphor. Events of historical, social, political, and cultural import (from the feudal countryside through Shanghai enterprise to revolutionary promise) occur in the theater that functions as a microcosm of Chinese society at large. Chunhua, Yuehong, and Jiang Bo stand in as "every woman," extraordinary because of their notoriety, but only a step away from the peasantry. The structural parallels are obvious but effective. The personal dramas of the stage sisters parallel the fictional worlds of the plays they perform, which, in turn, parallel the political changes occurring in Chinese society.

Perhaps the most important parallel to consider, however, is the connection between the aesthetic of the film itself and the aesthetic development of the fictional theatrical world it chronicles. *Two Stage Sisters* is itself very much like Chinese opera. Its episodic narrative structure, for example, relies on often disjointed, autonomous sequences to give it a sweeping scope and an ability to deal with all aspects of society.

Moreover, like opera, the film relies on music to both frame and underscore important dramatic moments and to place these moments within a broader social and narrative context. For example, the film opens with a sweeping crane shot that takes in the expanses of the Zhejiang countryside before settling on the opera being performed in the marketplace. A female chorus accompanies the crane shot. The same chorus also accompanies similar crane shots later in the film as well as several montage sequences that interrupt and comment on the narrative flow. Similarly, traditional opera narrative may be interrupted by arias or by physical-action sequences choreographed to instrumental music.

As in traditional opera, an orchestra punctuates moments of intense drama with percussion or full orchestral musical phrases. For example, the music swells when Chunhua and Yuehong face each other after Chunhua's acceptance into the opera troupe and at other similarly dramatic moments. In addition, the gestures, speech, and movement of the characters in *Two Stage Sisters* often take on the highly stylized air of traditional opera.

Opera training, for example, involves hours of exercises devoted to making eye movements more expressive by following a candle flame in a darkened room. Many of the eye movements within the film draw on this aspect of opera tradition (e.g., Chunhua's passionate glances at Yuehong when the latter begins to drift away from her in Shanghai and Yuehong's startled and terrified glance at Tang after he slaps her across the face before their appearance in court).

The similarity of the characters in *Two Stage Sisters* to some traditional opera heroines must also be noted. In many ways, Chunhua appears as a modern recreation of the *wudan* or *daomadan,* martial heroines like Mu Guiying, the famous female general. Like the female warrior characters she performs on stage, Chunhua is aggressive, physically powerful, morally upright, and inevitably victorious. In fact, the representation of the revolutionary heroine in the preponderance of films made in the PRC owes a great debt to traditional opera characterizations. Similarly, the villains take on characteristics of wicked generals, evil-spirited demons, or monks from their stage counterparts.

However, although *Two Stage Sisters'* aesthetics may be rooted in traditional opera in many important respects, the film also gathers stylistic momentum from the other developments in theater to which the film's plot alludes. In many ways, *Two Stage Sisters* owes a great deal to the same May 4th impulses that gave rise to Lu Xun's mature style, represented in the film by *The New Year's Sacrifice.* Like Lu Xun's novella, *Two Stage Sisters* uses central female characters to concretize all sorts of social ills. In addition, *Two Stage Sisters* makes full use of the naturalistic detail characteristic of May 4th literature. Seemingly insignificant images take on dramatic weight (e.g., laundry washed in the river after sunset, drops of blood in a bowl of water or on a white sleeve, the straw hats an abandoned woman must make to survive in the countryside).

Although epic in scope like traditional opera, *Two Stage Sisters* also has

the chamber quality of a literature influenced by Ibsen and Western critical realism. Jiang Bo cooks rice that boils over as she discusses sexism, class differences, and the theater with Chunhua. A montage sequence shows the daily
routine of the traveling troupe from calisthenics for martial roles to memoriz-
ing lines while walking from town to town. This attention to what may appear
to be nearly irrelevant detail creates a sense of the particularity of the social
fabric, a concrete feeling for the historical period, as it does in the best of critical realism globally.

Just as the narrative of *Two Stage Sisters* culminates with the performance
of *The White-Haired Girl* and the reunion of Chunhua and Yuehong, the aesthetic strivings of the film itself find their culmination in the performance of
this play. Mao's vision of a "revolutionary romanticism" is wedded to critical
realism. Indeed, it is tempting to look at *Two Stage Sisters* as an example of
revolution romanticism. The film's plot, for example, follows the trials of a
young peasant woman, who, instead of ending her life as an obscure beggar
like the peasant widow in *The New Year's Sacrifice,* almost magically transforms herself into a revolutionary heroine. With a few exceptions, *Two Stage
Sisters* deals with crystal-clear conflicts, between masters and servants, lords
and peasants, powerful men and helpless women, in which traditional power
relations are overturned. As in all revolutionary romanticism, the revolution
becomes the most important motive force for change. Its coming resolves virtually all of the narrative conflicts. Just as Xi'er joins up with her lover and the
Red Army in *The White-Haired Girl,* Yuehong, transformed by her suffering
at the hands of Tang, joins up with Chunhua and the revolutionary opera troupe
at the end of *Two Stage Sisters.* Individual concerns find public resolution in
the political arena.

Two Stage Sisters seems to conveniently contain the seeds of its own aesthetic unraveling within its plot. On closer examination, however, it becomes
clear that this discussion does not do justice to the aesthetic complexity of the
film. Although profoundly indebted to traditional opera, the May 4th
Movement, and Mao's revolutionary romanticism, *Two Stage Sisters* takes up
aesthetic concerns that transcend Chinese drama. Like most Chinese films of
its era, *Two Stage Sisters* walks a tightrope between indigenous dramatic forms
and foreign influences, between revolutionary romanticism and what Godard
has called "Hollywood Mosfilm."

During his sojourn in China, Jay Leyda found himself quite taken aback
by the Chinese film industry's indebtedness to Hollywood:

The influence of Hollywood, and in one of its worse aspects, was a shock. First, it contradicted everything that I heard and read here about the poisons and falsehoods of Hollywood being discarded by a revolutionary, bold, new Chinese cinema. The Soviet cinema had been occasionally tempted in the same way, but never so unblushingly as here. And I was shocked to find here a part of the past revived that was long since judged as a sham and embarrassment, while a new important Chinese film [*Song of Youth* (*Oingchun zhige;* dir. Cui Wei and Chen Huaikai, 1959)] turned away deliberately from the progress being made in world cinema, even so near as Moscow and Warsaw. (1972, 247)

The influence of Hollywood on *Two Stage Sisters* cannot be denied. In fact, if the character of Jiang Bo and the revolution were erased from the script, the film could quite easily be mistaken for a Hollywood backstage melodrama. It has all the classic elements of that genre, for example, the hard struggle to the top of the theatrical profession, the bitterness of the aging actress' lot, the inevitability of decline, sour romances, misguided ambitions, competition, romantic needs vying with the dream of theatrical success, the hardships of exploitation by unsympathetic bosses.

In addition to this indebtedness to Hollywood and despite Leyda's comment that Chinese film tends to ignore Soviet cinema, *Two Stage Sisters* also owes much to Soviet socialist realism. In fact, a careful examination of the film underscores the similarities as well as the fundamental differences between classical Hollywood realism and Soviet socialist realism.

With some exceptions, for example, *Two Stage Sisters* strives for that transparency and clarity so prized by both Hollywood and socialist realism. The film creates a self-contained world. It is lit, photographed, composed, edited, and scripted in a self-effacing, Hollywood style. Characters are not as psychologically complex as their Hollywood counterparts, but they are more than one-dimensional. The narrative is linear, if episodic. The familiar codes of narrative and aesthetic form allow disbelief willingly to be suspended.

Despite their similarities, Hollywood classical realism and socialist realism differ fundamentally. Like other films of its era, *Two Stage Sisters* perhaps owes a greater debt to Moscow than Leyda would be willing to admit. Characterization in *Two Stage Sisters,* for example, follows many of the conventions traditionally associated with socialist realism. Each character represents a certain class position and the contradictions associated with a specific historical period. Lord Ni and Tang, for example, represent a position of power through ownership, and they exploit the women peasants and workers in the film. Although individually quite distinct, these characters function as "types," exemplary of the ruling order in both rural and urban prerevolutionary China.

Typification by gender and class does not rubber stamp a character. It does, however, allow for possible points of identification. Each character embodies a particular idea and has a certain abstract potential. Chunhua, for example, functions as an icon beyond the narrative, an abstraction of a "typical" woman's awakening into class and social consciousness. She represents both a psychologically credible Hollywood-styled character and an abstract idea, that is, a type in the socialist realist mold.

With history foregrounded as a narrative force in socialist realism, other classical realist narrative techniques also change. In the socialist realist text, a tension surfaces between polemics and plot; plot structure becomes subordinated to the rhetorical necessity of making a political point. Narrative structure seems to be transformed by this injection of history and the necessity for generalization and abstraction operative in socialist realism.

For example, although *Two Stage Sisters'* narrative is, for the most part, linear, it certainly does not follow the Aristotelian dramatic unity so dear to most types of classical realist fictions. In order to broaden the geographic, temporal, and social scope of the issues dealt with in the film, the episodic narrative presents incidents often only tangentially related to the development of the principal plot line. The device of the itinerant theatrical troupe provides an excellent vehicle for this. Both before and after the revolution, the troupe drifts along the river in the countryside, encountering peasants and wealthy landowners. Characters appear, are used to make a point, disappear, occasionally reappear to make another point, or simply vanish.

In addition, the film structures events into a series of dialectical relationships. Chunhua's and Yuehong's lives not only parallel one another, for example, but have a profound effect on one another. They each represent distinct choices and attributes that contradict one another at an abstract level. By seeing their lives juxtaposed, the viewer can synthesize certain ideas about the treatment of women, the limitations on their lives, and their struggles.

In the cases of Chunhua and Yuehong, two approaches are explored. Thus, Chunhua's choice to work against the system is understandable only in relation to Yuehong's decision to live within it. When the two clash in the courtroom, the whole system explodes, and the revolution arrives in the streets of Shanghai in the following scene, a direct result of the dialectical conflict within the narrative.

The Brecht Connection: Chinese Opera and Epic Theater

After looking at *Two Stage Sisters'* roots in Chinese theater, Hollywood melodrama, and socialist realism , the aesthetic sum of all this seems to be something rather different from the aggregate of its parts. Xie Jin has taken from a genre at the edges of Hollywood classicism—the melodrama. The place of the melodrama within the tradition of classical Hollywood realism must be taken into account in order to better understand the textual operation of *Two Stage Sisters*.

Recent criticism has pointed out that melodramas often strain the formal foundations of classical Hollywood realism to their limits (Pollock et al. 1977). If *Two Stage Sisters* resembles classical Hollywood cinema or Soviet socialist realism, it remains at the edge of those forms. It must be placed at the boundary between classical realist conventions and something quite different.

There seems to be something within the formal structure of *Two Stage Sisters,* coupled with the film's revolutionary politics, that places it very close to Brecht's notion of epic theater. Although Xie Jin would be the first to deny any conscious similarity between his work and Brecht's, a closer look at both the film and Brecht's writings reveals some interesting aesthetic parallels.

Despite the notoriety of his debates with Lukács on the applicability/inappropriateness of taking up the nineteenth-century realist novel as a model for socialist art, Brecht, while arguing against that form of realism, never placed his own aesthetic ideas outside of a broader realist tradition. Anti-illusionist and anti-Aristotelian rather than antirealist, Brecht sought to break down the illusion of transparency created by bourgeois theater as well as the emotional identification and catharsis invited by Aristotelian drama.

Instead, Brecht tried to distance the spectator from the drama by breaking the illusion of an invisible fourth wall. This was done by distancing the spectator from the actors on stage by making the audience constantly aware of the fact that the players were simply presenting a role constructed for them. In this way, Brecht hoped to create a critical distance between the play and the spectator, so that the playgoer would be inspired to think about the social and political issues under discussion rather than become overly involved with the characters as "real people" with individual problems.

Similar principles of distanciation can be seen at work in *Two Stage Sisters*. For example, the film revolves around the performance of other fictions, that is, operas, that constantly alert the viewer to the fact that the film, too, is a constructed fiction. Moreover, *Two Stage Sisters'* structure resembles opera; for example, it has disjointed episodes, major leaps in time and place, choral interludes, and many other elements that foreground its structuring principles and place it far outside Aristotelian traditions. Both the orchestra and the camera intrude self-consciously on the drama, acting as storytellers, commenting and reflecting on the characters' placements within the historical moment.

Also, just as Sirk and Fassbinder create compositions that frame characters within doorways and windows to place them figuratively outside the drama, Xie uses the same techniques for political analysis. This distance allows the viewer room for reflection on issues outside of any emotional involvement with the characters as individuals.

For example, after a scene that features a political discussion in Jiang Bo's apartment, a storm develops outside. Chunhua and Jiang Bo go to the rooftop apartment's doorway. The camera frames them inside and dollies back. With this shot, the camera figuratively places the characters' lives in perspective. The narrative comes to a temporary halt, allowing the viewer to reflect on the position of these characters within history, within the developing political struggle. Political changes break like a storm, and the implicit metaphor takes the viewer away from the drama for a moment. As Brecht hopes "the spectator stands outside, studies" in epic theater (1964, 37), Xie Jin's camera allows the viewer this same critical distance in *Two Stage Sisters*.

The similarity between *Two Stage Sisters* and Brecht's notion of epic theater goes beyond mere coincidence. However, although *Two Stage Sisters* postdated epic theater and achieves several of its hoped-for effects, it would be taking the argument too far to say that Brechtian aesthetics directly influenced Xie Jin. Rather, the common roots and purposes of Brecht and Xie must be kept in mind.

Brecht and Xie both owe a considerable aesthetic debt to traditional Chinese opera. Although originally a folk form, Chinese opera developed a high degree of stylistic sophistication within its long history. Outside of traditions of Western realism, Chinese opera formed its own aesthetic standards, with its own perspective on the relationship between art and actuality. Brecht particularly admired Chinese opera's aesthetic self-consciousness and delight in conventionality.

In an essay titled "Mei Lanfang, Stanislavsky, Brecht—A Study in Contrasts," Huang Zuolin notes that Brecht was particularly taken with the famous opera star Mei Lanfang's acting technique and with the Chinese opera's attitude toward performance in general. In fact, Huang traces Brecht's notion of "quotation" acting to traditional Chinese storytelling techniques:

In the course of his work, Brecht actually adopted a number of techniques from the traditional Chinese theater. One of these is his method of "quotation." He makes an actor "quote" the character played, like a traditional Chinese story-teller who steps in and out of the role at will, sometimes into the part, some-times making comments in the first person. This shifting of position facilitates the unfolding of the story, the delineation of character, and the elucidation of the author's intention. (1981, 16)

In his essay, "Alienation Effects in Chinese Acting," Brecht states:

Above all, the Chinese artist never acts as if there were a fourth wall besides the three surrounding him. He expresses his awareness of being watched. This immediately removes one of the European stage's characteristic illusions. The audience can no longer have the illusion of being the unseen spectator at an event which is really taking place. A whole elaborate European stage technique, which helps to conceal the fact that the scenes are so arranged that the audi-ence can view them in the easiest way, is thereby made unnecessary. The actors openly choose those positions which will best show them off to the audience, just as if they were acrobats. . . . The artist's object is to appear strange and even surprising to the audience. He achieves this by looking strangely at himself and his work. (1964, 91–92)

Similarly, in *Two Stage Sisters,* as the narrative bandies back and forth between onstage and offstage life, characterization takes on a quality of quotation.

In addition, the visual presentation of the self to be looked at by others operates as an "alienation effect." To cite one example, when Chunhua and Yuehong first arrive in Shanghai, they see Shuihua for the first time back-stage as she puts on her makeup. The camera's position allows the viewer to see Shuihua looking at her reflection in the mirror as well as the dumbfounded faces of Chunhua and Yuehong. Whether the two young actresses are open-mouthed because of the older actress' age or because they are simply star struck is never elucidated.

In this shot, however, the film viewer confronts a character, aware of being watched within the narrative, preparing to be watched within another fictional drama, that is, the opera to be performed on stage. Chunhua and Yuehong seem aware of their own similar positions as actresses aging within the theater. Perhaps the viewer becomes aware, at this dramatically charged moment, of yet another element, that is, the fact that all three are portrayed by screen actresses who may face similar career problems. (Since this film was not released to the general public until after the Cultural Revolution, this effect may have been further heightened by the fact that the actress who portrays Shuihua, Shangguan Yunzhu, had died during that period. Her death was subsequently blamed on the stress she underwent during the Cultural Revolution.) This moment allows the viewer to think critically about women's lives, class struggle, and the nature of oppression. The spectator can reflect on the drama as Shuihua reflects on her aging image in the mirror.

Two Stage Sisters' allusions to other dramatic works, its narrative ellipses, its stylistic self-consciousness must be regarded as very sophisticated aesthetically by Western standards. The film has certain affinities with Western modernism and international developments in Marxist aesthetics. Beneath this complexity, however, there is also an innocence, a moral directness, an ingenuous hope for a brighter future.

Coming from traditional theater and its folk aesthetic, *Two Stage Sisters* has a "naive" quality, and this quality finally brings the film close to Brecht's dream of a drama that is both didactic and popular, critical and supportive of revolutionary change. Alan Lovell has astutely observed: "Increasingly, Brecht described the quality he was searching for in his art as 'Naïveté'" (1982, 66).

Perhaps *Two Stage Sisters* comes close to Brecht's longing for "naïveté," since it draws on the folk art roots of Chinese opera to shape a modem aesthetic, to reform a relationship between art and the people obscured within modern, industrialized, commercial culture.

Two Stage Sisters and the Cultural Revolution

After tracing the aesthetic roots of *Two Stage Sisters* from folk opera through Lu Xun to Brecht and Mao himself, it seems unlikely that anyone could come up with another Chinese film indebted to as many strains of Marxist aesthetics so vividly described through narrative devices and cinematographic techniques. However, *Two Stage Sisters* was not released to the public until after the Cultural Revolution had ended, and the film was viciously attacked politically while it was still in production. In order to understand the reasons for the suppression of *Two Stage Sisters,* the film must be placed within the context of the political events going on at the time of its production.

In 1958, Mao Zedong launched China on an exceedingly ambitious project of reform called the Great Leap Forward. Designed to quicken the transformation of China into a model socialist society by increasing the size and power of both rural and urban communes, the program rather quickly collapsed the following year. In 1959, Mao stepped down as chairman of the People's Republic in favor of Liu Shaoqi, although Mao remained head of the Communist Party.[3]

Paul G. Pickowicz has noted that the end of the Great Leap Forward and Mao's temporary loss of power had some significant effects on the Chinese film industry (1985). Even though there was a decrease in production, greater emphasis was placed on quality filmmaking and carefully crafted stories.

As Pickowicz points out, the publication in 1961 of an essay by Xia Yan titled "Raise Our Country's Film Art to a New Level" ushered in the new era for the Chinese cinema. One of the best known of the "left-wing" film-makers during the golden age of the Shanghai studios in the 1930s, Xia Yan had risen in the party ranks after 1949 to become vice-minister of culture. In this 1961 essay, implicitly critical of the Great Leap Forward, Xia calls for greater autonomy for artists and for more diversity within the cinema.

Xia's directives had a definite impact. The period between the Great Leap Forward and the Cultural Revolution was characterized by a tremendous diversity in both form and subject matter within the cinema. Production ranged from domestic comedies like *Li Shuangshuang* (dir. Lu Ren, 1962) to dramas about life in prerevolutionary China like *The Lin Family Shop* (*Linjia puzi*; dir. Shui Hua, 1959). Stories about intellectuals and their romantic as well as political exploits like Xie Tieli's *Early Spring* (*Zaochun eryue*; a.k.a. *Second Lunar Month, Threshold of Spring*, 1964) were produced alongside films about revolutionary activities like Xie Jin's *The Red Detachment of Women* (1961).

This period came to a rather abrupt end, however, with the reassertion of Mao's power in the mid-1960s. The Cultural Revolution saw the mobilization of youth in the guise of the Red Guard, further radicalization of peasants and workers, dismantling of huge chunks of the bureaucratic superstructure, and purge of many party cadres.

Interestingly, many of the Cultural Revolution's most heated battles were fought in the aesthetic realm, and the Shanghai film industry became one of the prime targets. In fact, during much of the Cultural Revolution, feature-film production ceased. Because of his calls for reform after the Great Leap Forward, Xia Yan stood out for censure. As Xie Jin has pointed out, *Two Stage Sisters* fared particularly badly because of Xia Yan's association with the project:

"Wutai jiemei" [*Two Stage Sisters*] and "Zaochun eryue" [Xie Tieli's *Early Spring*] were attacked above all because of Xia Yan who had made corrections and suggestions on the screenplay. By attacking the films, they wanted to attack him. For "Wutai jiemei," Xia Yan not only helped me a lot in writing the screenplay, but it was he himself who encouraged me to make the film. And that was one of the "crimes" of which he was accused during the Cultural Revolution.[4]

Jiang Qing, Mao's wife and head of the "Gang of Four" in power during the Cultural Revolution, had a particular dislike for Xia Yan that extended back to her days as an actress in Shanghai. Beyond the personality clashes, Jiang Qing also had very clear and firm ideas about what a Chinese revolutionary drama should look like. The controversy became divided along geographic lines, which paralleled political camps. Revolutionary art outside the boundaries of the aesthetics developed in the Yan'an soviet during World War II lost all validity and was thought of as somehow "impure."

If *Two Stage Sisters* is looked at not as a harmonious mixture of Yan'an and Shanghai influences but as a battleground between two notions of what a politically progressive art should look like, then perhaps the bitterness of the film's condemnation can be better understood. Although indebted to Yan'an's *The White-Haired Girl* and Mao's "revolutionary romanticism," *Two Stage Sisters*' aesthetic heart remains in Shanghai, and this aesthetic debt assured its condemnation.

Even in works like *Two Stage Sisters* that so fervently support the party and the revolution, the Cultural Revolution's proponents could unearth a bourgeois, Western sensibility. In literary and dramatic works, characterization became a politically charged issue. A notion of the "middle" class character developed. In *Two Stage Sisters,* for example, Yuehong stands out. Neither heroic nor villainous, she aids her own oppressor because of avarice and sheer stupidity. She is, however, sympathetic. She is a victim and a "sinner" who is eventually "redeemed" by the love of her stage sister. The morally ambivalent nature of this character places her somewhere outside the realm of heroics or infamy. In the "middle," her moral ambivalence leads to textual ambiguity and, in turn, the possibility of counterrevolutionary readings. Likewise, the illusion of psychological complexity that characterizes the "middle character" places Yuehong squarely within a Western tradition of naturalism. Descriptive detail outweighs didactic precision, and, once again, the possibility of a subversive reading appears.

In retrospect, this reasoning seems strained, to say the least. More importantly, however, no degree of censure should rob *Two Stage Sisters* of its right to be taken seriously within the history of Marxist aesthetics. In its attempt to locate a peculiarly Chinese socialist aesthetic that can do justice to the representation of women, *Two Stage Sisters* merits attention. Beyond this, *Two Stage Sisters* remains at the cusp of aesthetic currents that still rage not only within Chinese cinema but within cinemas committed to social change worldwide.

Notes

This article was first published in *Jump Cut* 34 (1989): 95–106. Copyright © 1989 by *Jump Cut* Associates. Reprinted with permission.

1. *Two Stage Sisters*' Chinese title, *Wutai jiemei*, is also translated as *Stage Sisters, Two Actresses, Sisters of the Stage*. At the time *Jump Cut* decided to devote two special sections to cinema from the People's Republic of China in 1986 and 1989, little existed in English on Chinese language film. Since this essay was first published, however, there has been a welcome blossoming of scholarly works on Chinese cinema. Thankfully, Xie Jin and his oeuvre have not been ignored. See Berry 1991, Browne 1994, Da Huo'er 1989, Semsel 1987, Tung 1987.

2. Raphael Bassan, "Ombre électrique sur la cite interdite: La longue marche du cinéma chinois," *La revue du cinéma* 380 (February 1983): 77. Gina Marchetti's translation.

3. For more information on the relationship between revolutionary politics and aesthetics in twentieth-century China, see Spence 1981. Chapter 12 includes extensive background information on the period under discussion here.

4. Marco Muller, "Les tribulations d'un cineaste chinois en Chine," *Cahiers du cinéma* 344 (February 1983): 19.

Two
Hibiscus Town
(*Furong zhen,* dir. Xie Jin, 1986)

Screenplay Ah Chen, Xie Jin
Cinematography Lu Zunfu
Producer Shanghai
Cast Liu Xiaoqing, as Hu Yuyin (Sister Hibiscus)
Jiang Wen, as Qin Shutian (Crazy Qin)
Xu Songzi, as Comrade Li

H *ibiscus Town,* an adaptation of Gu Hua's novel of the same title, was a big box-office hit in 1987 when it won the Best Picture awards from both Golden Rooster and Hundred Flowers. Jiang Wen, who was only eighteen when he played the much older Crazy Qin in this film, won Hundred Flowers' Best Actor award, and the two female leads, Liu Xiaoqing and Xu Songzi, both were designated Best Actress.

In the post-Mao era, director Xie Jin became an important early critical voice on-screen of the Party's political errors since the 1950s. The influence of his films became so dominant in post-Mao (but pre–Fifth Generation) filmmaking that many contemporary films would follow the so-called Xie Jin model—a realistic, subtle, and well-planned drama showing a believer's passionate condemnation of past political abuses within the Party, a firm support of the new Party policies of reform, and a faith in a bright political future.

Hibiscus Town, a retrospective of China's recent political history as lived in a small southern town, was Xie Jin's grandest epic. To understand this film, one needs to know the following dates and events:

1957: The Anti-Rightist Campaign. Started as a reaction (known as "correction") to the excesses that occurred during the preceding Hundred Flower period, when the Party-sponsored democracy generated criticism of the Party's bureaucratization and the suggestions that China should have a multi-party political system. Intellectuals on all levels were condemned, imprisoned, or sent away as forced labor.

1963: A Campaign of Cleansing. Meant to "cleanse" the corruption within the Party and the "capitalist tendencies" in the Chinese economy.

1966: The Cultural Revolution. This power and ideological struggle within the Party took the form of a long period (officially a decade) of mass campaigns, conflicts, bloodshed, exiles, political extremism, ideological terror, cultural deprivation, and economic chaos.

1979: Smashing the Gang of Four. The foremost figures (including Mao's widow) of ultra-leftist political control since the Cultural Revolution were put under house arrest. Deng Xiaoping started to emerge as the "architect" of the reformist politics of post-Mao China.

Suggested readings for *Hibiscus Town* are as follows:

Pickowicz 1993
Ma 1994
Silbergeld 1999, 188–233

Director's Notes

Hibiscus Town is a tragedy, a unique tragedy that has occurred only in China and nowhere else in the world. Why is this the case? This is the foremost question we need to ask and an important topic for a retrospect when we shoot this film.

This tragedy contains comic elements and touches of absurdity. The laughter these elements elicit is tragic; it is the kind of laughter that should lead us into deep reflection.

This tragedy combines realism and symbolism. [In adapting Gu Hua's original,] we cannot use much of his verbal narration but must rely on our shots, frames, and figurative means to express the subjective feelings of the characters and to influence the audience's associations and contemplation. Certain sounds, such as that of the gong, the grinding stone, the bugle, and the baby crying, are all given symbolic implications.

This tragedy is lyrical for glorifying human nature, humanitarianism, the beauty of the human heart, and the human struggle to survive. (Xie Jin 1987, 3.4–3.5)

Society and Subjectivity: On the Political Economy of Chinese Melodrama
Nick Browne

A study of filmmaking in the People's Republic of China will, almost inevitably, take as its starting point the relation of the character ("the self") to the social space in which it moves. The assumption that this dramatic relation is also, at bottom, ideological is evident in contemporary Chinese cinema through the continuity with and conflict between the pre-Liberation traditions of Confucianism and the post-Liberation ideologies of socialism, a continuity and conflict that turn on the relation among the self, the family, the workplace, and the state, the fundamental terms of any image of the social totality. Starting from these premises, this essay argues that the most complex and compelling popular film form that embodies the negotiation between the traditional ethical system and the new state ideology, one that articulates the range and force of the emotional contradictions between them, is what is known in the West as "melodrama." Because this category is not part of the Chinese genre system, its use entails a shift of cultural perspective.[1]

The legacy of Western criticism of melodrama in literature and film is complex and contradictory in its theoretical formulation of the affective foundations of subjectivity. For Elsaesser, melodrama is the representation of the subjectivity of the European bourgeoisie in its struggle against the authority of a declining feudalist system (1985). That is, melodrama is a passionate meditation on the historical experience of bourgeois subjection to the economic authority of the ancient regime, an account of action and subjectivity in the social formation from the standpoint of loss and from the point of view of its victims. This representation of historical victimization as a social catastrophe is registered by narrativizing the subjective and ethical aspect of the drama within an economic interpretation of class relations and by viewing the story's individual protagonist as an overdetermined ideological figure. The shape of the story underscores a fate of suffering and of eventual social insistence on reconciliation through conformity that locates this sentimental drama and its protagonist within an ultimately oppressive social order.

The main alternative to Elsaesser's understanding of melodrama emerges from Peter Brooks's psychoanalytic account of the melodramatic imagination.[2] On this account, "melodrama" is founded on the (French) postrevolutionary attempt to institute in the Republic a morality founded on an ethical imperative centered around a new and troubled figuration of the self in its relation to the unconscious. Melodrama is a theater of social misfortune in which personal virtue is contested, hidden, misrecognized, or subverted, a form of theater that seeks within the confining and largely recalcitrant parameters of the old society to restore and recenter the ethical imperatives required of the bourgeois age. The personification of innocence and villainy constitutes the dramatization of the democratic reverberations of a newly emergent, post-traditional mode of romantic individuality. In this, melodrama is a *mise-en-scène* whose system of figuration is caught between restoration and reform. For Wylie Sypher (1965), melodrama, seen from a political point of view, is the characteristic form of nineteenth-century bourgeois aesthetic thought that marks out the impasses and the paralysis of Western revolutionary programs and aspirations, informing even the theatrical metaphors and schemes of Marx's *Kapital*.

For contemporary film studies, melodrama indicates a site of ideological critique centered on the representation of sexual difference.[3] Its logic as an aesthetic ideology is founded on the contradiction between a potentially transgressive feminine sexuality and a social system that seeks to delimit and contain it. As a transcription of the tragic into the domestic order, melodrama exemplifies the instability of the ideology of private life under capitalism and, from women's perspective, the domains of affect and action within the nuclear family. The dominant explication of the conflict of law and desire is founded on the psychoanalytic paradigm of the (white) bourgeois patriarchal family. The "social" itself—the workplace, politics—enters the familial configurations of subjectivity through the mediation of the father. The specifically aesthetic impasse of melodrama, and to a certain extent the limitation of its critique, consists of the form's failure to constitute the family in a clear or comprehensive relation to the larger social formation.

From a feminist perspective, melodrama is a dominant mode of mass culture and the site of the central contradictions of patriarchy. Owing to the centrality of its figuration of women's experience, it has been the chosen ground for the delineation of the affective stakes of social constraint and transgression. Hollywood melodrama's aesthetic ideology, in distinction to the strongly marked class oppositions characteristic of its European prototypes, reflects the democratizing of its cultural scope and generic meaning.

Even with certain ambiguous precedents, the translocation of the critical/aesthetic category of "melodrama" from its Western inscription to a contemporary Chinese context is hardly unproblematic. On what basis can an aesthetic ideology so embedded in the popular entertainment forms of Western culture—Christian and capitalist—be treated as significant, culturally speaking, to the form and meaning of contemporary Chinese film? Strictly speaking,

the Chinese system of genre classification and its categories are incommensu-
rable with the Western system. The comparability of critical terms like "genre"
is not simply a question of formal similarity, but one related to recognizing both
significant similarities and differences in literary *and* cultural contexts.[4] It is true
that important conventions of both Chinese *spoken drama* and *butterfly fiction,* instances of popular, vernacular entertainment that influenced Chinese
filmmaking in the early decades of the century, are arguably Western influenced
(Link 1981). Though the terms "melodrama" and "family melodrama" have
been used rather widely in the 1980s in discussions of films from Hong Kong
(to emphasize sacrifice for family order) (Li Cheuk-to 1986), I am unaware of
a general account of the cultural or critical genealogy of the term in relation to
Chinese aesthetics.

Ma Ning's analysis of contemporary cinema of the People's Republic shows
how what he calls melodrama renegotiates the relation between tradition and
modernization in a narrative that introduces a justification for a new economic
order, represents a transformation of power relations within the family order,
and shows this change from the vantage point of an established power structure.
This social order, he argues, is ultimately subordinated to the system of hierarchy and patronage that supports the political power of patriarchal socialism
and its new, ideological imperatives.[5] The constitution of the family drama calls
on a system of family ethics that serves in turn the project of ideological legitimation. But a depiction of the designated conflicts within the family does not,
it seems to me, constitute in a sufficiently clear way the melodramatic problematic as it has been enacted in Western cultures. The "other" can be reduced
to the "same" only at a price. That is, though important elements associated
with Western melodrama are present in films in the People's Republic, these
films do not exemplify its distinctive, constitutive features—the form's schematization of good and evil, its emotional effects, its mode of theatricality and
spectacle, its mode of characterizing the individual as victim, and its mode of
understanding the relation of the individual to the social as a matter of justice.
At best, the term "melodrama" indicates a rough critical analogy.

I express this reservation about the relevance of Western melodrama to an
accounting of Chinese film forms for several reasons: in order to motivate a
move toward a more specific account of the constitution, function, and interpretation of these forms as works functioning within the culture in which they
originate; to qualify the colonizing power and domination of Western critical
theory for an accounting of the specificity of Chinese film and culture; and
within the discipline of film studies, to work toward a new model of figuring

melodramatic structure and affect in the Western context, through an alternative to its familial focus, namely through the juridical. To the extent that Western theory of melodrama has privileged the nuclear family and its psychoanalytic account of the private sphere of "sexual difference" and "subjectivity," it has lost sight of the broader social conditions of the meaning of the form. I want to proceed, in other words, on the premise that what has been called the genre of Chinese "family melodrama" is neither a true analogy nor the exclusive site for the expression of what we might call the "melodramatic mode." Cross-cultural exchange/interpretation of what is meant by "melodrama" can be elaborated by considering the form of what I will call "political melodrama" as it is dramatized in the work of the Chinese film director Xie Jin. In this way, we might treat "melodrama" as an expression of a mode of injustice whose *mise-en-scène* is precisely the nexus between public and private life, a mode in which gender as a mark of difference is a limited, mobile term activated by distinctive social powers and historical circumstances.

The political melodrama that I want to consider is best exemplified in Xie Jin's films focused on the figure of the rightist, the nature of his crime, punishment, and process of political rehabilitation. In the 1980s, this thematic is an authorial preoccupation in *The Herdsman* (*Muma ren*, 1982), *The Legend of Tianyun Mountain* (*Tianyunshan chuanqi*, 1980), and *Hibiscus Town* (*Furong zhen*, 1986). Indeed, *Hibiscus Town* addresses the emotional complexity of the central ideological question of the post–Cultural Revolution era—the place accorded to individual entrepreneurship within the socialist order.

Hibiscus Town tells how a young woman laboriously and diligently builds up a small business (a bean curd restaurant), then is denounced by the local Party leader, who is jealous of her large income. She loses her business, her house, and her husband (who is persecuted to death), suffers years of ostracism, becomes sick and slides into despair, falls in love with a fellow street cleaner (an old rightist who cares for her), becomes pregnant, is illegally married, is judged and condemned again by the Party (it isolates her and imprisons her new husband), and bears the illegitimate child. At the end of the Cultural Revolution, she has her second husband, home, and business restored to her. The "text" of *Hibiscus Town* narrativizes these events through a sexual, economic, and political description of the organization of the society of a small Chinese rural town from 1963 to 1979. The film centrally dramatizes the relation between "subjectivity" (self) and society as it is organized and mediated by the Communist Party.

At the very outset of the film, the population of Hibiscus Town consists of three groups: the "people," the "bad elements," and the Party. The action proper begins with the arrival of local Party Secretary Li, a woman, under the banner of "class struggle," and the initiation of her investigation of Hu, the small restaurateur. The latter is building a new house with her business profits on land bought from a local Party official, Wang, a land-reform activist who lives elsewhere in a dilapidated section at the edge of town. Li's investigation moves forward with a public accusation of Hu's "illegal" self-enrichment (realized, it is alleged, through favorable terms she had negotiated with the local manager of the state's granary stores). The state confiscates Hu's property, condemns her as a "bad element," "a newly rich peasant," and sets her to work cleaning the town streets. Three years later with the onset of the Cultural Revolution, Secretary Li is herself stigmatized—as a slut (she protests saying she is a leftist)—and is publicly humiliated. In 1979, with the close of the Cultural Revolution, Li returns to the town to carry on Communist politics.

In posing the question of how, fifteen years after the founding of the socialist state, hard work leading to the purchase of a house can be regarded as a crime, the film points directly to the contradictory ideology and practices of socialism in the reform years. Indeed, the film's complexity consists of the fact that the sexual, economic, and political systems that comprise this social network are almost completely imbricated and intermixed. Notwithstanding this, the film is organized around distinctive binarisms, identified and labeled as "rightist" and "leftist."

Most important, these political categories (which are also economic categories) intersect with moral categories. That is, in the film's principal reversal, the oral perspective contradicts the long-standing correspondence of "Left" with "good" and "Right" with "bad." Indeed, the film inverts the dogmatic formula of the 1950s in which the Party leaders come to the small village and liberate the people from an oppressive feudalism by dissolving the forced marriage contracts that serve as the quintessential emblem of feudal patriarchy. *Hibiscus Town* inverts this formula by showing that the Party system of social control through classification by type leads to persecution and criminalization of a marriage between two persons freely choosing each other outside the authority of the Party. In *Hibiscus Town* the agents of the Party are designated as oppressors.

The personification of the moral and sexual conflict between Right and Left is realized in a dramatic comparison between two women—New Rich Peasant Hu and Secretary Li. Each woman is authoritative in her own sphere of work. Hu, the younger, is married both at the beginning of the film and at the end; Li is older, more severe, and unmarried throughout. Li's political comrade and lover Wang is a boastful, self-important toady, imperious in his own sphere but wholly subordinated to her power. The film's evident inversions of traditionally subordinated power relations between women and men underscore and thematize male masochism.

In conjunction with the moral evaluation of political positions is a moral evaluation of sexual relations. In this way, the personal and sexual characteristics of the two leading women contribute to an understanding of the legitimacy—and even the rectitude—of their political status. In one central difference—not of gender but of politics—the film points up the superiority of Confucian morality over socialist pragmatism. That is, the ethical perspective at work in the film contends with the political system.

The narrative of *Hibiscus Town* is organized around three major clusters of events that can be summarized as crime, punishment, and restitution. Hu's trajectory through the film marks them out: the allegation of criminal self-enrichment through the sale of state property; her punishment and suffering through the loss of business, house, and husband; and the restitution and restoration of her home, a new husband, and the birth of a boy child. The film supplies a detailed and comprehensive literal accounting of the economic foundations of Hu's bean curd business that includes the cost of raw materials, gross sales, and so forth. Indeed, her product is explicitly analyzed as a commodity. The fact that the business is part of the food cycle puts the enterprise in close proximity to a biological understanding of the requirements of maintaining life. Indeed, attention to food—both its lack and its abundance, its necessity and its symbolism (as in the wedding feast)—grounds this film, linking it to one of the dominant preoccupations of the Chinese cinema and underlining its foundations in the representation of scarcity. This sequence of narrative events, then, is the figuration of a political interpretation of economic events: acquisition, loss, and return of objects of value (literal and symbolic).

Hibiscus Town shows a fundamental and strict understanding of the political economy of the social order—its modes and relations of production organizing goods, social relations, and indeed "subjectivity" within the framework of the same system. The narrative intelligibility of this Chinese text as a system of signs is predicated not only on a series of motivated consequences, but also on a system that correlates its objects with modes of subjectivity. In this sense, the political classification scheme is coextensive with the order and hierarchy of the social body, and is a means of deciding individual obligations and privileges. Social positions and subjectivity are named and determined by the political system; the Party's political criteria provide a legal justification for the assignment of persons to social ranks. The film shows in methodical, narrative detail the deprivation of life and goods by a political machine that serves at the same time as a judicial apparatus.

In the Chinese political melodrama, the political process is narrativized as a trial that occupies the thematic center in the way that the family conflict does in the family melodrama. Here the drama arises from the Chinese institution of crime and punishment worked out through socialist culture. The film represents the Party's action on the social body. But in the contemporary period, a political perspective vies with and is contested by the ethical one. In this sense Xie Jin's narration and point of view include a perspective on the world of the characters that includes a historical critique. At stake in this form of melodrama is a definition of the self and of the relation of the individual to the social as a fully public matter. Melodrama is the mode of representation of a historical experience that inscribes "subjectivity" in a position between the expectations of an ethical system (Confucianism) and the demands of a political system (socialism), a condition that typifies the Chinese dilemma of modernization (Stacey 1983). The form's principal significance lies in the affective dimension of the self's relation to the social order, catalyzing two affective regimes that are acted out in the narrative as intensified performances of betrayal, disappointment, or defeat. Chinese melodrama's mode of arbitrating the relation of subjectivity/society is, in other words, a specific cultural formation.

Confucianism's traditional ethical doctrine linked the social body at all levels, modeling the responsibilities and duties of self, family, and state on an analogical "great chain of being." Socialism has undertaken to remodel these relations without abandoning them, recruiting film as a state ideological apparatus for the representation of this new, ethical system and its corresponding prescriptions on subjectivity. In this sense, Xie Jin's films work explicitly to monitor and readjust these new ideological premises to old ethical standards and—through a cultural critique of ongoing antirightist violence—to explore the limits of the political administration of socialist justice. *Hibiscus Town* lays out the political process of justice—crime and punishment—but it also subjects that process to a critique that puts politicization itself on trial from an ethical standpoint. For its audience, the film is a kind of judicial hearing with its own rules of evidence and argument. The film, both as a narrative institution and as a legal institution, mediates the relation of the audience to the abuses, disturbances, and injustices of the real, ongoing events of the Cultural Revolution.

In what way, we must ask, can the representation of the experience of Western capitalism viewed from a Christian perspective be analogous to the representation of the experience of contemporary Chinese socialism viewed from a Confucian perspective? The cultural specification of "subjectivity" and of victimization in melodrama implies, from the first, the concept of the "person." In the ethical and political writings of these two traditions, the treatment of this concept is traceable to the difference between Western "subjectivity" as the private, personal, and perspectival representation of a single mind and the Chinese definition of the person as a set of conventions, social relations, and transactions within the group (mind serving as the ground of social relatedness) (Munro 1985). The Kantian foundation of ethics in individual responsibility defines the moral autonomy of the self as a matter of choice based in a universal faculty of reason beyond or above social convention. What grounds this personal ethical autonomy, legally speaking, is an acknowledgment of rights. Western individuality is treated as a freedom from social and governmental control, surveillance, and the like, and hence individual autonomy is closely associated with the sphere of privacy. In its ideal form, the law guarantees and institutionalizes these freedoms and rights.

In Chinese culture, traditional writings on Confucian individuality underscore the transitive obligations between subjective terms within a hierarchy that regards the person as a social function, a position placed within the five cardinal relations of domination and subordination that draws its meaning and its codes from hierarchically organized social practice, and not from the status of the person as an agent of free choice. This tradition of ethics based on the cooperation of person and group and institutionalized by social practice is the basis of Confucian legal and administrative theory, a theory that posits human improvement through the exemplification of virtue and correction through education. Confucian legal doctrine[6] was elaborated over several centuries in conflict with an alternative, secular "legalist" theory that called for equal treatment of all before a uniform law and an ethical system backed up by rewards and punishments. Confucian ethics, in contrast, was constituted almost entirely as a code regulating *hierarchical* social relations within and beyond the family. It was the basis of the legal theory in one fashion or another that was inherited by the Communist social administration. Legalist theory, however, with its democratic instincts and its doctrine of reform through punishment, provided in some measure one of the intellectual resources for Communist administrative reform of Confucian feudalism.

We might ask, then, about the form of individualism implied in Xie Jin's political melodrama and how it stands in relation to Chinese models of justice. Who are Xie Jin's characters? What is his mode of characterization? First, people's social and political positions are designated by titles: Secretary Li, Director Gu, etc. The society understands the importance but also the superficiality of identity through this kind of symbolic positioning—and the problem of personal identity is articulated in the film around a cinematic topos constructed by distinguishing between the space of the house and that of the street. The spatial coordinates of personal identity are "inside" and "outside," "home" and "workplace." Xie Jin's revisionist mode of socialist spatialization—of construction of the lived relation between person and environment—both deconstructs and institutes the frontier between private and public spaces and the equivalent distinction within the *mentalité* of the social subject. In this sense, the project of revising established conventions of socialist spatialization (i.e., there is *only* public space) seeks to locate the self in the spaces of both the house and the street. In *Hibiscus Town* cinematic *decoupage* articulates the revision of the political valence of space.

The main interest of the film, then, lies in the problematic of the marginal characters, the social and political outsiders. What is the form of their social nonbeing? *Hibiscus Town* provides significant representations of the life of these outsiders. For a long time, one feels, they have lived in the streets. Indeed, in the long midsection of the film that traces the development of Hu and Qin's relationship, exterior social space and its representation are transformed lyrically. The bodily movement of the work of sweeping becomes the dance of the courtship ritual. This part of the film opens onto a strangely isolated cultural space that is roughly divided in equal parts between the street and Hu's room, between long shots of alleyways receding into the depth (largely bluish gray), which serve as the narrowed space of romantic choreography, and the smallish, rose-tinted scenes of the interior, nondescript private space in which the bed and the hearth are the most evident furnishings, the site of passion and its consummation. Outside this room, on both sides of the door, are posters announcing the place to the public as the residence of a "black couple." That is, the place of the outsiders explicitly signed as a space apart is the space of a criminalized marriage. Thus, the space of the social outsider is, in a way, indifferent to the discrimination between house and street. At the same time, there is a single space of romance, of song, and of sexual pleasure. This middle section of the film is composed through what we might think of as a romantic comedy centered around the formation of the transgressive couple.

Politically speaking, however, the spatialization of this interlude is contradictory and paradoxical and stands as the film's central instance of a mode of subjectivity at the margin of official discourse. It is the space of unauthorized and indeed transgressive assertion of individual choice. It, alone, is the space abandoned to the private and is explicitly, I think, the "space of human rights" as it might be understood in the West.

The theme of the rights of political outcasts to marry is repeated and underlined in Xie Jin's work in the 1980s. In *Hibiscus Town,* with Hu's announcement to Qin that she is pregnant, the couple seek permission from Party authorities to marry. The request is received by Wang with astonishment at "class enemies screwing on the sly!"—and is refused. Qin protests that even members of the "five bad elements" have the right to marry and have children. Qin's assertion of this right is assigned special status—differentiating the human as such. Marriage, however, requires legitimation by civil authority. Old Gu, former Party secretary, observing that no one else would dare to attend the wedding of a "black couple," performs this office. Subsequently, the couple is condemned by the Military Commission for "threatening the dictatorship of the proletariat" and the man is sent to jail. The space of romantic privatization is illusory and short-lived, and is soon rearticulated with the larger public space of the *mise-en-scène* of trial and punishment. The dark result, announced on the steps of a municipal building in the rain to the assembled community, underlies the Party's real power—if not over biology itself, then over the definition of the social status of human relations. It is part of Xie Jin's humanism to depict the injustice of this eclipse of the space of the human.

Two scenes underline the authority of the Party to decide the propriety of individual action: the early night scene of Secretary Li's public denunciation of New Rich Peasant Hu and the late scene pronouncing the verdict on the couple. Both have a similar formal design traceable to the explicit theatricalization of juridical politics—the official speaker is center stage and points out the accused both to incriminate and to condemn. The scene of judicial decision is presented theatrically to an assembled audience as a public lesson for didactic purposes. The *mise-en-scène* of human rights exists in the relation between the empty streets of political nonbeing and the private room, and the administrative display of public and formalized deprivation and castigation. The two spaces—of being and administration—are dialectically related.

The subjective state of the victims that corresponds to these public sanctions is ambiguous. Generally, Confucian punishment rests on the premise of corrective reeducation through shame rather than guilt as a *social* means for the production of conformity. Guilt, a private emotion, seems more consistent with the punitive theories of Western individualism. The film depicts the couple's refusal to accede to either punitive state. Rightist Qin, the town's artist manqué and poster maker, having had more experience at being an outcast, teaches Hu the way to bear this public sanction when he writes and then posts outside their own door the signs announcing the residence of a "black couple" to the assembled public. Qin's comic resilience, bemused distance, and elevated indifference to these self-authored critiques (an attitude carried, as well, in the movement, gesture, and carriage of his body) give form to a personal style of Chinese autonomy. It is a style of resistance to public sanction. He must bear the injustice, but it does not touch him or alter his fundamentally comic and ironic outlook on life.

This is a form of melodrama founded on the concept of the "person" apart from gender per se. The chief antagonists are both women, though one is "masculinized." In both Xie Jin's *The Legend of Tianyun Mountain* and *The Herdsman,* the political victims are men, although the women are the active figures and the ones who sacrifice themselves to maintain the men. The evident victim in *Hibiscus Town,* the one whose misfortunes are recounted, is the woman Hu, while it is the man, already stigmatized, who supports her. The dynamics of Xie Jin's victimized couples, between male and female, passive and active, are not irrevocably fixed. The woman suffers, as does the man, but neither sacrifices him- or herself for the other. Both characters adopt an ethic of survival, living when necessary like animals. Although in *Hibiscus Town* the woman is victimized, the man, the rightist, is the reference point for Xie Jin's humanist critique. The two figures are in a sense condensed in an emblem of social injustice. The Party's amnesty returns Hu's confiscated property and provides her with a legitimate husband. With his return, the family as a social unit is reformed and the bean curd business resumed. The formation of the family, with child, however, stands outside the strict terms of literal accountability. No price can be put on their suffering. In Xie Jin's hands the political melodrama concludes with the restoration of the family, embedded in a profitable, small entrepreneurial business.

The humanist ideology of the film is simultaneously transparent and complex in its relation to the processes of both socialist revolution and modernization in China in the 1980s. Contemporary Western film criticism since 1968, heavily invested in ideological critique, has not generally confronted the problem of the critique of socialist representation. Following Althusser, Western Marxism in its cultural criticism has treated ideology as a discourse of mystification justifying the capitalist order by naturalization. The spectator, on this account, is forced into an implicit agreement with the terms of the text's construction, one that precludes a critical reading. This process of ideological interpellation is literalized by an account of the functioning of cinematographic apparatus (Baudry 1985). This paradigm has become an article of critical faith across a range of "progressive" perspectives. Yet what can the Western critique of bourgeois ideology and its associated critical technology achieve in application to Chinese film? And more to the point, what from a Western point of view constitutes an adequate critical model of the relation of film and ideology in the People's Republic? Socialist "ideology," it would seem, is hardly in need of demystification—it is explicit and taught as such. This fundamental difference of perspective indicates that a political reading of *Hibiscus Town* as a melodrama and as ideology should proceed in close relation to the political time and culture in which it is embedded and not simply as the transcription of a Western critical problematic.

Soviet analysts of China in the 1920s and 1930s were undecided about the terms of analyzing the potential for Marxist revolution in China because of its complicated and entrenched mix of feudalism and capitalism (Dirlik 1978). *Hibiscus Town,* however, appears in a postrevolutionary culture, after the Liberation. It is a given that the feudal order so evident in many mainland films (especially those in the leftist tradition of the 1930s and 1940s) has been dismantled. Indeed, in this earlier period there was another version of Chinese political melodrama in which the central antagonist that victimizes the main characters is the feudal order itself. But in the film under discussion, "class struggle" is waged by the socialist victors against the defeated remnants, practices, and personnel of the prerevolutionary period.

Melodrama centered around such persons as Hu and Qin as victims seems possible only retrospectively—after the socialist revolution and after the shift of policy that permitted in the 1980s what was prohibited in the 1960s. "Modernization" as it is understood in China in the 1980s necessitated a change of ideology and, in particular, the process of de-Maoification. The new socialism borrows a moral perspective from Confucianism in order to criticize the old ways and to justify a new concept of the self appropriate to the new economic order. However, the film argues that this mode of subjectivity is not new, but is found in the villages of the past. What is new is the ideological task of introducing the legitimacy of individual entrepreneurship.

The Cultural Revolution in the film is a negative political reference mobilized as a framework in which to present the case for a more local and particular change—the process of modernization. The relationship of the form of political melodrama to the process of modernization is as complex as its relation to revolution. This fact puts the form of Chinese socialist melodrama, and

Hibiscus Town in particular, in relation to a certain historiography. The fictional form of the film is articulated around the contrast between past and present, by the process, told in multiple interrupting flashbacks, of Hu remembering scenes from an earlier and happier life. The narrative itself is marked out by a series of dates—1963, 1965, 1979—that organize the entire film and put this melodramatic form in relation to the audience's popular memory of contemporary history. The film restates the problems of the Civil War and Liberation through its figuration of the Cultural Revolution and its aftermath. In this, socialist historiography confronts the ambiguities of the post-Liberation period. Assistant Party Secretary Wang, driven crazy by events, is left wandering the streets, banging a gong and shouting his prophetic announcement of the return of another "movement." History, as seen by the film, threatens social dismemberment by repetition of the struggles that led to Liberation.

It is difficult to consider the film as fully a part of the new ideological campaigns of the 1980s. It looks backward—and in Xie Jin's account, the Party is assigned responsibility for the strife and suffering of the past. Yet the film stages an alteration of the social category of the "individual" that answers to the needs of both the past and the present. It is precisely the redefinition of human rights of citizens, that is, civil rights, that Xie Jin formulates in the film.

We have detailed the system for figuring the emotional content of the characters' experience in terms of the relation of personal subjectivity to social structure, and treated it as a matter of victimization. The film explores the scope and content of the "space" of human rights through an analysis of complicating relations between the two large systems of ethical/political thought, Confucianism and socialism, that operate in some composite form in contemporary Chinese society. In this, the film indicates the affective basis of Chinese political melodrama. Suffering is linked ultimately to the injustices of the political administration of social power. In this sense, subjectivity is part of a new political language of the post-Cultural Revolution period. It indicates an aspect of the person beyond that of the citizen. From this perspective we can see the justice of designating Xie Jin's project, as Esther Yau has aptly suggested, "rehumanization." Economic modernization, to the extent that it includes a cultural redefinition of the sphere of the personal or the private, indicates a future, yet to be realized, of both rights and desires.

The film's fundamental choice to proceed by dramatizing the central conflicts of a certain historical moment through the representation of women indicates the contradictory cultural symbolism of the figure of Chinese woman.[7] Secretary Li is a personification, no doubt, of the detested figure of Jiang Qing,

Mao's wife, the leader of the Gang of Four, and the film puts the blame on her for the persecution of the couple. In this regard, the film depicts the disfiguration of the social caused by the "phallic woman." By contrast, Peasant Hu, the entrepreneur, carries the extraordinary virtues of her type. In depicting cultural and economic change through the tropological opposition of two women, Xie Jin extends the Chinese practice of representing socialist ideological change by a reduction of sexual difference to an epiphenomenon of the social formation. "Woman" is an ambiguous figure of the Chinese cinema: liberated by the Party, she has been a traditional justification for Chinese socialist domination. Xie Jin's critique of social deformation in the past neither excuses the Party nor supports a call for dismantling it. The film is situated on the cultural horizon of the 1980s in quite a different way than many of the radically conceived films of the Fifth Generation in their refiguration of the role of the political. Xie Jin remains squarely within the recognizable terrain of Han culture, and the familiar contours and problematics of a socialist vision of life, while succeeding in formulating an ethical discourse that works closely in the space between popular sentiments of disappointment or cynicism and the regime of the politically possible. For some Chinese critics and filmmakers, this form of socialist humanism and the Hollywood mode that supports it constitute a cultural monument to the past and designate the limits of sustainable cultural critique.

Notes

This article was first published in *New Chinese Cinemas,* edited by Nick Browne et al. (Cambridge: Cambridge University Press, 1994), pp. 40–56. Copyright © 1994. Reprinted with the permission of Cambridge University Press.

1. For important contemporary statement on the question of cross-cultural method, see Yau 1987–88, Jameson 1986, Rey Chow 1986–87.

2. Peter Brooks, *The Melodramatic Imagination* (New York: Columbia University Press, 1985).

3. A thorough orientation and survey of the field from this point of view is Christine Gledhill 1987.

4. Plaks 1977, 309–52. For a justification of the use of the term "melodrama" in relation to Chinese fiction, see C. T. Hsia 1984, 199–240. On the relation of literature to film more generally, see Leo Lee 1991. For a general study of the performing arts, see McDougall 1984.

5. Ma Ning 1989. In his Ph.D. dissertation, "Culture and Politics in Chinese Film Melodrama: Traditional Sacred, Moral Economy and the Xie Jin Mode," Monash University, 1992, Ma Ning argues that, "although Chinese film melodrama in its development in this

century was subject to Western influences, it also embodies a culturally specific mode of imagination related to Chinese metaphysical, ethical, aesthetic and political traditions." It is the site in which the moral economy of traditional Chinese culture (an economy rooted in traditional Chinese cosmology and ethics) asserts itself in the area of mass cultural production. Ma argues for the specifically Chinese way of ideological domination.

6. The classic study is T'ung-tsu Ch'ü 1961. See also Valk 1956. For a penetrating account of the status of rights within the liberal framework, see Kelman 1987.

7. For recent analyses of Chinese women by women, see Yau 1989a, Yau 1989b, Kaplan 1989. On nonwhite women more generally, see Teresa de Lauretis 1988.

Three
Farewell My Concubine
(*Bawang bie ji,* dir. Chen Kaige, 1993)

Screenplay Lilian Lee, Lu Wei
Cinematography Gu Changwei
Producer Tomson (HK) & Beijing
Cast Leslie Cheung, as Cheng Dieyi
Zhang Fengyi, as Duan Xiaolou
Gong Li, as Juxian
Ge You, as Master Yuan

After some commercial failures with his philosophical and fable-like experimental films, such as *King of the Children* and *Life on a String*, Chen Kaige eventually had a commercial success with *Farewell My Concubine*, a three-hour epic adaptation of the best-selling novel by a Hong Kong writer, Lilian Lee. Chris Berry compares Chen's change in film style to that of Italian director Bertolucci who "revived his career after the fiasco of *La Luna* by sacrificing cinematic innovation to the Hollywood historical epic formula" (1993, 21). Yet in Chen's newly-adopted epic formula, some of his earlier themes remain. The interplay of these themes with the epic formula, what Wendy Larson describes as the feminized, thoughtful but powerless male at the mercy of the dominant cultural power, offers us a key for penetrating the epic facade of this new film by the innovative Chen Kaige.

Farewell My Concubine traces the relationship of two Beijing Opera stars from their boyhood to old age, that is, from the late Qing dynasty to the post-Mao era. The two stars' performances at different times of their favorite opera, *Farewell My Concubine*, offer a thematic consistency in the epic scope of the film. The concept of loyalty dramatized in this opera helps comment on the complexity of the part of Chinese history that they are witnessing. To understand this interplay of opera and history, we need to examine both.

The Beijing Opera was originally a local theater in south China. A theater troupe was summoned by the emperor Qianlong to perform in Beijing in the late eighteenth century; it became extremely popular and has been considered China's national theater ever since. Chen Kaige's film records the high point of this theater.

Farewell My Concubine, a favorite piece in the Beijing Opera repertoire, is based on a story of five years of competition for national supremacy between the king of Chu and the king of Han. The king of Chu tragically lost the war, and the Han dynasty, the first unified dynasty since the First Emperor, emerged out of his misfortune. The opera records the last of the king of Chu's losing battles. The king of Chu is discovered in a military camp with his concubine, Yu Ji. Although knowing that the morale of the soldiers is low, Yu Ji still tries hard to cheer up her royal spouse. When the enemy starts to attack from all sides, the king asks Yu Ji to take a carriage and leave with him. Yu refuses, not wanting to make this crucial escape difficult for her king. Then the king suggests that Yu go over to the king of Han for safety, which greatly irritates her. "Your Majesty is wrong," she sings. "A faithful minister will not serve two sovereigns; a virtuous woman will not marry twice. Since you are aiming at an empire, why should you lose heart for a woman? I beg from you the sword to end my life in return for your love and to relieve you from thinking of me." Diverting his attention, she seizes the sword and takes her own life.

What follows are some important dates within the epic scope of the film:

1911. A revolution overthrew China's last dynasty of Qing and ushered the country into its modern era of drastic social change and civil war. During this time, the powerful eunuch patrons of theater were ousted from the Forbidden City in Beijing.

1937–1945. During this eight-year-war of resistance against Japanese invasion, parts of China were occupied by Japan.

1949. The founding of the People's Republic of China ended the civil war on the mainland with the nationalist government and troops retreating to the island of Taiwan.

1966–1976. This decade of social chaos is known as the Cultural Revolution. One part of this revolution was an extremist cleansing from Chinese culture of its "feudal dregs," including using modern subject matter to replace the traditional subjects of classical operas.

Suggested readings for *Farewell My Concubine* are as follows:

Lau 1995
Zha 1995, 79–104
Kaplan 1997

Tam and Dissanayake 1998, 11–22
Benzi Zhang 1999
Silbergeld 1999, 96–131

Director's Notes

I found the novel to be somewhat skimpy, and I was ill at ease on reading it. To begin with, Lilian Lee had neither a clear idea of the situation in China nor of the Peking Opera itself. Nor again did she have any kind of personal feel for the Cultural Revolution for the simple reason that she wasn't there when it happened! Moreover, there was a problem of language too—a problem that showed up a writer with an external view of the happenings in the country; I, therefore, significantly developed the relationship between the characters, particularly the relation between the prostitute Juxian and Duan Xiaolou, one of the actors whom she marries. In the book she emerges as a rather pale figure; but I felt that without a consistent female character the film would not hold. After all, the trio—Juxian and the two "brother" actors, Duan Xiaolou and Cheng Dieyi—constitute the basic structure of both the film and the book. (Qtd. in Max Tessier 1993, 16)

The Concubine and the Figure of History: Chen Kaige's *Farewell My Concubine*
Wendy Larson

Eugene Yuejin Wang has pointed out an ironic cross-cultural situation: it is precisely the films of the Fifth-Generation directors, films that posit a "cultural identity that the current Chinese public are reluctant to identify, and which they keep at arm's length" that have received acclaim abroad as a "cinematic representation of Chinese culture" (1989, 36). Wang elaborates the cinematic codes that bear cultural specificity to China—understatement in emotional rhetoric, exploration of emotional subtlety, indulgence in faint sadness, a "distracted" narrative structure, and the evocation of familiar lyrical motives from traditional poetics, as well as other common characteristics such as lyricizing about departure, absence, and memory (37–39). It is these codes that are broken in some Fifth-Generation films such as *Red Sorghum,* which through "the bold indulgence in violence with sound and fury" and "the shift from the quiet back alleys of townscape to the dusty and naked land" constructs a radically new cinematic code and national identity (38). Eventually himself sliding into the position of the Fifth-Generation directors, Wang claims that while earlier films "lick the wounds" of the Cultural Revolution, *Red Sorghum* violently shatters any illusion of an innocent utopia and shows how the "indulgence in emotional delicacy for its own sake" and the traditional virtues of restraint and concealment are in fact historical restraints that limit action and fulfillment (39).

Wang is careful to point out that the so-called Chinese cinematic codes are neither absolute nor unchanging but are really a combination of traditional Chinese theatrical consciousness, the "grammatical mold" of classical Hollywood, Chinese didacticism, and Soviet dogmatism (36). Nonetheless, he sides with the Fifth-Generation directors in their implicit critique of the "physiology and the pathology" of the Chinese social psyche and situates this bent against the fact that now cultural identity is only meaningful when it is "posited against the Western Other"(39)—to do something else is an "indulgence" that results in complacence. As Wang implies, entry into the Western film community occurs only through identity and specificity. Western viewers want from China a film *about* China.

It is along these culturally specific lines that Chen Kaige's *Farewell My Concubine* has entered the international film arena, sharing with Jane Campion's *The Piano* the Cannes Palme d'Or award in May 1993 and, like a limited number of Fifth-Generation films before it, playing widely in art theaters. In the United States, *Farewell* is mostly read as a film about Chinese civilization; commentators often interpret it as a historical epic. The twentieth-century setting, which progresses historically through the decades and recognizes the two major political and cultural events of the Japanese invasion and the Cultural Revolution, leads many reviewers to comment that this is indeed Chinese history and thus, China.

Kevin Thomas, writing in the *Los Angeles Times,* sums up this approach to *Farewell* and thus links it to Chen Kaige's *King of the Children* and *Yellow Earth:* "the films possess an epic scope much like 'Farewell My Concubine,' which spans half a century and covers a sizable portion of China itself. That's because they are subtle, understated journeys into the heart, soul and mind of their people" (Jan. 17, 1994). Calling the Fifth-Generation directors the "greatest and bravest in [Chinese] history," Nigel Anderson quotes Chen Kaige's comment on the filming of *Yellow Earth* in a remote area where cameras had virtually never been before: "People were very quiet, very guarded, very austere. Yet reading their faces was like 'reading Chinese history'" (1994).

In interviews with Western writers, Chen Kaige does nothing to debunk the film's reception as a Chinese epic; over and over he links *Farewell* with his personal experience in the Cultural Revolution and a broader history outside the Cultural Revolution that he knows intimately. The entire film, he claims, is a result of his present anger at being "duped" and, like the rest of the Chinese population, falling victim to revolutionary ideology. Chen places himself in the position of the characters for whom "the opera means everything" yet who have "paid a huge price to be part of the spectacle."[1] The term "spectacle" is used not only by the film's director but also by others commenting on the film's success or failure; in awarding *Farewell* the International Critics' Prize as well as the Palme d'Or judges seemed to paraphrase Chen's words, praising the film for "its incisive analysis of the political and cultural history of China and for its brilliant combination of the spectacular and the intimate" (Canby 1994).

What is the "spectacle" to which Chen, as director and critic, and other commentators refer?[2] Is it Chinese history itself, or the exhibit of history within the film, which provides a night out more pleasurable than reading an academic book and is easily accessible to those who know little? From the perspective of Yuejin Wang's incisive analysis of the Chinese cinema's entry and translation into Western film's interpretive field, *Farewell* has convinced Western viewers that it is an authentic portrayal of Chinese history.[3] Yet at the same time, the film continually turns the viewer's attention away from deep historical analysis toward an ahistorical consciousness and a gendered subjectivity-under-power.[4] In its persistent use of historical referents to panoramically parade the past before us, the film presents itself as "about" Chinese history; still, it offers no persuasive historical explanations to show why things are the way they are. The ending of the film belies such a notion and has raised the ire of officials in China, who demand that Chen explain why the main character has to kill himself in 1977, just as Deng Xiaoping comes to power and "history" is changing.

This essay investigates the way in which *Farewell* appropriates the past to reject history in favor of fantasy as the means through which Chinese national subjects who want to enter transnational culture must produce personal and cultural narratives. Contradictorily both in and out of history, Peking opera players are from the past yet are not its real actors. A character such as Cheng Dieyi exists as if drugged—and actually does fall into a drugged stupor in the story—and in a time warp, ostensibly outside the demands of contemporary global and domestic politics, purely within the realm of personal and symbolic desire.

In somewhat misleading ways, the film's category of fantasy corresponds to that used in Western psychoanalysis. Jacques Lacan constructed a formula for fantasy which "encourages us to understand that psychic formation as a mechanism for plugging the hole of symbolic castration or lack by positing a particular object as the cause of desire" (Silverman 1992, 4). After his symbolic castration, Cheng Dieyi fixates on Duan Xiaolou and strives to keep intact the "particular syntax or tableau" that allows him to assume the desiring position (6). However, the necessary tableau is the opera, a craft that, because it is uniquely Chinese, shifts the film's critique away from focus on the individual or even the acculturated subject in Chinese society and—unlike the work of Jacques Lacan, where the psychologized subject is universal—toward the specificity of (Chinese) cultural form itself.[5] The category of fantasy is an answer to this question: In an age of transnational capitalism, under what circumstances can local or national culture be staged?

In order to keep his fantasy of pure cultural form—here symbolized by the opera—alive, Cheng Dieyi lives the concubine's subservient position. This archetypical feminine position is the essence of Chen Kaige's new and compromised transcultural consciousness and is created and developed through a series of films he directs. What has been given up is precisely the historicized understanding of the communist past, which orders events into a progressive narrative and represents the story's authority through a male figure—in this case the king of Chu, Duan Xiaolou.

Western viewers see Chen's films as Chinese and, because of the historical references and their mimetic power, authentically so. At the same time, through an intense emphasis on the male characters' subjective sense of lack and disorientation, the films deviate from emphasis on Chinese social and historical issues. The films embed the narrative into a framework the Western viewer would identify as specifically Chinese at the same time as they replace a historicist presentation with a crisis of consciousness. *Farewell* is the first of Chen's films to organize the central male character's fractured being into two characters and to try to redeem the broken side of consciousness through the artistic, active, sensitive Cheng Dieyi.

In *Farewell,* the reticence and withholding characteristic of traditional cinematic codes are enveloped into the aesthetic of the opera and the appeal of the main character, with the Fifth-Generation trademark "sound and fury" all relegated to the falsely accentuated shell of history, where it functions as a domestic critique and as a hook for the Western film community. At the same time, the failure of history to act as an organizing and unifying principle brings forth a ruptured male consciousness that then molds itself into a new, if ultimately untenable, possibility. The symbolic castration and gendering of Cheng Dieyi as female and the overwhelming and ahistorical nature of his conflation of art with life, along with the resulting vulnerability of this feminine position, utilizes the opera's specularity to speak to the precarious entry of "Chinese"—national—film into the international world of prizes and transcultural interpretation. Cheng's arduous training, a lived experience that allows him access to supreme artistry and the ability to reproduce and represent the heart of Chinese culture, becomes a rarefied consciousness that turns into entertainment and exotic color when presented in film abroad and when presented within China is easily used and manipulated by political agendas. Eventually, this art even fails to maintain a viable connection to Chinese social life itself. Such, the film implies, is the fate of "local" cultures in the transnational field of film and perhaps in other cultural arenas as well.

Femininity: A New Male Possibility

A great deal has been written about masculinity, femininity, and the post–Cultural Revolution national crisis of Chinese identity. In his *Zhongguo wenhua de shenceng jiegou* (The deep structure of Chinese culture) Sun Longji constructs the theory that Chinese men have all been turned into eunuchs, and Kam Louie points out that in fiction and film, a number of writers and directors from the 1980s have focused on redeeming male sexuality, a strategy Louie believes is simply a concern with power and control.[6]

Chen's films generally feature a male character attempting to effect a cultural act that engages a central narrative of modern China. Such actions fall within Chen's category of *history.* In *Yellow Earth,* Gu Qing collects folk tunes from the people to be rewritten as anti–Japanese Communist Party songs, thus embodying the archetypical act of the party going to the people. Lao Gan takes over the role of teacher in *King of the Children.* In *The Big Parade,* a series of male characters in the lead roles attempt to ritualistically display the power and representational unity of the People's Liberation Army (PLA). And in *Farewell My Concubine,* the staging of Peking opera by Cheng Dieyi and, to a lesser extent, Duan Xiaolou is the quintessence of Chinese cultural form.

In all four films the male characters have an originally simple connection to a seemingly simple goal. Their initially unproblematic desire to act—a direct appropriation of the logical narrative of history into consciousness—becomes, as the films progress, complicated. In each case, the masculine, action-oriented character is *feminized,* compromised with complex knowledge, a split subjectivity, and the inability to realize his goals through planned action. Although characters are not deepened in terms of inner psychology—that is, they do not have progressively more profound understandings of their motivations or actions, and we "discover" nothing about them or their pasts—their subjective

existence is made complex. This feminization process occurs only with biological males. Biological females are excluded from this process because within cultural creation, they do not occupy positions of power. Chen's films all possess
profound and overarching narratives of potential unity, and each proclaims
itself serious as art and as critique. And from *Yellow Earth* through *The Big
Parade, King of the Children,* and *Farewell My Concubine,* the male character
or characters are increasingly problematized and feminized.

In *Yellow Earth* Gu Qing has the simple goal of collecting folk songs for
assimilation into the anti-Japanese efforts of the Chinese Communist Party
(CCP): the rewriting of the folk. The *suanqu,* or sour tunes, will be engaged on
behalf of the revolutionary redefinition of the people. As Esther C. M. Yau
points out, the party ban on erotic involvement—one of the rules of the party-
to-people narrative—between soldiers or cadres and the people underlies Gu
Qing's refusal to help Cuiqiao escape from her impending marriage.[7] The line
of potential action through which the male is galvanized into national and cultural production through an erotically catalytic relation with a woman, so successfully exploited by Zhang Yimou, ends with barely a glimmer in Gu Qing's
eyes.[8] The main connection in *Yellow Earth,* as in all Chen's films, is between
male characters; the older male undergoes the feminizing, complicating process
of consciousness and loses his ability to empower the younger. Hanhan—and
the viewer—struggles in vain as Chen Kaige makes Gu Qing try three times to
come over the hill in his return to the village; Cuiqiao presumably is dead. Gu
Qing's mind has been made complex by his new awareness that he lacks control over even his own simple narrative (CCP to the people), and that the narrative itself may indeed be a myth; he can accomplish the single cultural act of
collecting and recreating the sour tunes, but he cannot make the liberation narrative work as it should. In order to do that, he would have to construct a fantasy within which his efforts could succeed and use it to displace the history of
Communist narratives.

In *The Big Parade,* many of the male characters preparing for the parade,
especially the citified boys, express doubt about the meaning of their rigorous
training. One criticizes from a modern viewpoint, focusing on the anachronis-
tic nature of military ritual in contemporary life; one frames the military not as
glorious battle but as sheer careerism; one flees and in this act wordlessly foregrounds the dehumanizing nature of military training. Yet all continue to prepare and ultimately perform. Through one critical stance or another, the
potential soldiers profess to see through military ritual and its rationale, yet its
historically sanctioned form alone propels them forward. Chen Kaige's origi-

nal ending, where the sounds of the parade accompany scenes of a blank Tiananmen Square, was changed into a vision of plentitude because of PLA objections.

With the male of action and authority subsumed into the entire military structure, the female—barring the added female soldiers viewed in the altered ending—becomes a hazy moment of disembodied fantasy, an unidentifiable experience outside articulation. Women stand at the edge of the historical PLA narrative and seem to offer relief from the duplicity it demands from all participants. When the young soldier develops a fever and runs away, he seamlessly joins in with a group of peasant women working in the fields, and although their lips move, their voices are replaced with an insistent extradiegetic noise. The viewer immediately perceives that the trainee is escaping from a seemingly cruel and needlessly rigorous ritual to something more basic and good, something connected with the land. The peasant women are so divorced from military sensibility and so unaware of anything outside their own charmed, natural existence and work that they are not even surprised that a stranger has joined them. *King of the Children* takes a rather ordinary, slightly cocky novelistic character and gives him a vagueness and dislocating sensibility that borders on the insane. Time and again Lao Gan, obfuscated by his growing awareness of the impossibility of true teaching or learning, laughs at inappropriate times, loses his way in speech, or stares out into space. As in *Yellow Earth* and *The Big Parade,* the male character is shot through with a disorienting knowledge that seems to come from the land and air itself; we see many shots of barren mountains and the river in *Yellow Earth,* of the parade training ground in *The Big Parade,* and of the countryside in *King of the Children.*[9] Lao Gan's mission is one of the most overdetermined within Chinese culture: the education of children and the transmission of texts. This process becomes so fractured that the actual building block of written language, the Chinese character, breaks apart under the stress of new meaning and reforms itself in a directly mimetic representation. Lao Gan's new written form is "cow water," a nonexistent character that represents urine.

In *King of the Children* as in *The Big Parade,* the ideological critique is only too apparent. The extreme feminization of Lao Gan and the placing of a very muted (yet vociferous) erotic desire totally onto the plump Laidi and distant from the male character, however, draws our attention away from overt criticism of Chinese education and texts. The humanistic interpretation of one American critic, who claims that Lao Gan "has transformed the lives of his students," is difficult to document; in fact, Lao Gan fails to have much influence on the children, who continue their parroting (of the chant) and copying (of the dictionary) (*Los Angeles Times,* Jan. 17, 1994). Only the mute refusal of social organization and its power, as shown through the cowherd and his sullying gesture of peeing without comment, can prevent the ritualizing discourse of education from overwhelming its students and teachers.

Lao Gan's historical "meaning," both as an intellectual sent to the countryside and then as a teacher who disseminates texts, is intense and overdetermined. Because he transmits texts and creates song lyrics (against Laidi's music tunes), Lao Gan's connection to cultural form is primarily linguistic. In *Yellow Earth,* Gu Qing's political and cultural mission also is linguistic, and like Lao Gan he is stymied by a first hidden and unrecognized and then revealed meaning of the significance that comes from melody (sour tunes) and the land. While Cuiqiao's tunes have words that tell of her unhappiness, Laidi is incapable of writing the words and assigns that job to Lao Gan. In *The Big Parade,* the women are pure presence, without access to any words or sound.

Chen's films construct symbolic femininity as a means through which male subjectivity can be deepened and made aware of its own lack of belief in or control over the history that has been produced through central narratives. As Rey Chow shows, the film *King of the Children* excludes biological woman, who herself cannot be in the problematized subject position.[10] Nonetheless, the unification of being and representation is faintly original with biological woman. Cuiqiao sings out her misery, and has the agency to act against it. Laidi can write melodies and sing songs as long as Lao Gan can provide the words. The wordless women in *The Big Parade* work in the harvest with no apparent recourse to a story about their actions. In all cases women, because they do not enact the modern unifying narratives, are not responsible for them; although they embody the more primitive and pure knowledge of lived experience, they cannot possess the deeply fractured consciousness of the central male characters. Chen's construct defines biological woman as this ahistorical, nonritualizing, existence-based understanding. As is best shown in *Farewell My Concubine,* however, when male characters are feminized, they do not imitate this woman's naturalness, but rather become the shattered victims of what was once a unified consciousness.

The Concubine and Cultural Position

Corresponding almost exactly to Kaja Silverman's analysis of marginalized but superaware male consciousness (such as that of gay men), Cheng Dieyi accedes to an extreme state of lack only when he can admit that he is by nature a girl, not a boy. Such a superb and delicately aware state of being is not open to the king, who plays the traditionally powerful but historically fallen male of authority, the king who should hold the mandate of the political and cultural body. After Dieyi becomes like a woman, he does not need a problematized consciousness like that of Gu Qing in *Yellow Earth* or Lao Gan in *King of the Children*. Rather, Dieyi has actually *become* the feminine itself. Looking back from *Farewell* it becomes clear that the central male characters in Chen's earlier films are not just weakened in terms of action or complicated in terms of consciousness but are feminized in relation to the discourse of historical cultural form. Dieyi is still very young—a boy, not a man—when his digital excess is chopped off, he enters the masked art-world of opera, and he is forced to admit that he is a girl; thus he can embody the feminine position in totality. Dieyi has the best possible circumstances under which to admit his lack: he is poor, parentless, small, young, and weak, plus he is under initiation into a feminine role in the most stylized, ritualistic, and costumed art of the culture. Even so, the admission proves difficult, and Dieyi must undergo symbolic rape with a pipe before he can proclaim his femininity and begin his cultural servitude as a sexual object and cultural concubine.[11] At the end of the story Dieyi once again says the wrong words, collapsing the fantasy he has maintained for so long.[12]

Cheng Dieyi becomes a symbolic woman but, like the women in Zhang Yimou's "red" films, pays with his life.[13] In *Farewell My Concubine,* biological woman possesses an even fainter sense of originary being and is utterly unproductive, both biologically and culturally. Juxian takes on a role—much feared by Cheng Dieyi—that is more similar to that of the domesticating woman so common in American western film and fiction, a woman who lures the man away from a creative power associated with the wild west. Juxian wants to get Duan Xiaolou away from Cheng Dieyi's contaminating influence and his tendency to drag Xiaolou into the overwhelming and obsessive practice of the opera. Although Juxian does not have the appealing naturalness of Cuiqiao, Laidi, or the women in *The Big Parade,* she is not a negative character. Many times she steps in to redeem both Xiaolou and Dieyi, to mediate between the two, and ultimately to cradle Dieyi as if he were her lost child and rescue him from a self-destructive opium addiction. Juxian's face shows pain and empathy as Xiaolou betrays Dieyi during a Cultural Revolution struggle session; she dies under Xiaolou's betrayal when Dieyi does not.

Juxian's suicide is different from that of Dieyi. She kills herself because, under terrible but historically limited pressure, Xiaolou says that he does not love her. Although Juxian is a deep and feeling character, a woman dying for the love of a man is only a common human situation. Juxian and Xiaolou have an offstage relationship that is warm and true; as they bum their clothes and destroy the wine cups they have drunk from together in preparation for a Red Guard investigation—and thus show themselves willing to cast off an illusion sustained by the past—we clearly see their strong mutual affection and physical love, developed through time and shared experience. Dieyi also views the scene from outside the door, and it throws him into despair. Dieyi and Xiaolou have a different loyalty and affection based on the bitterly shared experience of operatic discipline. Dieyi kills himself not for the excellent but common human kind of love, which is what Xiaolou and Juxian share, but because he cannot continue to be a concubine. This role is taken over by his own revolutionary son and cannot be restored after Xiaolou's betrayal, a nearly voiced proclamation that Dieyi played the concubine/lover to the corrupt official Yuan Shiqing (also called Yuan Siye).

Cheng Dieyi does become Yuan's private prostitute, but only when he can paint Yuan so that he looks like the king of Chu. In the "real-life" court of law, Dieyi refuses Yuan's life-saving patronage, which Xiaolou elicited to rescue Dieyi from the consequence of being branded a traitor for performing for Japanese officials. Japanese officials, the clearly marked imperialist presence in China, readily exchange the king of Chu for a single performance by the concubine.

The scene with the Japanese military officials brings out the implications of specificity in cultural form within a global arena. The authority of the king of Chu can be maintained only when the concubine prostitutes her art—the essentially Chinese art—before the art-loving audience, whose imperializing position corresponds to that of the international (Western) film spectator and critic. While in the West, we mark Chinese film as Chinese culturally and historically and enjoy it as such, the playing out of what was once a unified historical imperative that existed of itself through the staged, revealing, and betraying spectacle of film results in the demeaning of the concubine's art and life. The fantasy of specificity in culture cracks—the play is not the king and the concubine's to be performed for and by them but can be coerced and manipulated—until the Japanese are gone. What remains is Xiaolou's suspicion that Dieyi played the concubine not only to foreigners but also to the corrupt Chinese state represented by Yuan Shiqing.

In order to preserve Xiaolou's independence and life, Dieyi must specularize his art/self before foreigners and before the Chinese state. Thus Dieyi's attempts to maintain the powerful specificity of culture is shown to be an unsustainable fantasy. Whereas Xiaolou eventually may be able to excuse the performance for the Japanese as virtually unavoidable, Dieyi's continuing relationship with Yuan Shiqing exposes the fantasy to its spectacularly rotten core.

As Wai-yee Li describes in a study of *qing* (sentiment, love) in Chinese literary genres of *fu* (narrative poetry), *chuanqi* (tales), and *xiaoshuo* (fiction), the concubine traditionally is associated with both a moral purpose and the "'way of concubines' *(qiefu zhi dao)*, the use of devious ploys of self-abnegation to please, flatter, and seek favor" (1993, 19–20). Excessively adorned women are linked to culture through direct metaphors that align them with writing. Li refers to the critic Yang Xiong's (53 B.C.–A.D. 18) "oft-quoted" criticism of *fu*: "'Or put it this way: a woman has beauty; does writing have beauty also? The answer is yes. The worst thing for a woman is to have her inner beauty clouded by cosmetics; the worst thing for a piece of writing is to have its rules and proportions confounded by excessive rhetoric'" (19). The concubine carries not only this cultural meaning but also a political significance that arises through the role of the court poet, who represents the subservient in his relationship to the emperor and generally is assigned a feminine role in literature. Indeed, "[t]o represent the ruler-subject relationship in gendered terms (e.g., the emperor as the absent lover, the poet-minister as the abandoned woman) came to be a standard practice in Chinese literature" and is a convention that began with *Encountering Sorrow* (*Li sao;* by Qu Yuan, ca. 340–278 B.C.) (Li 1993, 19). The theme of *Encountering Sorrow* is the quest for the divine being, a search that has secular, political, and allegorical meanings; the "deity acquires an aura of high seriousness as the 'symbolic other' in the dramatic quest for the fulfillment of political ideals." Although the deity is false, the poet possesses a "fervent and uncompromising political idealism" (Li 1993, 6).

Li's research can help us decode the meaning of Chen's screen concubine, who is both the deceptive betrayer and the mark of idealism. *Farewell My Concubine* contains inside it the operatic performance, which itself is a quasi-historical reference to one of the earliest forms of Chinese culture in the state of Chu. Chu culture, which was magical and shamanistic, was followed by Han Confucianism and its correlative cosmology, "the most relentless order-building in Chinese cultural history." The spirit journey represented in Chu literature is a direct communication of the poet with divine powers; as Li notes, such "intense ecstatic experience cannot be easily accommodated within structures of order, where the relationship with the divine-numinous realm is regulated through officially sanctioned ritual" (1993, 6).

The film draws a clear parallel between the sociopolitical world of modern

China and the opera's cultural-historical representation, and the concubine carries both the unification of bodily cultural ecstasy with political purity and loyalty and the morally suspicious posturing of the adorned female. Although in
these four films directed by Chen Kaige, men construct and reconstruct historical culture, their two contemporary sides are eventually split into the two characters Duan Xiaolou and Cheng Dieyi. Duan is the historically authoritative
male who has been disempowered first by foreign imperialism and its challenge
to traditional values, second by Chinese revolutionary culture itself, and third
by the impossibility of keeping alive a vital, nonspecular national culture in an
age of transnational economic capitalism. At the film's end, in the contemporary post-Mao period, the benighted king does not really know that he just cannot reassume his throne. In fact, while not a bad sort, from the beginning Duan
carries no moral presence, implying that the entire enterprise of twentieth-
century cultural China has been built on illusion. In the three earlier films,
Duan's character is subsumed within the historical narrative itself and its cor-
porealization in the male character *before* he senses that the mission he is
attempting to carry out is impossible or false. Cheng is the alternative consciousness based on lack that arises from the realization that history is duplic-
itous. Again, in the three earlier films, this alternative consciousness is also
contained within the central male character *after* his ability to act on the narrative is impaired. In these films, however, this alternative consciousness does
not cast itself into a discrete role with a positive goal. It remains a negative and
enfeebling knowledge within the same character who once was engaged fully
within the historical project.

In *Yellow Earth, King of the Children,* and *The Big Parade,* the cultural
and historical missions of the male characters eventually are infected with the
fantastic, concubinal lack, but in *Farewell My Concubine,* the parts are separated, with the positive values of mystery, fascination, and artistic discipline
assigned to Cheng Dieyi. Only *Farewell* theorizes the meaning of the new consciousness were it to be actually performed. As long as it is staged within the
trope of opera, the fantasy of a live cultural form can live on. The object of
Cheng Dieyi's loyalty is not the Chinese state; in separating the state from the
core of historical cultural power indicated by Duan Xiaolou as the king of Chu,
a trade-off is established as one possible action. The historical Chinese political body can be split: on one side is the corrupt and unworthy state, represented
by Yuan Shiqing, and on the other is the naive, weak, but still honest cultural
nation, symbolized by Duan Xiaolou. This break is relatively trivial and as a
political cliché around the world is easily represented: the government is bad,

but the nation/people is good. We viewers, however, see from the beginning that Duan Xiaolou is not worthy of Cheng Dieyi's efforts, because Duan is too weak to protect Cheng from the ravages of political and cultural change, too clumsy and unintelligent to really comprehend the meaning of the trade-off, and too lazy to make the sacrifices necessary to sustain the fantasy. What seals the fantasy's doom, however, is that, once inserted into the situation of global film spectatorship, the concubine—whose mediation as purified cultural process is absolutely necessary if the king is to retain his throne—becomes not a unified expression and practice of the cultural nation, but only a disembodied and debased indicator of cultural and historical difference, a kind of local color parading itself before delighted viewers.

In her foreword to *Male Subjectivity at the Margins,* Kaja Silverman must defend herself for writing a book about men in order to investigate femininity. Her argument states that while women's inroads into cultural construction are significant, with most recognized culture still created by men, one of the most interesting places to look for a radically new, positive, and demasculinized consciousness is in the work (film, fiction, etc.) of men who are socially marginalized by unorthodox sexuality or historical, racial, or other social trauma. Thus Silverman analyzes classical Hollywood film to see how it first displays post-World War II male lack and then recoups it through representing feminine efforts to brace the fallen man. She then compares this approach with the work of the nonmainstream filmmaker Rainer Wemer Fassbinder, who begins from a marginalized subjectivity and uses film "as an instrument for the 'ruination' of masculinity" by "returning to the male body all of the violence which it has historically directed elsewhere" (Silverman 1992, 9).

In somewhat the same way, *Farewell* stages a symbolically feminized consciousness that is an attribute of a man who already "knows" of lack and is completely possessed by his marginalization. Contrasting with him is the still-deluded historical man. The strong, complex female character of Juxian tries, as do Silverman's female characters, to prop up the lacking man; she also represents a positive, a less illusionary way of life, a road possible only if Dieyi's fantasy and illusion of pure cultural form can be discarded and replaced by the intimacy Juxian shares with Xiaolou. This female road is, of course, deficient in imagination and creative reproductive power, and herein lies Chen's own misogynist vision.

In focusing on the performance and specularity of national art forms, *Farewell* goes a different direction than the films that Silverman analyzes; it presents complex issues of cultural representation that are precisely those problems foregrounded at the juncture where Chinese film enters the international market. *Farewell* succeeds not only by furthering the domestic critique of history and culture for which Fifth-Generation filmmakers and roots writers such as Ah Cheng (on whose novella *King of the Children* is based) are famous, but also for implicating the global film economy in the now impossible staging of local culture. When Chinese film is positioned within the transnational and transcultural market, any innocent notion of cultural representation immediately becomes simplistic and reductionist and reinforces the consumerist commodification of culture.

Notes

This article was first published in *Transnational Chinese Cinemas: Identity, Nationhood, Gender,* edited by Sheldon H. Lu (Honolulu: University of Hawaii Press, 1997), pp. 331–46. Copyright © 1997 by University of Hawaii Press. Reprinted with permission.

1. Adam Mars-Jones, "A Visually Stunning Portrayal of the Peking Opera: *Farewell My Concubine,*" *The Independent,* Jan. 7, 1994. Mars-Jones is the sole reviewer I could find who specifically denied that the film was a historical epic, instead calling it "visually-magnificent, downbeat soap opera for international consumption."

2. I refer to Chen Kaige as "director and critic" not only because the collaborative nature of filmmaking, with its large number of actors, technicians, and various experts, does not allow a "pure" authorship but also because in contemporary times, filmmaking demands an understanding of technology, sponsorship, and the market. As a director, Chen exercises some control over the film's production, and through mass media presentation, his interpretive comments can create or reinforce meanings he believes are in the film or those that should be directed toward a particular audience. Thus when being interviewed for an international publication, Chen may focus on the spectacle of the film; when speaking with Chinese Communist Party cadres he may take a different line. Because Chen's comments are widely quoted as authoritative statements and presented to international audiences as "expert" testimony, his words become quite significant in determining the film's "meaning." I thank Patricia Sieber for her enlightening comments on this issue.

3. Commenting on both the historical and gender-bending nature of the film, Caryn James writes that "The most stunning aspect of the film is the deft way that Dieyi's confusion—of sexual identity, art and life—becomes a metaphor for the identity crisis of China itself, as the film goes from the days of the warlords to the end of Mao's Cultural Revolution." Caryn James, "You Are What You Wear," *New York Times,* Oct. 10, 1993: H13.

4. Mars-Jones, "A Visually Stunning Portrayal," notes that again and again "historical cataclysm coincides with personal crisis."

5. An example of focus on an acculturated subject would be Lu Xun's *Ah Q zhengzhuan*

(The true story of Ah Q), in which Ah Q and others carry the cumulative cultural effects of thousands of years of—in Lu Xun's view—devastating cultural ideas.

6. Kam Louie, "The Macho Eunuch: The Politics of Masculinity in Jia Pingwa's 'Human Extremities," *Modern China* 17.2 (1991): 165. Louie quotes Sun Longji's popular text on culture published by Jixianshe, Hong Kong, in 1983.

7. Esther C. M. Yau, "*Yellow Earth:* Western Analysis and a Non-Western Text," in *Perspectives on Chinese Cinema,* edited by Chris Berry (London: BFI Publishing, 1991), 66.

8. See Larson 1995 for an investigation into Zhang's use of women as erotic fulcrums to propel men into nationally significant action.

9. Zhang Jia-xuan describes the filmic technique thus: "First of all, the opening shot of the film is a low-angle extreme long shot of a huge parade ground with soldiers training. As the shot fades in, the camera begins to move slowly forward to reveal more and more of the same ground, thus underscoring its spaciousness, while the angle and distance of the shot make the figures of the soldiers appear so tiny that they form a striking contrast with the huge parade ground. Moreover as the camera continues to move forward, it also slides up and down, seemingly creating a sense of pressure." See "The Big Parade," *Film Quarterly* 43, no. 1 (1989): 57.

10. Rey Chow identifies biological woman as an excluded nature and reproductivity that is part of Chen Kaige's—and others'—fantasy of male symbolic cultural production. Chow also wonderfully elucidates that symbolic meaning of urine and cows through references and images that have been used by twentieth century writers and politicians. See Chow 1995, 108–41.

11. See Mars-Jones, "A Visually Stunning Portrayal."

12. There are several reasons why I believe Cheng Dieyi's difficult proclamation that he is a girl, and his subsequent behavior, should be regarded as feminization rather than homosexualization. First, following the trajectory of Chen's filmic presentation of the male character, we see that weakness and fragmentation become a symbolically feminine position through a series of characters acting in different story lines, and in some cases differing radically from the novels out of which the characters are adapted. Second, *Farewell* emphasizes the position Cheng Dieyi holds relative to the other characters and to the discourse of national cultural form, rather than any essentialized desire. Third, Cheng Dieyi's position, and that of the other fractured males in Chen's films, is one of weakness and inability to act, or symbolically that of the feminine within the social arena. However, for a well-argued discussion that focuses on homosexuality in the film, see Sang Zelan (Sang Tze-lan) 1994, 54–60.

13. The women in Zhang Yimou's three "red" films *(Red Sorghum, Ju Dou, Raise the Red Lantern)* all die or go insane.

Part Two

Speaking for the *Other*
Changing Allegorical Roles for Women

Qiuyun in *Woman, Demon, Human (Ren gui qing)*, directed by Huang Shuqin, 1988. Courtesy of China Film Archive, Beijing.

W hile gender issues could be explored in the discussion of every film in this book, the four films in this section specifically illustrate the changing allegorical roles of women. The focus here is not gender per se but an aspect of film representation that shows how certain tropes employ female characters at particular points in filmmaking history. This historical perspective illustrates the fact that in Chinese cinema, women rarely speak for themselves on-screen but are often used as metaphors to refer to various social, cultural, and political issues. Although women are often at the center of Chinese films, they have little voice for themselves—the *Other,* here meaning broader issues that are not necessarily gender-specific, speaks through them.

In leftist filmmaking before 1949, the representation of women was related to the leftist filmmakers' obsession with the socially oppressed and with social ills (see overview). Women were often used in tropes for social injustice concerning the oppressed and in tropes for the national fate, wherein China as a nation had fallen prey to imperialist powers. The portrayal of women as victims of a patriarchal culture often also spoke of anxiety about the future of China as a nation; thus, the representation of women supports various national allegories. This dominantly allegorical representation of women, in the meantime, also opened up a special site of cultural production since it often needed to present a changed image of women, known then as "modern women" *(modeng nüxing),* "new women" *(xin nüxing),* or the "Chinese Noras." This last reference indicates an interesting phenomenon: the translation and performance of Norwegian playwright Henrik Ibsen's *A Doll's House* sparked a feminist fad wherein the educated women wanted to leave behind their "doll houses," that is, the Confucian confinement of women, arranged marriage, and dependence on men. In his study of the new women images on-screen during this period of Chinese cinema, Yingjin Zhang suggests that these images are both disruptive and productive forces in a cultural production for a modern China—disruptive, because they challenge traditional Chinese values, and productive, because they open up a new space of modern knowledge and predict social change (1996, 185–231).

Street Angel, the first film in this section, illustrates a typical melodramatic use of women in which their possession becomes an allegorical battle between China and Japan, Chinese culture and the invasion of foreign cultures, the socially oppressed and the social oppressors. The two central female characters, a singer and a prostitute, represent inspiration and misery, the two aspects that womanhood offers to melodramatic allegories. *Three Women,* the second film, was produced toward the end of the leftist filmmaking era in Shanghai.

Contrasting three types of women, it was the leftist cinema's concluding remark about the "new woman." The film intertextually leads our attention to some earlier titles on the same subject, such as *The New Woman* (*Xin nüxing,* 1935). Vivian Shen's essay discusses this earlier title's relation to *Three Women* in detail and helps us understand how in different representational roles "Chinese women are required to serve Chinese society, but only in the ways that leftist Chinese men spell out."

The representation of women in PRC cinema before 1966 presents a paradox. Women are both elevated and subjugated—elevated because gender-specific issues such as women's rights in marriage and work become so visible, subjugated because the representation is politicized to promote issues from the Party's official agenda, often at the expense of women's existential reality. The Chinese women's gender experience is tailored and exploited in order to better carry the overwhelmingly heavy burden of political and ideological indoctrination, delivering such messages as the Party as savior, the achievement of social progress through equality of the sexes, and the abandonment of the old mode of family-based production in exchange for socialized collectivism.

Numerous historical factors may have contributed to this representational position of women in the PRC cinema. Let us consider two factors here. First, this representational position was useful in China's socialist construction since women accounted for a significant percentage of the labor force. In the countryside, for example, along with the collectivization of the labor force and the setting up of the People's Communes, women were forced to join in the production of the collective units rather than continue to work in the traditional economic units of the family. Second, this representational position of women was promoted because it conformed to the class-struggle ideology. Since women's lower position in the family structure resembled the working classes' lower social status, in order to relocate the family in the PRC's socialist construction, the family conflicts between the sexes were often politically exploited in representation—women became the potential initiators of a family revolution, and men became the potential obstacles to change.

Although no film included in this section illustrates this aspect of Chinese cinema (films of this era have not been subtitled), the central female character of *Two Stage Sisters* (see chapter 1) embodies a certain militant-era spirit of this cinema. When this militant spirit is applied to the subject matter of the early PRC era, the films often fall into a "socialist-feminist" narrative mode that foregrounds gender issues and assigns the female to stand for the ideological calls and the male to function as the potential obstacle. This narrative mode was pushed to the extreme during the Cultural Revolution. Mao's wife, Jiang Qing, supervised the configuration of quite an array of political superwomen who controlled the representation of the period. It is important to have some general knowledge of this representational tradition in order to properly understand gender representation in the post-Mao new cinema, especially a certain sexist orientation of this cinema that may offend Western feminist taste but that is actually a rebellion against the earlier representational oppression of the male. I will discuss this aspect of gender representation as related to masculinity in the introduction to Chinese Western films and roots-searching in part four.

Ideologically, the socialist-feminist convention is related to the anti-individualistic efforts of the Communist Party, as Chris Berry observes, for the rule of consensus leaves little room for differences and contradictions (1988a, 8). When the specificity of the individual is overlooked, the specificity of gender is also put aside. As the art of a counter-discourse, the representation of women in the post-Mao new cinema develops a paradigm that is the direct opposite of the anti-individualistic tradition, that is, the paradigm of the individual's desire versus a repressive consensus, be it political, social, or cultural. This new individualistic paradigm occupies a central position in the representation of women but may not be gender-specific itself: gender is still often represented as an emblem for some broader issues facing both sexes. In the female-written and - directed *Sacrificed Youth,* a film selected in part three, femininity is rendered so as to express a sense of loss and mourning: through this film, subjects of "socialist feminism" (the female writer, director, and main character all grew up with the PRC's early cinema) reexamine the repressive nature of this ideology in a minority culture and reflect on the losses and gains of being such subjects. The Han women's social position, compared with those of the Dai women, may have improved, but their other desires, shown in the film as the desire for beauty and love, are denied. *Sacrificed Youth,* nevertheless, overlooks feminine experience by using it as a political critique that applies to the feelings of a whole generation of youth. As some Western scholars have remarked in their interviews with Chinese women film directors, Chinese artists do not seem to be very enthusiastic about asserting gender specificity. The director of *Sacrificed Youth,* for example, emphasized the expression of self in an interview: "Being a woman is part of that, but I don't think it should come before everything" (Berry 1988b, 21).

In the post-Mao new cinema, although women still often play allegorical roles and although some male-directed depictions of female sexual desire often reflect more of a cultural search for masculinity and empowerment, women's dilemmas in everyday life also become a subject of cinematic exploration. *Sacrificed Youth, A Good Woman (Lianjia funü,* 1985), *Army Nurse (Nü'er lou,* 1985), *Zhenzhen's Beauty Parlor (Zhenzhen de fawu,* 1986), *Woman, Demon, Human (Ren gui qing,* 1988), and *Sunshine and Showers (Taiyang yu,* 1988), among others, reflect this exploration. Such an exploration differs from the PRC's socialist-feminist convention of using women for propaganda and pays more attention to individuality, ambiguity, and women's vulnerability in life. *Woman, Demon, Human,* the third film in this section, well exemplifies these characteristics in showcasing the difficult career of an actress. This female-directed film has surely delivered certain gender-blind messages of cultural critique, such as a general pessimism about human relationships. This film, nevertheless, remains a powerful allegory for the predicament of femininity: Qiuyun, the protagonist, is empowered onstage playing a male role, and offstage, she remains helpless, besieged by a sense of guilt for being a woman.

　　Ju Dou, the fourth film in this section, provides an interesting case of the more recent complex allegorical roles played by women. Seeing the Chinese government's efforts to censor and ban this film as a way to control "representations of 'China,'" W. A. Callahan describes the film as a political allegory invoking both the patriarchal systems of Communism and Confucianism (1993, 52–53). Jenny Kwok Wah Lau, in her essay included in this book, explains that the offensiveness of the film lies not so much in its allegorical challenge to patriarchy as in the fact that a "bad woman," violating such cultural notions of *zhen* (loyalty), *jie* (chastity), and *xiao* (filial piety), is what the allegory is all about. And Rey Chow comments on how the film provides the Western audience with "mythical pictures and stories to which convenient labels of otherness such as 'China' . . . can be affixed" (1995, 170–71). If *Ju Dou* is an allegory of China, Chow believes, its Chineseness "is already the sign of a cross-cultural commodity fetishism, a production of value between cultures" (170). As more new Chinese films got into international film markets, Chinese women's allegorical roles on-screen also started to prompt cross-cultural issues

Four
Street Angel
(*Malu tianshi,* dir. Yuan Muzhi, 1937)

Screenplay	Yuan Muzhi
Cinematography	Wu Yinxian
Producer	Mingxing
Cast	Zhou Xuan, as Xiao Hong (singer)
	Zhao Huishen, as Xiao Yun (prostitute)
	Zhao Dan, as Xiao Chen (trumpeter)
	Wei Heling, as Lao Wang (newspaper vendor)

*S*treet Angel demonstrates the sophistication of Chinese leftist filmmaking in the 1930s with its distinctive cinematography, unique editing, and superb acting. Challenging Hollywood domination, *Street Angel* was actually based on an American cinematic romance of the same title (1928) that was popular in Shanghai. The Hollywood version, starring Janet Gaynor and directed by Frank Borzage, is about an Italian girl who flees from police, joins a traveling circus, and meets and falls in love with a young painter who finds her an inspiration. Film scholars, such as Ma Ning whose article on *Street Angel* appears later in this section, have long noticed how director Yuan Muzhi used *Street Angel* to arouse the audience's expectation of Hollywood formulas only to twist these formulas (for example, by adding montage elements) for a critique. "Regardless of its source," film historian Jay Leyda comments, "Yuan made the film in his own style, with sharply incised characters, spare dialogue, an always alert use of sound, and story points indicated in gesture or camera movement; the film opens with a long camera movement, from the highest roofs of Shanghai to the cluttered surfaces of a canal" (1972, 106).

Yuan Muzhi, who in a few films worked as both director and actor, refrained from stepping out of the role of scenarist and director this time and yielded the male leads to Zhao Dan and Wei Heling, two stars who continued their acting well into the PRC era. The nineteen-year-old Zhou Xuan, who plays

Xiao Hong, grew up poor and orphaned in the Shanghai of the film; Xiao Hong
was once her real name. Popularly known as "the Golden Voice," she was both
a singer and a film actress. Through this film, she popularized the song by Tian
Han and He Luding, "Song of Four Seasons" *(Siji ge)*. Zhao Huishen, who
plays Xiao Yun, had her screen debut with this film. She had previously been
popular as a stage actress playing Fanyi in Cao Yu's play *Thunder Storm*.

An Outline for Viewing *Street Angel*

So far, an English-subtitled video of this film is not available on the American
market. Despite this obvious obstacle, we can still easily understand the film
via the following outline. Although produced in 1937, well into the age of the
"talkie" (which started in China in 1931 with *Singsong Girl Red Peony*), *Street
Angel* still retains heavy traces of the silent movie.

> A "family" of five: Chen—a trumpeter, Wang—a newspaper vendor, a bar-
> ber, unemployed #1 & #2
> The two sisters: Xiao Hong—a singer, Xiao Yun—a prostitute
> The "parents" who are actually the owners or employers of the two sisters
> Gu—a local despot, and his valet
> 1. Establishing shots
>   After recording the Western presence and influences in Shanghai, the
>   camera moves from the highest roofs of Shanghai to the cluttered
>   surfaces of a canal: here is the underground Shanghai contrasting
>   with a Shanghai that is soaring to the sky (note the extremely low
>   angles of the camera in showing this).
>   The wedding processions.
>   Presenting the main characters in relation to the wedding processions:
>   the trumpeter (Chen), the newspaper vendor (Wang), and the singer
>   (Xiao Hong).
> 2. Xiao Hong is summoned away from the window of a tea-house.
>   "Come over here, Xiao Hong. You're a big girl now and your heart is
>   still wild."
>   Xiao Hong sings "Song of Four Seasons."
>   Gu and his valet are in the audience. Gu: "The girl is nice."
>   Valet: "I know her father."
> 3. The "family" of five gathers and lines up in front of the barber's shop.
>   Following the trumpeter, they march back home.
>   Greeted by the landlady.

Their "family" picture turns up after having been missing.

After inscribing the picture (see Ma Ning 1989), they see the sun's reflection that Xiao Hong has sent with a mirror from a window facing theirs: "Here comes our wireless signal!"

4. The window of the family of five becomes a stage for presenting a show to Xiao Hong.

5. The two sisters' family: the father (knowing Gu's local influence) asks for money for socializing with Gu.

6. Xiao Yun on the street, unable to attract clients.

   Xiao Hong sneaks into the trumpeter's place across the roofs.

   "What shall we do for fun?"

   They find an ad for an amusement park in the paper and decide to go.

   Xiao Yun evades a cop on street.

   Xiao Yun stops Xiao Hong, forbidding her to go with Chen and Wang.

7. Xiao Yun returns home in the morning.

   "Father" to Xiao Yun: "Your mother knows what's happening between us. I can't help you now."

   Communicating through the windows that face each other, Chen and Xiao Hong sing their favorite song, "Street Singer."

   Their chorus is interrupted by the entrance of a miserable Xiao Yun.

8. At the barber shop, Xiao Hong is brought in by her "father" to see Gu.

   Gu offers to take Xiao Hong out for fun.

   They are followed by Chen's friend.

   Chen is enraged to hear that Xiao Hong is happy with Gu.

   Chen and Xiao Hong exchange harsh words.

9. Tea house. Chen is drunk.

   He orders Xiao Hong to sing their favorite "Street Singer" song against her will.

   Chen leaves with a broken heart.

10. Gu visits Xiao Hong's parents.

    He wants to buy Xiao Hong as his concubine.

    The two sisters overhear him.

11. On the advice of her sister, Xiao Hong seeks Chen's help.

    Chen and Xiao Hong are reconciled.

    "Don't you worry. We can rescue you."

    Wang brings their attention to a piece of news in the paper: "Adoptive mother prosecuted for selling her daughter to a brothel."

    They decide to go and see a lawyer.

12. Lawyer's top-floor office. "It's heaven here."

The two friends don't know how to tell the story and discover that they
can't afford a lawyer.

13. "What can we do since we do not have money?"

Wang brings their attention to a want ad in the paper for a fugitive.

"Yes, let's 'run away.'"

While Xiao Hong resists the idea, Chen is enraptured by it.

The family of five gathers together.

With the window curtain as their screen, they perform a shadow show of
a scene of rebellion.

14. The two sisters.

Yun: "Don't cry. Go with them. They are good fellows."

Hong: "How about you? Come along."

Yun: "They hate me. They look down upon me."

15. Xiao Yun is left alone.

She sneaks across the street to talk with the landlady only to find that
Chen's "family" has left.

Her parents see her talking with the landlady.

She is interrogated by her "mother" who orders her to take off her
clothes for a beating.

Her "father" informs Gu of Xiao Hong's elopement.

16. In her new home in the same city, Xiao Hong has her hair done.

Members of the family of five: "What gift shall we give to Xiao Hong?"

Engagement drinks.

Chen performs a sleight of hand: a silver dollar disappears but comes out
of his mouth. He describes his game as "exporting silver" *(baiyin
chukou),* a pun on China losing money to foreign countries.

17. "Silver exported!"

While Wang sells the newspaper with Chen's help, the barber demands
back salary from his shop owner.

Wang meets with Xiao Yun and asks her to join her sister.

It starts to rain.

Outside Xiao Hong's new home, a policeman follows Xiao Yun.

Inside, Xiao Hong is listening to Chen's horror story when Xiao Yun
enters, evading the policeman.

Chen is angry that Wang has told Xiao Yun of their whereabouts.

The police comes in to inquire about Xiao Yun: "Does this woman live
here?"

Chen is forced to say yes.

18. The two sisters at the new home.
    Wang comes back early and brings some medicine for Xiao Yun, who
        has been ill and sleeping in the attic. They stay there to chat.
    Chen also comes back early, eager to be with Xiao Hong.
    The landlady comes to collect the rent.
    Her husband comes again to ask for a different kind of currency.
19. The owner of the barber shop is forced to close the shop because he can-
        not pay the lease.
    The family of five offers to help him.
    "Great discount for hair cuts!"
    They are seen by Xiao Hong's "father."
20. Xiao Hong's "father" tells Gu about what he sees.
    They search the neighborhood and find Xiao Yun.
    "Father" stabs Xiao Yun.
    Gu sneaks off when he sees that Xiao Yun is dying.
21. Wang wants revenge but is stopped by Chen: "For this kind of woman?"
    Wang shames Chen, takes Xiao Yun back, and leaves for the doctor.
    Xiao Yun accepts Chen's apology, saying: "We are all unfortunate. There
        is no need to apologize."
    Xiao Yun: "Is Wang back now?"
    Chen: "No, it is a policeman passing by."
    Xiao Yun is terrified and dies.
    When Wang comes back, he is told that Xiao Yun is asleep.
    Wang tells his friends that the doctor won't come because he has no
        money.
The end.

The Textual and Critical Difference of Being Radical: Reconstructing Chinese Leftist Films of the 1930s
Ma Ning

Asian cinema criticism in the West as a cross-cultural discipline needs a cultural perspective. The normal approach is to think of it as an object of knowledge for a thinking subject (the Western man/woman). Any attempt at understanding Asian tradition and Asian culture through cultural texts, such as film, requires a special kind of dialogical engagement with the life worlds of the peoples of Asia. As a fusion of horizons, the assumptions of the Western-thinking subject come into dialogue with those of the Other so that the interpretation process becomes more inclusive and comprehensive and potentially more rational (if radical thinking can be defined as a more rational way of thinking).

In this essay I would like to argue for a localized reading that will focus attention on domination inherent in a regional or national cinema. The works under examination are the Chinese leftist films of the 1930s which were to a certain extent influenced by the "radical" movement of Japan in the late 1920s. By examining these films in relation to the local popular discourses of the time, the films' relationships to the Hollywood model, and the ways in which these texts are reconstructed in the decades following the establishment of the People's Republic in 1949, I hope to provide an alternative approach to the problematic radical art practice in Asian cinema.

In Western critical discourses on Chinese leftist films, a compromised view prevails. A radical function in the historical context of the time is acknowledged, but its radicalness is undermined by the appropriation of the formal system of Hollywood cinema.[1] In recent years, however, there has been an attempt to reassess the leftist films of the 1930s by relating them to the concept of Third World cinema. Chris Berry, for instance, locates these films in the social context of the time and points out the similarities between the socioeconomic circumstances of China in the 1930s and those of Third World countries in the 1960s where a different use of the film medium was practiced with very practical aims. However, he concedes that the strategies used by the Chinese filmmakers and those of the Third World countries are quite different. What is significant about his work is his strong emphasis on an adequate understanding of the Chinese critical discourse on film (1989).

According to this critical discourse, represented by film historian Cheng Jihua, the Chinese Communists operating in Shanghai at the time argued that film must be studied and understood as a basically Western art form brought to China by foreign businessmen in the wake of Western Imperialism. As such, it was an integral part of a culture whose economic and political system had at that point made China a semi-colonial and semi-feudal state. The Western domination of the Chinese film market was such that by the 1930s intellectuals in China, especially those with leftist leanings, realized the disastrous consequences of this form of cultural domination. As a result, a number of well-known leftist artists who had been active in theatrical circles entered various small Chinese film production companies.[2]

Contrary to the general understanding that leftist filmmakers were concerned with getting "the progressive message" across to the audience, most leftist filmmakers saw their task as a dual one: to transform the mode of film expression, as well as the mode of spectatorship (Leyda 1972, 63). They regarded the film audience of the time as basically conservative due to class positions. The task of transforming the audience was one of the major concerns of the May Fourth New Literary Movement around 1919, a background shared by most leftist filmmakers. Most of the leaders of the movement had gone abroad to study medicine or science. They turned to literature and drama when they realized that without changing people's minds there could not be significant social change.

One of the leading authors of the May Fourth New Literary Movement, Lu Xun, recounts a viewing experience he had in 1906 while studying in Japan. It had an enormous influence on his literary career and his perception of the film medium. He saw a documentary about the Russo-Japanese War fought on Chinese territory in Manchuria, in which the local Chinese were shown as witnesses to the execution of those Chinese supposedly working for the Russians. Lu Xun was struck by the indifference of the Chinese spectators and their readiness to accept the status quo. He was later to find the same attitude in the movie houses of Shanghai in the late 1920s (Leyda, 13, 464).

The main theoretical framework these leftist film artists worked in was the Marxist theory of social contradictions. It was argued that by the early 1930s, the political situation in China had been dramatically changed by the Japanese occupation of northeast China and its military action in Shanghai. The Communists regarded the conflict between the ruling and working classes as a set of social contradictions between China as a semi-feudal and semi-colonial state and Japan as a newly emerged imperialist power seeking territorial expansion. The Communists saw the feudal forces in China as accomplices to Japanese imperialism and the bourgeoisie as a potential ally in their political struggle. But they argued that the Chinese national bourgeoisie was too weak to lead the alliance. They therefore sought moral and political leadership in all areas through the creation of an active, direct consensus by adopting the interests of the popular classes.[3] For example, the KMT [Nationalist] government, for fear of provoking further Japanese military action in China, decided to censor any artwork that openly expressed anti-Japanese feelings (Leyda 1972, 89). The Communists saw patriotism as the particular form in which a cultural hegemony could be achieved.

Looking at them as a body of politically-oriented works, it is interesting to examine the ways in which the process of narration in these texts addresses its middle-class audience and makes reference to the social context of the time. It should be noted that at the time there was a totally different and at the same time rhetorically powerful mode of film narration available to filmmakers—the Soviet cinema of the 1920s.[4] Although the leftist filmmakers were subject to its influence, they opted to work within the Hollywood tradition. But the ultimate political goal of filmmaking for them meant that they had to deviate from the norm of Hollywood filmmaking.

The task of transforming the mode of film expression with the purpose of transforming the audience can be seen in the opening sequence of *Street Angel* (1937), one of the acknowledged leftist film classics. The film opens with a marriage procession that includes a Western brass band and a traditional Chinese band. In this sequence, camera displacement creates a series of mismatches such that the procession seems to continually crisscross its own path. The sense of disorientation is reinforced by the incongruity between the Western military brass band and Chinese band. Not only do they march in different directions, but the music they play, the march music and folk music, is consistently contradictory. The sense of confusion and contradiction forms a powerful and ingenious allusion to the social milieu of China as a semi-feudal, semi-colonial state with divided foreign influences.

What is interesting about the above sequence is that of a total of 52 shots, 36 contain on-lookers, inserted as two series of shots, each consisting of eight rapid cuts of medium shots or closeups of spectators in the street. The spectators inscribed in these shots are frozen in rapt enjoyment of the spectacle (a projection of the typical Chinese spectators similar to Lu Xun's description). But significantly they are denied any vision. On the other hand, the actor-character, the trumpeter Chen, the news vendor Wang and the singer Xiao Hong, are active and also have visions in which they are even more active. The most interesting of these involves Chen, who slips out of the brass band and manages to take a look into the palanquin. His subjective point of view entitles the viewer to this privileged vision: the bride wrapped up in the palanquin is cross-eyed, which fully reveals the inherent irony in this spectacle of a metaphorically forced coupling of Chinese feudalism and foreign powers.

Even more interesting in this sequence are the form and meaning of the POV structure as they fall into two of the categories identified by Edward Branigan: open and closed POV structures (1984, 103–21). In the sequence, the establishing shot that shows the marriage procession in its entirety comes after the initial mismatches. Aside from its narrative function in situating the action in a coherent spatial-temporal framework, this shot also serves as a link between looker and vision. The shots that present the grotesque spectacle of the procession can be seen as a series of POV shots without a designated point of authority (the looker). The shots of spectators as lookers occur immediately after the establishing shot, and inscribe a point of authority deprived of any vision. Thus both fall into what Branigan calls the open POV structure. The deliberate breaking of the link between the looker and his vision in these open POV shots is significantly replaced by the closed POV structure associated with the trumpeter and his friend, the news vendor.

This closed structure consists of three shots: the first shows the looker; the second reveals what he sees; and the third renders the effect—his own eyes have crossed. This structure is the key link of the whole procession sequence. It not only reunites looker and vision in a new way that enables the viewer to perceive marriage as a significant social event that will eventually affect his/her life, but also provides the rationale for the shot organization of the whole sequence. The sense of confusion generated by the mismatches, like the vision of the now cross-eyed looker, is the effect of the grotesque social realities of China in the 1930s. The juxtaposition of closed and open POV structures, exemplary of the formal structure of the leftist film texts as a dialectic process of openness and closure, is a unique Chinese synthesis of Soviet montage and Hollywood continuity editing. As a form of political rhetoric, it effectively alienates upper- and middle-class viewers from their normal way of looking, inculcated by their nightly exposure to the cheap American film products that dominated the cinemas of China at the time.[5]

The process of the transformation of Hollywood conventions occurs on other levels as well. It has been pointed out that the leftist films all operate within the Hollywood melodramatic tradition (Ellis 1982, 80). Although this is the case (*Street Angel* has incorporated certain motifs from Frank Borzage's films of the late 1920s such as *Seventh Heaven* [1927]), the formal system of the leftist films cannot be totally explained in terms of classical codes.

Formally speaking, narration in melodrama, as Bordwell points out, is quite unrestricted in range and closer to an omniscient survey so that the film can engender pity, irony, and other dissociated emotions (1985a, 1985b). In Hollywood melodramas, this omniscience is also omnipresence. But they are, in most cases, generally bound by diagetic time and space. The narrative strategies usually aim at personalizing time and space to comply with classical narrative dependence on psychological causality.

Narration in leftist films, however, deviates from this norm in its construction of a social allegory that frames the melodramatic narrative of the text. The presence of a broad, sometimes rather abstract, ethico-political scheme, made possible by blending different artistic modes through various extradiagetic intrusions and explicit social references, socializes the diagetic time and space of the melodramatic narrative.

Allegory as a specific mode of narration in which extended structural patterns of a text are intended to refer to correspondingly complex patterns of intelligibility has two dimensions: vertical and horizontal. The vertical dimension of the allegorical text is created by various allusions and associations or metaphors. It is realized in the development of the narrative, which contextualizes the isolated symbolism. Formal features fundamental to the allegorical form can be identified in leftist texts: characterizations as a bundle of stereotypes with certain class or institutional affinities; striking attention to the particulars of visual imagery matched by a deep concern for extradiagetic referents; action interspersed with implicit or explicit commentary; and finally, central contradiction between random accumulation of incidents and a systematic movement toward change.

The master narrative of Chinese leftist films is quite similar to Elsaesser's allegorical reading of Western melodrama in its early form (1985). It features a class conflict between corrupt feudal forces and an enlightened bourgeoisie (or a bourgeois projection of the working classes in certain leftist texts), which is realized in the narrative in sexual terms. The role of women is essential in this power struggle. The adoption of the classical codes presents the female protagonists in these films as objects of male desire. Their bodies are the battlegrounds where the power struggle between opposing social forces is waged. The alliance between the local feudal forces and foreign powers results in their superior political and economic power to possess the women, while the rising lower and middle classes try to secure their relationships on moral and emotional terms. Acknowledged classics of the leftist film movement like *Big Road* (1934), *The Boatman's Daughter* (1935), *Cross Street* (1937), and *Street Angel* are cases in point.

To approach the leftist texts as allegory depends upon an understanding of the cultural and artistic codes at play in these films. It is noted that Chinese film is characterized by an admixture of generic modes (Rayns 1980, A9). With the incorporation of a set of different discourses circulating at the time, especially the journalistic discourse and the popular discourse, a new system of comprehensibility emerges that gives the text its artistic unity. Such a unity cannot be located in terms of Western generic norms.

Contrary to the melodramatic plot that unfolds in purely personal terms (love relations between characters), both the journalistic and the popular discourses present the political situation of the time as another narrative that frames the melodramatic element. The journalistic discourse in these films in the form of news items such as newspaper headlines and historical footage, because of its quasi-objective nature and its emphasis on individual rights and the supremacy of law, can be identified as that of the Chinese bourgeoisie. On the other hand, popular discourse manifests itself in such cultural forms as folk songs, shadow plays, wordplays and magic shows that can be seen as proletarian because of its collective nature and its appeal for radical actions.[6]

The incorporation of these two different discourses at various moments in the leftist text not only forms a larger system of intelligibility that gives the text its allegorical structure, but also transforms the Hollywood conventions the text utilizes in presenting the melodramatic narrative. Because these two discourses represent the interests of different social groups in China, their realization in the text often forms a dialogical relationship of confirmation and contradiction. The process of generic transformation and the intricate relationship between these two discourses are worth examining in detail.

The melodramatic conflict in *Street Angel* unfolds in the restaurant singing scene after the initial marriage sequence. After the girl, Xiao Hong, bids Chen and his friends good-bye and returns to the restaurant, she is asked to sing the "Song of Four Seasons" (which prefigures the cycling structure of the narrative). The scene can be characterized as a juxtaposition of a realistic space and a subjective space in which the personal and the social narrative converge. The allegorical dimension of the scene is generated by the interaction of the popular discourse in the form of a lengthy folk song. Here the realistic space organized by the shot/reverse-shot format unfolds the melodrama and the folk song. This authorizes the insertion of a subjective space articulated through the privileged vision of the actor-character through which the social narrative unfolds. In this scene, just before Xiao Hong begins to sing, the local despot, Gu, and his valet come into the restaurant. The eye-line match which establishes the spatial relationship between the despot and Xiao Hong also construes the girl as the object of sexual desire as is often the case in the Hollywood cinema. The facial expressions of the characters in these shots suggest the conflict to come. The girl's folk song unfolds a social narrative on a much broader temporal and spatial scale through her subjectivity. Her subjectivity, however, is inter-subjective and differs from the subjective POV shots found in Western cinema because her vision is at the same time retrospective and prospective and has a degree of omniscience and omnipresence beyond individual subjectivity. Here the female body becomes the point where the horizontal and vertical dimensions of the text converge, allowing the girl to take on an allegorical meaning. She is not only the virgin over whom the feudal forces and the lower classes contest, but also Mother China, who is now being violated by the Japanese invaders.[7]

The homologous structure of these two narratives symbolically reenacts the dual tasks facing the Chinese Communists: the struggle against feudal forces at home and imperialism abroad. It also helps make a point about the alliance between the Chinese feudal forces and Japanese militarism. Essential to these two narrative structures is the mediating role of the women. Here, as in other leftist texts, gender relations as a metonymy of domination and exploitation also become signifiers of the power relations of domination and exploitation in terms of class and race. The textual system articulates the power structure of domination and exploitation in terms of sex, class and race in a hierarchical order so that women's liberation, a prominent theme in leftist texts, is closely related to other equally pressing social issues.

Although the realist space is largely organized according to the classical principle of continuity, there is a moment when this principle is deliberately violated. When the employer of the singer (Xiao Hong, adopted by him, calls him father) gestures to the girl, who is offscreen left, to come and meet the local despot, the mismatch of shots caused by camera displacement leads the viewer to think the girl is looking and walking in the opposite direction. The mismatch highlights the potential conflict between the girl and the despot.

The problem of social reference is another major concern of the leftist filmmakers. Through shifts in levels of narration realized in different discourses which sometimes confirm and sometimes contradict each other, the social context referred to is constantly constructed and deconstructed. The photo inscription sequence in *Street Angel* offers a good example in which the popular discourse confirms as well as contradicts the journalistic discourse.

In this sequence, popular discourse takes the form of a word play. The four sworn brothers finally find their group photo and decide to give it an inscription: "To share joy and adversity together." However, Chen, who is doing the writing, does not know the character "adversity."

> *Chen:* Do you know the character "Nan" [meaning adversity, danger, suffering]?
> *Wang:* That's easy. It looks like the character "Ji" [meaning chicken]. Half
> of it is the character "beauty" as in the phrase "the talented scholar and the
> beautiful lady" [an implicit comment on the right-wing literary school of
> Mandarin Duck and Butterfly and their followers in the film circle, who
> advocated at the time a form of writing that is nonpolitical] and the other
> half is like the other half of the character "hai" [meaning sea] as in Shanghai.

> Oh, no, the other half of "Jin" as in "Tianjin." Now I remember the charac-
> ter appeared in yesterday's newspaper. [The shot of the newspaper headlines
> comes on screen: "OUR NATION IS NOW IN DANGER, EVERYONE OF US HAS THE
> RESPONSIBILITY TO SAVE IT"—along with the item on the problem of
> Manchuria.]
> *Chen:* You got the character, all right, but the other half of it is not the other
> half of "Shanghai" or "Tianjin" but "Han" [meaning China or the Chinese
> nation] as in "Hankou".

The use of Chinese ideograms, especially in the dialectic principle of word composition, inspired Soviet filmmakers like Eisenstein (1979). Yet while Eisenstein's
theory of montage is basically a constructionist theory, what happens here is a
process of deconstruction, that is, the breaking down of a Chinese character to
reveal the contradictory meanings of its component parts, which the character
as a whole has suppressed.

The new meanings generated by the popular discourse in the form of this
play on words confirm, but at the same time, contradict, the journalistic discourse in the form of the news item suddenly inserted through an extreme
closeup, which allows the viewer not only to read the headline but also most of
the text. In the sequence, all the names for cities refer to those ports partially
under foreign control generally known as "the foreign concessions." The viewer's
attention is drawn not only to the fact that Japan had occupied northeast China,
but also to the fact that other Western powers also had entrenched interest in
the country. This reveals that leftist filmmakers, contrary to general understanding, do not necessarily regard newspaper headlines as a reliable source of
information.[8] In the above sequence, the headlines, while mentioning that China
was under the threat of Japanese aggression, conceal or take for granted those
parts of China already under foreign control, especially these territories con-
ceded to the Western powers under unequal treaties in the 19th century.

How these two discourses contradict each other can be seen in the middle
of *Street Angel*. When Chen learns that Xiao Hong is to be given to the local
despot by her adoptive parents, he is at a loss as to what to do. After scruti-
nizing back issues of the newspaper that Wang used to cover the walls, the news
vendor draws the others' attention to another piece of news: "Madame Sued by
Adopted Daughter for Being Used for Prostitution." They decide that legal
action could save Xiao Hong and go to a lawyer located in the western quarters of Shanghai. However, they quickly discover they cannot afford the legal
fees. Here the narrative development comments on the idea implied by jour-

nalistic discourse that social justice can be maintained by the intervention of law. The social dimension of this comment, completed by the Chinese audience of the time, is its allusion to the KMT government's effort to affect League of Nation intervention in Japanese military actions in China in the early 1930s.

The incorporation of journalistic and popular discourses that interact with the melodramatic narrative can be found in other leftist films of the 1930s such as *Big Road, Plunder of Peach and Plum* (1934) and *Cross Street*. The social narrative as a framing device not only defines the narrative potential of the melodramatic element and its affective mechanisms (such as misunderstanding and misrecognition, which generate much of the pathos of the text), but also produces a new mode of spectatorship in the process of semiotics.

The social narrative as a framing device is clearly seen in the visual motif of the newspaper-walled dwelling where the melodramatic relationship unfolds and the characters make plans for the future. For instance, when the possibility of legal action fades, Wang draws attention to another news headline about a runaway employee. However, the idea of running away is instantly rejected by the girl. Her determination to remain is further reinforced upon her return to the village. There, her friends perform a shadow play that reenacts a drama of popular revolt. The play clearly demonstrates that Xiao Hong's rebellion can only lead to the death of her sister. (The inclusion of the shadow play was tolerated by the KMT censors only because the explicit contents of the drama could be interpreted as a reenactment of the revolution of the Northern Expedition, which established the KMT regime in Nanjing.)

Social contradictions inherent in the formal contradictions between different discourses remain dormant in the specific historical conjuncture of the early 1930s. The narrative does not dramatize any one of them. The leftist films of the thirties do not provide the narrative with a resolution in the Western sense of the word. This is because the main purpose of the leftist text is to invite the viewer to relive those social and political contradictions unresolved by the text. Such a journey was a central organizing motif in most leftist films of the time.

Street Angel, for instance, opens its credits sequence in the western quarters of Shanghai where most of its intended Chinese upper- and middle-class audience resided. The first shot after the credits sequence shows a skyscraper. The camera tilts downwards from the top of the building until it reaches an underground canal with the subtitle: "The Underworld of Shanghai, 1935." The narrative interest moves from a marriage ceremony to an elopement and, finally, to the ritual of death. The camera, after lingering outside the window of the room where the newlywed couple and their friends mourn the death of their sister, rises again and returns the viewer to the first shot of the film: a skyscraper on the edge of a canal leading to the underworld of metropolitan Shanghai.

The incorporation of a set of discrete discourses in the melodramatic narrative also poses interesting questions about the subject-positioning of the leftist texts. Interesting to note is that the incorporation of the indigenous art forms in such popular discourses as Shadow Play and Magic Show inscribes a theatrical mode of spectatorship which comes into a dialectical relationship with that of the cinematic mode. As we know, theater inscribes a different mode of spectatorship in terms of the viewers relation to the spectacle: both authors and audience are present in the same temporal and spatial framework. This contemporaneity of actors' performance and audience viewing, where each party watch through opposite sides of a window, as well as a case history of the character as actor-audience, when inscribed by the movie camera, forms a mirror structure of double viewing, theatrical and cinematic, that implicates the viewing subject in specific social and cultural processes.

Further consideration of the inclusion of both journalistic and popular discourses in the text leads me to suggest that the radical function of Chinese leftist film does not lie in the textual production of a new mode of spectatorship based on anti-illusionism. Rather, the function is in the mode of actual social experience which the viewer relies on to form his/her critical judgment—a judgment which articulates contradictory discourses at a particular historical conjuncture. The subjective positioning of the text is a process of constant change. The set of formal contradictions that are overdetermined by social contradictions turns the text into a contradictory discursive space. This space provides the fertile ground for radical art practice as well as debates about it.[9]

Chinese critical discourses on the issue of radical art practice in film also focus on these leftist texts. In the decades following the establishment of the People's Republic there have been many attempts to reconstruct the leftist texts for quite different political purposes. An examination of this process unveils the extent to which the reception of the leftist texts of the 1930s, because of their unique formal qualities, are deeply implicated in Chinese politics and to a certain extent, world politics.

The major Chinese critical text on leftist films is a two volume book, *The Development of Chinese Cinema,* written by Cheng Jihua with two other authors, and published in 1963. Their affirmative view of leftist texts as part of the Chinese revolutionary art movement was fiercely attacked by ultra-leftists who opposed Mao Zedong's temporary dominance in Party politics. In their criticisms, they argue that Cheng's history deliberately overstates the role played by Communists in filmmaking. They say the book obscures the fact that the actual Communist position was a compromise between the "proletariat" and the "bourgeoisie," so that these films meant for the urban middle class of the thirties were no longer suitable for redistribution. The thrust of the criticism is aimed at the Party leadership in the arts (most of them were themselves leading artists of the leftist literary movement of the 1930s) which officially authorized the view expressed in Cheng's book. On other occasions, it emphasized the importance of learning from the West, of which the leftist texts were seen as an example. The ultra-leftist critics further pointed out that the Party program on the arts formulated in the early 1960s was in direct opposition to Mao's aesthetic position of art made accessible to peasants, which was, of course, part of Mao's total program of world revolution.

After the ten years of Cultural Revolution (1966–1976), the new regime negated the Maoist program of world revolution and turned to the West as a possible source of assistance, as well as a model for its modernization drive. This restructuring of power relations, both domestically and internationally, led to a reevaluation of the leftist films of the thirties. Consequently, the leftist film texts of the 1930s, the embodiment of a political alliance of different classes, became the classics of revolutionary art in China. They were not only redistributed in China in the early 1980s, but were also approved for inclusion in retrospectives of Chinese film in Western countries. This change in policy has put the reception of these leftist texts of the 1930s into a world context.[10]

Notes

This article was first published in *Wide Angle* 11.2 (1989): 22–31. Copyright © 1989 by Ohio University: Athens Center for Film and Video. Reprinted by permission of the Johns Hopkins University Press.

1. Leyda 1972, 60–113; Pickowicz 1974, 328–35; Ellis 1982, 79–83.

2. Cheng Jihua's account has been summarized by Berry 1989 and Pickowicz 1974.

3. My account here is based on the Chinese Communist analysis of the social contradictions of China in the 1930s and the cultural policies formulated based on that analysis. Relevant documents can be found in Mao 1967, vol. 2 and vol. 3; Cheng 1963, 4–6.

4. The introduction of the Soviet cinema of the 1920s to China is recorded in Cheng 1963, especially in the sections "Soviet Cinema and Soviet Filmmakers in China" (137–46) and "Soviet Film and Film Theory: Its Dissemination and Influence" (193–94).

5. Here a comparison with the Japanese cinema of the 1930s, especially the films made by Ozu, is helpful. In the Chinese leftist films the disjunctive elements such as camera displacements occur only at certain significant points of the text so that the sense of disorienta-

tion is very striking. While in Ozu's works, the construction of film space, as David Bordwell has noted, is different but systematic so that the viewer can easily adapt to the film system and no longer experience the disjunctiveness highlighted by Burch and others (especially the local audience).

6. In China in the early part of this century, newspapers were one of the major means with which the Chinese bourgeoisie disseminated their views. These newspapers also provided the progressive writers in the major cities a chance to publish works such as poetry, short stories and essays. As such these newspapers became very influential in literary and art circles. In this essay, the term "journalistic discourse" refers specifically to the use of those news stories and documentary footage approved by the KMT censors. The class nature of this discourse is rather ambiguous due to the complex class relations in China in the 1930s. The basis for my definition is that its readers were basically the upper and middle classes. In the 1930s, the literacy level of the working classes was very low. This definition also helps me to make comparison with the Communist literary movement launched in the late 1920s and the early 1930s in the vast rural areas of China. The aim of this movement was to educate the large illiterate peasant class through popular art forms and to mobilize them in the mass movement led by the Communists. The theory on which this movement is based was first formulated by Qu Qiubai (Ch'u Chiu-pai), who was responsible for the Communist cultural activities of the time. Because of his literary reputation, he was able to influence some members of the leftist film movement in Shanghai in the early 1930s. For more details see Paul Pickowicz (1974, 1981).

7. A similar narrative strategy can be identified in *Big Road* (1934).

8. The narrative of *Plunder of Peach and Plum*, for instance, can be seen as a self-conscious deconstruction of the news story of a former student turned murderer featured in the opening sequence of the film. In *Cross Street,* the news stories not only cover the social situation of the time but also concentrate on the working conditions of the female laborers in the cotton mills of Shanghai. While giving credit to the contents of the stories, the narrative concentrates on the bourgeois pretensions and hypocrisy of the author of these news stories in his actual dealings with one of the female workers in the cotton mills of Shanghai.

9. In the early 1930s there was a heated debate on what constitutes revolutionary art by the left-wing writers in Shanghai.

10. For more detailed accounts see Clark 1987b and Berry 1989. For sample criticisms of the ultra-leftists in the 1960s, see *Renmin ribao* (People's daily) 1st April 1966, 3–6; 19th April 1966, 6.

Five
Three Women
a.k.a. *Women Side by Side*
(*Liren xing,* dir. Chen Liting, 1949)

Screenplay Tian Han, Chen Liting
Cinematography Wu Weiyun, Han Zhongliang
Producer Kunlun
Cast Sha Li, as Liang Ruoying (once a Chinese Nora)
Huang Zongying, as Li Xinqun (member of underground resistance)
Shangguan Yunzhu, as Jinmei (raped by Japanese soldiers)
Zhao Dan, as Zhang Yuliang (Ruoying's former husband)
Lan Ma, as Wang Zhongyuan (Ruoying's current husband)

hree Women is an adaptation by Tian Han of his play of the same title, done in collaboration with Chen Liting, a Second Generation director who wrote on film during the war years and who vigorously started his own directing work in post-war Shanghai.

A craze for behaving like Ibsen's Nora—to slam the door and leave behind any "doll's house" that did not respect women—was a legacy of the May 4th New Cultural Movement, which took place at the beginning of the twentieth century, when China was on the threshold to modernity. Since then, any modern woman in China was labeled a Chinese Nora, and this figure was employed differently in all kinds of representation in contrast with the harsh Chinese social and cultural reality. *Three Women* is leftist filmmaking's interesting conclusion to its involvement with the "new woman" issue. This film was produced toward the end of the leftist filmmaking era as the PRC's early revolutionary cinema was taking over. Two earlier films are necessary references for a better under-

110

standing of this conclusion: *Three Modern Women* (*Sange modeng nüxing*, 1932), also by Tian Han, and *The New Woman*, starring Ruan Lingyu, who also played in *Three Modern Women*.

Three Modern Women contrasts the different types of new women: Yu Yu is a materialist looking for pleasure; Chen Ruoying is a sentimentalist seeking love devoid of social responsibility; Zhou Shuzhen is a working woman who has social concerns. One man, Zhang Yu, links them to each other. Evading an arranged marriage, Zhang leaves his home in northeast China for Shanghai, where he lucks out and becomes a big film star. Zhou, his arranged bride, soon also leaves for Shanghai because of the Japanese invasion, where she becomes a phone operator. Meanwhile, Zhang is dating Yu, a wealthy woman from Shanghai's high society. And Chen is a fan of Zhang's who becomes love-crazed for him. With China's fight to defend itself from Japanese invasion as the back-drop, the film shows how Zhang is constantly educated by his arranged bride to become more socially oriented. Eventually, he distances himself from the materialist woman, declines the love of the sentimental woman, and gets closer to the social woman. He takes an interesting detour to "date" and to learn how to appreciate his family-arranged bride.

The New Woman is a melodrama about an independent woman's difficulty in making a living in a society that exploits women. Wei Ming, the protagonist, is a single mother abandoned by the husband she selected herself in protest of a family-arranged marriage. She is writing a novel while teaching music. Her life is full of complications: her manuscript is accepted only when the publisher sees her picture; he uses it without her consent to attract readers. Her male editor becomes her good friend, but she is hesitant about walking into another mar-riage with him. At school, she is constantly harassed by her boss, Dr. Wang, who eventually fires her when she won't give in to his advances. The unem-ployed Wei Ming reluctantly decides on prostitution in order to pay her daugh-ter's medical bills, only to find that her first client is Dr. Wang himself. She feels greatly humiliated and swallows a handful of sleeping pills. The doctors can't save her life. Outside the hospital, female factory workers led by Wei Ming's female housemate, another factory worker who once wrote a song with Wei Ming's help, march in the street in the morning sun and sing a proletarian song declaring a different kind of new woman. The individualistic subjective position of a new woman is proved tragic in the film, which proposes a collective sub-jective position available for revolutionary women.

As a conclusion to these two earlier films, *Three Women* fills that proposed subjective position with a female revolutionary, Li Xinqun (literally meaning "new masses"). As an underground organizer for a war of resistance, Li contrasts with two other women: Liang Ruoying, a former Chinese Nora who returns to her "doll's house" because she lacks willpower, and Jinmei, a factory worker who has not joined the organized social revolution and falls victim to both her national and social-class enemies.

Suggested readings for *Three Women* are as follows:

Chan 1993
Yingjin Zhang 1996, 185–231
Harris 1997

From "*Xin nüxing* to *Liren xing:* Changing Conceptions of the 'New Woman' in Republican Era Chinese Films"
Vivian Shen

Gender politics in the male-dominated world of republican era leftist filmmaking is exemplified quite well in cinematic portrayals of the New Woman. Throughout the 1930s and 1940s, the concept of the New Woman conveyed in Chinese films shifted so dramatically that a study of the changes sheds considerable light not only on male-female relationships, but also on the general social and political context of that era.

Two films deal explicitly with this subject: *Xin nüxing,* or "The New Woman," released in 1935, and *Liren xing,* or "Women Side by Side" released in 1949. Both films were written and directed by prominent left-wing Chinese male filmmakers and produced by left-wing film studios.[1] During the 14 years between the making of these two films, there were many wars and battles in China (namely, the Sino-Japanese War of 1937–1945 and the Chinese civil war of 1945–1949 which caused great tensions in Sino-American relations). But issues related to the characterization of the New Woman need to be traced back to the May Fourth Movement of 1919. During this movement, women's liberation became one of the central issues. Such periodicals as *The New Women* and *The Women's Bell* appeared to "rouse women as a means of reforming society" and to educate women and enable them to take part in the progress of society" (Tse-tsung Chow 1960, 180). After the May Fourth Movement, doors started to open for girls and women to become independent. Coeducation made it possible for girls to go to college. By 1922, 28 universities and colleges admitted female students. As Tse-tsung Chow has written, "Professional opportunities for women increased. Free marriage was practiced more often. Morality concerning the sexes started to change, and the concept of birth control was introduced" (1960, 258). In February 1921, the Women's Association of Hunan was established and "posed the realization of five rights for women, i.e., equal right of property inheritance, right to vote and to be elected to office, equal rights of education, equal rights to work, and the right of self-determination in marriage. This was later known as the 'five proposal movement'" (Tse-tsung Chow 1960, 258–59).

Young women who were educated in the modern style lived in urban centers, had the freedom of love and marriage, and, thus, challenged the traditions that had sustained Chinese society for thousands of years. Such women came to be regarded by many as liberal, bourgeois, modernizing, and pro-western. In the 1920s, these sorts of women represented the new ideal for the more socially progressive forces in society.

But, according to *Xin nüxing* and *Liren xing,* this kind of New Woman of the May Fourth tradition was likely to become disoriented and helpless once she became detached from school, lost the financial support of her family, and stepped into the world of real life. In the 1930s, it appears, May Fourth–type New Women fought a war for their independence, but lost. In the 1940s, their energies were re-channeled to help fight a war against foreign imperialists. In the process the May Fourth prototype lost her glorious title as New Woman. Left-wing filmmakers introduced alternative models: the leftist, factory worker of the 1930s who is highly class conscious, and the nationalist fighter of the 1940s who is militantly anti-imperialist, multi-class conscious, and an advocate of united front politics. The image of the New Woman was undergoing constant transformation in the republican era.

Xin nüxing: The Battle of the Sexes in the 1930s

Her slender body is wrapped in a long gown, often made from fine silk. The dress has a mandarin collar, buttoned in the front of her swanlike neck. There are two slits on both sides of the dress just above her ankles. The dress is fashionably lined and hemmed. When she moves, the laced slip inside gently follows her body movement. She has the perfect stretched "s" shape body line, slim in the middle, full at both front and back, but not so obtrusive as to destroy the symmetry of the line. It is difficult to say whether her beautiful body and demure manner make the dress look gorgeous, or the first-rate custom-made garment accentuates the lines of her body.

This is the image of Wei Ming, the eponymous May Fourth "New Woman" (played by the legendary Ruan Lingyu) when she wears a *qipao* dress in the film of the same name.[2] Throughout *Xin nüxing*, she is seen wearing many different *qipao*. No other woman made this Chinese dress look so good before or after Ruan Lingyu made her appearance in it. However, one needs to look closely at this fashionable Chinese garment: it is the two slits on the sides that allow the woman to move her legs. If the slits are high, it looks indecent; but if they are too low, she is not able to walk. Even a perfect slit would not give her too much freedom of body movement. Therefore, peasants and workers generally did not wear the *qipao*, even in the 1930s. Aying, the factory worker in *Xin nüxing*, for example, never wears a *qipao;* she always wears a jacket and pants. It appears strange, therefore, that Wei Ming, this liberated New Woman, is "imprisoned" by her clothing on a daily basis. What is happening here is that the left-wing filmmakers are trying to use the trope of the stylish *qipao* to criticize the May Fourth bourgeois model of women.

Liberated by the writings of Ibsen and the May Fourth spirit, Wei Ming was highly educated in the new style in Beijing soon after the May Fourth period. She learned from the painful experience of her sister, who was the victim of a traditional marriage. Wei Ming became a product of the new liberal wave. She fell in love with a May Fourth–type young man. When she became pregnant, her father urged her to commit suicide. Instead, she eloped with her lover and they got married. But she soon learned that such a marriage did not guarantee happiness. Less than three years later, her May Fourth husband abandoned her and their daughter. After this experience, Wei Ming left her daughter in the care of her sister and came to Shanghai.[3]

When Wei Ming starts over again, she is 27 years old and alone, working as a music teacher at the Shanghai Yueyu Girl's Middle School. All the "isms" and options advocated during the May Fourth Movement have failed her. What she faces is the cold reality of modern living in a capitalist metropolis. In the years before the narrative begins, Wei Ming had already been exposed to the May Fourth trends initiated by male intellectuals. Ching-kiu Stephen Chan, who studies ideological representations of the New Woman by May Fourth writers, points out:

> It is little but hindsight for us to suggest today that the misguided practice of the May Fourth iconoclasts was partly rooted in their (the writers') failure to posit a concrete historical as well as textual place for the new women of China. But for the intellectual iconoclasts writing at that particular juncture in history, where contradictions were lived as part of everyday reality, the paradox of representation was a fundamental and critical one. Their choice was most difficult

to make—between representing the symbolic liberation of women and disrupting the dominant mode of discourse that had initiated the very act of subversion in the first place.[4]

Detached from her family and husband, Wei Ming struggles to make a living, aimless and resentful in the 1930s (a time described by a film critic in 1935 as being *kongqian weiyou de hunluan* or "of unprecedented chaos") and adrift in both the upper and lower levels of the society of Shanghai (a place depicted by another film critic in 1935 as *nanxing zhongxin de shehui* or "a male-centered society"). In this time and place, Wei Ming's worst enemy is men. In her spare time, she likes to do creative writing. But because she refuses to reveal her true identity as a woman, or, sometimes, because the publishers, all men, are not interested in an unknown author, her manuscripts are rejected. One publisher agrees to publish her latest book, entitled *The Grave of Love (Lian'ai de fenmu)*, only after he realizes how attractive this female author is.

The Grave of Love expresses this May Fourth liberal woman's total disillusionment regarding love and marriage. (This novel contrasts sharply with Feng Yuanjun's novel, *Juanshi*, of 1923, which openly celebrates the romantic love of young women). In everyday life, Wei Ming lives in great contradiction and confusion. She does not believe in love, but still, she seeks out Yu Haitao (played by Zheng Junli), an editor at the Shanghai Publishing House who also came from the May Fourth tradition. Yu Haitao prefers to focus all his energy on his work, and suggests that Wei Ming do the same. On one occasion, he asks Wei Ming to learn from Aying, the leftist factory worker. Throughout the movie, he appears to speak in the left-wing patriarchal voice. But in reality, he is revealed as an emotionally and sexually castrated man who fails to respond to Wei Ming's romantic overtures. Once again, Wei Ming, a liberated, bourgeois New Woman, is abandoned by a May Fourth intellectual man.

Yu Haitao's rejection pushes her close to Wang, a returning Ph.D. from America (played by Wang Naidong) who pursues her relentlessly. Wang lies to Wei Ming about being married. On a lovely summer evening, when Haitao, as usual, refuses to go out with Wei Ming, Dr. Wang shows up and fills the emptiness that Haitao leaves in her. They arrive at a newly opened seaside night club. A few drinks later, she begins to dance madly. After they leave the ballroom, Dr. Wang confidently takes her, by now half-drunk, to a grand hotel. When she realizes where she is, she becomes furious with him, jumps into a rickshaw and goes directly home.

This costs her dearly because Dr. Wang serves on the board of the school where she works. He pressures Principal Wu, offering her two thousand *yuan,* not to extend Wei Ming's contract. To make the situation worse, at precisely the time Wei Ming learns that she is jobless, her sister comes to Shanghai for help, bringing Wei Ming's daughter. Her financial and emotional burdens are enormous. The little girl caught a cold on her way to Shanghai, and, because of the lack of proper and timely care, she has now developed lung problems. The medical bills are over 127 *yuan.* There is no way Wei Ming can afford this.

The physical location of Wei Ming's apartment, like her position in society, is between Aying (played by Yin Xu), the progressive female worker, and Xu Taitai, an old lady who lives off her daughter's prostitution.[5] Aying, one neighbor, teaches female workers at a night school run by the factory. While Wei Ming is lost in her own thoughts at a dance, listening to the popular erotic song "Peach Blossom River," there is a reverse shot of Aying teaching woman workers a revolutionary song titled "Huangpu River." The other neighbor, the old lady Xu, regards Wei Ming's youth and beauty as commodities, and suggests that Wei Ming exchange them to get a rich husband.

Nevertheless, individualism and the other modern notions that Wei Ming has accepted from the May Fourth Movement make her unwilling to follow in the footsteps of a mere woman factory worker. Wei Ming is much more interested in her own happiness and the pleasure to be found in the city. On the other hand, the purely pragmatic and materialist life that Xu Taitai advocates is too vulgar for her highly educated and sensitive mind. Wei Ming struggles between these two kinds of women and two kinds of lives, hoping to find a new social space for herself.

Unfortunately, Wei Ming never finds one. She cannot even find another job. And the cold her daughter caught has now become pneumonia. Xu Taitai takes advantage of the situation and eventually talks Wei Ming into selling her body for money. To her shock, her very first customer is Dr. Wang. Wang is surprised, too, because just a few days before, Wei Ming had rejected his marriage proposal and his expensive diamond ring.

This situation, coupled with Wang's verbal insults, leads Wei Ming to desperation. She runs out on him and tries to kill herself in her apartment, only to be stopped by her sister. Half curious and half vengeful, Dr. Wang shows up at her residence and continues to abuse her verbally. When Aying comes to her rescue, Dr. Wang and Aying get into a very intense physical confrontation. The proletarian Aying is strong and fearless, and she breaks the bourgeois Dr. Wang's walking stick and throws him out. This is a very symbolic scene. Aying not only saves another woman, but also physically and spiritually overpowers a "modern," upper class man. Not many left-wing films have projected the conflict between men and women, upper class and lower class this directly and intensely.

Although she is saved from Dr. Wang's attack, and her first book, *The Grave of Love,* is in print, Wei Ming's misery does not end here. Eventually, her daughter, Xiaohong, dies from lack of medical attention. Moreover, taking his revenge against Wei Ming, Dr. Wang lies to Qi Weide, the editor of the Shanghai Publishing Company, about having had a relationship with Wei Ming. Like those of Dr. Wang, Qi's earlier sexual advances to Wei Ming were fruitless. So, the journalist wants to get even with this woman, who is now quite helpless. Totally desperate, Wei Ming has taken sleeping pills after her daughter's death. As the doctor tries to revive her, Qi comes in and records the event. Ironically, while Wei Ming is still alive in the hospital fighting for her life, her photo and Qi's article reporting her suicide appear in the newspaper.

All the bourgeois men in the story fail Wei Ming. These figures are all May Fourth–type modern men. Wei Ming's struggles against them only lead to self-stigmatization and self-destruction. This further indicates that the so-called bourgeois women's liberation movement failed to generate a society in which women can realize their hopes for equality with men and for independence.

Left-wing and Proletarian: Redefining the New Woman in the 1930s

As a New Woman, Wei Ming has failed in every sense. The May Fourth dream turned into a nightmare. Wei Ming tries to detach herself from her motherhood. She leaves her daughter, Xiaohong, with her sister so she can freely pursue her dreams in Shanghai. In *Xin nüxing,* Wei Ming's motherly devotion comes into focus very slowly. When her sister is forced to bring Xiaohong to Shanghai, Wei Ming first puts them in a hotel, so no one will learn of the existence of the little girl. Her sister and Xiaohong move in with her only when she has no other choice.

One is tempted to side with Chan and "read the dilemma of modern Chinese realism as a crisis in the formation of 'self' for the women within a 'new' sociocultural space still very much organized by a language that spoke of despair through the patriarchal voice."[6] In the movie, Wei Ming's failure as a New Woman makes it necessary for the male left-wing filmmakers to redefine the term. It is in this respect that Aying claims our attention.

The comparison between the two women is developed gradually. Unlike some May Fourth literature of the early 1920s where the New Women's physical attractiveness often works to their advantage, Wei Ming's beauty in the 1930s always invites unwanted sexual advances. Aying appears plain by contrast. She does not take over the spotlight, yet she is omnipresent. Wei Ming is highly educated and often associates herself with people from "the upper class." Aying is proletarian and seeks out people who work with their hands. As an individual, Wei Ming's helplessness and self-destructiveness contrast sharply with Aying, who is more constructive and lives in the company of many other women. This contrast further signifies a shift in the definition of the New Woman. Wei Ming enters the story as a fancy New Woman from Beijing who has been immersed in the new ways of thinking, while Aying is introduced as an ordinary worker and night school teacher. Keeping in mind the reality of Shanghai in 1935, when this film was made, one realizes that the concept of the New Woman has shifted from Wei Ming to Aying.

This displacement of positions occurs early in the movie, when Wei Ming returns in the morning after dancing with Dr. Wang. She meets Aying, who is on her way to work, at a street corner. The two women exchange a few words of greeting and then depart. Wei Ming watches Aying walk away, carrying some books under her arm. The morning is very quiet, and there are only a few workers cleaning the streets. From Wei Ming's perspective, we see Aying's shadow (carried out with a rare ultra-close up) projected on a wall, so huge that Wei Ming is totally overshadowed by it.

From helping Wei Ming to saving her, and ultimately replacing her in the story, Aying sets a new standard for the New Woman. The movie gradually shifts its focus from Wei Ming to Aying, from the May Fourth, educated bourgeois woman to the 1930s proletarian woman. Aying, the factory worker, is the one who possesses real strength and power. As Wei Ming lies in the hospital bed shouting "I want to live!" and "I want my revenge," life continues at the night club she once visited, where we see Dr. Wang with a new dance partner. As Wei Ming is dying, she hears politically progressive songs echoing from Aying's classroom.

The final replacement of the May Fourth New Woman of the 1920s by the proletarian New Woman of the 1930s is realized the morning after Wei Ming's death. Dr. Wang throws the previous night's newspaper out of his car. A little girl in the crowd sees the picture of Wei Ming in the paper and, curious, starts to pick it up, only to be stopped by an older woman worker next to her. The paper is then stepped on by many feet. Finally, the wind blows the newspaper away. Wei Ming becomes a forgotten page of history, gone with the wind. At this moment, we see Aying among a group of many workers headed to the factory. The morning sun shines on them.

What, then, is the message of *Xin nüxing*? Although the movie does not

offer an explicit discussion of the subject, "The Song of New Women," the striking tune sung by Aying and the other women factory workers, underscores the
evolving definition of the New Woman. In the film, Aying writes the song and
Wei Ming composes the music. But in real life, all of these jobs were done by
the left-wing Chinese male filmmakers.[7] The song has six parts. The first three
describe the hard life of New Women (mainly urban factory workers). They get
up while other people are still sleeping. They go to their factories before the sun
rises. They work twelve hours a day. They repeat this routine regardless of the
weather. Their lives are just as hard as men's. Of special interest is the fourth
part, which warns women not to enjoy any emotional or material pleasure, and
encourages them to work:

> No matter if we have time or not,
>> we should try hard!
> Don't be afraid of heavy burdens,
>> we should throw out our chests!
> Don't dream about romantic love,
>> we should respect ourselves!
> Don't live a parasitic life,
>> we should work!
> New Women,
>> born in suffering;
> New Women,
>> born in wakening!

Part five suggests that women should not be slaves of wealth, power, and
deception all their lives. By working they will never be poor. Part six, the core
of the song, advocates that New Women be the pioneers of a new society:

> New Women,
>> are the female mass of production;
> New Women,
>> are the workers of society;
> New Women,
>> are the pioneers of building a new society;
> New Women,
>> should be like men in the changing storm of time!
> Storm! We should use it to waken our nation from its dream!

Storm! We should use it to build a gallery for women!
Don't be slaves,
> be masters under heaven!
No division between men and women!
The world in great harmony!
New Women,
> bravely march forward;
New Women,
> bravely march forward!

Liren xing: The War Between New Women and Japanese Imperialism

In many ways, *Liren xing*, translated as "Women Side by Side," can be considered as a sequel to *Xin nüxing*. The liberal New Woman of the May Fourth era, and the urban proletarian New Woman of the 1930s reappear in *Liren xing*. The difference is that while *Xin nüxing* highlights the war of the sexes, *Liren xing* calls for a reunion of the sexes. This is because the left-wing male filmmakers in the 1940s had a new political agenda in mind: the united front and the battle against the imperialists, mainly the Japanese and the Americans.[8] Although *Liren xing* was released in 1949, the story actually takes place in 1944, during World War II.[9]

The gender conflicts we see in *Xin nüxing* had changed dramatically by the 1940s. Throughout *Liren xing*, Chinese men and women are seen living and working together. Unlike *Xin nüxing*, *Liren xing* does not feature a war of the sexes. In *Liren xing*, three women of different backgrounds, Ruoying (played by Sha Li), Jinmei (played by Shangguan Yunzhu) and Xinqun (played by Huang Zongying), are married to men who share their social backgrounds and tastes. Factory worker Jinmei is married to an iron worker, Yousheng (played by Zhang Yi), and Xinqun is married to a revolutionary patriot, Meng Nan (played by Zhou Feng). The May Fourth–type bourgeois New Woman, Ruoying, is married twice, first to Zhang Yuliang, a resistance fighter, and then to Wang Zhongyuan, a banker. Meng Nan is seen as Xinqun's comrade, working with her side by side. Yousheng saves Jinmei twice and loses his eyesight defending his wife. Yuliang is somehow able to tolerate Ruoying's decision to live with Zhongyuan after Yuliang left Shanghai to join the resistance. All this indicates that many left-wing filmmakers were no longer preoccupied with the war between the sexes.

Their focus had shifted to imperialism. *Liren xing* opens with factory worker Jinmei's rape in 1944 by two Japanese soldiers in Shanghai. This misfortune starts a chilling chain reaction. Jinmei's boss fires her. To support her aging mother and her blind husband, Jinmei tries many odd jobs and eventually ends up as a prostitute. As a consequence, her husband kicks her out of the house, which causes her to attempt suicide. Throughout *Liren xing*, Jinmei is portrayed as a simple, but sympathetic, target of the Japanese imperialists, the victim of a bitter time. According to Tian Han, the screenwriter, the creation of Jinmei's role was inspired by actual events (Cheng Jihua et al. 1963, 2:234).

Ironically, Jinmei's way of life is consistent in many ways with the ideal of the New Woman advocated in *Xin nüxing* in the 1930s: she gets up early, works many hours a day, and her life is as hard as her husband's. She does not enjoy many material pleasures, nor does she live a parasitic life. She works hard, but she is still poor. She fights, but she is still a hopeless victim. Unfortunately, the ideal sketched out for the modern proletarian woman in the 1930s does not bring fulfillment to Jinmei in the 1940s. Compared to Aying, the class-conscious, leftist of *Xin nüxing*, Jinmei is something of an embarrassment to Chinese Marxist film historians.[10]

The bourgeois Ruoying's marriage to her first husband conforms to the May Fourth ideal: she declared war against her wealthy parents in order to marry her lover, Yuliang (played by the famous actor Zhao Dan). They had a daughter. Later, Yuliang went inland to participate in the national resistance against Japanese imperialism, leaving his wife and four-year-old daughter behind. Ruoying, then a school teacher like Wei Ming in the earlier film, could not single-handedly tolerate the hardships of living in Shanghai during the Japanese occupation. Like Wei Ming, she met a wealthy man (a banker named Wang Zhongyuan, played beautifully by Lan Ma). But unlike Wei Ming, who rejected Dr. Wang's marriage proposal, Ruoying did not turn down Wang Zhongyuan. They soon began living together in the occupation environment as husband and wife. Like Wei Ming, Ruoying also lives in contradiction. While she is materially secure living with Zhongyuan, she is still emotionally tied to Yuliang. Ruoying enjoys material comfort, so she stays with Wang Zhongyuan, but she feels spiritually empty living with him. Each of her men provides her with some of what she needs: the ex-husband with spiritual fulfillment and the current husband with material satisfaction. When her material welfare is threatened, she is eager to associate herself with Wang Zhongyuan. "If I am not Mrs. Wang, what am I? What am I?" she says. But, interestingly, it is the woman Wang is living with after he rejects Ruoying at the end of the film who mocks Ruoying's previous identity as a modern, May Fourth–style, liberated, New Woman.

Ruoying is definitely sympathetic to the Chinese national resistance. Two important people in her life, the father of her daughter, Beibei, and her friend, Xinqun, are both active in the resistance movement. When Zhang Yuliang comes to Shanghai to visit his daughter after seven years of separation, Xinqun arranges to have Yuliang and Ruoying meet at her place for security reasons. This reunion is interrupted when the two, mistaken for Meng Nan and Xinqun, are arrested by the Japanese Secret Service. Now, a pair of handcuffs lock the two together in the center of the screen. At this moment, Yuliang comments sarcastically, "I didn't realize that it would take this to reunite us." This is the fate of the May Fourth New Woman: her reunion with a May Fourth–type man, now a nationalist fighter, has to go through the rigorous test of the wartime 1940s. This time the test is not about backward Chinese cultural traditions and social forces which the May Fourth–type woman must overcome. Now, the enemy separating her from the man she still loves is Japanese imperialism. She asks Yuliang, "Do you think there is a future for us?" This nationalist fighter answers stoically: "If the resistance has a future, then every one of us will have a future."

In this regard, Ruoying is a victim of the Japanese imperialists who create a barrier between her and the one she loves. At a more personal level, after being arrested Ruoying has to go through physical and emotional torture and humiliation in the Japanese jail. By now, both Ruoying and Jinmei, that is, the New Woman of the May Fourth tradition and the New Woman of the 1930s proletarian tradition, share the same misfortune. As the intertitle at the beginning of the film states, these women live in the same difficult age: "They suffer as Chinese women and bear the nation's fate."

In order to get Ruoying out of jail, her husband Wang Zhongyuan, who always claims to be "politically neutral," agrees to work with the Japanese for the newly established East Asian Press. This step makes him a traitor to China. After Ruoying was jailed, Zhongyuan began to live with Lizhu, a divorcee who had an intimate relationship with Suzuki, the leader of the Japanese Secret Service in Shanghai. With Yuliang at her side, Ruoying bravely survives her jail time. However, after Ruoying gets out of jail, she cannot quite decide whether she should follow Yuliang, the man she loves, or return to her husband, Zhongyuan, to arrange for Beibei's educational expenses. Yuliang immediately indicates that he wants their daughter to go with him. "What about me? Are you going to leave me like this?" Ruoying asks him. To that, Yuliang answers: "I won't have a peaceful life. I don't want to get you in trouble." "Didn't I already make it through jail?" she quickly reminds him.

At least on the emotional level, Ruoying wants to be with Yuliang, the man she still loves. And she is willing to go through many hardships to be with him. All she needs is one gesture of encouragement from him, but she never gets it. Later she reaches out to him once again, asking his advice: "I am going to have a talk [with Wang Zhongyuan], then I'll be back, what do you think? . . . Why don't you say something?" To that Yuliang answers incongruously while chewing and swallowing his food: "I am hungry." Here, again, a May Fourth liberal woman is being ignored by a May Fourth bourgeois man, now a nationalist fighter.

So Ruoying goes back to Zhongyuan. But this step leads her to further degradation when she discovers that her husband has another woman. All of this leads to her attempt to commit suicide. By then, Ruoying is echoing the cry of despair made by Wei Ming in the 1930s. On the battlefield with another woman, Lizhu, and striving to keep her husband, Wang Zhongyuan, Ruoying has lost to a woman who is a traitor to China. Ruoying is aware of the existence of "the other woman" at the beginning of the story. But she does not intend to end her relationship with Zhongyuan until she learns that, by working for the Japanese, Wang has become a "cultural traitor to China." It is also at this time that she, like Wei Ming in the 1930s, decides to end her life; once again this appears to be the fate of the May Fourth–type New Woman.

What did Wei Ming and Ruoying do so terribly wrong that would drive both of them to their deaths? The only explanation I can think of is that, although these educated, liberal, bourgeois new women were in the spotlight during the May Fourth period, by the 1930s and 1940s they were a social embarrassment and an economic burden to progressive, intellectual men, the same social force that played a leading role in the invention of the "modern woman" in the 1910s and 1920s. Why? Because these women never stop cultivating their individuality and pursuing their personal happiness. Often, however, they cannot support themselves and their children, especially after their men abandon them and the children to pursue other "noble" causes in life. This is why Ruoying blames her first husband Yuliang after seven years of separation by saying: "*Wode tongku ni yeyou zeren*" (You are also responsible for my suffering).

With the suicide of Wei Ming in the 1930s, the character of Ruoying in the 1940s seems redundant. However, the portrayal of Ruoying in *Liren xing* is not totally superfluous. Left-wing male filmmakers, in an effort to confront Japanese and American imperialism, felt the need for a greater united front which would bring together Chinese women from all walks of life. The introduction of Ruoying at the very beginning of the film suggests that filmmakers

Tian Han and Chen Liting had this intention in mind. She is seen sitting on a couch talking to Zhongyuan, holding a publication entitled *Baofengyu zhong de xin funü* or "New Women of the Storm." Later, after her ugly fight with Lizhu, her husband's "other woman," Ruoying picks up a second publication entitled *Kangzhan zhong de xin funü* or "New Women of the Resistance."

This also explains why Ruoying, the May Fourth–type liberal woman, saves Jinmei, the urban proletarian worker, from trying to drown herself after Jinmei is kicked out by her husband. (In *Xin nüxing*, of course, it is Aying, the leftist proletarian, who saves the bourgeois Wei Ming. This, and similar left-wing films of the 1930s, anticipate Chinese communist literature and art of the 1950s and 1960s where workers, peasants, and soldiers overwhelm Chinese intellectuals.) This "misplaced" relationship between a bourgeois woman and a factory worker was unthinkable during the Cultural Revolution (1966–1976). Is it likely that the left-wing Chinese filmmakers of *Liren xing* realized that in the 1940s the urban proletariat was in a difficult position to play a leading role in the anti-imperialist movement? Is it possible that the need for the united front to fight against the imperialists created a new role for Chinese women, especially bourgeois woman like Ruoying? In other words, is it possible that male left-wing Chinese male filmmakers brought the May Fourth New Woman back in the 1940s to serve nationalistic purposes?

However, in order to play this new role, Ruoying is forced to destroy her old identity as the May Fourth–type bourgeois New Woman. When Ruoying finally "turns around" (Xinqun's words) and comes to join Xinqun and her female comrades in the classroom toward the end of the film, her very first line to everyone is "I have already died." Ruoying has been transformed. By now, she has broken off from Wang Zhongyuan. "I want to live. I want to be with you." Ruoying utters these sentences in one breath, as if, in order to live, she has no choice but to join these women and their cause. She asks Xinqun, "You won't despise me because of my bourgeois habits?"[11] Xinqun hugs her affectionately and replies, "We will criticize you. But we will also love you. After all, you are one of our sisters!" Ruoying is thus surrounded by the multi-class united front of women. None of the men in the story, including Yuliang, the revolutionary fighter, ever reaches out to her as these nationalist women fighters do. It is in this space that Ruoying finally feels at home.

Jinmei is seen at this moment resting in a room adjacent to Ruoying's classroom. She has tried to commit suicide by jumping into the Huangpu River after her husband kicked her out of the house when he learned about her activities as a prostitute. She is saved by Ruoying and others, and is eventually taken to

Xinqun's school. Jinmei, like Ruoying, has also undergone a symbolic death. Is this the end of her sufferings? Or is it being suggested that the urban proletariat also has to undergo a transition in order to be a part of the resistance against imperialism? Again we see a classroom setting, again we see women students, just as we do in *Xin nüxing* of the 1930s, but this time the role model for the New Woman in the 1940s is neither Jinmei nor Ruoying. The united front resistance against imperialism has offered both of them the promise of a new future.

Nationalist Fighters: Redefining the New Women in the 1940s

Aying, the model of the New Woman of the 1930s, could not save Wei Ming, who lost her battles against men and the darkness of Chinese society. It is obvious that the character of Aying lacks femininity in both her appearance and behavior. And she does not have a male companion throughout the film. Does this mean that Chinese women have to give up their femininity in order to serve Chinese society? Does this mean that the best "New Woman" is a man? The portrayal of Aying reveals the radical, yet impractical, proposal for Chinese women put forward by left-wing filmmakers.[12]

In contrast, Xinqun in *Liren xing* is portrayed relatively fully and in more depth.[13] One soon realizes that she is the latest model of progressive womanhood of the 1940s. On the surface she works for China Press. But she is also an underground revolutionary fighter against the Japanese imperialists. Married to Meng Nan, she wears both a *qipao* and western clothing. She possesses femininity and bravery, spirituality and physicality. In the Chinese war against the Japanese imperialists, she is the only one who is not a victim. Speeding along on her bicycle, she personifies female strength and modernity.

In her daily life Xinqun, like Aying, helps other women. She takes care of Jinmei after the latter is raped by Japanese soldiers. She arranges for Ruoying and Yuliang's release after they are arrested. Throughout *Liren xing,* Xinqun is portrayed as a woman warrior. Worker Jinmei, linked to the proletarian archetype of the ideal woman of the 1930s, cannot withstand the complications of the foreign invasion and occupation of the 1940s. Like Ruoying, Xinqun is educated (they were classmates); like Jinmei, Xinqun is often associated with the working class. Like Aying in the 1930s, Xinqun is a teacher of women. But Xinqun is also capable of many tough and dangerous revolutionary tasks. For example, she distributes propaganda bills in the streets. When Yuliang went inland to fight against the Japanese imperialists, he also left his daughter Beibei behind. Seven years later, when he returns to Shanghai to reclaim his daughter, Beibei no longer recognizes him. It is Xinqun who bridges the gap between father and daughter, a task that neither Ruoying nor Yuliang is capable of doing. In the end, Xinqun attracts both Ruoying and Jinmei to her side and points out a new group and collectivistic direction in life for them—to join the forces against the main enemy in their life: imperialism.

Both Wei Ming and Ruoying defy tradition and contribute to Chinese social progress by pursuing free love and marriage. Unfortunately, their positive contributions are short lived. Time soon passes them by. But they are not able to redefine their role in society. For Wei Ming, her novel, *The Grave of Love,* says it all.

Neither Aying nor Xinqun has children. Their noble roles in urban production and the urban underground nationalist resistance and their associations with their women students indicate that they have both channeled their energy to a higher mission in life. This approach was converted into a stereotype by communist filmmakers after the People's Republic was established in 1949. Does this mean that a woman had to sacrifice her womanhood in order to conform to the new model? What we see is that the various portrayals of the ideal New Woman in both 1930s and 1940s reveal the patriarchal attitudes of male, left-wing filmmakers.

Both Wei Ming and Ruoying had daughters after marrying the men of their choice. Their children are the tangible result of their choices. In *Xin nüxing,* Wei Ming gives her daughter, Xiaohong, a doll called *budao de nüxing* or "Bounce Back Woman." This is all Wei Ming can hope for her daughter in the 1930s. Ironically, as Yingjin Zhang points out, this doll is still a "plaything" (1996, 201). In *Liren xing,* Ruoying's daughter Beibei is made to choose between her May Fourth bourgeois mother and her nationalist fighter father. Ruoying asks her daughter, "Beibei, don't you want your mother?" The young girl answers, "I want (my) father, I want mother to go with father." Ruoying leaves a suicide letter for Xinqun in which she specifies that she does not want her daughter to follow in her footsteps. By selecting Yuliang, her revolutionary father, Beibei formally accepts the guidance and leadership of left-wing, male patriarchal forces. Ironically, just a few months prior to Yuliang's arrival in Shanghai, Beibei had no evidence that her heroic father ever existed. Who informs her that Wang Zhongyuan, the man she affectionately calls father all this time, is not her real father after all? Who informs her that Zhang Yuliang, the man who literally left her and her mother seven years earlier when she was only four years old, is her loving father? What forces drive this sheltered school girl to despise her stepfather (who has been doting on her) and to be intimate with her birth father (who is a stranger to her) almost overnight? There is a huge gap in Beibei's transformation, but the film clearly implies that Xinqun is behind Beibei's change. Interestingly, Beibei not only quickly accepts the leadership of the left-wing male patriarchal forces, but also soon becomes a spokesperson for those forces. Later, in her letter to her mother, she asks Ruoying, "Mother, when are you going to join us?"

In *Xin nüxing*, Wei Ming's daughter Xiaohong dies in childhood, eroding the legacy of the May Fourth New Woman in the 1930s. In *Liren xing*, Beibei's life and choice mark a further erosion of the legacy of the May Fourth New Woman in the 1940s. In the end, the roles that the New Woman of the May Fourth tradition played are finally outmoded.

Xin nüxing and *Liren xing* were written and directed by left-wing men. In the first film, they want urban Chinese women to merge with the proletariat to acquire proletarian consciousness and to become independent; in the second film, they urge urban women to join the war of resistance against the imperialists. Wei Ming, an example of the May Fourth–type woman, cannot function in the 1930s. Similarly, Aying, the 1930s model of new womanhood, cannot accomplish the kind of work Xinqun undertakes in the 1940s. In all these cases Chinese women are required to serve Chinese society, but only in the ways that leftist Chinese men spell out. It is no surprise, therefore, that the definition of the New Woman underwent constant transformation in the first half of the twentieth century.

Notes

This article was first published in *Asian Cinema* 11.1 (2000): 114–30. Copyright © 2000 by *Asian Cinema*. Reprinted with permission; courtesy of *Asian Cinema* (John A. Lent, editor) and Vivian Shen.

1. *Xin nüxing* was written by Cai Chusheng, directed by Sun Shiyi and produced by the Lianhua Film Studio in 1935. *Liren xing,* based on Tian Han's screenplay, was directed by Chen Liting and produced by the Kunlun Film Company in 1949. For background information relating to these screenwriters and directors, see ZDX 1982, vol. 1, 65–70, 338–49; vol. 2, 55–66, 237–44.

2. After the release of the film, Chinese film critics had many heated debates regarding its content and style. As Chen Wu, a prominent left-wing film critic of the 1930s, pointed out, the reviews of *Xin nüxing* created a situation of unprecedented confusion. See Chen Wu, "Guanyu *Xin Nüxing* de yingpian, piping ji qita" (Regarding the film *New Woman*, criticism and other matters), in Chen Bo 1993, 570.

3. *Xin nüxing* is based on the real life story of actress Ai Xia, a talented young starlet who was featured in several movies, including *Zhifen shichang* (The cosmetic market) and

Chuncan (Spring silkworms). Ai Xia was born into a large old-style family in 1912. She received a modern education and became socially progressive. After graduation, she fell in love with her cousin. The relationship produced one child. However, after her family strongly opposed the union, her lover abandoned her. Like Nora, she left her wealthy family to go to Shanghai by herself. She soon worked in the Shanghai film world. During her spare time, Ai Xia did much creative writing, including screenplays, which invited both admiration and attack. Not able to deal with her situation, Ai Xia committed suicide on February 12, 1934, at the age of twenty-two, by consuming raw opium. See Cao Maotang and Wu Lun 1987, 166–75.

4. Ching-kiu Stephen Chan, "The Language of Despair: Ideological Representations of the 'New Woman' by May Fourth Writers," *Modern Chinese Literature* 4.1–2 (Spring-Fall 1988): 23.

5. Film critics from the 1930s noted three types of New Women in the film: Zhang Xiuzhen (Dr. Wang's wife), Wei Ming and Aying. (See Chen Bo 1993, 339–41.) In my view, though, Zhang Xiuzhen and Wei Ming are from the same tradition; the difference is that Xiuzhen is portrayed as still living in a world of male deception and bourgeois dreams.

6. Chan, "The Language of Despair," 36.

7. Sun Shiyi, the screenwriter for *Xin nüxing*, wrote the songs, while Nie Er composed the music.

8. Because of the political tensions that existed between the United States and China when this film was made in 1949, many of the anti-Japanese references were actually anti-American in thrust.

9. *Liren xing* is based on the stage play of the same name by the famous left-wing dramatist Tian Han. Tian Han wrote the play between 1946 and 1947. This play can be found in *Tian Han wenji* (The collected works of Tian Han), Beijing: Zhongguo xiju chubanshe, 1983, vol. 6, 157–279.

10. For example, while praising Jinmei's noble nationalistic integrity, Cheng Jihua, Li Shaobai and Xing Zuwen indicate that "the portrayal of Jinmei is open to questions." See Cheng Jihua et al. 1963, 2:233.

11. The actual words Ruoying uses here are *"Nimen buhui xian wo zhifenqi zhong ba?"*

12. Chen Wu complained that the role of Aying "is not a real person of blood and flesh; she is a person constructed from an ideal." See his article in Chen Bo 1993, 345–46.

13. According to Tian Han, the character of Xinqun was inspired by the real life of Communist Party member Mao Liying, who participated in underground activity during the Japanese occupation. See Cheng Jihua et al. 1963, 2: 233.

Six

Woman, Demon, Human
a.k.a. *Human, Woman, Demon*
(*Ren gui qing,* dir. Huang Shuqin, 1988)

Screenplay Huang Shuqin et al.
Cinematography Xia Lixing et al.
Producer Shanghai
Cast Pei Yanling, as Zhong Kui
Xu Shouli, as Qiuyun
Wang Feifei, as Qiuyun (child)
Gong Lin, as Qiuyun (teenager)
Li Baotian, as Qiuyun's stage father

Upon graduation from Beijing Film Academy, Huang Shuqin (b. 1939) started her film career in her hometown at Shanghai Film Studio in the mid-1960s. Shuqin comes from a theatrical family. Her father, Huang Zuolin, studied theater in Britain and returned to teach it in Shanghai in the 1930s. After the founding of the PRC, he served for decades as the head of the Shanghai People's Art Theater and was called the Chinese Brecht not only because he shared Brecht's admiration of Beijing Opera but also because, inspired by Beijing Opera's role in Brecht's new kind of theater, he advocated the idea of transforming Chinese contemporary theater by integrating the traditional theatrics into the modern spoken drama. The theatrical influence of such a father is unmistakable in *Woman, Demon, Human,* Shuqin's tour de force about the life of a theater actress. Here, her love for theater gives her an interesting angle through which to express her concern with the gender experience in China. She represents the dilemma of a woman through traditional Chinese theater's transvestism (here a female playing a male role): how she finds her voice onstage (impersonating a male) but not off (being a female).

The film was inspired by the true story of an actress, Pei Yanling, who opened an unconventional career path by playing Zhong Kui, a supernatural character traditionally played by a male. After reading the story of this unusual woman, Shuqin visited her to learn more about her past and traveled with her to further experience her theatrical life; in the meantime, Shuqin drafted her film script. Later, she shot all the Zhong Kui footage with Pei herself in the role, a theatrical feast that lends the film a distinctive artistic flavor.

Filled with lyrical intensity and subtlety, the film presents a striking juxtaposition of light (the stage, shiny costumes, candles, and lanterns) and shadow, of fantasy and reality, of the grandeur of the male ghost and the weakness of the female performer. Stylistically, the film is an interesting mixture of tradition and modernity: its representation of traditional drama and legend is done through a strikingly modern cinematography and accompanied by unconventional music blending Chinese and Western instruments.

The mythical figure of Zhong Kui and the folklore of his marrying off his sister is crucial for a proper understanding of Shuqin's film. Zhong Kui's portrait is often found in Chinese households, especially on doors. His image illustrates two major aspects of Chinese demonology *(gui)*: the ghosts of unavenged victims and evil spirits. Though stories about him vary, Zhong Kui has been widely believed to be a sort of "ghostbuster," a god overlooking the administration of examinations and the protector of travelers against evil spirits. His stories contain an examination and a journey. It is said that Zhong Kui was a talented martial artist and ranked first in a military exam. Being extremely ugly, however, his candidacy was denied after the interview; this rejection led to his suicide. In the underworld, the king of Hades pitied his rejection, loved his talent, and made him *zhanchong jianjun,* the general in charge of policing evil spirits. Before Zhong Kui left for his military exam, he had been the guardian of his unmarried younger sister because their parents had both died. Now as a ghost, he still thinks about his unfulfilled human duty and sets out on a journey to find his sister. His sentimental meeting with her, while he is a ghost, is an opera scene that is repeatedly performed in the film.

Director's Notes

When I directed my first film in the early 1980s, I was already 40 years old. Why did I start so late? As we know, the Cultural Revolution had halted our economy and culture for over a dozen years; the return to normal life and the start of reformation and opening to the outside world started in the early 1980s. I had waited for 17 years for a chance to direct since graduating as a director from Beijing Film Academy. I started with a film about contemporary social reform, then did one about high school girls in the 1950s, one about war-time kids and their loss of innocence and love, and even one "pure fabrication" about capturing a foreign hit-man in Beijing. Critics noticed the candor, subtlety, and lyrical flow of these films, attributing these qualities to my being a woman director. But I knew these films had not really allowed me to explore myself in earnest; they did not really have my individuality in them.

I was then drawn to the story of an actress who specialized in performing male or even demon roles. Onstage, she was big and heroic; offstage, she was quiet and weak. Her story allowed me to contrast and merge male and female, stage and life, human and demon. The perspective in this film was that of this woman; this film was about her desire for an ideal male and her lonesome soul. The film was completed by the end of 1987 and was warmly received. Critics commented on its unique structure and depth but said not a word about its female perspective and gender consciousness. It was only abroad, at a film festival in March 1989 in France, that a consensus was quickly reached that the film was thoroughly feminist—critics wondered how such a self-consciously feminist film could be produced in mainland China.

There are two reasons why our critics don't talk about feminist films. First, Chinese society discourages feminist consciousness; nobody bothers with it. Second, critics believe that the "feminist consciousness" limits and even demeans our understanding of a particular film. Till now, people have been advising me not to talk about my films as feminist so that they might be understood on a higher level. I don't believe that it is a matter of high and low but rather an issue of specificity, a cultural specificity out of the mainstream.

This mainstream is the traditional culture (films included) prevailing in our society. Because the male has dominated our society for thousands of years, this mainstream will surely present a male perspective on the world. The images of this world are accepted by the absolute majority of the audience (including most women), whom the mainstream trains and influences. If we want a film to have individuality, the director surely has to merge him/herself into the film. Here we encounter gender, which contains individuality. How can one really talk about individuality if gender is erased? [Following this logic,] even female-directed films, including my previous ones, may not necessarily produce a gender-conscious narration but may cancel out their creators' femininity by unconsciously identifying with the mainstream ideology. These female directors may also not be able to create a new vocabulary but repeatedly enhance the male-dominated status quo, wandering within this thousand-year-old, super-stable mainstream, never able to leave it.

I would like to use an analogy. Perspective is just like the directions of the

windows of a house. The Chinese are very particular about this; they value windows facing south: here, from the most expensive, the biggest, the brightest and
the most important window, one may get a frontal view of the garden and the
road. If this is the male perspective embodying thousand-year-old social values,
the female perspective will be the window facing east: sunshine comes in here
first and one views the garden and the road from a different angle. This view
has a special sensitivity, beauty, softness, strength, and durability. Films with a
feminine consciousness should appear to open a different window. A female
director may benefit from art's constant requirements for something new:
exactly because people have not bothered with how a woman looks at the
world, a unique feminine perspective will help the audience discover the other
half of the meanings and feelings of the world, making it more complete.
(Huang Shuqin 1995, 69–70)

Human, Woman, Demon: A Woman's Predicament
Dai Jinhua (Translated by Kirk Denton)

1. The Subject of Woman

The subject of woman is, it would appear, first and foremost one of silence. The
subject of woman is always metaphoric: the "madwoman in the attic," the
woman confined and silenced, who has only fiery rage to transform her prison
into ruins. Everything about her, including her interpretation, is given her by
"Rochesters," that is, by men. She is labeled a madwoman and thus stripped
forever of discursive power, the ability to self-narrate.[1] The subject of woman
is also that young woman in the ancient Chinese folk legend, "Unknotting the
Red Bundle Behind Her Back" *(Beijie hongluo).* In a period of state decline,
incessant warfare, and imperial dissolution, she has escaped selection as an
imperial concubine by not registering her name in the official census, and thus
become nameless. But to save her aged father from the emperor's threat, she
stands before the crowd of people in the Imperial Hall and, hands behind her
back, unties a knotted and buttoned red bundle, a "gift" from a powerful enemy
state that, were it to remain tied, would be a declaration of war. Of course,
because with that act she saves the people from disaster, she is selected into the
palace anyway, and appointed "imperial consort." She is rendered nameless
and speechless once more. With a fleeting appearance in male history, she falls
forever wordless into the very tragic fate she had sought to flee. Her deeds and
their narration [her story?] occur "behind the back" of History, embellishments
on the beautiful painted screen of the male story, or as its distant and obscure

background.[2] The subject of woman is also the shadow of a naked woman rushing through the sleeping dreams of men, silent, never having existed in the past, never to appear in the future. For the Italian writer Italo Calvino, humanity's civilized city is built for her, built to imprison her, a city where she is fated to be forever absent.[3] Chinese and world history and civilization are replete with images of women and discourse about women, but the real bodies and discourses of women are forever "absent in their presence." As in the contemporary Chinese woman writer Wang Anyi's novel *Documentation and Fabrication (Jishi yu xugo)*,[4] the endpoint of a pursuit of a matrilinear order may be where the memories of the living and oral legend disappear; extending that pursuit into written language the extant textual fragments of civilization—reveals only the shadows of male ancestry.

So the subject of woman is once again about the *subject of self-expression.* If we say there exists a female memory that is severed, suffocated in History/male discourse, then a feminist cultural struggle is that which intends to give voice to this silent memory, to give it expression. To be sure, in mountainous south China there once was a "women's writing" *(nüshu),* a written language that belonged to a sisterhood. An as yet unauthenticated legend of this script tells of an "imperial consort" who, having had the "fortune" to be selected to enter the palace, and to tell her sisters remaining outside about the complexities of the palace, its jungle of prohibitions, and the many ways women in it suffered, created a form of writing that only women could write and recognize.[5] This ancient, meandering form of writing existing beyond male History—official and unofficial historiography—was finally "discovered" in contemporary China and banned. Deaths of the last old women able to write and recite passages verbatim in this language means "women's writing" is quickly receding into a miracle that had once existed in memories of a female world and in the documents of literati and male scholars. It is like the "golden voice" of the various sisterhood legends and speech patterns only women were alleged to have had. In the struggle for discursive possibility, women living in civilized society have often encountered the so-called "plight of Hua Mulan,"[6] for we have no chance of creating a new heaven, an/other linguistic system, within patriarchal culture.[7] This is the predicament of a female discourse and narration, the very predicament of female existence. Cultural tradition places women in a city of mirrors. For "women" to be women in the mirrored city is to be forever off-balance, wounded, mired in distress. In the mirrored city, "real women" appear onstage either in men's costume and speaking in men's voices or are "returned to my former female self" and so rendered forever silent. In terms of expression, a women's "reality" does not exist. This is first because the reality of women cannot be narrated through male, phallocentric and logocentric, discourse. And second, a female reality cannot be an essence, normative and pure. The predicament of women originates in the prison of language and the prison of norms, in the difficulty of self-recognition, in besiegement and the perplexity of these multiple mirrored images. Female existence is often a kind of mirrored existence: not the perplexity that comes of narcissism, nor the psychological trauma suffered in tragedy, but a kind of coercion, an intense pressure, a civilized violence that transforms women's flesh and blood bodies into butterflies pinned to death.

It is in this sense that Huang Shuqin's *Human, Woman, Demon* becomes an exceptionally interesting feminist text. In many senses, it is to date the first and only "feminist film" in China. It concerns narration and silence; and it is a story about the fate of a real woman, as well as a metaphor of women, especially the historical fate of modern women.[8] A woman who rejects and attempts to flee the fate of women, a successful woman who succeeds because she performs the role of a man, is still, in the end, a woman and thus beyond salvation. The director, Huang Shuqin, clearly had no intention of making an experimental feminist film. Nor in the process of producing the film did she ever evince any self-consciousness about feminist film per se. She accepted an essentialist, irrefutable "commonsense" view of gender—that a woman's happiness comes exclusively from marriage, which is the "natural product" of heterosexual love. Yet at the same time, a wrenching pain intuited from the experience of being female and an intensely condensed, profound empathy for the real fate of an actual woman artist, Pei Yanling, infuse every scene and every detail of the film, thus questioning essentialist gender expression, questioning the hypocritical and fragile sexual landscape of patriarchal society. The film is not a self-conscious pose from the margins nor an effort at resistance. It is a window opened up on a bricked-up wall where through the opening there materializes a new kind of landscape—the landscape of women.[9] The protagonist, Qiuyun, is in no way a female rebel. Nor is she, nor can she be, a "madwoman in the attic." She just goes after what she wants, stubbornly and irrepressibly. Hers is not a mad cry, but a slight, mournful laugh lacking any modicum of self-pity, filled with silent compassion. This is the self-portrait of contemporary Chinese women. Theirs is both a longing and dream born in patience: the desire for salvation, but with a profound understanding that salvation will not fall into their laps. In a sense, it is a retelling and reenactment of the Hua Mulan story.

2. Choice and Lack

Human, Woman, Demon opens with a scene at once bewitching and night-marish. After the first frame there gradually appear in a close-up shot three makeup jars filled with red, white, and black oil paint. In the dressing-room mirror the attractive, handsome face of a young woman, Qiuyun, enters the frame. She removes her milky-white jacket, binds up her head of lovely hair, and with a practiced hand begins to paint her face with a make-up brush. Each tiny stroke of the brush covers the face of the woman and replaces it with a painted visage of machismo and martial valor. At every twitch of its features, this face reveals a wondrous grotesqueness. The dresser applies the various lay-ers of the costume, and gradually the woman's delicate shape disappears beneath a long red gown. When the headdress and beard are placed on her, this woman no longer exists. In her place is Zhong Kui—a wondrous, ugly, ulti-mately male figure, fierce and intense, shrouded in silent grief and an aura of grandeur and might. As this Zhong Kui sits down before the mirror, we see reflected there many Zhong Kuis; as though perplexed, Zhong Kui leans for-ward for a closer look and now sees in the mirror numerous Qiuyuns wearing milky-white jackets. As the camera slowly pans away, we see Qiuyun seated alone at the mirror looking intently at the Zhong Kui in the mirror, then Zhong Kui outside the mirror staring at a Qiuyun in the mirror. Qiuyun and Zhong Kui alternate before the mirror. Qiuyun and Zhong Kui are both within the mirror. Stepping into a hall of mirrors, or falling into a nightmarish world: woman? man? true self? role? human? nonhuman? demon? Clearly a moment of descent into the confusion of the mirrored images, this is not merely the intoxicating experience of an artist becoming her role, it is the quandary of a modern woman who must perform, indeed can only perform. The tragic question "Who am I?" seizes the moment, but the "I" or subject speaking, asking the question, is specif-ically a woman whose difficulty with recognizing her gendered identity and social role is what defines her. This is not the manifestation of a split in a fren-zied psyche, nor the consuming conflict in a disturbed mind between self-love and self-hate. "I" registers perplexity rather than shock; a prolonged, hidden suffering rather than madness. Indeed, the opening scene of *Human, Woman, Demon* presents a nightmarish situation that constitutes nothing less than a metaphoric statement about the circumstances of modern women's existence. From the film's first moment, definitive notions of gender and gender landscape have already broken down to reveal interlocking fissures.

Human, Woman, Demon is a narrative of growing up. It is the tale of a woman artist's vocation. In thrall to an uncontrollable desire, Qiuyun throws herself so deeply into the theater that she must rend her life, cast aside all attachments to perfect her dramatic role, make herself into that "role." At the level of meaning this is a woman's tale. As the narrative of a "real" or "normal" woman, Qiuyun's life is more a despairing adherence to or revision of the patriarchal gender order than a transgression of or affront to it. Because of this she becomes a successful woman who, though unfortunate, never bemoans her fate. Scripting and interpreting Qiuyun's life, Huang Shuqin certainly did not resort to the current "explanation" in contemporary China that, for a woman, career and life (in blunter terms, marriage) are doomed to incompatibility; nor did she represent it as the allegedly female choice between professional success or personal happiness. If we say that a "woman is not the moon, and does not rely on the radiance of man's reflection to illuminate herself," then in this film, in Qiuyun's career, in her universe, there has never shone a male sun.[10] Qiuyun's narrative of escape is a story of refusal; to avoid becoming the kind of "good woman" that exists only in fantasies, she seeks to escape the fate of women. Yet because of this she must also refuse the path of a traditional woman. Indeed, she even refuses to play a woman character onstage.

A classic Freudian "primal scene" occurs during Qiuyun's first escape.[11] The headstrong little girl ends a game of "marrying the bride" announcing, "I won't be a bride, not for any of you!" As Qiuyun flees the pursuing boys she runs headlong into her mother and another man, clearly not her "father" (in actual fact this man turns out to be Qiuyun's biological father) making love in a haystack. Shrieking, she flees once again. This scene is not a simple female statement or self-narration of a constituting, traumatic life experience, though it certainly smashes any idealized images of a happy nuclear family Qiuyun may be harboring. Self-narration follows in the consequent conflict with the boys. If we accept this primal scene as indeed constituting the opening of a kind of tragic female life, it is a wholly social one. It is Qiuyun's first encounter and escape as she confronts and seeks to elude the reality of women. It is also her first naming as woman and her mother's daughter. This will even prove to be her nail, her historical and social cross to bear. This sort of fate brings humiliation and the chance that at any time she might be banished by Ur-society. As a social woman, what constitutes Qiuyun's traumatic life experience is certainly not the scene of her mother's love-making, but the scenario of her conflict with the boys. These boys who once adoringly surrounded her suddenly become a band of fiends. Instinctively, she turns for help to a male, the "little man" Erwa, who to this point in her life, has always served as protector and authority and who is her close childhood playmate. Traumatically for Qiuyun, after only a moment's hesitation Erwa joins the ranks of the "enemy." This does not just hurt Qiuyun, it is a banishment. She despairs. Then she fights back, and "of course" she loses. Just as she had earlier come to grasp woman, she now also comprehends man. This moment of cruel play devastates all her notions of an idealized world: if as common sense has it, man equals power, then for a woman man signifies protection, as well as possible devastation or harm. The question hinges on circumstantial social and historical conventions: a woman cannot expect to unite with men when she opposes society for the sake of her sex. Unfolding before this little girl is the truth of this metanarrative.

The first time Qiuyun flees in shock and terror, but the second time she chooses for herself, refusing to play women characters in order to refuse women's fate. Once she decides on a stage career, Qiuyun meets with her father's all-out opposition. The profession makes him anxious, and he warns her about what happens to girls and women in it: "How can girls learn performance, what good comes from women actors going onstage! Even if you avoid the bad ones who want to take advantage of you, you'll eventually turn into the sort of person that your mother is." Apparently, then, only two kinds of fates can be predicated in advance for Qiuyun: to be a "good woman" and consequently humiliated and hurt; or to "degenerate" into a "bad woman" where, subjected to humiliation, she will be spurned and banished. In this, to be a woman is a tragic role from which one cannot escape. And though her father's advice is steeped in sympathy, it constitutes yet another metanarrative of womanhood: it denies happiness to the "good woman," salvation to the "bad," and vitiates all other possibilities beyond these two constituents of the double bind. But Qiuyun approves the advice and makes her choice: "Then I won't play women's roles, I'll play men." An intriguing image in this scene is Qiuyun, exhausted, lying on a haystack; with nothing on but a red undershirt, a little boy enters the frame and peers curiously at the motionless Qiuyun. At this point, the edge of the frame cuts off the boy's torso, turning his naked lower body into a sexual index. And yet, conveyed here is certainly not Freudian "phallic worship" or a feminine complex of "lack," but a simple factual statement: Qiuyun can escape a woman's fate and refuse to play the female role, but this choice cannot change her sex. What it means is simply choosing another, more difficult, thorny path, a path of no return with "no regrets whatever one encounters, even death." A woman cannot escape the fate of women: this is a kind of social "fatalism."

The ingenuity (or *textual* trickery) of metanarrative's construal of women lies precisely in the ways these stories end. Each love story must conclude with a wedding ceremony: "The couple bow to each other and enter the nuptial chamber!" Music fills the air. The curtain slowly falls. Or "The Prince and Snow White (or Cinderella, or Thumbelina, and so on) have a grand wedding and live happily ever after." The potential story of the marriage lies forever in the obscurity of the extradiegetic.[12] Any tale of a woman's performance always terminates after the lines "I replace my martial attire with the garments of my former days,"[13] and then the male (real or performative) world and the female world are situated into two separate spatialities, two temporalities. In classical metanarrative, even the many Hua Mulan stories, there is no pain or confusion. The world manifested in *Human, Woman, Demon,* a feminist film, however, is never clear or easy. Although little Qiuyun refuses female roles, even renounces women's attire and throws herself into the itinerant life of the artist, dressed as a stubborn boy, despite even a series of humiliating misrecognitions (for instance, the tragicomedy of being mistaken for a boy as she emerges from the women's public washroom), she will grow up and become a young woman, will love, and desire to be loved. Qiuyun longs to be recognized and named as a woman; recognition and naming signify an affirmation of the life and value of a woman (with Huang Shuqin there is a clear and immobile pattern—love and marriage). When Qiuyun finally gains this confirmation ("You are a good-looking girl, very feminine") from Maestro Zhang (the only man, besides her father, who, if he doesn't "dazzle" her, at least "discovers" her sex and feels tender toward her), she stages her third refusal and escape. Recognition and naming still imply erotic love (as when Zhang says, "I feel as though I will never tire of gazing at you"). This scene also takes place at night among the haystacks, and once again Qiuyun flees in a state of shock and terror. In a point of view shot (POV), haystacks like flickering ghostly shadows seem to rush toward her, and press down on her from above.[14] She has refused; she is terrified and loathe to repeat her mother's social fate. Yet this time she will grasp that the "scarlet letter" of shame her mother (women) wore, also, contrarily, offers its own happiness and rewards. To be a "normal" woman yet to refuse women's fate means to accept the lack in women's lives. In *Human, Woman, Demon,* Qiuyun's actions as a performer exact a price beyond the stage. Yet there is still more to this. She can refuse the sexual advances of Maestro Zhang and still have no means of escape: as a woman, she encounters social punishment not just for what she does, but for what she does not do. She is again named as a woman, the daughter of her mother, an impure, shameful woman. As a result of Zhang's advances and her retreat Qiuyun becomes "homeless." The intense atmosphere of the stage, public display under dazzling bright lights, come with a price: loneliness offstage and banishment to a state of voicelessness. The punishment the Ur-society beyond the stage inflicts even insinuates its way onto the stage. When Qiuyun, numb and empty, performs the play *Three-Forked Road (San cha kou)* to the sound of gongs and cymbals, a parallel montage shows Maestro Zhang quietly slipping away into the dark of the night, his family in tow, to leave her forever.[15] In a close-up shot a nail appears upright on the stage table. Backstage—in the middle ground between the world of performance and the real world—countless (male) faces concealed under makeup glance expectantly at each other, a shot that defines the nail as a punishment meted out by a metasocietal conspiracy. Finally, as she brings her hand down hard on the table top the nail pierces Qiuyun's palm. She completes her performance, bearing the pain without tears, and the mass of painted faces surround her as if to show concern, but in fact to enjoy, to confirm the punishment. In a close-up shot, the eyebrow of a mask drawn on the forehead of another painted face moves in a peculiarly lively and wicked-looking fashion. Suddenly, all the "painted faces," their task fulfilled, vanish, leaving Qiuyun to suffer the cruel form of discipline in wordless banishment. Nearly insane, she grabs the red and black oil paint and smears it on her face; she stands upon the table unable to cry, shouting hoarsely toward the oppressively low ceiling and waving her arms in utter despair. Through the entire scene the swinging ceiling lamp casts a sense of confusion and desolation. This is truly a scene from the life circumstances of modern women who choose the path of social achievement. Punishment still exists. It may no longer involve the extreme cruelties of the past, the public parades or forced drownings: it is just a nail, but a nail that pierces your spirit as it pierces your flesh.

In another rhetorical cinematic strategy, Huang Shuqin inserts an idiot who serves as a witness into each tragic scene involving Qiuyun: the conflict between Qiuyun and Erwa, when Qiuyun is dragged out of the women's washroom, when Maestro Zhang sits desolately in the waiting room of the train station. The idiot image is masculine and a metaphor of the historical unconscious (this is to some degree the same rhetorical [textual?] strategy used in 1980s "roots literature" and the "Fourth" and "Fifth Generations" of Chinese filmmakers).[16] The idiot is always laughing aloud, jostled in a crowd, unmoved and ignorant of all the "small" tragedies visited on Qiuyun.

Qiuyun succeeds. She earns success with her wondrous masculine image. It is not, of course, what her father had hoped for when he told her, "All you need to do is become popular, a famous actor, then everything will sort itself out." The price of Qiuyun's success is that she will forever lack a female life. In plot terms, Qiuyun marries and becomes a mother. On the discursive, textual level, however, Qiuyun's father and husband—these two key men in her "normal" female personal life history—are absent. Her so-called "father" is not her biological father. The biological father appears on-screen only as the back of a head; he never faces the spectator or Qiuyun, has never been a father to her or been named as such. Her husband, appearing only in a wedding photo at the very margin of the screen—an image within an image, an imaginary signifier in all senses, absent in his very presence—serves an indispensable discursive function in the debt collector's report about "Qiuyun's happy family." The husband never appears on-screen. Apparently he never really "exists" in her life apart from being an obstacle ("if she acts male parts, he minds the ugliness, when she acts female parts, he worries about her"), a burden to her because his chronic gambling burdens her with debt, though he is the father of Qiuyun's two children. To be a woman, to fulfill a role, implies that one must become the role. Acting on the stage of life means acting the part of a woman, since in life the stage lights never go off. When she performs her success, she still must play-act the happy and perfect woman, assuming all the heavy burdens and losses of womanhood. In this sense the film reconfigures and deconstructs the Hua Mulan story.

3. The Performance and Loss of Salvation

In many regards, Qiuyun is both a female success and failure. Even as she expresses herself, she is silent. Living and performing onstage are obviously a form of linguistic agency: playing men, she expresses herself and derives her success there, and yet while playing men she uses that male image of presence to create the very absence of her femininity. She pays the price of the absence of a female discursive subjectivity when she expresses herself as a woman.

The textual strategy is that Qiuyun does not perform men in any ordinary sense. Rather she brings to life ideal maleness as it is encoded in the old world, traditional China. Her first male role is Zhao Yun from *Changban Slope (Changban po)*, who is a hero alone in a sea of armies, the metadiscursive protector and savior of the weak (here, a woman and child, Madame Mi and Ah Dou, respectively)[17] in the classical narratives. Zhao Yun in his shining armor is also an ageless icon of youth from traditional Chinese culture. Subsequently, she also plays the part of Zhuge Liang, a symbol of male intelligence and military strategy, and Guan Gong, perfect male virtue, the embodiment of Confucian morality and righteousness.[18] This expressive agency offers Qiuyun a kind of distorted female discursive subjectivity. It reiterates classical male discourse and gives a roundabout enunciation of female desires, while at the same time gently mocking patriarchal discourse. A male image performed through a female subject, an image that exists as the object of female desires, itself constructs a paradox, a peculiar form of irony. This is a circumstance in which a lack is fated to be because of an incommensurability between the subject and an object. The only exception in *Human, Woman, Demon* is a scene in which Maestro Zhang performs Gao Chong, like Zhao Yun, a traditional Chinese icon of youth, from the opera *Overturning Chariots (Tiao huache)*.[19] Qiuyun and the young women in comic female *caidan* attire are standing in the wings watching. When he exits the young women surround him and, for the first time, Qiuyun evinces a certain listlessness as she slowly removes the grey beard she is wearing in her role as Xiao En.[20] She appears in the next scene, seated before the dressing-room mirror putting flowers in her hair; dressed as a caidan she is the feminine complement to Gao Chong. This is not merely an illusory love, but the final wish of a disgraced youth.

Yet what *Human, Woman, Demon* relates is not in the end a story of desire. Its real narrated theme is women and salvation. The film contains another network of levels: the story-within-the-story, the staged Peking opera *Zhong Kui Gives His Sister Away in Marriage (Zhong Kui jia mei)*. This opera appears at every important moment in Qiuyun's life. Zhong Kui and Qiuyun are not two subjects, between whom there is a misrecognition, a blurring, a mirrored confusion of role and performer, but rather, they form a relation of subject and object that will be forever marked by mutual lack, because the role and the performer cannot coexist. As a minor god in the pantheon of traditional Chinese secular mythology, the Zhong Kui of legend is exceptionally talented and passes the civil service examinations with first-place honors. He is expelled, however, because of his extraordinarily ugly appearance; then and there he slits his throat (or smashes his head on the steps, in another version) and dies. Following his demise, the Jade Emperor honors Zhong Kui with the title "General Who Chops Down Evil Spirits," and gives him a retinue of 3,000 soldiers who specialize in killing the evil spirits who haunt the human world.[21] Now Zhong Kui is a popular figure who grew out of folk legend and the pantheon of religious spirits in a nation where people were not meticulous about worship and taboos. Paintings, dramas, and fiction surrounding this figure center on two core plotlines: catching ghosts and giving his sister away in marriage. The latter plot relates how before his death Zhong Kui had promised his younger sister to the scholar Du Ping. Even after his death and apotheosis, Zhong Kui does not forget his sister's holy matrimony, since in feudal times a woman with no elder brother or father could look forward to a life of spinsterhood. So he prepares a wedding orchestra of reed pipes, flutes, and drums, and on New Year's Eve he returns again to the human world to marry his sister to Du Ping. In the film's signifying system, Zhong Kui serves as an idealized protector and savior of women. "I have been waiting for you since I was small, waiting for you to beat away the ghosts and save me," Qiuyun, narrator in the film, declaims. "My perfect Zhong Kui has only been able to fulfil one task, his role as go-between. Do not mind Zhong Kui's ghostly appearance. The fate of women is enormously important to him and so he must find a good man for his sister." That is Qiuyun's dream, neither abnormal nor extravagant—the dream of an average yet uncommon woman.

The cinematic rendition of *Zhong Kui* adds not only a wondrous, dreamy hue to the film but, more significantly, it injects into the original ancient story a tragic, desolate quality that it had lacked earlier. To the clamor of gongs and drums, in a cascade of color, with a performance at once poetic and terpsichorean, Zhong Kui appears to ruminate in solitude on his extraordinary loneliness and despondency. An allegorical narrative common to Chinese art films of the 1980s, this is obviously an index of the nation's existential state as well as a metaphoric image of the existential condition of contemporary women, or so-called liberated, successful women. In the signifying structure of the film, Zhong Kui becomes that figure in which Qiuyun cum woman lodges her dreams; but he is *not* an object of her desire. The male and female protagonists in *Zhong Kui* are a brother and his younger sister. His status as older brother prohibits him from being her image of desire; also he is an exceptionally ugly man and so not a possible subject of female desire, broadly speaking. At the same time, he is a famous ghost, a nonhu(man). If we say that he nonetheless appears in the guise of a man, then it is as an incomplete man. Zhong Kui is nonetheless still an idealized male in the story of this woman, a "most perfect man," in a dream that haunts Qiuyun throughout her life.[22] Perhaps the purpose of the text's web of meaning is to suggest that for the traditional Chinese woman the ideal male image, her "most perfect man," is always a father or brother and never a "prince on a white horse." This ideal man can protect her in the face of trials and humiliations. He shows concern for her happiness and will indeed complete her happiness. There is no romantic sentiment here, only tenderness and intimacy. It is the Chinese woman's longing for a feeling of security, belonging, salvation. One explanation to be drawn from this predicament of modern women disclosed in *Human, Woman, Demon* is that, despite being free in name, even liberated, Qiuyun still names her nameless suffering after the tragedy of Lin Daiyu: "So piteous that my parents died early and I have no one to take responsibility for me."[23] Yet clearly, though Qiuyun is no stubborn rebel, she certainly does not long to have her fate determined by "parental commands and the words of a go-between." Apart from representing the cultural unconscious of Chinese women's devotion to natal kinship ties à la Qiuyun/women's dream savior, Zhong Kui actually serves no more than an empty and hopeless ritual of naming, an obscure utopia about salvation. ("Actually I think that women should be allowed to marry a good man.") As the performance of man, Zhong Kui is nothing less than an empty signifier on to which lodge the nameless suffering of contemporary women, their situation indefinable, an uncertainty that comes from their not belonging anywhere, a longing for happiness and salvation. Only the specter of an elder brother, a ghost, a nonhu(man) can fill the role of woman's benefactor: and we can especially see, when this nonhu(man) compels a woman to perform him, how the prospect of the patriarchal order not only splinters, but is itself already revealed to have been as fragile and insubstantial as the background stage scenery.

A stage performance of *Zhong Kui* appears first during the film's initial major narrative sequence and it constitutes a part of the idealized, harmonious images of family surrounding Qiuyun just then. It is New Year's Eve. A village outdoor stage. Onstage Qiuyun's mother and father are performing *Zhong Kui*. In the wings, Qiuyun and Erwa stand entranced at the performance. Everything is jubilant and auspicious. Only when a zoom-in shot to a column standing on the stage gradually reveals the old adage "Husband and wife, a sham marriage from the start" do we begin to detect a fissure in this scene of old world perfection. *Zhong Kui* is performed a second time, but then the jubilant mood is washed away, leaving nothing but wreckage. When Qiuyun's father as Zhong Kui returns to the human world and knocks on the "door of his old home," calling out, "Sister, open the door," no one reappears onstage, indeed backstage is in a total state of chaos. Like some black comedy, as the elder brother, the savior, finally arrives, it turns out that his object for redemption has already fled with her lover. The Zhong Kui onstage, Qiuyun's father, despondently fends off the fritters, fruit peels, and old shoes the audience sitting below the stage hurl at him while he attempts to continue the performance single-handedly. Qiuyun witnesses her father's pathetic plight from the wings and cries out loud. Her mother/Zhong Kui's sister cannot be located, nor is any trace of Erwa to be found. The third enactment of the same scene unfolds offstage as Qiuyun encounters her former playmates, the group of boys, beside the little bridge over the stream. This time, in a cruel comic imitation of the scene titled "Zhong Kui Gives His Sister Away in Marriage," the boys force little Qiuyun onto the planks that cross the stream, then shake the boards and splash her with water, chanting in unison, "Sister, open the door. I am your brother Zhong Kui returned." When Qiuyun timidly calls on Erwa for help, the boys chorus sings, "Sister, open the door. I am your brother Erwa returned." Erwa responds: "Who's your brother! Go look for your bastard father." And then the boys begin cheering, "Go look for your bastard father." Absent now is precisely that elder brother, Zhong Kui, who brings salvation, safety, a loving heart. This is also the scene where, as little Qiuyun forces Erwa to the ground, her despairing, pleading eyes drift off into an indistinct distance. And then in Qiuyun's POV shot the story-within-the-story appears for the first time, in a wondrous scene from *Zhong Kui*. Sword raised, breathing flames in the darkness, Zhong Kui severs the heads of the demons, and materializes as Qiuyun's idealized redeemer here for the first time in the film.

In the operatic story-within-the story, a key rhetorical strategy is the perennial absence of Zhong Kui's sister. Neither the meeting of the brother and sister nor the marriage ever actually occurs. A joyous occasion—the wedding ceremony and the event of marrying off the sister—is forever deferred beyond the diegetic. Salvation never occurs in the end, never reaches completion. The first time Zhong Kui appears in a scene within the film proper is after Qiuyun has performed *Three Forked Roads* in which the conspiratorial and punitive nail has pierced her palm. As she screams hoarsely with tearless despair, Zhong Kui appears backstage, lit in a ray of bright, strange light. Striding toward her half-closed dressing-room door he peers inside and in a desolate timbre sings: "I've arrived at my home, the house so very cold. I want to knock on the door, but fear startling my sister. Tears flow and swallow up my words." In a close-up shot, tears of passion well out of Zhong Kui's eyes. In the dressing room, Qiuyun seems momentarily to take the position of Zhong Kui's sister. Yet the male costume she is wearing and the red and black paint she has smeared on her face situate her between these two figures, Zhong Kui and the sister beckoning him. In the real-life scenario, Zhong Kui—absent male savior—and his younger sister from the staged scene or story-within-the-story—absent object of salvation—point simultaneously to the destruction and the redemption of these ancient gender roles.

In scenes pertaining to Qiuyun's life, her father and Maestro Zhang are obviously characters constructed as Zhong Kui foils. Though they serve the roles of father and elder brother in Qiuyun's life, the text's narrative structure makes them appear in a certain sense incompletely male. Long before Qiuyun's mother escaped, her marriage to Qiuyun's father had become a sham; he isn't even Qiuyun's biological father. When Qiuyun discovers her mother making love with "back of the head" in the haystack and rushes back to the old temple where the opera troupe is billeted, a close-up shot shows Qiuyun's "father" lying alone on his bed facing the wall. In what is clearly a POV shot, the camera rolls to shoot the feminine, bared arms of a figure in a dilapidated wall mural; the scene articulates the desire of a sexually frustrated man. He has raised Qiuyun to maturity and in the end lets her go because this choice is her only avenue toward completion. Maestro Zhang nearly replicates the actions of Qiuyun's father. On two occasions, projecting the gender misrecognition of Ur-society, he also mistakes Qiuyun for a woman, and, in so doing, he protects her right to "be a woman," so in the end he, too, must give her up. Her father sacrifices his only relative for the sake of her future; Maestro Zhang gives up his position as "the leading actor of martial role" and leaves it for Qiuyun as an empty space, a gift. Like Qiuyun's father, Maestro Zhang also renders up the very thing in which he has vested his every emotion. All they can complete for her is her career, never her happiness. This loss or absence of the male sex— subject and savior in the classical gender discourse—will indubitably rupture the traditional female world. A woman planning to repair this fractured image can only do it in performance, playing an ideal male image; but to play this role implies that she cannot even be at the same time a female subject who occupies the position, an object position. A modern woman, who must save herself but cannot, falls into the empty fissure that opens up between acting and the absence of a self, female expression and silence, the glittering light of the new world and the complete dilapidation of the old. Qiuyun/woman and the male savior Zhong Kui/man can only, as in the film's prologue, gaze at each other from within and without the mirror.

In the film's final sequence, Qiuyun and her "father" meet again. The room is alight with countless candles, casting a rich, warm hue. As though steeped in happy emotion Qiuyun imagines: "In tomorrow's performance, you play Zhong Kui and I'll play his sister. You marry me off." It is the last time that Qiuyun will ever seek to repair an ideal image of gender *difference*. Performing Zhong Kui's sister she seeks to fill up this always absent, empty position; she relies on her father to "name" her a happy woman onstage. Yet this nomination reappears immediately, though differently, by way of the naming process of the Ur-society; and it indicates disappointment, points out that women have not moved out of their position as the "second sex." While father and daughter steep in their happiness, a dark, crooked shadow enters screen left, finally enveloping Qiuyun's entire body. It turns out to be old lady Wang, who helped in Qiuyun's birth: "When you were born the only thing visible was your big mouth, crying with all your might, as though in song. Your father thought you were a boy. But I saw you were lacking that little thing and so I knew you were a girl." In the Ur-society's naming, woman is still the incomplete gender. So Qiuyun, a modern, even successful woman, can only harbor one simple, utopian desire: "Actually, I have always felt a woman should marry a good man." The hope of salvation is still vested in a man, though the man is incomplete, a protoman. The metadiscourse is still classical: the woman "is returned to where she belongs."[24] The predicament of a modern woman appears in the film but at the same time the film uses a classical discourse to deconstruct classical images of gender.

At the film's end, the narrator finally allows Zhong Kui to face Qiuyun onstage. In unison they speak: "I've come here to marry you off." Yet Qiuyun's response is: "I'm already married to the stage." "Any regrets?" Zhong Kui asks. Her answer: "No." A modern woman unwilling to adhere to traditional gender roles, who will not take the "returning" course. Regretless? Certainly, though not without a sense of loss. If we say that Zhong Kui's last performance finally completes the scenario, bringing the (pseudo) male savior and the saved woman together visually, then what is interesting is that the two figures face-to-face on-screen are actually both women: playing Qiuyun is the actress Xu Shouli, and Pei Yanling, who performs all the Zhong Kui scenes, was in fact the model of the story of Qiuyun as performed in the film. Once again, contrary to expectation, narrative completes the women's story, completes the expression of incompletable women.

Human, Woman, Demon is by no means a radical feminist film that derives pleasure in destruction. It recounts the story of a woman in what Zhang Ailing has called the Chinese style of simplicity and splendor, and in this appears the female predicament of being between the devil and the deep blue sea. In the ruptures and fissures of the metanarratives of the past, windows open up on walls to expose a world and a human life in the female perspective. Cinematically the other's salvation of woman does not materialize, nor can it. Yet perhaps self-redemption for a woman lies in ripping apart historical discourse, to allow the real process of her memory to take shape.

Notes

This article (translated by Kirk Denton) was first published in *Cinema and Desire: Feminist Marxism and Cultural Politics in the Work of Dai Jinhua,* edited by Jing Wang and Tani Barlow (London and New York: Verso, 2001). Copyright © 2001 by Verso. Reprinted with permission.

1. See Charlotte Brontë's *Jane Eyre.* See also Sandra M. Gilbert and Susan Gubar 1979. The Chinese version is *Nüquanzhuyi wenxue lilun* (Feminist literary theory), Hu Min, Chen Caixia, and Lin Shuming, trans., Changsha: Hunan renmin wenyi chubanshe, 1989, pp. 113–25.

2. *Unknotting the Red Bundle Behind Her Back (Beijie hongluo)* is a well-known opera performed in various regional theatrical traditions. [Looking for an excuse to attack, an enemy of the Song sends them a bundle tied together with a series of impossibly complex buttons and knots, demanding that it be untied by someone behind their backs or they will invade. A minister is ordered by the emperor to find someone to fulfill the task, or his head will be chopped off. Unable to find anyone, his daughter finally comes forth to save his neck. Her name had never been officially registered because her father had wanted to spare her being selected as a concubine for an immoral emperor. The daughter succeeds in unraveling the bundle and saving the empire, but in the process she gains a name and is selected as imperial consort.—Trans.]

3. From Italo Calvino's *Invisible Cities,* cited and discussed in Teresa de Lauretis 1984, 12–56. Dai is clearly indebted to de Lauretis, who writes: "Calvino's text is thus an accurate representation of the paradoxical status of women in Western discourse: while culture originates from woman and is founded on the dream of her captivity, women are all but absent from history and cultural process" (13). Chinese translation in "Cong mengzhong nü tanqi" (Opening the discussion with woman in a dream). Wang Xiaowen, trans., *Dangdai dianying* (Contemporary film) vol. 4, 1988, 13.

4. Wang Anyi, *Documentation and Fabrication: One Way of Creating the World (Jishi yu xugou—chuangzao shijie fangfa zhi yi zhong),* Beijing: Renmin wenxue chubanshe, 1993. [This book is in the form of an autobiography that is at once factual and fictional.—Trans.]

5. See Zhao Liming, "Preface" *(Xu)* in Zhao, ed., *Encyclopedia of Chinese Women's Writing: A Compendium of Materials on a Unique Form of Women's Writing (Zhongguo nüshu jicheng: Yi zhong qite de nüxing wenzi ziliao zonghui),* Beijing: Qinghua daxue chubanshe, 1992, 15–17. [Dai Jinhua relates here only one of the several legends about the origins of this writing system.—Trans.]

6. Her father ill and unable to serve the emperor in his war against the invading barbarians, Hua Mulan disguises herself as a man and battles in his place for twelve years. When victory is won, she returns home and dons again her female attire. See Julia Kristeva, *About Chinese Women* (New York: Marion Boyars, 1974), 93.

7. For related discussion, see Laura Mulvey 1985. [Dai Jinhua may have in mind Mulvey's discussion of psychoanalysis and its relevance to feminist criticism. The question for Mulvey is how to fight patriarchy "while still caught within the language of patriarchy. There is no way in which we can produce an alternative out of the blue, but we can begin to make a break by examining patriarchy with the tools it provides" (199). For the Chinese text, see the translation by Zhou Chuanji in *Yingshi wenhua* (Visual culture), vol. 1, 1988.—Trans.]

8. The prototype for the story comes from the real-life experiences of the female artist Pei Yanling (who performs Zhong Kui in the film). See Dai Jinhua and Mayfair Yang's inter-

view of Huang Shuqin in *positions: east asia cultures critique* 3.3, 1995. For the Chinese original, see "Zhuiwen ziwo" (Self-queries) in *Dianying yishu* (Cinematic art), vol. 5, 1993.

9. From notes taken at a lecture by the director Huang Shuqin at a conference organized by the Film Department at UCLA on April 2, 1995. Huang Shuqin said that she hoped her own films would express a female perspective, as if opening an eastern-facing window in a house that ordinarily only had windows facing north and south, revealing perhaps some different scenery.

10. The play "A Friend Arrives in a Storm" ("Fengyu guren lai"), by the woman playwright Bai Xifeng, describes the choices made by a mother and daughter in their life experiences as women intellectuals and the conflict between their professions and loves. When the play was performed in Beijing in the early 1980s, it gave rise among audience members of both sexes to very heated reactions and one of its lines of dialogue ("woman is not the moon, and does not rely on the radiance of man's reflection to light herself") became for a time a popular turn of phrase among urban women. In a certain sense, "A Friend Arrives in a Storm" was a rather early self-conscious feminist voice of opposition to appear in the post-Mao period. See *Bai Xifeng juzuo xuan* (Selected plays of Bai Xifeng), Beijing: Zhongguo xiju chubanshe, 1988.

11. Freud's "primal scene" is the witnessing of or fantasy about parents copulating.

12. "Diegesis" is commonly used in film criticism to refer to the world created by a film's narrative.—Trans.

13. See the *yuefu* "The Ballad of Mulan" ("Mulan shi"): "Ten thousand leagues she marched to the borderland, flying over mountains and through passes. War drums echoed through the bitter cold, the winter light shone on coats of mail. Great generals of many battles perish, foot soldiers return after years of battle. . . . I open the east gate and sit on my bed in the western chamber. I replace my martial attire with the garments of my former days. By the window I do my hair, before the mirror I place a yellow flower there. She went out and greeted her comrades, who were all shocked, for they knew not the one with whom they had traveled for twelve years was the woman Mulan." From Shen Deqian, ed. *Ancient Poems (Gushi yuan)*, Beijing: Zhonghua shuju, 1963, 326–27.

14. A point of view (POV) shot is taken from the perspective of a particular character.—Trans.

15. *Three-Forked Road (Sancha kou)* is a famous Peking opera derived from the long *pingshu* narrative *Yang Family Generals (Yang jia jiang)*. It recounts the story of General Yang Jianye of the Song dynasty leading his troops to Liao; because the rations don't make it to the front, he loses the battle and he commits suicide. The Yang family sends a general to find out where Yang Jianye's body was buried. The general puts up for the night in a small inn in foreign territory. Xiao Er from the inn is a Song loyalist who mistakes the Song general for a foreign general, while the latter mistakes Xiao Er for a Liao spy. With this misunderstanding, they begin to fight each other. In the end, the misunderstanding is cleared up. This was originally a comic martial opera but later performed as a serious martial opera.

16. As part of the "cultural reflection movement" in the early and mid-1980s, roots lit-

erature and Fourth and Fifth Generation films often used the idiot as a metaphor for the ignorance of traditional Chinese culture or the historical unconscious. The most typical of these
are Han Shaogong's novella "Dad, dad, dad" ("Ba, ba, ba") and the Fifth Generation filmmaker Zhang Zeming's *Swan's Song (Juexiang)*.

17. *Changban Slope (Changban po)* is a well-known Peking opera derived from the classic novel *Three Kingdoms (Sanguo yanyi)* by Luo Guanzhong. The story is about Zhao Yun,
a great general under the command of Liu Bei, who as a youthful hero fought a bitter, solitary
battle at Changban Slope against the great army of Cao Cao to protect Liu Bei's wife, Madame
Mi, and their son Ah Dou; hence, the famous act "Saving Ah Dou at Changban Slope."

18. In the film, Qiuyun performs Zhuge Liang and Guan Gong (Guan Yu) in the two
famous Peking operas *Qunying hui* (A meeting of heroes) and *Huarong dao* (The Huarong
road), respectively, both of which derive their material from *Three Kingdoms*.

19. A famous martial piece from the Peking opera repertoire. The story takes its material from the classic Chinese novel *The Biography of Yue Fei (Shuo Yue quan zhuan)*. The
Southern Song general Yue Fei leads his troops to battle against the invading Jin army. The
Jin obstruct them with an articulated armored vehicle (also called a pulley car, *hua che*). The
Song general Gao Chong breaks through their formation alone and pushes over their pulley
cars with his long spear; when he tries to push over the tenth, his horse collapses and he is
crushed to death by the pulley car.

20. Xiao En is a principal character in the famous Peking opera *Fisherman's Revenge
(Da yu sha jia)*, which takes its material from the classic Chinese novel *The Water Margin
Revisited (Shui hu hou zhuan)*, one of the many sequels to *The Water Margin (Shui hu zhuan)*.
The story takes place after the heroes of Mount Liang Marsh have been given amnesty by the
court. The former hero of the marsh, Xiao En, takes his daughter home to earn his living as
a fisherman, but corrupt officials press them with heavy taxes leaving them no way out but
to kill the corrupt officials and rebel again.

21. See the section on Zhong Kui (#49) in Ma Shutian, "Daoist Gods" ("Daojiao zhu
shen"). In *Gods of China (Huaxia zhushen)*, Beijing: Yanshan chubanshe, 1990, 265–79. The
entry on Zhong Kui in Zong Li and Liu Qun, *Chinese Folk Gods (Zhongguo minjian
zhushen)*, Shijiazhuang: Hebei renmin chubanshe, 1986, 231–41, cites the Song dynasty writer
Shen Kua's "Mengxi bitan" ("Bu bi tan") and many other classical collections of anecdotes
which recount the legend of the Tang artist Wu Daozi painting for the Tang emperor
Xuanzang a picture of Zhong Kui catching ghosts. The legend has it that after the emperor
returns to the palace from Li Mountain he falls ill and cannot be cured for a long time. One
night he has a dream in which he sees two ghosts, one big, one small. The small ghost steals
the imperial concubine Yang Guifei's purple perfume bag and the emperor's jade flute, circles
the hall, and flees. The big ghost, wearing a hat and blue clothes (sometimes a black face completely bearded, a tattered hat and blue gown), grabs the small ghost and first digs out its
eyes, then splits him in half and swallows him. The emperor asks the big ghost who he is and
he responds "Zhong Kui." When the emperor awakens, he is cured; so he orders Wu Daozi
to paint Zhong Kui as a door god.

22. In the film, Qiuyun hangs Zhong Kui's painted face in her home and pays no heed to her husband's and friends' opposition to her determination to perform Zhong Kui, and in her dialogue [with her child] says: "Your mother wants to perform a most perfect man."

23. See chapter 32 (In which "Bao Yu demonstrates confusion of mind by making his declaration to the wrong person; And Golden shows an unconquerable spirit by ending her humiliation in death") of Cao Xueqin's *Dream of the Red Chamber (Hong lou meng)*, Beijing: Renmin wenxue chubanshe, 1957, 331–32: "Upon hearing these words Daiyu didn't know whether to be happy, alarmed, regretful, or sorrowful. . . . Sorrowful because though there are things of burning importance to be said, without a father or a mother I have no one to say them for me." For an English translation, see *Story of the Stone.* 5 vols., David Hawkes and John Minford, trans., Hammondsworth: Penguin, 1977.

24. In ancient Chinese a woman who lives with her husband's family is said to "return." To marry a woman off is also called "returning." In the *Book of Odes (Shi jing)*, (*Guofeng*, "Nanshan"), there is a poem which reads in part: "The road to Lu is easy and broad, / For this lady from Qi on her wedding way *(gui)."* *The Book of Changes (Yi jing)* contains the hexagram "Guimei" (Returning bride).

Seven
Ju Dou
(dir. Zhang Yimou, 1990)

Screenplay Liu Heng
Cinematography Gu Changwei
Producer China Film Co-Production,
Xi'an & Dejian Bookstore (Japan)
Cast Gong Li, as Ju Dou
Li Wei, as Yang Jinshan (the old guy)
Li Baotian, as Yang Tianqing

*J*u Dou caught international attention in 1991 when it was honored as Chinese film's first Oscar nomination, but at the same time, it was banned by the Chinese government. This phenomenon could well be the point of departure for a discussion. One could consider why the film offended the Chinese authorities and became a politically sensitive issue. One could also consider what the resemblance is between the film's "cultural China" and today's political China: how both Communism and Confucianism demonstrate patriarchal systems of domination.

Named after its female lead, *Ju Dou* is adapted from Liu Heng's novel *Fuxi, Fuxi*. The title of the novel suggests the primary theme and subject matter for both the book and the film. In Chinese mythology, Fuxi and his sister, Nüwa, are the human-headed and snake-tailed creators of human beings and of civilization. Nüwa is supposed to have created human beings out of clay and mended the "leaking roof" of the universe for them. Fuxi is given a more intellectual job; he is supposedly the author of the basic trigrams contained in the *Yi jing*, that is, the *Book of Changes*. He also "invented" measuring instruments and the calendar. Reflecting the national minorities' influence on this particular piece of ancient mythology, Fuxi and Nüwa are also brother and sister who decide to get married. A Tang dynasty (A.D. 618–907) book records this part in some detail: "Long ago, when the universe had first come into being, there were no people in the world, only Nüwa and her brother on Mount Kun-lun. They considered becoming man and wife but were stricken with shame. And so [Fuxi] and his sister went up on Kun-lun and [performed a sacrifice], vowing: 'If it is Heaven's wish that my sister and I become man and wife, let this smoke be intertwined. If not, let the smoke scatter,' whereupon the smoke was inter-twined, and his sister did cleave unto him" (see Plaks 1976, 35–36.) Obviously, Ju Dou and Tianqing, the stepmother and stepson (addressing each other as aunt and nephew in the film) who fall in love, are violating the same taboo that the ancient mythology touched upon.

Compared to the festive tragedy of *Red Sorghum*, Zhang Yimou's debut in film directing, the tragedy of *Ju Dou* has a much more somber tone. Zhang's allegorical filmic world—colorful, fanciful, ritualistic, and carnivalistic—has turned from a celebration of human vitality to an examination of human con-finement. On-screen, the dye mill's stone walls confine the lustful display of col-ors. They also keep the carnival "overthrowing of the ruler" only within the walls. The ritual no longer endorses any fantasy but becomes repressively real—the funerary procession showcases the power of social conventions and the pain of the lovers who are at the mercy of these conventions.

Gong Li, the Chinese actress best known to American audiences, contin-ued to act for Zhang; she actually played in all of Zhang's first seven films before eventually moving out of his orbit. Although still active in the mainland Chinese film circle, she has ventured into the international market and acted, for exam-ple, with Jeremy Irons in Wayne Wang's 1998 film, *Chinese Box*. As for her earlier performance in Zhang's films, *Ju Dou* demonstrates Gong Li's acting at its best. Her contribution to the impact of this film was complemented by Li Baotian, who did an equally superb job as Tianqing. Since the mid-1980s, Li Baotian, once an acting instructor at a drama school, has become China's num-ber-one actor by popular and critical consensus. In March 1997, eight institu-tions (including the prestigious Beijing Film Academy and *Film Art* journal) sponsored a week-long film festival showcasing his films as well as a confer-ence on his art of acting. Students who enjoy his acting will have another chance to observe it in *Woman, Demon, Human,* also selected for this book.

Suggested readings for *Ju Dou* are as follows:

Callahan 1993
Huot 1993
Lau 1994
Rey Chow 1995, 142–72
Cui 1997

Director's Notes

What I want to express is the Chinese people's oppression and confinement, which has been going on for thousands of years. Women express this more clearly on their bodies *(zai tamen shenshang)* because they bear a heavier burden than men.

I was so excited when I discovered the walled gentry mansion [where *Red Lantern* was filmed], which is hundreds of years old in Shanxi Province. Its high walls formed a rigid square grid pattern that perfectly expresses the age-old obsession with strict order. The Chinese people have for a long time confined themselves within a restricted walled space. Democracy is still very far off, and it will be slow in forming here. We have a historical legacy of extinguishing human desire *(miejue renyu)*. (Qtd. in Mayfair Yang 1993, 300, 301–2)

The human nature in *Red Sorghum*—a freedom of creativity, a wild craze of life, an elaborated disobedience to disciplines and controls—is filled with idealism. One can hardly find it in the real Chinese, not even the contemporary Chinese. Liu Heng's *Fuxi, Fuxi,* nevertheless, is different. It is about the realistic mentality of those who are genuinely Chinese. Although it is a story about the past, it has strong realistic implications [for today]. [The reason that I turned the book into my film was that] I was touched by the book's realism and felt that the real Chinese were the characters in this book. Yang Tianqing is a typical Chinese. He has the desire but not the guts. He sneaks, hides, and fears any suspicion from outside the walls [of the dye mill]. He is heavily burdened, and repressed, and shows a distorted mentality. Yet he can't restrain his intuitive urges and desires either. He is like a muffin being toasted from both sides, and ending up by being burnt on both sides. Such a character represents the Chinese mental reality best. The film will project Yang Tianqing's shadow on everyone of us. (Zhang Yimou 1996, 386)

Ju Dou—A Hermeneutical Reading of Cross-Cultural Cinema
Jenny Kwok Wah Lau

In 1988, China's open-door policy was at its peak. Director Zhang Yimou had just created a huge controversy over his film *Red Sorghum*. In mainland China, supportive viewers came out from cinemas mimicking the drunken palanquin carriers from the film and singing their indecent songs that worried the patrolling police. In various cities, security teams were called in especially for the movie screening.[1] The film caused a few officials in the China Film Bureau to raise their eyebrows, and outraged viewers accused the director of insulting the Chinese in order to please Westerners. (The film won the 1988 Golden Bear Award at the Berlin Film Festival.) It was *Red Sorghum*'s flouting of traditional sexual norms that elicited these responses. For a brief period, fan magazines and newspapers were full of discussions about the film—its plot, history, chauvinism, sex, violence, and so forth—but the director himself remained silent. No one would have guessed that two years later Zhang would turn out yet another project, *Ju Dou,* that would be even more problematic than *Red Sorghum.*

Ju Dou is a film that has generated tremendous international attention not only because of its merits (it was the winner of the Cannes Film Festival, the Chicago International Film Festival, and was nominated for the Foreign Language Oscar) but also because of the controversy it has aroused among Chinese film officials. The China Film Bureau, which serves, among other things, as a censoring committee for all films screened in mainland China, decided that the film was not good "for the image of China" and attempted to withdraw it from the Oscar nominations on the ground that it had not yet been commercially released in China. But the Academy Awards Committee argued that there had been a paying public, however small, for the film, presumably in Hong Kong.[2] The main Chinese audience for *Ju Dou* was indeed the Hong Kong Chinese, who saw the film upon its release there in the winter of 1990. The response was lukewarm. Some mainland Chinese were able to see the tape of *Ju Dou* when they visited Hong Kong. From the author's experience, the response of these mainland viewers was unfavorable. In the People's Republic of China itself, the film's audience has been confined to officials from the China Film Bureau, who, although they have failed to prevent *Ju Dou* from being shown in the rest of the world, have to this day denied the film's primary audience, the mainland Chinese themselves, the opportunity of seeing it.

The fact that *Ju Dou,* a film that has won admiration from its Western audience, has caused uneasiness among its Hong Kong Chinese viewers and has so totally antagonized mainland Chinese officials is a challenge to the interpretation of the film. Some in the West have speculated that the film was too sexually provocative for the authorities. Other Western critics, in seeing the film as a tragedy of feudalistic marriage, have assumed that the Chinese officials were offended by its metaphorical allusions to the present autocratic regime. But a close study will reveal that neither the level of nudity nor the explicitness of sexual acts in the film was unprecedented on Chinese screens in the eighties. Furthermore, films that emphasize the oppressive nature of feudal institutions, including marriage, such as *A Good Woman* (1985) and *Widow Village* (1989), are favored by the socialist officials and welcomed by the public. In *Ju Dou,* at least at first glance, adultery is not presented favorably. The couple is, or could be interpreted as being ultimately penalized by death and separation. In accord with Chinese didacticism it is then perplexing why the film could not be screened after some cuts, as was suggested at one point by the Film Bureau. Finally, some Western reviewers have tended to dismiss the case as yet another power showdown after the June 4th incident in Tiananmen Square, even though the production contract of the film was signed after June 4th.[3]

In a brief interview during the "Oscar controversy" Zhang commented that the reason Chinese officials find the film to be problematic is not so much because of the actual depiction of sex but because of the "somber" tone of that depiction.[4] This statement provides an interesting insight into the issue. One finds that the explicit erotic content of the film—beginning when Ju Dou deliberately turns around to expose her naked body to the peeping Tianqing—is not derived from a simple act of narcissism. Indeed, her tired, dirty, and bruised body, together with the melancholy accompanying music, offers no "visual pleasure" for Tianqing or the film audience. Ju Dou's turning around represents a decisive move against the gerontocratic and patriarchal rule that operates against her. And I propose that it is her implicit attack on this rule that has aroused the Chinese authorities' antagonism and the Chinese audience's unease.

However, these different explanations of the meaning of the film expose the difficulties and errors that are often made in the cross-cultural reading of a text and call for a theory of reading that can account for the wide divergence of opinion between audiences of the East and West. Brian Henderson has pointed out that "[critics] most often proceed by invoking or creating paradigms absent from a text in order to illuminate it."[5] My question here is how one can justify an extension of a paradigm onto a given text and claim validity. It is therefore important to clarify the question of methodology or interpretation before a solution can be proposed.

The comparative literature scholar Heh-hsiang Yuan, in his effort to bridge the study of the literature of the East and that of the West, has noticed some erroneous tendencies among comparativists which I find to be relevant to the field of Chinese film study. He notes that an analyst heavily reliant on Western critical tools may impose already established Western models on Chinese film analysis. The comparativist may also find or draw attention to different types of formal or content expressions that superficially resemble those of the West while ignoring the cultural and philosophical conditioning of these forms and their meaning. And finally, a scholar, demonstrating a kind of cultural chau-vinism, may simply rule out the possibility of any comparison that is appro-priate to the study of films in both China and the West (1980, 1–24). While these practices may create instant gratification of some kind, they hardly lead to any genuine understanding of a different culture or its cinema.

My starting point is to take a film as a text. But contrary to the structural notion that the text is autonomous and may generate ahistorical readings, I fol-low the philosophy of Paul Ricoeur in maintaining that a text is an inscription of a discourse in which both meaning and intersubjective exchange take place (1971, 1976). That is, a text has a double world. As an inscription, the text has a "world of its own" that can be analyzed structurally or semiotically. As a dis-course, there is the meaning of an experience being transferred from one sphere of life to another. The text, as a dialectic of the two, can be analyzed not only semiotically for structure but also semantically for meaning that transcends the text itself and points toward a vision of the world.[6] Interpretation is a dialectic between the semiotic sphere, which explains what is said, and the semantic sphere, which appropriates the world projected by the text.

But even when one is working purely within the sphere of structural expla-nation one still has to select constitutive units, segments, and antinomies that have existential bearing to ensure that the text has meaning as a narrative of sig-nificance. For the reading of a film such as *Ju Dou*, which explicitly portrays a sexual relationship, understanding the Chinese concept of sexuality becomes essential. According to Chinese scholars such as Sun Longji, the idea of "Yin" (excessive sexual feeling or action) and "Zhen" (female sexual purity, the oppo-site of Yin) is vital for understanding the Chinese approach to the subject (1983).[7] In traditional Chinese thought, the Confucian Code of "Li jie," an ethic structured around the notions of "Zhong" (loyalty to one's country), "Zhen" (loyalty to one's husband), and "Xiao" (filial piety), forms a major foundation for human relationships.[8] In observing these disciplines a good Chinese exhibits the quality of "Li" (propriety) and "Qing" (consideration for others).[9] In this essay, I argue that the antinomy of Yin and Xiao, which is nonexistent in Western criticism, is the cornerstone according to which the story and meaning of *Ju Dou* are structured. However, the sources from which these elements are selected are extratextual and, in fact, mostly cultural. It is therefore an under-standing of Chinese culture and not merely its politics that is necessary in order to comprehend the power of the film to entertain/persuade/agitate its audience.

The film is a story of doomed lovers in rural China in the nineteen-twen-ties. A young woman (Ju Dou) is purchased by and married to a sadistic old man (Jinshan) who desperately wants an heir. The old man has an adopted son (Tianqing), whom he enslaves in his dye factory. Soon Ju Dou and Tianqing fall in love, and Ju Dou becomes pregnant with a child (Tianbai). The old man is overjoyed with what he assumes is his ancestral blessing.

The secret affair between Ju Dou and Tianqing continues until one day Jinshan is partially paralyzed by a stroke. He subsequently learns of the affair and discovers that Tianbai is not his own child. Enraged, he tries to kill the couple and the child. Then, one day, while playing with the child, he accidentally drowns. His disappearance leads to gossip among the townspeople about the relationship between Ju Dou and Tianqing. And as Tianbai grows into a teenager he turns against his adulterous parents and finally kills his father. Ju Dou, in despair, burns down the dye factory.

Western assumptions about Chinese reactions (both official and popular) to this story are based on Western readings of Chinese attitudes toward sex and politics. But I am going to show that it is not so much as a political metaphor that the film is problematic (or else all other feudalistic marriage films are politically problematic), nor as an illicit morality play. Instead, it is because of its "Chinese quality"—its unique use of Chinese symbols, its challenge to basic Chinese beliefs, and the shrewdness of its argument based on Chinese logic— that the film is able to criticize Chinese culture harshly enough to cut deeply into the psyche of many Chinese.

Yin, as a Gesture of Self-Liberation

"The biggest Sin of all sins is Yin and the greatest Virtue of all virtues is Xiao" is a folk saying familiar to most Chinese. It is this notion that defines what it means to be "human" and it is the notion under scrutiny in *Ju Dou*. As a context for such an interpretation, one can look at *Fuxi, Fuxi,* the contemporary novel on which the film is based.[10]

Fuxi is one of China's earliest and most important mythic deities. His marriage with Nüwa generates the universe and the human race from a formless mass. They are brother and sister, the Yin and the Yang, the separate and the inseparable. The incestuous marriage of Fuxi and Nüwa, about which they initially feel morally uncertain, is actually blessed with offspring, always a sign of heavenly approval. To juxtapose Fuxi with Ju Dou already reflects a concern with the moral issue of Yin. Ju Dou's union with Tianqing carries an incestuous overtone as well, although Tianqing is, in fact, not the biological son of Jinshan or the brother of Ju Dou. Their relationship, like Fuxi's, is also blessed by heaven. The parallel of the "marriage" of Ju Dou and Tianqing with that of the deities suggests that the former is morally correct. Fuxi's innocent marriage occurs in the archaic period, when civilization has not begun and artificial rules do not yet exist. Similarly, in the case of Ju Dou, a natural act becomes a sin only after the establishment of human-made rules.

The arguments presented in the film pivot around the contradiction between nature and human-made structures and the dialectic between a system and human beings, a system that controls and at the same time is controlled by humans. The issue of human-made structures is visually symbolized in the film by the very act of dyeing, an activity that is commonly found in some parts of China. The story takes place in a dye factory. Dyeing is an artificial imposition of color on what is natural. Dyeing is possible only if structures, machines, or apparatus are built.[11] The extreme close-up shots of different parts of the machine, its arms, wheels, etc., ensure that we recognize its dominance. Highly stylized, heavily sidelit shots reveal the wooden texture that elicits a sense of heaviness and clumsiness. The wide shots of the machine show its different parts coordinated in such a way that their movements are totally predictable and monotonous.

The machine, monstrous as it may seem, is closely but also dialectically related to human beings. Within the factory, workers and animals labor together under the same apparatus. The gigantic structure occupies the foreground while the humans in the background are small figures who have to adjust their movements to the functioning of the mechanical object. Huge pieces of cloth are hung in a systematic way, illustrating structure and order. But this apparatus, which produces beautiful fabrics and feeds the humans who work around it, is also threatening. Low-angle shots of hanging cloths look like Chinese funeral couplets, a symbol of death.[12]

On the other hand, the machine that, as a product of human endeavor, is powerful and structurally complex is also highly vulnerable. For the whole structure relies on a simple block and notch mechanism (repeatedly shown in several close-up shots) whose removal can result in the collapse of the whole operation.

Despite the power of the system, the life force cannot be permanently blocked off. The medium low-angle close-up shots of Ju Dou with a strong back light coming from the bright sky portray her as a woman of vitality. Her natural beauty contrasts with the artificiality of her environment, which her marriage epitomizes. It is natural that Ju Dou repels the old man who sexually tortures her. And it is natural that she is attracted to the young man who cares about her. Yet her emotional affinity is unacceptable to society. The common Chinese term used to describe Ju Dou's sexual behavior is Yin, which has a negative moral-istic connotation under the Confucian institution of marriage.

Yin is the original word for active lovemaking, sexual feeling, or erotic activity. The character has a meaning of "an uncontrollable/excessive (flow of) torrent of water." The film uses this character almost literally. When Ju Dou and Tianqing make love for the first time by the dye vat, the whole structure of human architecture collapses as Ju Dou accidentally kicks off the guarding notch of the dye machine. The endless piece of cloth that flows down like water is impossible to stop. Yin is as inevitable as an object falling under the force of gravity.

Contrary to the opinions of those who hold that *Ju Dou* is a story about "lust," or "taint," the film itself does not make any moral judgment here. Visually speaking, the unraveling of the long bolt of red fabric even celebrates Ju Dou's ecstasy, although the somber flute solo which fades up slowly at the end of the scene reveals yet another level of comment—that this natural act is a tragic one.

The correlation between innocence/guilt and the man-made system is sym-bolically dealt with again a few scenes later when Ju Dou's child is born and the village elders, following a Chinese tradition, gather to give the newborn a name. After a long search in the family book of names—another aspect of an artificial system—Ju Dou's son is named Tianbai. The irony is that the elders choose the name Tianbai because of the connection between this name and his "brother's" name, Tianqing: the two names placed together form the idiom "qing-bai," which means "innocent from any guilt." "Tian" (heaven) connotes an anthro-pocosmic relation, which again directs one to the archaic story of Fuxi. This allu-sion to the Chinese vision of cosmogony provides the background from which the film criticizes the Confucian patriarchal and gerontocratic society.

Xiao, as Root of Oppression

The naming tradition, which defines relationships and hence power, is sharply and critically examined in the film. Under the designation husband/wife/son are contained major pairs of antinomies: powerfulness/powerlessness, harsh-ness/placidity, inflicting/caring, oppressor/oppressed, fertility/aridity, and pub-lic/private. Power ostensibly resides in the position of husband. However, these relations between characters reverse themselves at two distinct points—first, when Jinshan, the "father," loses power after his stroke and second, when his "fatherhood" is reestablished through Tianbai's practice of Xiao. The double reversal pushes the narrative to close almost at its original equilibrium—except for the last shot, which, by destabilizing the closure, brings the film to a tragic conclusion.

In the beginning it is Ju Dou and Tianqing who are the placid, the powerless, the oppressed, and at the same time the caring and the generative, the ones who respond directly, simply, and naturally to the human instinct of sexual attraction, while Jinshan represents the other end of the spectrum. Even his sexual relation with Ju Dou is public, for the latter's screaming, which is heard during the wide shots of the empty courtyard, connects the private space with the public one. But the whole relation undergoes a 180-degree reversal after the old man is immobilized. Assuming that little harm can come from their oppressor, the young couple openly defy his surveillance and place him in a powerless and oppressed position. His inability to speak confines him to his private world of anguish and bitterness, while the couple's flirtatious laughter floats out from their room. In this stage even the husband/wife/son relationship is reversed, with Ju Dou and Tianqing becoming the couple and the old man, who now has to be fed, bathed, and carried around, turning into their "son."

But this momentary liberation due to the fall of the "father" is very precarious or even dangerous. (When Jinshan first attempts to kill the baby the flute solo is replaced by the diegetic sound of thunder and rainstorm. During the other two attempts the Chinese gong, a nondiegetic sound effect, creates a sense of suspense and horror.) Since Tianqing is unable to make his relation with Ju Dou public and is psychologically incapable of disobeying the principle of Xiao, which bonds him to Jinshan, the struggle between the young couple and the system is antagonizing and never-ending. It is reflected in their battle with Jinshan, and later with Tianbai, whose maturing consciousness becomes a psychological time bomb.

The relationship of the three characters is reversed again when Tianbai first learns to call the old man "Ba" ("daddy"). Jinshan immediately seizes on the natural innocence of the child and uses it as a tool for revenge, declaring in front of the child that he himself is the father, Ju Dou the mother, and Tianqing the brother. Jinshan reestablishes the former relationship of husband/wife/son and reverses the relation of the oppressed/oppressor, powerless/powerful.

It is interesting to see how a world is defined with a single utterance of a child. This practice becomes possible in a male-made symbolic world that embodies the ideology of Zhen (sexual purity) and Xiao (filial piety). According to the logic of Zhen, Ju Dou's sexual relation with Jinshan is the only legitimate one and her relationship with Tianqing is denied. Xiao for its part, ensures that it is Tianbai's duty as a son to recognize and give allegiance to his "proper" father, Jinshan. This symbolic system is in fact creating reality by determining what Ju Dou can or cannot do. Under the patriarchal system men continue to inflict pain upon women. The wide shot of the courtyard reappears. One hears the familiar screaming of Ju Dou. A somehow abusive sexual activity begins again, but this time it is with Tianqing. The latter's patriarchal identification puts him in the oppressor position, in which he participates through slavish regard for the rule of piety. Patriarchal identification prevents him from seeking any solution for Ju Dou that would violate his Xiao toward Jinshan. He feels obliged to save Jinshan in various critical moments when in fact he could have harmed him in order to help Ju Dou. His identification becomes abundantly clear when he slaps Ju Dou because she criticizes his lack of reflection in adhering to the norm of filial piety. Ju Dou responds to the violence with a sharp recognition that in this circle of oppression she is always the victim. As she heartbrokenly says, "Now you are beating me too. Revive the old man and you can both beat me!"

The man-made system dominates by suppressing nature. While in the first part of the film Ju Dou gives birth to a child despite the impotence of Jinshan, the second part, although she has now gained some room for herself because of the old man's stroke, depicts the loss of her childbearing option. And although Jinshan cannot biologically have a son, he is, by manipulation, slowly "creating" a "son." For it turns out that Tianbai is emotionally linked to him, while Tianqing and Ju Dou, though biologically capable, do not dare produce any offspring because of social pressure.

The question of Xiao depicts the complexity of the father-son relationship. In the beginning the "son," Tianqing, engages in a sexual relation with his "mother" and on various occasions talks about killing his "father." This, however, is not to be confused with the Western Oedipal narrative, although later in the film Jinshan is drowned in front of his "son" Tianbai and Tianbai kills his father Tianqing. Looking at these relations in more detail, one notes that Tianqing is unable to harm Jinshan, who is anyway not his biological father. (Jinshan, in trying to kill his "son" Tianqing, ends up accidentally drowning himself.)

When he murders Tianqing, Tianbai has already irrevocably identified himself as the "son" of the old man. The identification, dramatically portrayed in the highly stylized funeral shots shown earlier in the film in which Tianbai sits on top of Jinshan's coffin, also constitutes a reincarnation ritual. Tianbai is now the father—or at least the surrogate father—who kills the son, Tianqing. Structurally speaking, the plot parallels what has been termed in Chinese mythology studies the Chinese "Inverse Oedipus complex," in which the father kills the son.[13] The theme is quite consistent with a tradition built on Xiao.

The power of gerontocratic rule asserts itself through a symbol that does not require the actual presence of the old man to enforce it. The funeral ritual of "blocking the coffin," in which Ju Dou and Tianqing, as widow and adult son of Jinshan, have to try to stop the latter's funeral procession by rolling under it forty-nine times, is a dramatized declaration of the superiority of the dead. The scene is composed of a montage sequence of repeated close-up low-angle shots with the coffin, the carrier of gerontocratic power, as the dominating force to which the couple has to submit. (The shot repetition reminds one of the Eisensteinian strategy of using repeated close-up shots of repeated actions for extradiegetic commentary.)

A woman's struggle against both gerontocratic and patriarchal power is futile. Her destiny is ultimately determined by the male, whether or not he hates, loves, or "honors" her (being Xiao toward her). Ju Dou is tortured by the three males in her life—her husband, her lover, and her son—who, by taking up the various roles in patriarchal system, end up destroying her. As long as the woman is left out of the circulation of power she has no exit. Even the suicidal act in the last shot, in which Ju Dou takes a torch and burns down the factory, is in fact a fulfillment of what the old man wanted to do in one of his murder attempts.

Although one may be tempted to summarize *Ju Dou* as consisting of two strands of narrative: romantic admiration-confession-consummation-persecution-separation—the story of unfulfilled love; and sadism-retribution-counter-retribution—the story of jealousy, it is noticeable from the above discussion that the structure of the text follows no simple linear form. This periodicity of narrative structure corresponds to a Chinese rhetorical device, one that, as Chinese literature scholar Andrew Plaks has observed, uses dichotomies not as a mechanistic alteration but as a process of constant flux. Here, the narrative ends at the same place it began, with the relation of oppressed/oppressor remaining unchanged. But the narrative has also described a life which experiences the ever-changing roles and characteristics of the powerful/powerless, harsh/placid, inflicting/caring, fertile/arid, that define each cycle. By keeping the character Ju Dou within the system and providing a tragic ending (unlike the woman character in, say, *Old Well,* who finally leaves her village), the film refuses to use any logic alien to the Chinese culture and forces one to recognize the limitations of a social system.

Let me return to my original question of why it is that *Ju Dou* is so offensive to both Chinese authorities and audiences even when it so incisively criticizes the feudal rule. Once again, one must turn to the underlying cultural substructure for an answer. The person who proves the absurdity of the system is not a heroine according to the Chinese model. Unlike protagonists in "acceptable" films, who fulfill the Confucian requirement for being a "good" Chinese, such as the heroine in *Good Woman,* who gains group recognition and exhibits Qing (considerateness) and Li (propriety), Ju Dou is far from satisfying these conditions. Like the protagonist in *Red Sorghum,* Ju Dou violates not only the institution of marriage but the basic Confucian Code of Li jie, which defines the fundamental being of a traditional Chinese. Consequently, it is highly uncomfortable, to say the least, for the audience to see someone who according to their model is a "sinner" proving the system to the wrong.

Ju Dou, as a simple story about a love affair, could be easily seen as a melodrama well crafted by its talented director. The audience may accept Ju Dou's affair as being a normal/obvious outcome of an abnormal marriage. While sympathizing with Ju Dou as a victim of her environment, the audience may either criticize her society as being unfair or feel frustrated at her inability to fight for her own rights. These criticisms, though not unfounded, do not in themselves cut deeply into the complexity of the issue. For what is involved is not only a depiction of an extramarital relationship, but how this affair is perceived and managed under the constraint of a set of social norms. It is, therefore, necessary to understand these rules in order to realize the fundamental problem in the shaping of the life of the protagonist. By reading the film against its cultural context one can discover the true nature of the conflicts and open up the subversive and culturally radical text.

Notes

This article was first published in *Film Quarterly* 45.2 (winter 1991–92): 2–10. Copyright © 1995 by The Regents of the University of California. Reprinted with permission.

1. *Red Sorghum* created such emotional response in China that the press called it the "*Red Sorghum* phenomenon." The vehement reactions in some circles can be found in the lively discussions in *Dazhong dianying* (Popular cinema), 1988, nos. 5 and 6.

2. For a report of the "Oscar controversy" see *South China Morning Post* (Hong Kong), March 26, 1991.

3. Ibid.

4. Ibid.

5. Brian Henderson, "Notes on Set Design and Cinema," *Film Quarterly* 12.1 (1958): 26.

6. For an outline of Ricoeur's position consult Ricoeur 1976. For a more comprehensive understanding, see Ricoeur 1970 and 1971.

7. Also consult Wolfram Eberhard 1976.

8. Strictly speaking, the Confucian Code that structures the Chinese moral system is that of Zhong and Xiao. However, Zhong, understood as "loyalty to the emperor," did not apply to women in the past, since they were not allowed to hold public office. Instead, the female rule is Zhen, which means "sexual purity." Under the feudalistic system, Zhen basically applies to females only and sexual purity for married women implies "loyalty toward one's husband."

9. For more discussion see Lau 1989.

10. The novel *Fuxi, Fuxi* is written by Liu Heng. In Wang Ziping and Li Tuo 1989, 80–171. The title of the novel draws on the name of a well-known and ancient Chinese mythical god. But the narrative of the novel does not follow the mythological story.

11. It is interesting to notice that the Althusserian notion of apparatus as a structure or institution for the perpetuation of a ruling ideology which supports the existing mode of life is used in a most literal and visual sense in this film.

12. Carried throughout the funeral ceremony, Chinese funeral couplets are long pieces of cloth on which poetic couplets are written to memorialize the deceased.

13. A lengthy discussion can be found in *Cong bijiao shenhua dao wenxue* (From comparative mythology to literature), edited by Ku Tim-hsuang and Chen Wei-hua (Taiwan: Dong Tai Publisher, 1984).

Part Three

Cinema Exotica
Ethnic Minorities as the PRC's "Internal *Other*"

Norbu in *Horse Thief (Daoma zei)*, directed by Tian Zhuangzhuang, 1986. Courtesy of China Film Archive, Beijing.

I n the mid-1980s, the Chinese new cinema produced quite a number of films about ethnic minorities living in the PRC: *Sacrificed Youth* about the Dai in Yunnan, *Horse Thief* (1986) about Tibet, *On the Hunting Ground* (1985) about Inner Mongolia, and *A Good Woman, In the Wujie Mountains* (1985), *Border Town* (1985), and *Girl from Hunan* (1986) about such peoples as the Miao, Dong, and Tu living in southern China. The intimate relationship of these minority films with the artistic innovations and cultural critiques of the time caught much critical attention (see Berry 1986 and 1992, Paul Clark 1987b, Yau 1989b).

Two related facts should be noted right away. First, China has over fifty ethnic minorities, including Mongolians, Tibetans, Uighurs, Koreans, Dais, Bais, and Miaos; living on the fringe of the land, they account for about 6 percent of the entire population. The Han remain the overwhelming ethnic majority. Second, the ethnic minority film has been an important genre in PRC filmmaking; from 1949 to 1965, over fifty films of this genre were produced.

In describing the American Western, Alan Lovell pinpoints a blending of three elements: a plot structure taken from nineteenth-century popular literature, involving hero, heroine, and villain; an examination of the history of the West; and a revenge motive or structure (1976, 164–75). Interestingly enough, Lovell's findings, with slight modification, may help delineate the Chinese national minority genre: an emotive structure vaguely influenced by turn-of-the-century popular literature, with such favored subjects as "mandarin ducks and butterflies," often enriched by exotic music, songs, and dance; a use of ethnic history to deliver social messages; and a love theme or structure involving a triumph over obstacles and misunderstandings.

In the leftist filmmaking prior to the PRC era, presenting the national crisis was among the dominant concerns of the progressive cinema. Sometimes, this issue would also be shown as it concerned minority subject matters. In wartime 1942, Ying Yunwei, a left-wing film director, produced a fairly popular minority film that both catered to filmgoers' curiosity about the exotic and responded to the contemporary call to resist Japanese invasion. Set in Chinese Mongolia, the film, *Clouds over the Border (Sai shang fengyun),* possesses the essential attributes of the would-be national minority genre, including a theme of love and misunderstanding and an intricate plot concerning a Japanese secret agent beguiled as a subject to a Mongolian king. The appeal of the exotic and the complexity of the ethnic relations help deliver the social messages more effectively. In a way, *Clouds over the Border* may well be seen as leftist filmmakers' use of one kind of exoticism (lives of the ethnic minorities appear exotic to the general filmgoers in China) to compete with the exoticism represented by the Hollywood films. In the early decades of the PRC, when the Hollywood films were banned, the national minority films flourished.

The PRC cinema produced so many national minority films that they started to qualify as a specific genre, and many films of this genre are considered classics, indicating their importance in PRC film history. Some examples are worth mentioning. *Five Golden Flowers* (*Wuduo jinhua,* 1959) supports the Great Leap Forward (a rather chaotic and disastrous push by the Party for economic growth between 1958 and 1960) by showing the enthusiastic responses it gets from within the minority area resided in by the Bai. A lovesick young man travels through the Bai area in search of his date, a young woman who calls herself "Golden Flower," whom he exchanged songs with a year before. Prior to finding his Golden Flower, the man is led to four other women who are also known as Golden Flower. During his journey, this young man witnesses the active participation of these women in the economic reconstruction of a new China.

Set in areas lived in by the Zhuang along the scenic Li River in Guilin, *Third Sister Liu* (*Liu san jie,* 1960) uses minority customs, particularly "dialogic singing" (or talking in songs), to present a musical, a rather rare form for Chinese cinema. Sister Liu, a popular singer in exile, arrives in a riverside village and soon uses her songs to gather around her all the poor villagers. With the wisdom shown in their songs, Sister Liu and her supporters humiliate the local landlords and their hired singers.

Serfs (*Nongnu,* 1963), set in Tibet, uses the general audience's unfamiliarity with Tibetan life to heighten the emotional impact of its portrayal of social class exploitation, to show the Party's resourcefulness in approaching the exploited people of a different ethnicity, and to celebrate the liberation of the serfs by the Party.

Visitors over Ice Mountains (*Bingshan shang de laike,* 1963), set in the Uighur area on the borders, uses a search for a lost love by a People's Liberation Army (PLA) border guard to tell a story of spying. The guard, Amir, is shocked to discover that the new bride of a local man may well be his childhood sweetheart, Gulandam. The details that he learns of this woman's life confirms his belief. However, he is soon shocked again to discover that the woman does not even remember the song that he and his sweetheart enjoyed singing years before. The woman turns out to be a spy working for the Taiwanese government. She has usurped the identity of the real Gulandam and is associated with a bandit trying to disturb the peace on the borders. With intricate plot twists and turns, the identity of the fake Gulandam is revealed, the bandits are arrested, and Amir is reunited with the real Gulandam.

Through the examples above, one can see that the national minority genre has been employed to embody the PRC's ideological myths: it warns of the threats of foreign spies and intrigue, it promotes the idealism of the Great Leap Forward in socialist construction, it rebukes class exploitation, and it calls for class struggle. Yet critics have also discerned the genre's inclination to deviate from the conventions. Paul Clark has noticed that certain national minority films produced in the 1960s "blur the theme of class struggle by tending to glamorize the exotic" (1987b, 21), and Esther Yau has pointed out that "the non-Han women on screen provided an exotic and convenient site for the representation of sexuality not assigned to the Han women's bodies" (1989b, 122). The exoticism of the genre, while not offering a bulletproof shelter from the demands of socialist realism, may deflect slightly the materials it processes. In the mid-1980s, this tradition of deflection made the genre attractive to directors of the post-Mao new cinema who sought to deviate from the by-now conventional socialist-realist filmmaking.

This renewed zeal for national minority films becomes even more interesting when we relate it to the contemporary rise of the Chinese Western film (see part four). The Chinese Westerns shared the national minority films' use of exoticism and their search for new cultural identities; both genres underscored similar sublanguages and designated a certain cultural consensus of the mid-1980s.

What is the defining feature of this cultural consensus? Contrasting the new national minority films with those produced in the 1950s, Ma Ning remarks that while the early films emphasized social change to justify Liberation (that is, the founding of the PRC in 1949), the new minority films manifest a strong interest in the "traditional social structures and cultural values" of the national minorities; while the early films reflected an attitude of Han superiority, the new films showed a "respectful and admiring attitude" (1987, 82). With a changed vocabulary of culture, customs, and humanity, the new fascination with this genre reflected a marked deviation from the class-struggle ideology and showcased a great dissatisfaction with the Han cultural status quo. In a post-Mao identity crisis, the Han ethnic majority used the national minority subject matter to gain perspectives for self-understanding and to find a path by which to rejuvenate the culture. This phenomenon is described by Rey Chow as an *internal othering*, that is, an effort to redefine the Han majority culture by comparing it with the minority cultures found within the borders of the PRC (1995). This Chinese case actually illustrates what has always happened between cultures: anthropologist Lévi-Strauss, while traveling from culture to culture, suggests that one always goes to the *Other* so as to better understand the Self. Yet considering the cultural sense of crisis found in the Chinese national minority films, what happens in this genre in the mid-1980s recalls more of what Susan Sontag says about the modern thought of the West: "Modern thought is pledged to a kind of applied Hegelianism: seeking its Self in its Other. Europe seeks itself in the exotic—in Asia, in the Middle East, among preliterate peoples, in a mythic America; a fatigued rationality seeks itself in the impersonal energies of sexual ecstasy or drugs; consciousness seeks its meaning in unconsciousness; humanistic problems seek their oblivion in scientific 'value neutrality' and quantification. The 'other' is experienced as a harsh purification of 'self'" (1966, 69). In national minority films, the same Hegelianism applies: a fatigued totalitarian ideology configured in Han culture experiences the minority *Other* as a harsh purification of Self.

Since the Self/Other relationship of the mid-1980s minority films has changed considerably from that of the earlier PRC films of the genre, Yingjin Zhang suggests that the term "minority discourse" should be used to describe the changed cultural role, played by mid-1980s minority films, in constructing a marginality that questions and challenges the centrality of State discourse.

> What eventually distinguishes New Chinese Cinema of the past decade is its tactful building-up of a profound complexity and ambivalence, by means of which it not only interrogates—at a national level—the 'grand myths' perpetuated in the previous films (e.g., the glorified revolutionary wars, the celebrated ethnic solidarity, and the exaggerated achievements of the socialist construction) but also problematizes—at a local or localized level—its own position as a knowing subject, an oftentimes individualized subject burdened with the task of reassessing the culture of the nation and of rewriting its history. (1997, 93–94).

This minority discourse still tells us less about the ethnic minorities and more about the changed relationship of the majority to these minorities; it remains a pity that the ethnic minorities in China have not had voices of their own on the Chinese film screen.

Three films have been selected for this section. Xie Fei's *Girl from Hunan* is about an abnormal marriage system found among the ethnic minorities in southwest China. Zhang Nuanxin's *Sacrificed Youth* is an interesting cross-cultural comparison of the Han and Dai. And Tian Zhuangzhuang's *Horse Thief* is an avant-garde cinematic allegory of humans, nature, and religion, set in Tibet.

Eight

Girl from Hunan
(*Xiangnü Xiaoxiao,* dir. Xie Fei, Wu Lan, 1986)

Screenplay Zhang Xian
Cinematography Fu Jingsheng
Producer Qingnian
Cast Na Renhua, as Xiaoxiao
Liu Qing, as Xiaoxiao (child)
Deng Xiaoguang, as Huagou
Ni Meiling, as mother-in-law

There once existed an abnormal marriage system among the ethnic minorities living in southern China: a bridegroom is often just a little boy who needs babysitting, and a bride, usually much older, becomes his babysitter "wife"; their marriage will be reaffirmed once the little boy grows into manhood. This abnormal marriage system attracted cultural scrutiny in both the May Fourth and post-Mao eras. Shen Congwen's 1929 short story "Xiaoxiao" and its filmic adaptation by Xie Fei and Wu Lan in the mid-1980s offer an interesting comparison of the two eras and their different explorations of human nature against a particular cultural backdrop.

Xie Fei, a professor at Beijing Film Academy, is also a noted leading Fourth Generation director. Starting from the mid-1980s, he has directed films every other year and moved from an idealism to a more sober depiction of social realities. One of his earlier films, *Our Land* (*Women de tianye,* 1983), depicts the relocated youth, during the Cultural Revolution era, who dedicated the best time of their lives to cultivating the vast wasteland of northeast China *(bei da huang)*. This film may, as Xie Fei indicates, express a sense of loss. But it also, as Xie Fei admits, is inspired by a revolutionary idealism in the first place (Xie Fei 1990b). Following *Girl from Hunan,* he directed *Black Snow* (*Benming nian,* 1989), a somber depiction of a young man's sense of loss in an urban setting. (For a discussion of this film, please refer to Xiaobing Tang's essay in this book.) In 1993, Xie Fei's *Woman Sesame Oil Maker (Xianghun nü),* a story of

171

a woman's dilemmas in life and career, won the Golden Bear Award from Berlin. His *Black Steed: A Mongolian Tale* (*Hei junma,* 1995) is another national-minority genre film based on a story by Zhang Chengzhi, a literary spokesman of Muslim culture in China. The film is a troubadour's recollection of his love for a woman he abandoned, a story of innocence, betrayal, sacrifice, and redemption. It won the Best Director award in the Montreal World Film Festival.

Although both show the same alienation from idealism, Xie differs from his colleague Zhang Nuanxin, who, with her *Sacrificed Youth,* advocated documentary aesthetics and prose films devoid of dramatic intensity. Xie, on the other hand, emphasizes the importance of narrative and characterization, insisting that innovation in film language should serve to reinforce them. *Girl from Hunan* is a beautiful film that mixes symbolic suggestiveness, realistic characters, and melodramatic tensions.

As a film of cultural scrutiny, *Girl from Hunan* showcases a structurally important high-angle view of the gray tile roofs of village houses that block each other into a closed whole. This frame suggests a tightly knit community with strict, unbreakable cultural rules, the nasty face of which is shown, for example, in the drowning of an adulterous woman. Yet the imagery of nature also reigns here to soften the intensity of such cruelty and allows time to erase its memory. The repeated motion of a water-driven punching device both punctuates the film's narrative turns and expresses the circular theme of the film. An interesting comparison is found with Huang Jianzhong's *A Good Woman,* a contemporary film about the same marriage system in the same area and showing similar rehumanization cultural concerns. The symbolism of *A Good Woman* often has a nauseating effect. For instance, it uses an offensive sound track (for example, the howling of cats) and a barren landscape to contrast human repression and desire. Huang's expressionist exploration dictates the use of this symbolism, which invites a distanced evaluation of a woman's dilemma. In contrast, *Girl from Hunan* makes nature a grand force that both foils and absorbs the intensity of the human drama.

English translations of Shen Congwen's "Xiaoxiao" are readily available in two versions: "Hsiao-hsiao," translated by Eugene Eoyang, in *Modern Chinese Short Stories and Novellas 1919–1949,* edited by Joseph Lau et al., New York: Columbia University Press, 1981, 227–36; and "Xiaoxiao," translated by Gladys Yang, in *The Border Town and Other Stories,* Panda Books, 1988, 102–19.

Suggested readings for *Girl from Hunan* are as follows:

Kaplan 1991
Berry 1994

Director's Notes

There has been a craze for "roots searching" in recent years. People have realized that micro-reflection and contemplation of what had just happened is not enough. To find the reasons for the withering and decline of our once great and glorious nation, to find the key to an understanding of why our culture became stagnant and regressive under the yoke of feudal ideology for two thousand years, we must explore the roots. We must have a macro-reflection of the formation, development and mutation of our national soul, i.e., our national culture and mentality.

We consciously relate *Girl from Hunan* to the mission of "recreating the national soul." We use this film to censure "obeying Heaven's command," which has long been the primary cultural spirit; to criticize "collective unconsciousness," which denies humanity and individuality; and to attack the "vicious circle" that encloses our culture in ignorance and backwardness. We use *Girl from Hunan* to warn people.

Girl from Hunan is about sexual repression and how this repression illustrates the damage done by feudal teachings of rites.

In our directorial plan, we decided to focus on the psychological trajectory of the country girl Xiaoxiao—her sexual budding, awakening, eruption, and extinction—and let it motivate the whole film. All the artistic means in the film helped depict this trajectory emotively. For her sexual budding with youthful desires, there are such details as the other's erotic serenading of her, her unconscious touching of her own body, her kissing of her "younger brother." For her explosion of desires, there are such scenes as the man's tearing loose of the bondage wrapped around her chest and her lustful holding of the man at night in the sugarcane woods. To allude to, to contrast, and to strengthen the depiction of human psyches, we also repeatedly used such images and sounds as the roller and its wood axle of the mill, the water gate, restless noise made by frogs, and sugarcane disturbed by breezes. Although Xiaoxiao's awakening is unconsciously vague, it is the only happy and illuminated moment in her life. It is only then that she is a genuinely free person confirming the value of her own life.

Later on, when she becomes a mother-in-law herself and leaves behind all her miseries in life, she is already dead as a person; she moves around like a corpse. We believe that this is the only way to reveal her tragedy—a tragedy that denies human nature. (Xie Fei and Wu Lan 1986, 85–87)

"Hsiao-hsiao" and *Girl from Hunan:*
Teaching Chinese Narrative, Not Just Chinese Fiction
Stephanie Hoare

Its recent worldwide critical acclaim demonstrates that Chinese film is beginning to be seen as an art in its own right. Yet in many college classrooms it is often still treated as an adjunct to Chinese literature, useful only for its concrete depiction of the scenery, costume, and customs described in great works of Chinese fiction. Literary adaptation is indeed a common activity in contemporary Chinese cinema, and the relationship between film and literature is remarkably strong. However, I believe that there is a more pedagogically efficient and rewarding way of using literary adaptation, one which furthers students' understanding of Chinese literature, but which also acknowledges filmmakers as artists with their own political and aesthetic concerns, and not mere imitators.

Film scholar Dudley Andrew points out that literary adaptation can reveal much about filmmakers' goals. Examining the kinds of literary works filmmakers choose to adapt, one may better understand what kinds of effects they wish to achieve in film, and by comparing a film's narrative with that of its "literary prototype," one may discuss the kinds of narrative choices filmmakers make (Andrew 1984, 104–6). Through this approach to literary adaptation, students can learn about Chinese aesthetics of different periods; they can identify narrative differences between, for example, a May Fourth literary work and its PRC film adaptation, and learn actively about the different narrative aesthetics, and the different political and ideological conditions, governing their making.

Elsewhere I have presented a comparison of Lu Xun's *Zhufu (The New Year's Sacrifice)* with the 1956 adaptation by Sang Hu and Xia Yan.[1] Film adaptations of May Fourth works from the 1950s illustrate well the narrative aesthetics of the May Fourth period and those of the early PRC. Using the same approach on 1980s adaptations, one may reveal important aspects of recent Chinese cinematic narrative.

Shen Congwen's 1929 short story "Hsiao-hsiao"[2] and its 1985 adaptation *Xiangnü Xiaoxiao (Girl from Hunan)*, directed by Xie Fei and Wu Lan, provide excellent material for such a classroom comparison, clarifying both Shen Congwen's aesthetic and that of an important 1980s film trend.

Like other May Fourth writers, Shen Congwen was concerned with the problems of Chinese society. However, as C. T. Hsia points out, Shen Congwen's fiction focuses on universal aspects of human nature, particularly a kind of "animal innocence" as a source of salvation, rather than dwelling on social ills, or offering a socialist solution to them (Hsia 1961, 199–203). The narrative of "Hsiao-hsiao" illustrates Shen's views of Chinese society. The heroine Hsiao-hsiao, a young peasant girl betrothed to an infant husband, moves in with her in-laws and helps out on their farm. As an adolescent, she becomes pregnant by a hired hand who is closer to her own age than her fiancé. Her condition is discovered, but her in-laws eventually allow her to stay on and raise her baby son as one of the family. Hsiao-hsiao is saved from a worse fate by her own innocent and happy nature, which gives her the will to keep on living through her disgrace, and by her family's ignorance of the Confucian law dictating the punishment for adulterous wives:

> By rights, she should have been drowned, but only heads of families who have read their Confucius would do such a stupid thing to save the family's honor. [Hsiao-hsiao's] uncle, however, hadn't read Confucius: he couldn't bear to sacrifice Hsiao-hsiao, and so he chose the alternative of marrying her off to someone else. (Shen 1981, 235)

Hsiao-hsiao's in-laws never do find her a new husband, however, and are eventually quite happy to keep her on themselves: ultimately they, too, are unconcerned with Confucian standards of propriety.

The image of the coeds, modern female high school students not bound by Confucian laws, appears throughout the story as a contrast to the lives of the peasants, but not necessarily in conflict with them. Hsiao-hsiao's in-law Grandfather describes the strange behavior of the coeds from the peasants' point of view, then teasingly tells Hsiao-hsiao she should become a coed herself. From this point on, Hsiao-hsiao thinks often about the coeds, and identifies with them. This identification does not make her dissatisfied with her peasant life; although she does try to run away to the coeds after she becomes pregnant, it is only her pregnancy that makes her think this way. Once the family forgives her for her transgression, she is content to stay on the farm. She reaffirms her connection with the coeds at the end of the narrative, but in a traditional way. As she watches the betrothal of her first son, she croons to her new baby son:

"Look, look! The coeds are here too! One day, when you grow up, we'll get you a coed for a wife" (Shen 1981, 236). Hsiao-hsiao and the coeds are both free from traditional constraints, for different reasons. Shen Congwen's solution to the problems of Chinese society incorporates a return to primitive innocence, rather than simple escape from, or eradication of, Chinese traditional values.

After three decades of strict control over the film industry by the Communist Party, greater freedom for film artists in the People's Republic during the 1980s encouraged innovative experimentation in Chinese cinema. Critical acclaim at home and abroad for films breaking out of traditional Chinese filmmaking modes helped make film a major form of narrative in that decade. Films by the so-called "Fifth Generation"[3] of young directors, and some of their older supporters, make a case for film as an art form equal to and independent from literature. Although many of the new films were based on works of literature, the directors strove to present their own messages through them and changed the original narrative models in significant ways in order to do so.

A common theme for the innovative films of the 1980s has been the oppression of women in prerevolutionary rural Chinese society; this theme serves as a medium through which directors may subtly and safely criticize present day conditions in China. Stories of young women caught in oppressive arranged marriages have been a favorite choice of some of the most prominent innovative directors in 1980s China: Chen Kaige's *Yellow Earth* (*Huang tudi*, 1984), Huang Jianzhong's *A Woman of Good Family* (*Liangjia funü*, 1984), Zhang Yimou's *Red Sorghum* (*Hong gaoliang*, 1987) and *Ju Dou* (1990) are all examples of this type of film. *Girl from Hunan* is very much a part of this trend in innovative films. The style in which it is made lacks the heavy-handed melodrama of traditional Chinese films, and its plot focuses on the oppression of women in southwest rural China, painting a bleak picture of rural Chinese society.

Since Shen Congwen's narrative has quite a different emphasis, the filmmakers have had to change Shen's original narrative in several important ways in order to express their contemporary message. By investigating the changes, students can learn about the concerns of narrative artists of both the May Fourth period and the 1980s.

For example, students can discern that the filmmakers have altered characters in the narrative to emphasize the way traditional values oppress the young. In "Hsiao-hsiao," Grandfather, the head of Hsiao-hsiao's in-law family, brings the news of the coeds and their strange behavior to the farm, whereas in *Girl from Hunan*, it is the young man, Huagou (Motley Mutt), who imparts this information: in the film the impetus for change comes from the young, who have not yet been totally indoctrinated in traditional mores. The mother-in-law, an almost unheard-from character in Shen's story, become the enforcer of traditional oppressive laws in the film. She puts a stop to Huagou's tales of the coeds, keeps a sharp eye on Xiaoxiao's growth into womanhood, binding Xiaoxiao's breasts in an overt act of sexual repression. And when Xiaoxiao's pregnancy is discovered, it is mother-in-law who must be convinced by her young son to show mercy to Xiaoxiao. At the end of the film mother-in-law oversees the marriage of Xiaoxiao's toddler son to yet another adolescent girl. Mother-in-law thus embodies that oppressive tradition, so markedly absent in Shen's story, that the filmmakers wish to criticize.

And it is this tradition, not simply mother-in-law herself, that plays the villain in *Girl from Hunan*. The traditional values the film portrays have much less power over the characters in the short story; indeed it is their powerlessness in the face of that older, more natural quality of innocence that ultimately saves Shen's heroine. In *Girl from Hunan,* these values become an all-powerful negative force. Another obvious addition to the original narrative is a scene in which a pregnant Xiaoxiao and the hired hand, Huagou, witness the punishment of an adulterous couple. Condemned by their clan headman, the man is beaten until his legs are broken, and the woman is stripped and drowned in a lake as her young daughter cries for her. The camera shows us the horrified looks on the faces of Xiaoxiao and Huagou as they watch. This scene emphasizes the life-threatening nature of Xiaoxiao's predicament much more strongly than Shen Congwen's blithe narration, and therefore conveys a clearer message concerning the oppression of women in traditional China.

At the end of the film, we see Xiaoxiao's husband, now a young man, reacting negatively toward the marriage system. Walking home from school through the market town, he encounters some laughing coeds who tease him about his arranged marriage, which he denies. He returns home to the betrothal ceremony, but hangs off in the distance, broodingly watching the festivities. This added sequence further reinforces the film's social criticism: Xiaoxiao's husband is clearly discontent with his lot, but the old oppressive marriage customs continue.

Although the action in *Girl from Hunan* takes place in prerevolutionary times, the filmmakers' implication is that tradition continues to be an oppressive force in contemporary Chinese society. Unlike films of the 1950s and early 1960s that also deal with prerevolutionary social conditions, 1980s films about the oppression of women do not send a clear message that conditions have changed for the better since 1949. At the end of *The New Year's Sacrifice,* a voice-over narration announces that although the heroine died a victim of feudalism, the world she lived in no longer exists, thanks to the Chinese Communist Party. *Girl from Hunan* ends silently, with progressively longer shots of the rooftops and rice paddies of Xiaoxiao's village, scenes filmed in today's rural China. This ending contrasts both with traditional PRC filmmaking practices, and with the more optimistic ending of the short story "Hsiao-hsiao": it invites the audience to reflect upon the strength and endurance of oppressive Chinese traditions, rather than its demise.

The contrast between "Hsiao-hsiao" and *Girl from Hunan* can be used to elicit more specific issues of contemporary Chinese intellectual society. One strain of social criticism in the PRC asserts that the traditional value system that keeps China from advancing toward modernity places too much value or *yin*, or feminine, qualities in human behavior, to the exclusion of *yang*, or masculine, qualities. That is, Chinese society traditionally rewards passivity, weakness, and modesty, while punishing qualities such as aggressiveness, strength, and pride. Chinese social critics see the lack of balance in this value system as harmful to both men and women: as men take on, and identify themselves with, "feminine" characteristics, women become ciphers.[4] The trend in films about women's oppression is in part an attack on the overvaluation of *yin* qualities; for example, Eugene Yuejin Wang, in an article in *Public Culture*, shows that this is true of *Red Sorghum*. Like *Girl from Hunan*, most of these films feature young women trapped in arranged marriages with somehow impotent males: a little boy, in *Girl from Hunan* and *A Woman of Good Family*, a leper in *Red Sorghum*, an old man with venereal disease in Teng Wenji's *Song of the Yellow River* (*Huanghe yao*, 1990), or an infertile wife-beater, in *Ju Dou*. Invariably a younger, virile man is introduced into the plot, and the young woman's affair with him represents an attempt to right the balance, a return to natural behavior. In all cases except *Red Sorghum*, whose director has stated that this film is meant to contrast with present day social conditions (Zhou Youzhao 1988, 12), the traditional system is too strong, the union between the two young people is destroyed, and the result is suffering for everyone, especially the young woman.

Students can discern that the film adaptation of "Hsiao-hsiao" illustrates this type of social criticism in several ways. The directors chose to adapt a work that in one way fits the trend quite well: it features a marriage involving an impotent male, the baby Chunguan. Where Shen's narrative deviates from the directors' chosen message, they have altered it to reflect their own vision. There is a noticeable absence of masculinity in Xiaoxiao's film family. The directors have deleted the grandfather character from the narrative and replaced him with the more malignant and more active character of mother-in-law. They have added the information that Xiaoxiao's father-in-law, another young bride-groom, lives far away from home and shows no sign of wishing to return to his wife and family. Moreover, the final scenes of Chunguan looking on suspiciously from a distance as the two women of the family perpetuate the traditional system through the betrothal ceremony place him firmly on the outside of the family power structure. Thus the bleak society that *Girl from Hunan* portrays is one noticeably lacking in masculinity. Whether or not the lack of masculine qualities in the society portrayed in films like *Girl from Hunan* is equally detrimental to men and women may also provide a topic for classroom discussion. Film scholar Chris Berry cites the final scene in *Girl from Hunan* to argue that the message of such films is not as positive in its attitude toward women as Eugene Yuejin Wang has asserted. Berry points out that by the end of the film, Xiaoxiao has clearly been indoctrinated into the traditional value system, and through it gains power, which she shares with her mother-in-law: the audience (along with Chunguan) watch as mother-in-law adjusts on a nervous, but proud and happy, Xiaoxiao the headdress of a matron, signifying that Xiaoxiao has become like her. It is Chunguan alone who wordlessly conveys to the audience the view of the directors, that something is wrong with the system. Literary adaptation thus lends itself to discussion, on a variety of levels, of fiction and film and of the intellectual and social contexts in which they were created.

The study of Chinese literary adaptation can function as much more than a means of gaining insight into the works of Chinese fiction upon which they are often based. In fact, it is more effective as a means of examining the aesthetic, narrative, intellectual and political concerns of the period in which the adaptation is made. The method of comparison outlined above helps students learn a great deal about contemporary PRC aesthetics, and about the relationship between literature and film, without underestimating the artistic and social importance of the latter.

Notes

This article was first published in *Journal of the Chinese Language Teachers' Association* 26.2 (1991): 25–32. Copyright © 1991 by *Journal of the Chinese Language Teachers' Association*. Reprinted with permission.

1. See Hoare 1991. For Lu Xun's novella, *The New Year's Sacrifice*, see notes on *Two Stage Sisters* in this book. For the detailed study of the adaptation of this story, see Kuoshu 1999b, 51–70.

2. In this article I generally use the pinyin romanization system, in which Hsiao-hsiao should be written Xiaoxiao. However, my references to Shen Congwen's short story are based on the translation found in Lau et al., *Modern Chinese Short Stories and Novellas,* the text I use to teach. The translator, Eugene Eoyang, uses Wade-Giles romanization; therefore, in describing the short story, I refer to the heroine as Hsiao-hsiao.

3. Critics and the general public in China use the term "Fifth Generation" to denote the relatively young directors who were the first group to graduate from the Beijing Film Institute after the Cultural Revolution, in 1981. The term includes such directors as Zhang Yimou, Chen Kaige, and Tian Zhuangzhuang. *Girl from Hunan* directors Xie Fei and Wu Lan, while not "Fifth Generation" themselves, were teachers of the "Fifth Generation" at the Beijing Film Institute.

4. Eugene Yuejin Wang, "Mixing Memory and Desire: *Red Sorghum,* a Chinese Version of Masculinity and Femininity," *Public Culture* 2.1 (Fall 1989): 31–53.

Nine
Sacrificed Youth
(*Qingchun ji*, dir. Zhang Nuanxin, 1985)

Screenplay Zhang Manling et al.
Cinematography Deng Wei, Mu Deyuan
Producer Qingnian
Cast Li Fengxu, as Li Chun
Feng Yuanzheng, as Ren Jia

Unlike Tian Zhuangzhuang's *On the Hunting Ground,* which represents the isolated life of Mongolians living according to a primordial code enforced by social customs on the grasslands, *Sacrificed Youth* by female director Zhang Nuanxin is an on-screen cross-cultural comparison of the Han and Dai; a young Han woman, Li Chun, is caught between the two cultures and experiences unresolved contradictions. She painfully seeks redefinition by negotiating the two cultures but ends up suffering the sensual and actual losses of a loving surrogate mother and of her two beloved young men—a Dai, referred to as Dage, and a Han, named Ren Jia.

Based on female author Zhang Manling's semi-autobiographical novella *There Exists a Beautiful Place* (1982), *Sacrificed Youth* is Li Chun's recollection of her youth spent in a remote Dai village during the Cultural Revolution. This recollection through the novella and the film, with three years between them, marks an interesting trajectory that vindicates the relationships among *scar literature (shanghen wenxue), zhiqing literature (zhiqing wenxue,* literature about the young urbanites in the countryside during the Cultural Revolution), and *roots-searching literature.* Emerging from the first two literary trends, the novella drifted away from its predecessors' overt political and often melodramatic orientations by focusing on the coming-of-age process of a politicized Han subject in the relatively depoliticized and pastoral environment of the minority Dai region. By the time the film was shot, roots-searching had confirmed the desire to depoliticize and had encouraged this "prose film" of cultural scrutiny. Direct engagement with the political past was brushed aside.

This past, in a way, became the specter behind roots-searching, accounting for its desires, interests, and restraints.

Documentary aesthetics, shown in the film's preference for on-location shooting, natural lighting, and some nonprofessional actors and actresses (for example, Ya), is accompanied by a strong subjective touch of memory. Wanting to make this film "a piece of lyric prose" and "a dream-like recollection," Zhang enjoyed using unusual camera angles and added a slightly red tint to suggest the subjective perception in the general dominance of the natural green. Strict on-location shooting, however, was frequently violated. Zhang found it hard to locate the idealized Dai world, which was supposed to contrast with the off-screen Han reality: the Han reality shows itself everywhere in the Dai region as unsuitable images. She often had to give up her fondness for documentary aesthetics to create a "pure" Dai world.

Music by two talented composers, Liu Suola and Qu Xiaosong, also made this film unforgettable. Liu herself was a noted experimental novelist in the early post-Mao era. Her love for avant-garde music served this film well in a peculiar melody that conveys a primitive aspect of Dai life.

Suggested readings for *Sacrificed Youth* are as follows:

Berry 1986, 1988b
Semsel 1987
Yau 1989a
Yingjin Zhang 1997
Silbergeld 1999, 53–95

Director's Notes

As they are Han, the young women of Li Chun's generation have been brought up by the set standards of a modern civilization. They will never be able to really be like a Dai, that is, to pursue bravely what they love and display boldly what they are. The cultural tension between Dai civilization (primitive, natural, and close to human nature) and Han civilization (modern, hypocritical, and distorted) constitutes Li Chun's tragedy.

This film should be a lyrical prose. It is all about Li Chun's recollection—what she treasures in her memory and not real life itself. Memory is the key to the film, making it a dream-like recollection. (Zhang Nuanxin 1985, 135)

When we were young, we couldn't make ourselves attractive, nor could we express love. Why did I change the name [of this film] from "A Faraway Place" to *Sacrificed Youth*? Because I felt that our youth had been buried by those experiences then. I wanted to express that feeling, the tragedy of my youth, the tragedy of our whole generation. (Qtd. in Berry 1988b, 21)

What I would like to have happen after people have seen *Sacrificed Youth* is to have them say it is unexplainable, that it is all a matter of feeling. I want people to *feel* it, but to otherwise find it hard to talk about.

Film people often consider minority films to be a genre, but lacking in real depth of feeling for the people. Zhang Manling's work contains a great deal of compassion, and I tried to maintain that high level of feeling in the film. (Qtd. in Semsel 1987, 125–26)

Is China the End of Hermeneutics?; or, Political and Cultural Usage of Non-Han Women in Mainland Chinese Films
Esther C. M. Yau

Introduction

The Cultural Revolution in China in the 1960s has a convoluted history yet to be properly understood (Tsou Tang 1986). After 1979, the People's Republic opened its doors to international capitalism and put an end to the social forces generated by the monumental mass movement. However, to a whole generation of Chinese, and especially the Han people sent to the countryside, the experience of the Cultural Revolution was and still is important in the context and the collective unconscious of the 1980s and the 1990s.

In the West, efforts to construct China as an object of knowledge and as the "non-Western Other" are often limited by the tendency to interpret China's experiences according to liberal agendas (or conservative, or radical ones, for that matter);[1] by the benign but nonetheless narcissistic character of the venture; by dulled awareness of the slippery nature of cross-cultural articulations; and by the West's long-standing ignorance about ethnic differences in China, which takes "Chinese" for a single racial category.

From the perspective of Western self-critique, we need to be suspicious of claims that purport to recognize "the rich values of an ancient oriental civilization" or to acknowledge "those cultural differences which enable us [i.e., Western investigators] to learn something," assuming knowledge as a basis of superiority. Indeed, ventures into the still-unchartered "Third World" areas are becoming fashionable but no less questionable, as are generous inclusions of women of color within global (feminist or otherwise) definitions of liberation and sexuality. Many of these cross-cultural pursuits, prefaced by ritualistic self-critique, are oblivious to the neocolonial character of the ways they theorize the Others' differences (see Spivak 1987, 134–53). Readiness to accept "experts" who pay only lip service to historical and local specificities, and whose pro-forma apologies are complemented by uncritical use of native sources as truth, further attests to a troubling Western tolerance of superficial scholarship concerning the "Third World."

This essay, which examines the appropriation of national minorities in Chinese cinema, does not intend to seek out the recuperative values of under-represented groups as an alternative to the Confucian-based dominant Han Chinese culture. Rather, the purpose is to critique the appropriation and sub-jugation of minority cultures within the national boundary. Edward Said's *Orientalism* (1978) has stimulated many similar discussions concerning the ways aspects of non-Western societies have been interpreted and integrated into nationalistic and ethnocentric formulations of Western knowledge. Said's critique is invoked here to reflect on our participation in a similar process as we encounter the Other. China, according to the still-prevailing logic that equates the "First World" with the Self, is perceived by the West as the Other (and more so since the Chinese government crushed the 1989 public outcry for self-determination); however, when it comes to marginalizing minority cul-tures and creating the exotic, the dominant races and classes in China and the West are similarly culpable. Through reflection on the analogy, critiquing Chinese films' subjugation of the national minorities (as the "third realm" within China) could be inverted, so that reading the Other is turned into a con-frontation with the Self.

Context

To condense centuries of history into a brief narrative, one begins arbitrarily. The Han and their *huaxia* civilization of the northern plains of China rose from the battlefields. In different dynasties, the Han emperors and their army fought the surrounding tribes and countries as they established territorial domi-nation and claimed mandate from heaven. Etymology marks the Han's self-cen-tering efforts. The term *Zhongguo* literally means "the middle kingdom." The four most common terms for the surrounding tribes are *nu*, which shares the same character with "slave"; *di*, which is composed of the hieroglyph "animal" and "fire"; *yi*, which uses the character that means, in one context, "to flatten by destruction"; and *man*, which includes an ideogram "insect" in the charac-ter and denotes "uncivilized savages."[2] Thus, by defining the tribal Others as less than human, the Han have positioned themselves in the center of intelligence and cultural superiority. The supremacy of the Middle Kingdom's civilization was preserved at the expense of soldiers at war and beautiful courtesans dispatched as part of diplomatic *he fan* gifts to "keep peace with the aliens." In the years when the Mongolians ruled over China, the Han maintained that the inner strength of their culture would eventually bleach and convert the non-Han emperors.

By comparison, the modern, socialist version of Han cultural hegemony was apparently more benign. In the early 1950s, the People's Republic of China (PRC) government acknowledged that fifty-five nationalities lived in the country with the Han as the majority (approximately 94 percent of the entire population). The Common Program of 1949 and the Constitution of 1954 prohibited discrimination against the fifty-four non-Han nationalities officially named *shaoshu minzu* ("national minorities").[3] National unity and regional autonomy were dual goals in the Common Program, which dictated that "all national minorities [should] have freedom to develop their dialects and languages, to preserve or reform their traditions, customs, and religious beliefs."[4] The program also committed the government to attend to the minorities' economic and cultural well-being, and to be more flexible with the *xiongdi minzu* (brother nationalities).

The Soviet-inspired PRC's national/ethnic policy *(minzu zhengce)* of the 1950s attributed the reasons for inequality to uneven regional economic development. While Chairman Mao Zedong criticized Han chauvinism and stressed Socialist brotherhood, the government's long-term objectives stressed national unity and defense, appropriation of resources (notably minerals) in the "autonomous regions," elimination of local elites, and institutionalization of ethnic differences. Regional demands for self-determination were suppressed, silenced, or transformed by the mandate of integrating all nationalities within China (Herberer 1989). Defined as "*national* minorities," non-Han peoples who refused to comply with the government would be labeled political segregationists. As "national *minorities*," they were offered a contract without end—with terms arranged like those of a traditional marriage in which the bride (as the "minor") had no freedom to refuse but hoped to prosper by getting along. Overt and covert assimilation pressures kept transforming the sociocultural character of the "national minorities." In other words, military, organizational, and discursive forms of violence helped sustain the official-national constructions of unified struggle, harmonious coexistence, and cultural diversity.

The "National Minorities" Genre

From 1949 to 1965, the state-financed studios produced more than fifty feature films about the Mongolians, Tibetans, Kazakhs, Uighurs, Koreans, Dais, Miaos, Yis, Bais, and other "national minorities."[5] The productions involved non-Han consultants, interpreters, performers, and crew members. At the same time, Han control measures were omnipresent in every film: Han performers played national minorities' roles; slogans written in the Chinese language appeared in the scenes; a male Han cadre present in every story judged political and folk matters; and the government's agendas informed the narrative strategies. Together, the films purportedly represented the minorities' revolutionary struggles but subtly implemented nationalizing policies and constituted a special genre in China's postrevolutionary cinema.

The use of women as rhetorical figures in the national minorities genre was consistent with the Party's discursive use of women in general. Non-Han female protagonists, played by Han actresses, were set up as role models to suture narrative and visual interests with political functions. Ostensibly minority and actually Han, the performers with their mixed identities addressed both non-Han and Han viewers. Not surprisingly, only the strong and healthy bodies dressed in exotic costumes were selected as couriers of political messages. In films such as *Five Golden Flowers* (*Wuduo jinhua,* 1959) and *The Red Flower of Tianshan* (*Tianshan de honahua,* 1963), these women worked, sang, danced, suffered, and struggled in ways that whetted the Han viewers' voyeuristic interests in "primitive" cultures.[6] Inevitably, spectacles of beautiful and spontaneous women drew attention to themselves and provoked escapist fantasies. Thus, through attractive "minority" female protagonists, the didactic and the escapist functioned simultaneously, though probably more didactically for the non-Han spectators and more as escape for the Han ones.

The national minorities films invariably set up a triangular relationship that consisted of non-Han men and women and a Han cadre through which sexual transgression was negatively correlated with ethnic leadership. Among native elite men were oppressive slave owners, landlords, and Guomindang sympathizers who either raped or abused the powerless native women. While regional/ethnic authority was sexualized and constructed as male aggressiveness, compliance with Han socialism was presented as female vulnerability in need of Han official intervention as male chivalry. The virtuous minority woman, a Han supporter, has ethical and familial reasons for supporting the Party—a logic based on Confucian priorities. In short, good minority women were strategically produced to incriminate native men who resisted the government's regional policies. This nexus of ethnic, gender, and moral organization constituted the dominant paradigm of interethnic relations in the national minorities films from 1949 to 1965 and revealed the character of intranational "brotherhood."

Contrary to their prowomen stance, the films betrayed sadist interests in non-Han cruelty directed toward female protagonists. For example, in *The Dai Doctor (Moyadai,* 1960) a young Dai mother is punished and burned as a witch by the lustful tribal lord who failed to rape her; later, the superstitious villagers set fire to the family hut to expel both her husband and daughter. In *Visitors over Ice Mountains (Bingshan shang de laike,* 1963), a Tajikh woman—an impersonator and spy—is murdered by the Guomindang sympathizers in her own tribe. In *The Red Flower of Tianshan,* a Kazakh woman is whipped and later abandoned by her husband, who opposes her leading role in organizing the people's commune. These and other scenes of torture and killing underscore the Other's violence for purposes of discrediting the nationalist government, undermining non-Han men's power, winning women's empathy, and making charges against minority dissidents. Moreover, the "ethnic" characteristics of the violent acts consolidate the popular (mis)perception of the national minorities as "uncivilized."

Aside from political functions, non-Han women on screen provided an exclusive site for sexuality that was not addressed in other films. In most postrevolutionary films, Confucian morality continued to make the self-sacrificial mother the bearer of Han civilization and to condemn sexuality outside the institutions of reproduction and economic production. Moral and sexual crimes were often conflated with political crimes. The Party's attitude toward desire was codified in the calculated shrouding of women's sexual appeal on screen through costume, lighting, camera angles, and acting styles. Consequently, positive female Han types appeared uniformly and predictably virtuous. While most films observe rigid codes of female representation, the national minorities genre, which occupies a lower status in the hierarchy of Han postrevolutionary art, was sometimes spared by the strictest censorship of desire and sexuality and "licensed" to elaborate on beautiful and "exotic" female bodies. "Erotic excesses" invoked in scenes featuring national minority women acknowledged desires and smuggled them through Confucian and Party taboos, though, inevitably, they did not seriously threaten the codes of Han sexual propriety. In this manner, they also helped sustain both a segregationist logic and the austere codes of the hard-core revolutionary genres.

Significantly, the few early women directors working in the 1950s were just as faithful in executing Party prerogatives as their male counterparts and provided no distinctive "female" voices in the postrevolutionary cinema. So far, only two films of the genre have been identified as being codirected by women working with senior male colleagues: *Menglongsha Village* (*Menglongsha,* 1960) and *Eagle of the Plains* (*Caoyuan xiongying,* 1964). Since these films are similar to others in the genre, female directors' gender identity does not appear to be significant. *A Blade of Grass on the Kunlun Mountains* (*Kunlun shanshang yikecao,* 1962), a low-budget film directed by a woman director, Dong Kena, is, however, an exception. The film depicts the initial disappointments, frustrations, and struggles of two Han women who assisted male Han truck drivers working in the Qinghai Tibetan Plateau. The film advocates self-sacrifice and devotion in the face of harsh living circumstances, in line with the general call for perseverance in the early 1960s when the country was suffering from famine and from withdrawal of Soviet support. Dong Kena worked entirely within the sociopolitical parameters and did not question frontier development. Still, the film underplays the role of the male Han cadre (a deceased husband, he appears only briefly in a flashback), and it suggests that it was his widow's persistence and the companionship she offered to the newcomers that mattered in this unromantic frontier. Inadvertently, the film provides alternative insights into what it meant for the Han to be "settling happily" in the border provinces. Not a national minorities film, Dong's heroic portrayal of workers of the "autonomous regions" nevertheless makes an intertextual comment on the Han's frontier mentality. Still, the film does not question the politics of the national minorities genre, and Han ethnocentrism remains unaddressed.

Post-Cultural Revolution Introspection and *Sacrificed Youth*

In the post–Cultural Revolution "New Era" (which ended in about 1989), the government's modernization policy was accompanied by more autonomy given to filmmakers. Nevertheless, since the earlier, "classical" national minorities films did not challenge Han biases, more recent and "depoliticized" versions of non-Han cultures were not free of ethnocentric tendencies either. Still subjected to state censorship, films could not portray the national minorities' independence movements or the extent of harm done to them during the Cultural Revolution—these matters remained more or less oral history.[7] Of the many films that addressed the implications of the Cultural Revolution, only several reenacted the Han's traumatic "exile" to the autonomous regions and took pains to present the non-Han's cultural superiority. The ethnocentric tendencies in these films, which pursued cultural (and obliquely political) self-examination, suggest a complex introspective process.

Sacrificed Youth, an acclaimed film based on an award-winning novella written by Zhang Manling, who worked with the Dai nationality during the Cultural Revolution, is an example of the Han's self-critical efforts. Zhang Nuanxin, the film's director, was born in Inner Mongolia and is a graduate of and has been a lecturer at the Beijing Film Academy since 1958. Both Han women had lived in the border provinces, both were college-educated in Beijing, and both use the ethnographic mode for personalized narratives.

Zhang Manling's *There Exists a Beautiful Place (You yige meili de difang)* is semiautobiographical. It depicts in flashbacks the psychological changes within a young Han woman, Li Chun, who, during the Cultural Revolution, was dispatched from the city to work and live with the Dai natives in a Yunnan village. The narrative dramatizes the inner fears and anomie of a seventeen-year-old separated from her own Han community and drawn toward the friendly but unfamiliar Dai people, who live like the Thai. Li Chun's eagerness to observe and to mimic the Dai ways of living is motivated by political and survival needs (what the government required of the rusticated youths), by her own competitive character (especially with Yibo, the prettiest and most capable of the Dai girls in the village), and by her desire for a comforting acceptance badly needed since her own family members were forced apart by persecutions. In order to liberate herself from a homogeneous political upbringing and to explore a new identity, she puts on Dai clothes and becomes increasingly aware of her sexuality.

Li Chun's efforts to free herself from her Han background strains against the repressive mechanisms she has internalized. Dage, the son of her host family, a hunter and a brick maker, is infatuated with her but patiently awaits her initiative. However, the unstated reasons of class difference and interracial taboos sustain her distance from Dage. Her reluctance to give up her Han intellectual identity accounts for her friendship with Renjia, a Han youth whose fate is similar to hers but who is skeptical of the native life-style. As the novella maintains these split and repressed sexual interests without acknowledging their problematic nature, Li Chun's dilemma in the Han-Dai encounter is resolved by a narrative ploy: she comes under suspicion for money lost in the host family and, although the misunderstanding is clarified later, she leaves the village. (In the film version, Dage gets drunk and, venting his jealousy, beats Renjia.) In any case, a pretext is given that motivates Li Chun to move to another area. After many years, she returns to the city and enters college. But there is a mud-rock slide in the Dai village that hosted her, and Renjia is buried under it. At the end, educated and in her thirties, she regrets her ultimate separation from the perpetual youthfulness of the Dai. In her dreams, however, she remembers the lush green and the ever-flowing waters.

The novella presents positive and intimate details of Dai culture from a Han perspective. Li Chun is initially drawn to the Dais, while she has reservations about the Han. To a Han girl used to civil surveillance, an involuntary "exile" to Yunnan actually means gaining warm and trustful friends and protection from political strife. Yet, the romanticized Han-Dai relationship comes to an impasse when Li Chun's inability to become the Other is dramatized via the traditional (and sexist) device by which she has to choose between two men to signify identity and inscribe her loyalties. In other words, the novella suffers from its unconscious adoption of the dominant patriarchal perspective that prevents a woman from defining herself outside the restrictive realm of the family and heterosexuality. Li Chun's inevitable return to Han culture at the end, therefore, fulfills Han ethical prerequisites; but, sadly, she lives in a different form of "exile" as she has to give up the vibrant "non-Han" part of herself.

The novella's sentimental descriptions of Yunnan and the Dai natives are beautifully visualized in filmic terms by Zhang Nuanxin. Zhang shot her second film on location using the country's standard of a 3.5-to-1 shooting ratio, with a small budget from the Youth Studio of the Beijing Film Academy. *Sacrificed Youth,* a lyrical piece that set an important precedent for personal filmmaking long submerged in the self-effacing 1950s aesthetic practices, subtly expresses a middle-aged woman's sense of emotional loss. Through Li Chun's self-examination, Zhang shows that the naive notion of "beauty" had been distorted by repressive indoctrination and that a conceptual and visual restoration of that "beauty" is possible via a process of self-critique and inspiration from the (preliterate) rural southwestern Dai culture.

In a discussion of her directorial intentions, Zhang Nuanxin summarized the Han woman's (and her own) dilemma:

> Amidst the cultural conflict between the Dai civilization (that which is primitive, sincere, befitting to human nature) and the Han civilization (that which is modern, partly hypocritical, and distorting to human nature) lies the tragedy of Li Chun. She was awakened, but it made her feel even more painful. The clearer she knew, the more she felt her youth slipping away during the turmoil, and getting buried within the concepts which bind many. (1985, 135)

Zhang added that she was composing "an ode to the passing away of the youth of a whole generation of people." That is, her own generation, which spent its thirties during the Cultural Revolution, is "sacrificed youth." Nevertheless, the film does not confront the Han's mutual destruction during those years that led to the deaths of many; instead, it offers an intellectual audience disturbing cultural insights without trespassing political taboos.

Zhang Nuanxin's adaptation mixes reality and fiction, ethnography and memory, and the dramatic and poetic forms of realism. The subtle style and narrative ambiguity underscore the flow of Li Chun's consciousness. Zhang Nuanxin also experimented with practices new to the mainland Chinese at the time, including shooting in sync sound, setting up elaborate long takes, filming in extremely low light situations, and sensitively handling tones in a potentially monotonous subtropical environment. By asking the Dai people in Yunnan to play themselves, Zhang created what she calls "a real challenge to the professional Han actress who was trained to perform before the camera in more conventional ways." She also invited suggestions from the Dai people and welcomed improvisations from the 102-year-old Dai granny, who first encountered film on this occasion, and who turned out the best "performance" among the cast. Back in Beijing, she accepted her colleagues' suggestion to use dramatic shock as a concluding device, and reedited the ending, which now gives the impression that the whole Dai village has been eliminated by the mud-rock slide. In these various ways, Zhang Nuanxin actualized her notions of a modernized film language and ethnographic sensibilities, though, regrettably, she was not fully aware of the ideological implications of the film's new ending.[8]

Like most Han directors and some ethnographic filmmakers, Zhang Nuanxin's observation-participation techniques serve the ideology of artistic creation. Zhang recalled the hours and mileage the crew had spent on location reconnaissances, since many areas in Yunnan had been subjected to development and "they no longer look like they used to." Obviously, Zhang's thematic obsession with untainted nature obscured her perception of the everyday effects of Han presence on the Dai land, which keep jumping out as images "unsuitable" for her film. For, as the ideas about the Dai are beautiful, so their reality must be beautiful, too. Accordingly, the poetic, culturally introspective, and humanist film seeks out the Dai's primitive and positive virtues only; while the natives, like other national minorities, face the modern problems of colonization and deprivation. Thus, when the ideology of artistic reconstruction has replaced that of political didactics in the post–Cultural Revolution era, the objectifying processes are not automatically removed. A Han youth commented on the film's aesthetic project, "I know what it really means to be living in the beautiful borders and I do not need the intellectuals to tell me."[9] Yibo, the prettiest Dai girl in the film, acted on a similar attitude by leaving the village to join a cultural troupe after the filming.

In *Sacrificed Youth,* the prominent aspects of Dai life and culture are earthy, agrarian, and sensuous—qualities that feed into the bourgeois appeal of the film. The exotic connotations of the images are enhanced by the indigenous sounds of the Dai conversations, music, and songs, which create a subtropical ambience alluring to Han Chinese and Westerners alike. (Zhang told an American that most Chinese have never visited the Sino-Burmese border, and she had the Western audience in mind when she shot the film.)[10] Again, unconsciously, a "third realm" within China is "colonized" by well-intentioned Han artists and becomes a part of a "new Chinese cinema" that is being launched on an orbit of international marketing (hence indirect global colonization?) as well.

International glamour notwithstanding, privileges in cross-cultural encounters prove to be hard to give up. Still, for such encounters to be meaningful to the privileged, the latter must experience humility and learn; however, the experience remains superficial if the privileged refuse to give up their superior, centered positions. Such superficial experiences abound in fictional and ethnographic texts that depict figures that cross the racial and cultural boundaries. In relation to *Sacrificed Youth,* I shall focus on two different narcissistic articulations by identifying the tropes of "cultural disguise" and "familial projection" in two notable instances in which the Han woman undergoes psychological and emotional changes.

Earlier, in order to be included in the Dai girls' work team, Li Chun puts on a tight blouse and a long purplish sarong dress. Her attractive feminine figure, previously hidden by the grayish Maoist uniform, emerges, noted by musical accompaniment, and becomes a pleasurable site for gazes from within the diegesis and from offscreen. Instantaneously, the social relationships within the film work for Li Chun's benefit: Ya gives her a silver waistband and treats her as a family member; the arrogant Yibo admits her into the work team; and Renjia (the Han youth) and Dage (the Dai man) are attracted to her. In short, she gains full access to cultural-sexual exchange. While the Dai girls' difference initially displaces Li Chun's superiority, her adoption of Dai ways and mores, which has enlightened her, has also brought immense and immediate rewards. Evidently, the "superior" cultural figure's respect for the Other's difference enables the former to regain confidence and become the center of minority attention.

To describe the erotic power newly discovered when she discards the Maoist uniforms, Li Chun says in the voice-over that she is "like the Ash Maid [meaning Cinderella] in the fairy tale who has put on crystal shoes." The allusion to a Western fairy tale reveals the Han-Dai encounter as at once imagined in a narcissistic and romantic manner and legitimized by a fantastic (Western) figure.[11] What gives the Han character and viewers the pleasure of enlightenment is not just a departure from asceticism, but also the fantastic ability of a single Han body to take up and sustain two different cultural codes, one dominant and the other complementary. The experience turns out to be one of "cultural disguise"—a Han intellectual adopts a Dai identity and knows the Other from the inside, while power relations remain unchanged. That is, respect for the Dai turns into appropriation for the Han's benefit. Such a "cultural disguise" in this and other contexts enriches the privileged travelers, legitimizes their authority as "minority experts," and masks their appropriation of minority strengths as genuine facilitation of cross-cultural exchange.

The narcissism in the Han-Dai encounter, however, should also be considered alongside the dilemma of the female Han intellectual. That is, the personal voices in the text need to be historicized. After Ya's death, there are four sequences before the film comes to an end. They include Li Chun's mourning in whitish gray, a Dai funeral in fiery red climaxing in the cremation of Ya, a grayish gigantic mud-rock slide that erases all the traces of Dai life, and a lingering visual caress of the subtropical region in orange tones accompanied by the theme song. While the previous scenes have been carefully conceived with psychological nuances, realistic colors, and ethnic details, these four sequences have a different syntax and style extremely condensed, almost abstract in quality, and highly charged, they reorder iconic codes to produce distinctive changes in tonal scheme and emotional expression. It is at the film's very end that the death of the Dai granny, the burial of the Dai village, the passing away of Li Chun's youth, and the mourning for all the losses are chained tightly together. Together, they enact an emotional rupture that calls for further analysis of the film's oblique expression of a Han woman's bind in ways that cannot be further repressed or delayed by the film's narrative and aesthetic concerns.

Undoubtedly, the film deploys a surrogate mother as linchpin to the success of the Han-Dai encounter. In the body of Ya, the director found the perfect ethnographic realization: a real Dai offering the most genuine (m)otherly expressions to verify the film's sincerity, and an ideal maternal figure that naturalizes the Han's demands for a good mother who guarantees the productivity and prosperity of the household (Chu Tung-tsu 1972). The Dai community's openness and warmth contrast the Han's destructive behavior during the Cultural Revolution. The "familial projection," a romanticizing gesture, also offsets the film's apparent engagement with a different, autonomous, and sexual identity and reinscribes the Dai (as it does the Han) into a Confucian familial order. This inability to affirm any feminine existence outside the familial definition is indeed troubling. In as consciously self-critical a film as *Sacrificed Youth*, the imposition of a Han social-ethical scheme nevertheless reenacts the repressive mechanism that the film sets out to criticize and reveals its ideological fixation despite its conscious objectives. Moreover, projecting oneself on the Other, as the film uses the mythical Dai figure Ya for Han self-location, is ethnocentric indeed. Such inability to perceive or act outside one's ideological inscription despite having gained insights from the Others underscores ethnocentrism as a stubborn blind spot of the mind that may generate colonizing moves in cross-cultural encounters.

In a text as overdetermined by repressive cultural norms and by revisionist efforts of the early 1980s as *Sacrificed Youth*, the ending sequences finally come to an eruption. Even so, it was the death of Ya and her funeral as a spectacle of fire that provide "pretexts" or metonymic ways to articulate the feelings that Han women (the character used as an agent for both the writer and the director) have contained inside themselves for many years. Yet, even so, the pressures to prioritize the culture and the family rather than oneself have taken effect, so that this intimate moment of feminine self-revelation is tactfully placed, almost invisibly, within the "important scenes" of the mother's death and the mud-rock slide's ruthless destruction of Dai life. This "diminution" matches the choice of the "national minorities genre" for expression, though the film has taken crucial steps to avoid the clichéd images of the non-Han people. Still, as the middle-aged Li Chun cries in front of the overwhelming and silent site of the mud-rock slide, a deeply personal voice emerges that cannot be explained by the diegesis. This articulation of loss figured by a perpetual deprivation of contact with the spontaneous Dai can be historicized by relating it to the regrets of Han women who for years live within the binds of the Han political culture.

Ultimately, a sincere and deeply personal voice comes out in *Sacrificed Youth*'s representation of the Self: Chinese socialism as political culture has perpetuated a patriarchal dogma that trains women how to dress, behave, and think, and it produces forms of power they must learn to live in, especially since the demands of male leaders have influenced the men in their own families. What is repressed in the film's criticism of Han culture, then, is the criticism of sociopolitical ethics that keeps burdening the representation of the Self and Other. The discourses on cultural introspection and female sexuality in

Sacrificed Youth, complicated and contradictory as they are, constitute the fabric of a fictional Dai ethnography that is indeed suitable for our hermeneutic reading of the Han.

Concluding Remarks

When the relationship of domination and subordination remains unchanged, a better knowledge of the Other can become a form of rhetorical violation toward the Other viewed as an object of study. Thus, there is no consolation except that which is found in self-critical silence.[12] But a silence as refusal to colonize and to be colonized is very difficult when advanced forms of colonial discourse hardly pause in their benign global advancements in knowledge making.

Notes

This article was published in *Multiple Voices in Feminist Film Criticism,* edited by Diane Carson, Linda Dittmar, and Janice R. Welsch (Minneapolis: University of Minnesota Press, 1994), pp. 280–93. Originally published in *Discourse* 11.2 (1989): 114–36. Copyright © 1989 by Esther C. M. Yau. Reprinted by permission of the author.

1. Roland Barthes noted that "China . . . defeats the constitution of concepts, themes, names. [O]ur knowledge is turned into a figment of the imagination: the ideological objects that our society constructs are silently declared impertinent. It is the end of hermeneutics." Roland Barthes, "Well, and China?" *Discourse* 8 (Fall-Winter 1986–87): 117, an English translation of "Alors, la Chine?" privately published in Paris, 1975.

2. Southern China was traditionally the place of exile for the banished official class from the north.

3. See Chap. 3, sec. 4 of *The Constitution of the People's Republic of China* (Beijing: Foreign Language Press, 1983).

4. Article 53 in "The Common Program," adopted by the First Plenary Session of the Chinese People's Political Consultative Congress on September 29, 1949. *China Digest,* Oct. 5, 1949.

5. Those who can read Chinese may look at the synopses of feature films in ZDZ 1981.

6. Paul Clark also discusses the uses of "national minorities" in Clark 1987a.

7. The Chinese always use informal and orally circulated knowledge to bypass formal and official prohibition. See Herberer 1989.

8. The quotes in this and the next paragraph are cited from personal interviews with Zhang Nuanxin in Beijing, February and March 1988.

9. Personal discussion with Yao Xiaomeng in Beijing, February 1988.

10. See Zhang's comments in Semsel 1987, 124–28.

11. Although an old Chinese "Cinderella" story existed in about A.D. 850–60 (trans-

lated by Arthur Waley in *Folk-Lore* 58 [March 1947]: 226–13), Zhang Nuanxin's reference to the "Ash Maid" in *Sacrificed Youth* treats the wonder tale figure as a Western one.

12. Both Edward Said's "Intellectuals in the Post-Colonial World" and Gayatri Chakravorty Spivak's "Can the Subaltern Speak?" address the dilemma of the postcolonial intellectual.

Ten

Horse Thief
(*Daoma zei,* dir. Tian Zhuangzhuang, 1986)

Screenplay Zhang Rui
Cinematography Hou Yun, Zhao Fei
Producer Xi'an
Cast Cexiang Rigzin, as Norbu
Dan Jiji, as Norbu's wife

Tian Zhuangzhuang's first minorities film, *On the Hunting Ground,* has often been cited as illustrating *jishi meixue* (documentary aesthetics). *Horse Thief,* his second title in the same genre a year later, is striking in its expressionism. Although most of his Tibetan *mise-en-scènes* are equally authentic, this film is a mixture of the real and surreal, formalism and documentary approaches.

The film's literary base, Zhang Rui's novella "The Story of Horse Thieves," is a typical piece of roots-searching literature. Set in Tibet, it tells the stories of Norbu, a horse thief, and of his second son, prior to and after the Communist takeover. Driven out of the tribe because of his thievery, Norbu has to leave his homeland, Cherema pasture, to live in Mt. Oalar, believed by the locals to be the devil's realm. When his first son soon dies, Norbu believes this to be Buddha's punishment and voluntarily gives up thieving. Upon the birth of his second son, Norbu vows to give a big donation to the temple but finds it hard to keep his word. He feels forced to take up horse thieving again but is killed, leaving a widow and an orphaned son, Walgon. The son grows up under Communist rule among the poor herdsmen, who are nevertheless highly respected in the revolutionary community. He falls in love with the daughter of a former chief and social outcast. He witnesses a horse theft by a friend and finds out that the friend has done this to pay his mother's medical bills. Not wanting to betray his friend, he is suspected as the horse thief himself. The incident sets the Party's political machine in motion, which soon builds a case of class struggle as a warning to its citizens: Walgon's relationship with a former chief's daughter and his father's past as a horse thief are publicized in this campaign. Unable to bear the political pressure but wanting to follow his conscience, Walgon tries to follow in his father's footsteps by fleeing into the Oalar Mountains. He is captured and thrown into jail.

The novella is of interest because of its contrast of humanity subject to the Tibetan Buddhist temples and the Han totalitarian regime. It depicts how these institutions indoctrinate their subjects differently, but it also showcases an underlying commonality: the humanity, or a Tibetan style of humanity, which features a strong will, an aptitude for action, loyalty to one's words, faithfulness to friendship, and straightforwardness of character—what the rehumanization of the 1980s celebrated.

Tian Zhuangzhuang was first attracted to this Tibetan story by its depiction of humanity, but he did not particularly care for its comparison between the present and the past, the totalitarian politics and the Tibetan religion. At the very least, he wanted that to be off-screen, as he had done in his earlier film, *On the Hunting Ground*. He wanted his second minority film to be a spiritual exploration, an experience alien enough for the Han filmgoers and meaningful enough for him to contribute to his contemporary cultural critique.

Tian invited Zhang to turn the story into a film script with revisions that would distance the original from the present time, the Han influence, and the conventional story line in order to create an allegory of humanity represented through natural calamities and religious rituals. Once the script was drafted, Tian did not fine-tune it but decided to go on-site in Tibet and let the shooting experience itself be part of the exploration.

Once there, the film crew merged themselves into Tibetan life, especially the spiritual life. Their involvement coincides with the subjective color scheme and the viewing angle that Tian decided on for his film: while the residential area of the Tibetans is captured in cold gray tones, the spiritual realm—the temples and the rituals—are shot primarily from low angles and in the warm glow of lights. The Han perspective here invites an admiration of the spirituality of an alien culture.

The film's characterization of Norbu is subversive. On the one hand, it is consistent with the Fifth Generation's inclination to deliver rehumanization messages through traditionally negative characters. On the other, Tian's allegory of humanity alludes to the Han ideological reality and demands a rebel. Embodying humanity in a horse thief, the film makes Norbu both a hero for admiration and an underdog for sympathy. As a hero, he gallops with vigor. He worships Buddha. He doesn't kneel as his wife does when they are driven out of the tribe but silently starts an honest life. When natural disasters worsen and finally a lightning bolt destroys their mountain shelter, he stays calm. Even when he is fatally wounded during his last theft, he doesn't give up his aspiration toward heaven and Buddha: a trail of blood on-screen suggests that he has climbed onto the *tianzang* ground, the place for celestial burial, a Tibetan funeral ritual of feeding the corpse to eagles so that the soul may soar toward heaven.

In the meantime, Norbu has also always been a scapegoat. Early in the film, he is identified with *tianyang,* the goats that the Tibetans sacrifice to heaven: just as people drive *tianyang* uphill, Norbu is driven out of the tribe. His ousting also contrasts with the chief's *tianzang.* Whereas the chief is assured access to heaven, Norbu is barred from *tianzang* ground and fears that he may never find his way to heaven. His fear is choreographed into a long sequence of ghost dances while Norbu watches. Norbu also physically experiences this fear when, forced by the living, he carries the statue of *hegui* (a river ghost) into the water in a religious ritual while others throw stones at them. Norbu is overcome by this fear when his first son dies. Norbu dramatizes the pain of humanity: how he is torn between, on the one hand, the desire to be himself, to be heroic, and to live, and, on the other hand, the fear of being rejected by Buddha.

The allusion to the Han ideological reality leads to a series of paradoxes in characterizing Norbu, who draws out our conflicting responses to beauty and the cruelty of nature, sacredness and the folly of religion, as well as the significance and insignificance of human actions. Through these paradoxes, we sense how a pale and fatigued Han rationality projects onto the screen a piety that it both admires and resists. In a way, Norbu's difficult journey back to Buddha expresses the Han subjects' perplexed search for roots.

Suggested readings for *Horse Thief* are as follows:

Paul Clark 1987a
Yang Ping 1991
Xia Hong 1993
Tam and Dissanayake 1998, 35–45
Silbergeld 1999, 53–95

Director's Notes

I shot *Horse Thief* for audiences of the next century to watch. There are two aspects of any art: the popular and pure art. . . . [The relationship between a film director and the audience] should be a matter of getting close to each other. . . . Why can audiences abroad accept both commercial and art films, but not in China?

The theme of the film is very simple, in fact—the relationships between humanity and religion, and between humanity and nature. Its message is quite clear, too, otherwise how would we have been able to make sense of our fanaticism during the "Cultural Revolution"? (Qtd. in Yang Ping 1991, 127–28)

I believe that *Horse Thief* and my earlier work, *On the Hunting Ground,* are the only two films of their kind in Chinese filmmaking. I don't imply that they're very good films. But this kind of cinema, with nonprofessionals in the local area, and a very loose narrative, will probably never be done again in China.

My inspiration for *Horse Thief* came a lot from my experience in the Cultural Revolution. I think the Chinese people are all blindly following—not as in religion, and not like a cult of personality, but more like an ideal. This ideal is something that does not exist, that people don't experience themselves. It's not concrete at all. To me, when I was making the film, the most important question was how one faces life and death, as well as the conflict that evolves from religion. That's *Horse Thief.* (Qtd. in Robert Sklar 1994, 36)

Tian Zhuangzhuang, the Fifth Generation, and Minorities Film in China
Dru C. Gladney

Tian Zhuangzhuang, one of China's most controversial of the so-called Fifth Generation filmmakers, garnered the highest awards in both the Tokyo International Film Festival and the Hawai'i International Film Festival for his 1993 film, *The Blue Kite.* Tian's reputation was established by two earlier films that have been described as ethnographic and documentary—despite being feature films—due to their minority subjects and locations in Mongolia and Tibet. As Tony Rayns noted in his review of origins of the "New Chinese Cinema," these two earlier films, *On the Hunting Ground* and *Horse Thief,* were important departures from the earlier "minorities films" tradition in China in that they showed "the physical and spiritual lives of 'national minorities' in Inner Mongolia and Tibet, minus the usual mediating presence of Han Chinese" (Rayns 1991, 112). In this review article I suggest that the deliberate silencing of the Han Chinese voice in Tian's minorities films represents an important shift at the inception of the Fifth Generation films, a shift away from national narrative toward cultural critique. By moving his films to the geographic and national borders of China, Tian and many other filmmakers were able to effectively address critical issues gnawing at the heartland.

Tian's minority films have now been overshadowed by his award-winning *Blue Kite*. However, these earlier films, which became known as the Chinese Westerns, deserve attention precisely because they show the efforts of a young, relatively unknown filmmaker to address subjects both critical of Chinese culture and society, as well as highly visual in nature (both films were famous for their stunning cinematography and minimalist dialogue, didacticism, and narrativity).[1] Though Tian's films have been compared to others in the minorities films genres which preceded them, I argue here that Tian's films and the role they played in influencing and helping to form the Fifth Generation represent a significant departure, or to use Gayatri Spivak's term, a "strategic intervention" in apprising the state of the Chinese nation-state and film in China.

Tian's later film *Blue Kite* represents a more direct and devastating critique of the policies of the totalizing and vacillating Chinese state that led to such radical periods as the Great Leap Forward (1959–1961) and the Cultural Revolution (1966–1976) as well as the demise of the leading character's three successive marriages. And, if I read Tian correctly, he believes the state apparatus remains susceptible to similar swings of the political pendulum, which perhaps indicates why Tian is being sued by the central authorities for distributing the film abroad after it had been banned in Beijing. What is significant about Tian's earlier work is that he chose minority subjects to engage in a similar cultural and political critique, only more obliquely. In the political climate of the mid-1980s, it was still more acceptable to stand on the margins—literally, the geographical borderlands of Tibet and Mongolia—than to critique the state from the center. One may argue that *Blue Kite* is still a "safe" attempt at critical intervention, since it takes as its subject the officially excoriated Cultural Revolution. Even though Tian in almost soap-operatic style reiterates the now accepted themes about the mistreatment of intellectuals and the dissolution of families, it is still a topic not widely dealt with in the public sphere in China, and one that caused the government to ban the film and to sue Tian. By selecting such "marginal" and "safe" subjects, Tian clearly knew what he was doing.

Tian's *Horse Thief* is also worthy of another look because it represents an important, if not final, contribution of China's Fifth Generation filmmakers. These filmmakers are widely credited with having created a new era of filmmaking that deliberately used minority and rural settings as the backdrop for portraying larger constructions and deconstructions of Chinese society. Wu Tianming did it best perhaps in *Old Well* (Xi'an Studio, 1987), but Chen Kaige was most dramatic in *Yellow Earth* (Guangxi Studio, 1984). Zhang Yimou, perhaps the most famous of the Fifth Generation, created a similar distance by moving his films to rural and usually prerevolutionary China.[2] Tian set the *Horse Thief* in 1923 in minority areas to express his scathing critique of Chinese society and the roles its subject peoples play in cultural criticism. It is significant that Tian may have been the last of the Fifth Generation to have done so. Professor Zhou Chuanji, who taught many of the Fifth Generation filmmakers in the early 1980s at the Beijing Film Academy, stated that he believed *Horse Thief* was the last of the Fifth Generation films.[3] This was primarily due, Zhou argues, to the film's artistic quality, noncommercial nature, and reliance upon state funding. Later films by Zhang Yimou, Chen Kaige, and Tian Zhuangzhuang had substantially more funding, much of it foreign (from Hong Kong, Taiwan, and Japan), and were made with a view to international distribution and profits.

Horse Thief and Its Critics

Horse Thief stirred up extensive controversy in China, but for unexpected reasons. The subject matter was not the issue: the faraway, exotic minority subjects in *On the Hunting Ground* and *Horse Thief* confused and bored urban audiences. So much so that they stayed away in droves and wondered loudly why the state supported such obscurantism. The uproar in the popular press was not over content, but over the fact that Tian's films made so little money. They were duds. Chris Berry explains that most films in China make money not so much by box office sales as by selling prints to state-run theaters (1991, 114). An average film sells over one hundred prints. Tian's *Hunting Ground* sold two; *Horse Thief* sold seven. Both films were mainly purchased by the head offices of the China Film Corporation, who were already under contract to do so. The director Zhang Junzhao, maker of *One and Eight, Come on, China!,* and *The Lonely Murderer,* justified his more conservative and conventional films as necessary for political and financial survival. "*Horse Thief* and *On the Hunting Ground* lost tens of thousands of *yuan* between them, and no one went to see them," Zhang noted, and then asked, "Do you think the Xi'an Film Studio will dare to use him again?" (Berry 1991, 131). Zhang was apparently right, for Tian made his next film six years later, and financed it with outside sources.

Tian, and more importantly, his boss Wu Tianming, the head of Xi'an Film Studio from 1983 to 1989 and widely regarded as the father of the Fifth Generation filmmakers, argued that these were art films and deserved to be made "for art's sake." In Tian's defense, Wu Tianming explained: "There are three audiences that have to be satisfied in China. One is the government, one is the art world, and one is the ordinary popular audience" (Berry 1991, 122). He explains further that the government wants "reform films," the art world encourages "exploratory" films, and the popular market demands "Kung Fu" films. Tian's work was clearly too exploratory for China's popular market. In an interview with China's widely read film journal, *Popular Cinema,* Tian defended himself: "I shot *Horse Thief* for audiences of the next century to watch" (Yang Ping 1991, 127). Quoting Wu Tianming, Tian says he would rather "a film didn't sell a single copy, just so long as the quality is good." At least Tian's *Hunting Ground* sold two copies. "[T]he main problem," in Tian's opinion, "was the audience" (Yang Ping 1991, 127). Tian's *Horse Thief,* therefore, may mark the end of the Fifth Generation, not only due to its content, but also as a result of the subsequent institutional shift away from state funding dissociated from profit concerns, to films funded by transnational film corporations geared for financial success on the world market.

Minority Representation in China

I noted earlier that Tian's films indicated a significant departure from earlier minorities films in China. This category includes a wide range of state-sponsored educational and feature films set in minority areas and made from the 1950s through the mid-1970s. These films almost exclusively emphasize not only the color and beauty of their traditional cultures, but also their backwardness *(luohou)* and the oppression minorities experienced under the old feudal system, and their liberation by the communists. As such, they represent civilizing projects of the state not only for the minorities, but also for the cinematic public, who learn to distinguish between primitivity and modernity by viewing the "plight" of the minorities. In the 1950s documentary films were made in minority areas depicting strange and sometimes erotic customs, including matrilocal marriage and extramarital sex, often using minority and Han actors to dramatize what was thought to be "primitive" minority customs left over from the "feudal" era.[4] In the 1960s, feature films depicted the "soft" southwestern minorities such as the Yi, Miao, Zhuang, Dai, and Bai as the "happy, smiling" natives, including *Ashima (Ashima,* directed by Liu Qiong; Hiayan Studio, 1964), *Third Sister Liu (Liu sanjie,* directed by Su Li; Changchun Studio, 1960), *Five Golden Flowers (Wuduo jinhua,* directed by Wang Jiayi; Changhun Studio, 1959), and *Menglongsha Village (Menglongsha,* directed by Wang Ping and Yuan Xian; August First Studio, 1960) (Clark 1987a, 22–25). Northwestern minorities, such as the Uighur, Tibetans,

Mongols, and Kazakhs were featured in films that tended to stress "harder" themes such as class and political struggle in harsh and exotic environments, including *Visitor on Ice Mountain* (*Bingshan shang de laike,* directed by Zhao Xinshui, Changchun Studio, 1963), *Red Flower of Tianshan* (*Tianshan de honghua,* directed by Cui Wei, Chen Huaikai, and Liu Baode; Xi'an and Beijing Studios, 1964), and *Son and Daughter of the Grassland* (*Caoyuan ernü,* directed by Fu Jie; Beijing Studio, 1975). The disruption of the Cultural Revolution and the re-introduction of Western films into China in the late 1970s and early 1980s meant the decline of this traditional exoticization in service of the state. Chinese audiences could once again turn to imported films to satisfy curiosity about things foreign, and the minorities began to appear in Tian's and other films for different reasons.

Since the subject of *Horse Thief* is Tibet, an excellent contrast illustrating this transition in minorities film is provided by another film on Tibet, the classic *Serfs* (*Nongnu,* directed by Li Jun; August First Studio, 1963).[5] In this film, as in so many others, minorities are used to illustrate the social oppression in feudal society that the communists liberated in 1949. Here, a Tibetan serf, Jampa, is abused and humiliated by the son of his Tibetan landlord, who goes so far as to make him serve as his footstool, and even as his horse, with the son occasionally riding around on Jampa's back. Most of the film details this abusive relationship and the harshness and poverty of life on the Tibetan plateau, prior to direct Chinese Communist control.

Things change dramatically when the 1959 revolt forces the rebels, including Jampa's Tibetan overlords, to flee (presumably with the Dalai Lama leading the "oppressors" away from the "liberating" army). Jampa is forced at gunpoint to serve as his master's beast of burden, carrying him on his back as they flee. When Jampa resists by flinging off his oppressor, his master attempts to shoot him; a Chinese soldier intervenes and sacrifices his own life to save Jampa. Jampa returns to help the soldiers suppress the rebellion in Lhasa. He uncovers a cache of arms in a temple statue of a bodhisattva. Jampa himself thus becomes a metaphor of both the liberated and subjugated—an unwitting servant of yet another master, this time in an army uniform. *Serfs,* of course, makes it clear that the new masters in the green uniform are preferable to the old masters in saffron.

Serfs shares some key similarities with *Horse Thief* but the differences are more important. Both films exoticize the minority subjects, their lands, and life-worlds, but for very different reasons: one serves, the other challenges the Chinese state. One represents an attempt to "civilize" the primitive, the other suggests radical alterity, yet both claim to be ethnographic.[6] Jampa turns against his oppressor, and becomes subjugated to the state. The horse thief turns against his people, by preying upon them, and their retribution is based on their system of natural justice: he is abandoned to an ecosystem that he has violated by stealing from his own people, a nature that finally turns against him. The first film makes religion part of the oppressive feudal system, the second film naturalizes Tibetan religious experience, encompassing it within an exotic and harsh natural order that administers rewards and punishment. Both films use minorities in their quest to be politically and socially relevant to majority audiences who gaze at these minorities and the exoticized splendor of their surroundings.

The representation of the minority in these films and other public portrayals in China reflect an objectivizing majority nationality discourse that parallels the valorization of social and political hierarchy.[7] The widespread definition and representation of the minority as exotic, colorful, and primitive homogenize the undefined majority as united, mono-ethnic, and modern. Thus, although both *Serfs* and *Horse Thief* ostensibly use ethnographic subjects, they have little to do with Tibet, or the minorities themselves; they have much to do with the Han majority, and issues concerning their audience. The ethnic subjects in these and other minority films become modes for addressing controversial and sometimes taboo issues pertaining to the majority. The politics of representation in China reveal much about the state's project of constructing in the often binary terms of minority/majority an "imagined" national identity (B. Anderson 1991). *Horse Thief* suggests that we might learn much more about the construction of majority identity in China, and the state of society in general, by backtracking to the larger issues lying behind the film and the selection of minorities as its subjects.

China scholars have critiqued the often colorful and exotic portrayal of minorities in China as both demeaning to the minorities and supporting state policies (Diamond 1988; Thierry 1989). Such portrayals date back to imperial times (Eberhard 1982). Minorities have also played an important role in the formation of art history in China (Chang 1980; E. Laing 1988; Lufkin 1990). I suggest here that the representation of minorities in this exotic and romanticized fashion is more a project of constructing a majority discourse than of depicting the minorities themselves. Significantly, and here this study moves beyond Edward Said's critique of Eurocentric orientalism, the representation of minorities and the majority in Chinese art, literature, and media has surprising parallels to the now well-known portrayals of the East by Western orientalists, providing an alternative "oriental orientalism." This form of orientalism, and

the objectification of the minority Other and majority Self in China, is a "derivative discourse" (Chatterjee 1986, 10). It combines elements from not only
Chinese imperial traditions, but also Western (namely Marxist), and Japanese
ideas of nationalism and modernity. This approach rejects the dominant idea
that anyone who came into China—foreigner, minority, or "barbarian"—was
subject to assimilation, or "Sinicization" (Ch'en 1966; Lal 1970). In these typical configurations, Chinese culture was said to have absorbed and dissolved
foreign cultures. The commodification and objectification of minorities in China
is more than a response to consumer tourism and world capitalism, although
the market is certainly an important factor, particularly for the Fifth Generation
films that followed *Horse Thief*. Appropriation of the minorities provides the
state with symbolic and monetary capital (Bourdieu 1977, 6). The exoticization and representation of minorities is an enterprise that takes on an enhanced
salience with the rise of the Chinese nation-state and is central to its national-
ization and modernization project: a homogenized majority at the expense of
exoticized minorities.[8]

Backgrounding Minorities Film

The genre known as minorities film has played an important role in reforming
certain accepted norms of Chinese taste. Paul Clark, a noted critic of Chinese
film, argues that it is the "propensity of minorities film to explore normally
avoided subjects" that made them so successful and influential (1987a, 20). In
the Channel Four documentary, *New Chinese Cinema*, shown on British television, Wu Tianming, the director of the Xi'an Film Studio, where many of the
influential Fifth Generation filmmakers were working (including Zhang Yimou,
Tian Zhuangzhuang, and Chen Kaige), quoted the Chinese proverb, "When
there's no tiger on the mountain, the monkey is king," to suggest how distance
from the centers of power such as Beijing and Shanghai allowed his studio the
freedom for exploration.

Tian Zhuangzhuang defended his use of minorities as subjects for his films
precisely because they were exotic and different. He argued that people misunderstood his films because of the "foreign" subject: "It's an alien culture" (Yang
Ping 1991, 129). During an interview in the Channel Four documentary, Tian
Zhuangzhuang noted that although both *On the Hunting Ground* and *Horse
Thief* were dealing with exotic minorities, they were "actually about the fate of
the whole Chinese nation" (*New Chinese Cinema* 1988). Paul Clark argues that
the search for both "the exotic" and a "national style" *(minzu fengge)* generated minorities films (1987b, 11). Through the medium of the officially

approved film, Chinese national identity becomes clearly objectified in Tian's films. Objectifying the constructed minority as radically other, unrestrained, virile, beautiful, and at times brutally violent, also involves a critique of the repressed, bounded Han majority self.

Borderless Crossing: Exoticization in Chinese Film

Exoticization in Chinese film has important parallels to *National Geographic*'s portrayal of the exotic and erotic Other for a conservative readership which generally regards such portrayals of its Self as too extreme or even pornographic.[9] As Clark (1987a, 15–16) explains, "Film audiences could travel to 'foreign' lands without crossing the nation's borders." But there is more here than simple fascination with the exotic of *National Geographic*–style romanticization of the primitive, which one might argue is found in almost any society. In China, the state is intimately tied to, in control of, and a source of funding for the politicized process of portraying the Other (and in Tian's case, attempts to sue for damages). The critical question here is why the state explicitly supports such an enterprise. I argue that the politics of this representation of minorities is both an extension of political practices of the traditional Chinese state, and a product of China's emergence in the twentieth century as a nation-state.

In *Horse Thief,* Tian takes us to a faraway land to reveal the moral depravity of an overbureaucratized, urbanized Chinese core, which lacks beauty, vigor, and ritual. The pageantry, natural justice, and in the end, brutality of *Horse Thief* sends an unwelcome message to China's alienated urban populace. The film succeeds in convincing them that their lives are less spiritual, less natural, and tightly constricted by the vicissitudes of modernity. Yet the film also fails, precisely because its subjects are overexoticized, making them alien and unsympathetic to the audience. The message is too ambiguous; thus it was ultimately rejected by the broader population. Just as the singing and dancing, squeaky-clean minorities of an earlier genre failed to convince audiences that these people really were "liberated" by the party, and not just playing parts for a new director, so Tian's minorities films disappointed audiences: they both break with earlier representations of minorities and simultaneously reconstitute them.

The exoticized and even romanticized images of the harsh Tibetan landscape act to widen the gulf between the audience and the subjects of the film. Few in China could relate to Tian's portrayal of the uncrowded expanses, lawlessness, and isolation of Tibet and Mongolia. The distance between majority Self and minority Other is made unbridgeable. The absence of familiar Han cultural representations and characters makes the film alien and alienating to Han viewers. This is deliberate. Tian does not want his Han viewers to understand, establish empathy, or reach any commonality with his foreign subjects. He seeks to show alterity: by contrasting naturalized, primitive, and even barbaric minority life with the viewer's own domesticated, "modern," and "civilized" existences, Tian challenges the very basis of that contrast.[10] By the mid-1980s intellectuals in China had begun to openly readdress issues of urban alienation, democratization, sexuality, and cultural criticism that had been raised during the 1979–80 "democracy wall" movement and led to the 1986 and 1989 student democratic protests (Gladney 1996). The horse thief's freedom, disregard for the state and its laws, loyalty to his family and clan, and his close attachment to nature call into question assumptions and values of the film's audience: Is the modernized, urbanized, civilized life desirable and better? Only through driving the wedge between Self and Other as deeply as possible can Tian begin to force these issues on the audience. He certainly could not raise them directly.

In both the early minorities film genre and Tian's use of minorities in film, the minority subjects are still just that: subjects of a colonizing regime with a civilizing mission. And this project of civilization and modernization may be just as alien to the minorities as they are to the majority. Though Tian's film is more direct and critical of the state, it reaffirms the minority as a colonized, orientalized subject. As in earlier films, here the minorities speak Mandarin, though with a slightly northwestern accent. They have no "voice," literal or otherwise, of their own. The Tibetan language is reserved for singing, greeting, and cursing.[11] The Tibetans are shown to deal strictly in Chinese currency, language, and bureaucracy, readily accepting the Chinese administrative apparatus—the foreign overlordship of their land.

This issue, of course, is never politicized in these genres (lest they be even likelier candidates for the censor's knife), but in Tian's film, there is no device for even suggesting that it might be problematic for him. In both the earlier state-run minorities films and Tian's work, the minorities are useful and compliant subjects for larger projects that have more to do with issues concerning the majority *watching* the film than the minorities *in* the film.

Representing Minorities in the *Horse Thief*

Two cameos from *Horse Thief* epitomize Tian's manipulation of minority representation. I refer here to two scenes featuring the only other non-Tibetans in the film, Hui Muslim traders. Frequent travelers to Tibet have noted the extraordinary number of Muslim traders. These Hui Muslim merchants come from as far away as Qinghai, Gansu, Ningxia, and Xinjiang to exchange tea, religious objects, and manufactured items from inland China for hard currency, Tibetan handicrafts, and goods from India which are imported by Nepalese and Tibetan relatives in India. As elsewhere in China, the Hui are mediators in a small private economy that "fills the cracks of Chinese socialism" with Muslim entrepreneurialism (Gladney 1991, 149–60). Tian uses stereotypes for Muslims that are common throughout China. The film portrays Muslims as sly, stingy, and untrustworthy, especially in the first scene where they sell Tibetan goods at an exorbitant profit. The camera focuses on the bearded Muslim in white hat jingling and biting silver coins to be sure they are real, indicating mistrust of his clients. Furthermore, the Hui Muslim merchant readily sells Buddhist religious objects to Tibetans—anything to make a profit.

In the second and more dramatic encounter, three Muslim traders are surprised by Norbu and his accomplice on a distant trail and robbed at knifepoint of their goods and money. After being robbed, one Muslim feebly attacks Norbu with a small knife. Norbu later describes the wound as being inflicted by a dog. Norbu retaliates by attacking the Muslim with his more menacing Tibetan sword. Yet Norbu is compassionate in his victory: he offers money to the Muslims and donates most of the goods to the temple. The Muslim traders appear weak, cringing, and vindictive. The Tibetans by contrast are strong, ruthless, and possess a distinctive code of "honor among thieves." In a stateless region where the police are scarce and the laws of nature and clan prevail (laws to which Norbu ultimately succumbs), the Tibetans are clearly the masters of their harsh environs. Norbu may be a horse thief *(daoma zei),* Tian seems to imply, but he has more honor than these larcenous Muslims *(zei huihui).*[12]

Majority Agendas/Minority Subjects

Horse Thief begins and ends with close-up scenes of one of the grimmest realities encountered on the Tibetan plateau: the funerary rite of "sky burial." In both scenes we are given an intimate look at the Tibetan ritual of presenting the prepared corpse to be eaten by vultures, a practice believed to hasten one's eventual reincarnation or possible escape into the afterlife. While the corpse is not identified in either scene, the final scene suggests it is Norbu's corpse; and this is his punishment for stealing horses meted out by his kinsmen, and indeed, by nature itself. Despite his guilt at breaking the laws of the land, the film decisively portrays Norbu as a victim, not only of the vultures, but also of an environment so bleak that he is forced to steal in order to survive and support his family.

This tension between individual victimization and group survival, personal guilt and social exoneration, private attachment and public betrayal, thematically relates to the cataclysmic event intimately known by every viewer of the film in China: the Great Proletarian Cultural Revolution. Indeed, Zhou Chuanji and others have argued that the Cultural Revolution has set the Fifth Generation apart from its predecessors and successors. Tian joined the army during the Cultural Revolution and would have witnessed its excesses since the army was used to finally curb the escalating violence. Although the forty-one-year-old director was raised in a film family—both parents were actors and later officials in China's film industry—Tian did not enter the film world until he trained in the army as a still photographer, and then later as a cinematographer at the Beijing Agricultural Film Studio after he left the army at the end of the Cultural Revolution in 1975 (Berry 1991, 194–95). This is perhaps why his films stress the visual over the narrative. It also may suggest why the Cultural Revolution may serve as an important background to the film.

The Cultural Revolution is certainly a major theme that many younger directors have only recently begun to address, as in Chen Kaige's *Farewell My Concubine,* Zhang Yimou's *To Live,* and Tian Zhuangzhuang's *Blue Kite,* all banned in China. It may very well be that *Horse Thief,* which at the time could not deal with the Cultural Revolution explicitly, addresses it implicitly, serving as a grand metaphor for the brutal victimization of the Cultural Revolution, where the drastic shifts in party politics led to attacks not only between political factions, but between husband and wife, parent and child, friend and friend.[13] The harshness of the ecological environment of Tibet can be mapped against the brutality of the political territory of internal China, indicating to its audience that victimization is a natural expediency. And indeed, the final vulture scene might even indicate final exoneration. At one point during the film one of Norbu's clan members states that Norbu is so evil that even vultures would not consume his corpse. This final scene with Norbu as the probable victim may indicate that in the end he too will experience ritual rebirth. Might this be a hidden message of hope for Chinese society in general? If so, it was never noted by its critics.

We are left with a deeply complex film that few in China appreciated and even fewer attended. It became somewhat of a cult classic abroad for its revealing footage of life on the Tibetan plateau, but few have noted its significance either for China or for minority representation. Minorities are represented on film much as they are exoticized and stigmatized in the Chinese public sphere. It is just that Tian's exoticization has a point: cultural intervention at the center of Chinese society. Issues such as the Cultural Revolution, alienation, criminality, identity, religiosity, and spirituality were pressing concerns during the mid-1980s in China, and may still be today. But at the time, in order to explore these issues, Tian and other filmmakers, artists, and even tourists, had to travel to the margins—distant borderlands, which as this film shows, can reveal much about the heartlands of China.

Notes

This article was first published in *Public Culture* 8.1 (Fall 1995): 161–75. Copyright © 1995. All rights reserved. Reprinted by permission of Duke University Press.

1. Tony Rayns groups Tian's film with other Fifth Generation films, including Chen Kaige's *Yellow Earth* (Guangxi Film Studio, 1984), Zhang Zeming's *Swan Song* (Pearl River Studio, 1985), Wu Ziniu's *The Last Day of Winter* (Xiaoxiang Studio, 1986), and Huang Jianxin's *Black Cannon Incident* (Xi'an Studio, 1985). He argues they are all "new wave" for the following reasons: "They all minimize dialogue and trust their images to carry the burden of constructing meaning. They deliberately seek out subjects and angles of approach that have been missing from earlier Chinese films . . . a distinctively Chinese cinema, free of Hollywood and Mosfilm influences alike. Most important of all, though, they stand united against didacticism. They interrogate their own themes, and they leave their audiences ample space for reflection. After three decades of ideological certainty in Chinese cinema, they reintroduced ambiguity" (Rayns 1991, 112).

2. Until his most recent *To Live* (1994) and *Qiu Ju* (1993), both set in rural Shaanxi, Zhang Yimou's films all took place in prerevolutionary China, including *Red Sorghum* (1987) set in the Sino-Japanese war; *Ju Dou* (1990) set in rural Sichuan; and *Raise the Red Lantern* (1991) set in the early 1900s. For an excellent review of *Red Sorghum* that sets out themes often repeated in Zhang's later work, see Eugene Yuejin Wang (1989, 32–39).

3. Personal interview. I am grateful to Huang Hai-yen for arranging this interview with Professor Zhou Chuanji during his recent visit to Honolulu.

4. These films are no longer publicly shown and are now located in the archives of the Chinese Academy of Social Sciences, Institute for National Studies. These archives include such films as *Zouhun* (Moving marriage) shot among the Naxi (Nuoso), and other films on the Yi, Wa, and Miao in Yunnan, Guizhou, and Sichaun. For an excellent overview of Minorities Film in China, see Paul Clark 1987a.

5. This film is described in detail by Paul Clark (1987b, 96–99).

6. I am grateful to Michael Fischer for drawing my attention to the contrast in these strategies.

7. For a more extended discussion of minority/majority representation in China, see Gladney (1994).

8. This project has apparently met with success not only in China, whose census regularly divides the population into fifty-six distinct nationalities (*minzu,* a multi-vocal and prob-

lematic term; see Gladney 1991, 306–21), but also with Western scholars who readily accept the Han as China's ninety-four percent majority. See Eric Hobsbawm's classic restatement in his authoritative work, *Nations and Nationalism Since 1780,* describing China, Korea, and Japan as "indeed among the extremely rare examples of historic states composed of a population that is ethnically almost or entirely homogeneous." Hobsbawm continues: "Thus of the (non-Arab) Asian states today Japan and the two Koreas are 99% homogeneous, and 94% . . . of the People's Republic of China are Han" (1992, 66, fn. 37).

9. For an excellent deconstruction of the eroticized, exoticized image of the primitive in *National Geographic* see Lutz and Collins, *Reading National Geographic* (1993).

10. Tian reveals his deliberate ethnocentrism when he justified the horse thief's lawlessness as being part of his "alien" nature. When his interviewer points out that "horse-stealing is always wrong," Tian responds: "Horse-stealing is very common in Tibet, to the point where it's almost a profession. For reasons of physical geography and lack of economic development, horses are a form of currency in Tibet, and so horse-stealing happens a lot. For me to become a horse thief would be the same as becoming a carpenter, and I wouldn't feel there was any difference" (Yang Ping 1991, 130).

11. When I complained of the overusage of voice-over and dubbing in Chinese films, Zhou Chuanji suggested that the high rate of illiteracy in China ruled out using subtitles. Chinese characters on screen would not work because many Chinese could neither follow them, nor read them fast enough to keep up with the dialogue (even though in *Hunting Ground* and *Horse Thief* there is almost no dialogue). Perhaps to help correct this problem and reach a wider audience, recent Hong Kong films have begun to use not only English subtitles, but also Mandarin characters *and* special Cantonese characters as well, differing slightly from China's national script. These three lines of subtitles take up nearly one-third of the screen. Not much would be left of the screen if Tibetan or other indigenous languages were added.

12. This may be a play on the term for "thief," *zei,* which rhymes with, and is frequently combined with, *Hui* (pronounced *whey*). Hence the "horse thief" *(daoma zei)* is more crafty *(zei)* than the larcenous Hui *(zei Huihui)* with whom he interacts in the border regions.

13. See Anne F. Thurston's dramatic depiction of victimization in her account of the personal experiences of several prominent individuals and their families during the Cultural Revolution (1987).

Part Four

The Chinese Western
Roots Hidden in the Yellow Earth

Cuiqiao in *Yellow Earth (Huang tudi)*, directed by Chen Kaige, 1984. Courtesy of China Film Archive, Beijing.

I n 1983, Wu Tianming, the director of *Old Well,* became the head of Xi'an Film Studio, a lesser-known and smaller state studio with virtually no prestige and situated in China's distant midwest region. Eager for a breakthrough, Wu was ready to lead the tide that would change PRC filmmaking. In 1984, Zhong Dianfei, a film critic who had been a catalyst in renovating Chinese cinematic concepts, visited Xi'an Film Studio and suggested that the studio's journal be renamed *Chinese Western.* He wanted the studio to distinguish itself from the others by marketing a new kind of film that would be known as the Chinese Western—a Chinese version of the rough environment and tough-guy "cowboy" film.

The time was right for this kind of film. In the mid-1980s, the intellectual "oven" of the nation had been prewarmed by *wenhua re,* literally, in Chinese, a "cultural heat." Developed as a counter-discourse to the earlier ideological emphasis on class struggle, various explorations of broader cultural issues had emerged in the hope of better understanding China's past, present, and future. Certain of these explorations were known as "roots-searching," and they were initiated by a sense of crisis about China's political, social, and cultural status quo. Xi'an Film Studio's Chinese Westerns soon became a major cinematic version of roots-searching.

In promoting the Chinese Western films, Xi'an also co-sponsored the rise of Fifth Generation filmmaking. These young directors had already found their initial breakthrough at the even smaller and more remote Guangxi Studio with similar rough-type films as *One and Eight* and *Yellow Earth.* Now with Wu Tianming's arms open to them, they came to Xi'an and produced more critically acclaimed films. *Red Sorghum,* for example, won the Golden Bear Award in Berlin in 1988 and made Fifth Generation filmmaking an internationally known cinematic movement.

Compared with its Hollywood counterpart, the Chinese Western reflects a different cultural spirit. About this, Esther Yau notes: "While the American frontier appealed to the immigrants' evolutionist expansion of social and political organization over inanimate nature (according to Frederick J. Turner), the Chinese West evoked a non-aggressive self-reflection" (1987–88, 33). Unlike the American West that represents a wilderness awaiting conquering, the Chinese West presents not nature as wilderness but nature as containing a cultural alternative. The landscape here hides neglected history, legends, and folklore that need to be rediscovered, represented, and used as a mirror for the cultural center in looking at itself. Since the Chinese Western films showcased rough environments and tough guys to achieve this cultural purpose, let us focus on these two elements to illustrate the characteristics of this new genre.

If we use nature as a convenient term to refer to all the kinds of landscapes found in the Chinese Western films in particular and the roots-searching culture in general, Jing Wang has this to say about its heterogeneity:

> One can extrapolate endlessly from the nature cult in many orthodox *Xungen* [roots-searching] works. Perhaps this romantic syndrome is a manifestation of the displaced historical desire of the cultural subject denied its agency. In this light, the craving for the sublime may be nothing more than an allegory of the reconstructed National Subject in search of metaphorical means of empowerment. Or perhaps nature as a trope simply opens up the enclosed and oppressive sociopolitical space of quotidian reality in which the postrevolutionary subject still finds him- or herself helplessly fixed. (1996, 219)

The films in this section further illustrate this diversity. In *Yellow Earth*, the omnipresence of the earth itself overshadows and dwarfs the humans living on it. Clearly presented in a Taoist cosmology that believes that humans can only prevail by harmonizing with nature, the grand earth image in the film contrasts Chinese culture in two ways: first, with the Chinese revolution that defies nature with human will, and second, with the Chinese peasants' livelihood that has been overpowered by the domination of nature. The hope generated by these different responses to nature is to achieve a middle ground, a Taoist and Confucianist Golden Mean, one that might offer China a better future. With *Red Sorghum,* the desire for cultural renewal and empowerment becomes stronger. This desire is reflected, among other elements, in a confrontation between the fictitious landscape, where a Dionysian sorghum wine empowers individuality and free will, and a historical landscape, where a Japanese invasion reminds us of the urgency of Chinese cultural renewal. In *Old Well,* the harsh natural environment of a mountain village becomes a national allegory that, with a strong sense of ambiguity, attests to what people would, could, or have to do here. After all, in the Chinese Western, multifaceted nature plays crucial narrative roles that demand our attention.

As for the element of the rough guy, we need to examine it from the perspective of gender representation. In part two, we looked at how women in the PRC's early cinema were turned into politicized signifiers and how the gender experience was by and large ignored for, or at best subjugated to, the promotion of the Party's political agenda. In the conventions of socialist feminism, male characters who are not identical with state power are equally subjugated to the political agenda—and often via women. "If men also suffer from the need to submit to the demands of the state," Ann Kaplan reasons, "they are arguably emasculated by their situation. Given the prior phallic order, and given classical Oedipal rivalry with the Father, they may be harmed even more than women. State communism, in demanding male submission to the Law of the Father with little possibility for obtaining at least some parity with the Father position (as in free-enterprise capitalism), may produce men psychically damaged in deeper ways even than women" (1991, 153).

A film representing the socialist-feminist convention will serve as a point of departure to elaborate on Kaplan's reasoning. *Li Shuangshuang* (1962) is a film about family conflicts in the Chinese countryside. It tells the story of how Li Shuangshuang constantly fights with her husband, Xiwang, to eventually bring him in line with state interests in the socialist construction. Xiwang, the reformed husband, plays a typical, traditional conformist male. Better educated than most in the village, he wants to be a harmonizer in the life of the community and reminds us of a Confucian gentleman. Is he masculine? If we reflect on the spectrum of masculinity in traditional Chinese culture, we realize that masculine beauty seems to lie more in intelligence and gentility than in physical build and rough manners. Although the traditional metaphor of using *xiangcao* (a fragrant plant) to describe male beauty may appear a bit "sissy" to many today, the characters of this type, often known as *xiaosheng* (from a character type in traditional Chinese opera), have attracted female admiration in all kinds of legends and stories throughout Chinese history. In contrast, the characters on the other end of the spectrum, the rough guys, are often outlaws. Xiwang is basically a *xiaosheng,* and his role in the film shows that "socialist feminism" wants both to encourage and to revise the traditional masculinity. On the one hand, as women become the political signifier representing the Party's agenda, the conformist men's subjection to women in a reversed family structure aligns them with the same agenda as well. Although they function as obstacles to the agenda to begin with, they eventually need to display their conformity in order to be integrated into the new familial and social order. On the other hand, the dynamics of community life are changed: the conformist men need to revise their gentility and be absorbed into endless *douzheng,* or struggles, either between social classes or within a social class, to make sure that nobody in the community puts his own interest ahead of the state and the Party. In socialist feminism, while women give up their individuality through a political sublimity in representation, men do so with a certain servility.

The portrayal of the male characters in Chinese Westerns reverses that of a *xiaosheng;* men now generally have darker complexions, sturdier physical builds, and more personality. If we put Cuiqiao's father, the old peasant in *Yellow Earth,* side by side with Xiwang in *Li Shuangshuang,* we see the sharp contrast immediately. While Xiwang is fair-skinned, gentle, educated, well-dressed, articulate, and familiar with the Party's official discourse, Cuiqiao's father has a weathered complexion, a wrinkled face, a closed mouth that utters few words, a superstitious awe of nature, and no knowledge of the Party or the world beyond his mountain village.

This shifting of masculinity to the other end of the spectrum, to the rough type, occurred on-screen first in the national minority and Chinese Western genres, in somewhat alien *mise-en-scènes.* The shift was also often embodied in such unconventional protagonists as thieves, bandits, or murderers. In the Fifth Generation's precursory film *One and Eight,* a group of imprisoned bandits are turned into national heroes: as they are escorted to another prison, they demand the right to fight the Japanese invaders, to display their valor and humanity, and to die as martyrs. In another example, Zhang Yimou's *Red Sorghum* focuses on a rough-type seasonal worker and how he seduces the new bride of the owner of a wine distillery, rescues her by murdering her leper husband, weds her by showing his body to be stronger than those of the others working at the distillery, wins her back from bandits by courageously challenging their leader, and eventually loses her to Japanese bullets when the workers at the distillery ambush the invaders under his command. Here, the search for masculinity is merged into an allegory of national fate; both masculinity and nationality call for empowerment and revival. This need is expressed by Zhang Yimou when he describes how he feels like "an emaciated bug that has been starved for three years" in front of his legendarily masculine (read as "rough and tough") characters and how he worries about a "national resurrection" if people continue to be bug-like (Zhou Youzhao 1988, 12). The refigured masculinity indicates a gender desire to shed not only its earlier servility in representation but also its weak national-culture status.

The cinematic search for masculinity, when informed by such concepts as individuality, nationality, and resurrection, may often appear male-narcissistic, sexist, violent, and often at the expense of women. Wangquan, the young well-digger in *Old Well,* has the love of two women. An itinerant farm worker in *Girl from Hunan* seduces Xiaoxiao, the heroine, in a celebratory representation of human nature breaking cultural confinement and the girl reaching her sexual maturity. To a Western audience, many such scenes will remind them of classical Hollywood voyeurism, which renders the heroine as the object of the male gaze. Ann Kaplan, a Western feminist scholar, comments on how these scenes could be read "as a male fantasy of a female desire always awaiting arousal and happy to be satisfied by no matter whom" (1991, 148). She also notes how these scenes address "the contemporary male's unconscious desire for revenge on women for the new-found liberation in the communist state which insists on parity between the sexes in the public sphere" (148).

Eleven

Yellow Earth

(*Huang tudi,* dir. Chen Kaige, 1984)

Screenplay Zhang Ziliang
Cinematography Zhang Yimou
Producer Guangxi
Cast Wang Xueqi, as the soldier
Xue Bai, as Cuiqiao

In 1982, graduates of the first post-Mao class from Beijing Film Academy were assigned to various film studios, where they were expected to follow the rules of the studio system by starting their careers through a long apprenticeship. These young film artists, however, quickly became fed up with their assigned roles, the indoctrination process, and the film conventions of the time. They did not want to wait and found their breakthrough point at some provincial studios where there were less established directors. That same year, directing graduate Chen Kaige was on loan from Beijing Studio to Guangxi Studio where he joined his schoolmate, cinematography graduate Zhang Yimou, to try out their new ideas for shooting a film. The result was *Yellow Earth.*

The script assigned to Chen and Zhang to shoot was based on a prose article, "Echoes in the Deep Valley." It had a conventional subject matter: a Communist soldier ventures out from Yan'an into the neighboring countryside to collect folk songs. Chen and Zhang did not care much for the script but were very impressed by the land and the people they encountered while searching for a shooting location. Although they did not rewrite the script, the film turned out a far cry from the original. In the finished product, the presence of the land competes with the presence of the soldier. Eschewing conventional socialist realism, Chen and Zhang lent richer meanings to various images on their screen by emphasizing narration and visual impact. Although it did not do well at the box office in China, *Yellow Earth* proclaimed to the international community that the new Chinese cinema had arrived; it won numerous awards at international festivals and has ever since been considered the visual manifesto of the Fifth Generation filmmakers.

Suggested readings for *Yellow Earth* are as follows:

H. C. Li 1989
Rey Chow 1990
Yau 1987–88
Berry and Farquhar 1994
Tam and Dissanayake 1998, 11–22
Silbergeld 1999, 15–52

Director's Notes

We were working with the idea that life in Shaanbei, the northern region of
Shaanxi Province, could be equated to the position that China occupies in the
contemporary world. I wanted to express how the Chinese have lived for many,
many years. The location is a microcosm. That place is one of the most backward places I know, and China is backward.

We didn't do a lot of preproduction planning. Everything we shoot is in
Zhang Yimou's head. He didn't draw or paint anything. We didn't use a story
board. I don't agree with that approach as a working method . . . [but] we have
a great deal of trust of one another.

That broad, yellow land . . . had to become a vital part of the film. . . . The
land is the mother. The people who live on it have no way of changing it, no way
of transforming it. The earth is thick, but not fertile. It's beautiful, but it doesn't
grow crops. There are two things you can see here. First, the planting of the
soil, and second, warfare. . . .

It was very important for us to use cinematography as the basic means for
expressing the situation there and our feelings about the place, the poverty, and
slow pace—all its characteristics. (Qtd. in Semsel 1987, 136–39)

The "Hidden" Gender in *Yellow Earth*
Mary Ann Farquhar

Yellow Earth is regarded as a pioneering work in modern Chinese cinema. It
focused international attention on the burgeoning Chinese film industry; it influenced other young directors, known as "the fifth generation," whose collective
output in the eighties is a byword for the new exploratory Chinese cinema. One
of these directors, Tian Zhuangzhuang, said in 1986:

If it wasn't for *Yellow Earth,* then there wouldn't have been the whole debate about film aesthetics . . . [the film] represents the future of Chinese cinema now. (Yang Ping 1991, 127)

Tian's point is that *Yellow Earth* is "different." It was this difference which initially alienated and challenged Chinese audiences. For decades they were habituated to stereotyped storylines with overt political messages. But *Yellow Earth* emphasizes imagery over plot, symbolism and song over dialogue, and ambiguity over explicit didactic function. The director, Chen Kaige, put it most simply: "a single word sums up the essence of the *film's style: 'concealment'* (cang)" *(1984, 2).*

How, then, does an audience "read" a film which consciously "conceals" its meanings. Esther Yau uses western analyses of the narrative strands in the film but concludes that this reading does "not locate *Yellow Earth's difference* from other interesting Chinese films made during the same period" (1987-88, 32) (my emphasis). Throughout the article, she tantalizes one with allusions to alternative Chinese, that is, Daoist elements, which undermine her "western analysis." She refers to Chen Kaige's quote (it is actually a misquote) from the Daoist classic, *Dao de jing,* on the film's aesthetics:

Great music has no sound *(Da yin wu sheng).*
The great image has no form *(Da xiang wu xing).*[1]

From Chen Kaige's own perspective, the film may be read through key symbols and principles of Daoist cosmology, which traditionally regulated and explained the human and natural worlds and their inter-relationships, and constitute the informing philosophy for traditional Chinese art. Indeed, the natural world dominates this film. As one commentator wrote: "the main characters are not just people, but the yellow earth itself from which the Chinese people emerge."[2]

We could schematize the *Dao,* or way of life, concealed in *Yellow Earth* as shown in the figure on page 222. The narrative focuses on human relationships with each other and with nature, that is, heaven, man, earth, and the seasons. As Yau suggests, the narrative strands are inadequate to explain the film's meaning. The deeper meaning is embedded in visual images of sky and sun (male), and earth and water (female), which surround and determine the human stories within a hidden Daoist framework.

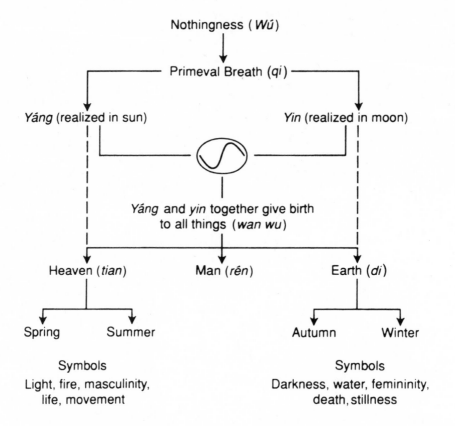

Nothingness (*Wú*)

↓

Primeval Breath (*qi*)

Yáng (realized in sun)   *Yin* (realized in moon)

Yáng and *yin* together give birth
to all things (*wan wu*)

Heaven (*tian*)   Man (*rén*)   Earth (*di*)

Spring   Summer   Autumn   Winter

Symbols   Symbols
Light, fire, masculinity,   Darkness, water, femininity,
life, movement   death, stillness

The two key principles of Chinese cosmology are *yang* (the male principle) and *yin* (the female principle). The superficial storyline is a Communist literary cliché: a Party cadre comes to a backward rural area in Shaanxi in 1939 to collect folk songs and re-work them for the anti-Japanese war effort.[3] He represents the possibilities of revolution and action and so belongs to the world of *yang*, which in Daoist cosmology corresponds to heaven, light, fire, masculinity, life and movement. But the film unwraps the package to reveal the hidden world of *yin*, the female principle realized in earth, darkness, water, death and stillness. The dominant images in the film are earth and water, the yellow earth of the title and the Yellow River, which nurtures, destroys and indeed symbolizes the Chinese people, according to Chen Kaige (1984, 2). The film ends with death, the drowning of the only female character, Cuiqiao, and crop failure through drought. The symbolic world of *yin,* the hidden gender, challenges the bright, active world of *yang* and by inference proclaims cosmological disharmony.

The Hidden Structure of *Yellow Earth:* Yin

Yellow Earth is adapted from an earlier story. Chen Kaige and members of the film crew went to northern Shaanxi (Shaanbei) in the heartland of China for background research. There they confronted the "mother" of Chinese civilization, the middle reaches of the Yellow River. "Early one morning, we saw an old man drawing a pail of water from the river's edge; from that moment we knew how the film would be and how to write it. For thousands of years, people have drawn water from the Yellow River. . . . In the film, the person who embodies this ideal strength is the main female character, Cuiqiao. . . . the river which drowned her is the same river which nurtured her" (Chen Kaige 1984, 2).

Whether intentionally or not Kaige sees the river as a mother and substitutes a young girl for the old man as the symbol of Chinese civilization. The feminine emphasis in the film is central to its conception, as well as its structure.

But *yang* and *yin* in Chinese myths are not the exclusive property of one sex. Rather, they are principles manifest in all things *(wan wu),* and cosmic order, including its repercussions on the natural and human worlds, depends on maintaining a harmonious relationship (Saso 1972, 8–15). Thus, the two rituals in the film, the (Yan'an) Drum Dance in its original form and the Rain Ceremony, for example, are rites which placate the gods and so ward off drought and pestilence. The *yang/yin* structure of the film is not one of fixed gender confrontation, or simple patriarchy, but one of disharmonious relationships.

The time span of the film supports this view. The film begins in early spring and ends in summer. Throughout China, the lunar year and its festivals and rituals were divided into two periods. The first (spring and summer) was dominated by the principle *yang,* ruled by heaven, and was the period of planting and growth of the crops. The second (autumn and winter) was dominated by the principle *yin,* ruled by earth and water, and was the period of harvest and rest (Saso 1972, 30). The action of the film takes place when *yang* has been reborn and reaches its zenith: early spring *(chu chun)* in Scene 1; the beginning of summer in the fourth month when Cuiqiao is unwillingly married out to an old man in Scenes 44 to 52; summer in Scene 56 just prior to Cuiqiao's death; high summer in Scene 67 where the director notes that it is to be played slowly "to increase the feeling of the molten heat" of the sun (in Chinese *taiyang* or "great *yang*").[4] This leads into the second last scene where the all-male peasants pray for rain to the Dragon King, the traditional "symbol of the productive force of moisture, that is of spring, when by means of genial rains and storms all nature renewed itself" (Charles Williams 1931, 131). The imagery is stark: a fiery sun and no water. As with the superficial story noted in the introduction, *yang* predominates but, in a reversal of the symbol, brings not life but death and drought.

The festivals and rituals in the film support this analysis. The first, in Scenes 13 and 14, is a wedding ceremony and the songs suggest that this joining of a man and woman is a natural and happy event.

> Pairs of carp drift in the stream,
> Pairs of goats run on the hillside,
> Pairs of plump pigs root in the trough,
> Fortune was smiling
> On this newly-wed couple.
>
> (Film Script, 110–11)

The pairing of natural and human images is a feature of Shaanbei folk songs and emphasizes the links between nature and people's lives in rural China. But Kaige's notes in the film-script state that "feudal weddings were happy on the outside but tragic on the inside" and this is shown, not by explicit statement but by the colors: red for happiness and *yang,* and black and white for unhappiness which is the color of the men's clothes (Film Script, 103). The bridegroom is thirty years older than the bride and Cuiqiao, a spectator, sees her own future as a young wife of an old man prefigured in these scenes. Her piteous songs in the next scene suggest natural and unseasonal abnormalities and then focus on her own situation:

> The ice in the Yellow River won't melt in June,
> It is my father who forces me to marry,
> As no grain is round like the pea,
> So girls' lives are the worst you can see,
> Poor girls, girls, oh.
>
> (Film Script, 112)

The second festival is Cuiqiao's own wedding. She has pleaded with Gu Qing to get permission to allow her to go to Yan'an and so escape her fate by trading her wedding shoes for straw army sandals. But he returns too late. Whereas the earlier wedding concentrated on its social ritual, this wedding focuses on Cuiqiao's own misery, particularly on her wedding night where all we see is a rough peasant male hand lifting Cuiqiao's veil and then her face full of fear. When Cuiqiao next appears she is running away to Yan'an and it is the first time she is explicit to others about her own life: "I am desperate *(ku),*" she says to her brother, Hanhan (Film Script, 185). For Cuiqiao, who drowns crossing the river to Yan'an, her wedding is all tragedy and no happiness—it brings death.

The third ritual, in Scene 53, is the Drum Dance at Yan'an. It is full of movement and vitality and is the only "lively" *(dong)* scene in the whole film.[5] It is also all-male and celebrates the vigor of *yang* and soldiers off to war.

The fourth ritual is the Rain Prayer ceremony at the end of the film following Cuiqiao's death. Yau claims that these all-male scenes, like the Drum Dance, celebrate "the strength and attraction of *yang*" (1987–88, 29). The prayers to the Dragon King for water are, I would argue, depicted much more ambiguously. Again, Chen's notes show that the Rain Prayer sequence is to be played as a contrast to the Drum Dance; "the Drum Dance is full of movement, the Rain Prayers are full of quietness" (Film Script, 193). The prayers are for rain to the Dragon King, symbol of moisture and sustenance or *yin,* as already noted. Thus the Rain Prayer scene is pervaded with sadness, quietness, death, the absence of water and the absence of women, all characteristics (in their presence or absence) of *yin*. The film ends with dearth of *yin*, not strength of *yang,* and crop failure through drought, not growth and maturation.

The human drama in *Yellow Earth* reflects this cosmic and seasonal disorder and the death of *yin*. The characters are Gu Qing, the Party cadre and the three members of the poor peasant family he stays with: the father, Cuiqiao, his twelve year old daughter and Hanhan, his young son. All the males are kindly, Gu Qing representing revolution and hope, the father embodying an age-old patriarchy and Hanhan offering a silent empathy to Cuiqiao. The plot follows Cuiqiao's story and reveals her feelings through the songs she sings which "fill the film's sound track—musical signifiers, narrating the sadness and beauty of *yin*" (Yau 1987–88, 29).

Songs and *Yin* in *Yellow Earth*

The collection and re-writing of folk songs is central to Chinese Communist literary theory. It was called "new wine in old bottles" and writers were to take traditional popular literature and art and re-write them with a revolutionary content. In this way the concealed folk tradition was to be made articulate and revolutionary. Chinese audiences would be fully aware of this context as revolutionary popular literature is the cornerstone of Mao Zedong's famous "Yan'an Talks on Literature and Art" (1942).

The discussion in the fields between Gu Qing and the peasant father sets the framework:

Father: What are you doing here?

Gu: Collecting Shaanbei folk songs.

Father: Sour songs?

Gu: Can you sing?

Father: Only when I'm in the mood.

Gu: There are hundreds and thousands of folk songs here. Can you remember them?

Father: I can because times are hard. Why are you collecting them?

Gu: When we find new songs we put new words to them. Let them be sung in the army by girls of Cuiqiao's age. People will know why we are suffering, why women are beaten and why workers and farmers need a revolution. When the Eighth Route Army hear the songs they fight the Japanese more bravely.

(Film Script, 140)

Shaanbei folk songs are called "sour songs" *(suanqu),* a term which emphasizes the hardship of peasant life in this region. The film, as artistic artifact itself, is set in the formative period of Chinese Communist artistic theory and practice and questions its effectiveness.

The initial two songs are sung by males. The first is a Communist stereotype about the bitter life of itinerant workers, laid off during the cold winter months. The second, partly quoted above, is a traditional wedding song. Thus, the first two songs introduce the world of *yang,* the need for revolution contrasting to feudal patriarchy in a rural setting.

The audience soon discovers, however, that there is a beautiful singer among the girls because Gu Qing asks Cuiqiao if she knows her. Gu Qing, in fact, suspects but never discovers that the girl is Cuiqiao herself. In ideological terms Gu Qing never utilizes the region's most important resource. It remains hidden from the Party, but not from the audience who hears Cuiqiao's songs sung for herself alone. At one stage she sings:

> The cadre living with us doesn't know I can sing,
> Like the eighteen green willow shoots,
> I have my own stories to tell,
> But I don't know, I don't know how to tell him,
> Poor girls.

(Film Script, 145)

The father, son and Cuiqiao finally sing for Gu Qing; the men's songs are public and about feudal marriages but the content of Cuiqiao's "public" song has been influenced by Gu Qing's message of revolution and escape. Whereas her sad, secret "sour" songs are about her own inner feelings *(xinshi)* and powerlessness, this public song is a plea to save her but she realizes that "folk songs will save no-one, not even me" (Film Script, 170). She dies singing the revolutionary song that Gu Qing has taught her and Hanhan:

> With sickle, axe and hoe,
> We open a road for peasants to go,
> Upon the wall the spotted rooster flies,
> Only the Communist Party can save the people's lives.
>
> (Film Script, 186–87)

She disappears in the middle of the word, "Communist." Hence, the male world of revolutionary ideology brings disappointment and death to Cuiqiao. This is further reinforced by the songs at the end of the film. The first is the song at the Rain Ceremony, which pleads with the Dragon King, not the Party, to "save the people's lives." The second is a repeat of Cuiqiao's last "revolutionary" song, disembodied between parched earth and empty sky, between the two major symbols of *yin* and *yang*. The song, imagery and symbolism leave a powerful impression of the emptiness and irrelevance of Party promises to ordinary people. In practice, but not in theory, the Party (Gu Qing) does not listen to the people (Cuiqiao's songs) even though "the mass line" was yet another cornerstone of Communist ideology.

Cuiqiao's songs are, therefore, the hidden component of the traditionally submerged folk tradition. Scene 21 is an example of Cuiqiao's hidden inner world where the cinematography and the sounds combine to deepen the feeling of stillness and darkness, qualities of *yin*. A single light shows Cuiqiao's face as she sits singing softly while she spins in the night. The whirring of the spinning wheel, a symbol of women's work for centuries, is the background accompaniment.

> Pairs of pigeons fly across the sky,
> Who is it that I miss the most?
> None but that mother of mine.
> Worthless as the melons in the valley, the gourds on the hill,
> I don't want to marry so I was beaten,

Beaten, oh poor girls.
Like a square purse embroidered but round inside,
If I don't marry my life may be bitter, but to me more sweet,
The spotted rooster sits on the window sill,
But I have no-one to tell, to tell, of these miseries,
Oh, poor girls!

(Film Script, 126)

In the notes in the film script, Cuiqiao is not desperately sad, perhaps because sadness is her everyday life. She listens to see she is alone but this is played ambiguously, perhaps she wants someone to hear. For such a poor peasant girl, "songs are her dreams" (Film Script, 126).

Cuiqiao's loneliness is echoed in references to the other women in her family, dead or married out. Her mother has died. Cuiqiao has been engaged since childhood and the betrothal money used to pay her mother's funeral costs and her brother's engagement. She is financially, not just culturally, trapped. Her elder sister has been married out; because she was beaten she ran away to her maternal home but was sent back to her husband. The lives of these women show Cuiqiao her own fate.

The father's song, sung for Gu Qing, generalizes these particular women's lives.

In the month of January, her big eyes open wide,
Her crescent brows are like bending bows,
You'll be saddened by the story I will tell,
Engaged at thirteen,
Married at fourteen,
At the age of fifteen, she became a widow,
For three days loudly she cried,
And everyone sighs,
For three days quietly she cries,
Then she drowns herself in the well.

(Film Script, 160)

Again, the song foretells Cuiqiao's early marriage and drowning. There is no escape except suicide for women in feudal China. Liberation and Yan'an offer the only alternative.

Hanhan's song is also about marriage from the girl's point of view but in this case the girl is married out to a child bride-groom, a "wet-a-bed."

When the pomegranate flowers, the leaves start showing,
My mother sold me off, without me knowing.
All I ever asked for was a good man to wed,
But what I've ended up with was a little wet-a-bed.
When you pee, I'll also pee,
Curse you, you can pee with me.
In spring next year, when flowers blossom red,
Frogs will start croaking under the bed.
Right to the East Ocean flows a river of pee,
To the Dragon King's palace under the sea.
The Dragon King laughs as he hears the pee:
"This little wet-a-bed is in the same line as me."[6]

Whereas Cuiqiao's songs are lingering and yearning, and the father's is fatalistic, Hanhan's song is ribald and hilarious. Nevertheless, the men in the family understand and sympathize with women's lives, offering different perspectives on Cuiqiao's own sadness. They are not enemies but both feudal and revolutionary societies "have their rules" *(you guiju)*, and both societies in this particular film offer Cuiqiao no escape. She does, however, try to escape and it is this which Chen Kaige says gives the film "hope" (1984, 2). But it is a very slim hope. In the end, everything soft, nurturing and maternal has disappeared or died.

Thus the men's songs wrap around the songs about women's lives and all these songs reverberate in the silence and vastness of the yellow earth and sky which surround the human lives from birth to death. It is this silence and emptiness which is a major feature of *Yellow Earth* and belongs to Daoist aesthetics.

Daoist Aesthetics and *Yin* in *Yellow Earth*

As in traditional Chinese landscape painting, the natural world overwhelms the depiction of its human inhabitants. The film begins with a shot of earth *(yin)* and sky *(yang)*, with the bare yellow loess hills initially dominating, then panning towards the sky before returning to the earth with its shifting horizons. The cinematography is simple, elemental and starkly beautiful. On the low horizon walks Gu Qing (sky dominating) and the camera slowly focuses on him as he hears a lingering folk song and takes out his notebook to record it. Within this forbidding landscape, Gu Qing offers the possibility of liberation in the Communist literary stereotype of this story.

The film ends with similar scenery but in reverse. In the Rain Ceremony, Gu

Qing once more appears on the horizon, continually coming but never arriving, and Hanhan strives to reach him against the surging crowd of worshipers. The following final scene "replays" the opening, a shot of sky and earth panning towards earth. There are no human inhabitants. Only the sound of the dead Cuiqiao's voice, full of desire and recorded with eerily beautiful echoes, fills the space between earth and sky. The song repeats that the Party will save the People but the audience knows by now that it has not saved these particular people. A parched earth and relentless sun have destroyed people's livelihoods, just as a rigid system has destroyed people's lives. Emptiness and space take on different meanings in their different contexts.

Emptiness or "nothingness" is a key concept in Chinese philosophy and aesthetics. In Daoist philosophy "nothingness" *(wu)* gives birth to the world, through "primeval breath" *(qi)* which forms the two principles *yin* and *yang,* the three sources, heaven, earth and man, the four seasons and so on. The union of *yin* and *yang* produces the myriad creatures. "Nothingness" or space in Chinese philosophy is, therefore, charged with the ultimate positive potential for creation; it is the force which makes manifest and defines all matter. Ryckmans explains the implications for Chinese aesthetics:

> "Nothingness" corresponds to what Western philosophy would call "being." "Being" can only be grasped in its hollowness: it is only its absence that can be delineated—in the same fashion as an intaglio seal shows its patterns through a blank: it is the absence of matter that reveals the design. The notion that the Absolute can only be suggested through emptiness had momentous implications for Chinese aesthetics. [The poet] does not explain, he does not narrate—he makes us see and feel directly. [The best painter] writes the meaning of things (instead of describing their appearances or shapes). The ideal painting is achieved not on paper, but in the mind of the spectator.
>
> This point leads us into another theme: the active function of emptiness—the role played by "blanks" in painting, by silence in music, the poems that lie beyond words. (Leys 1983, 6, 7, 13, 14, 15)

"Blanks," silence, meaning beyond words: all these are features of *Yellow Earth.* If we rethink the opening and closing scenes of the film, heaven, earth and man, then the reading becomes charged with a symbolism beyond the tangible images.

The shots of natural scenery, then, operate as "blanks" which give extra meaning to the more crowded images of the people's lives. Another example is the scene of Cuiqiao's death. The first shot is of the moon over the river at night, all characteristics of *yin*. Then we see Cuiqiao, desperate but not so desperate that she does not remember to give presents to Hanhan and think of others. Hanhan breaks his silence to stop her crossing the dangerously eddying river, we hear her song break and Hanhan's heartrending cry, "Sister." Then we see again the swirling waters of the river now empty of Cuiqiao and the boat. The inference is she has downed. Thus, the moon, night and water are the images beyond discrete form which surround and shroud the human drama. The predominant sound is that of flowing water which, in the *Dao de jing*, represents both *yin* and the power of *Dao* which seemingly soft and fluid overcomes all else.

Silence is another feature of *Yellow Earth* which sharpens the sounds, whether song or dialogue. As Kaige said, "great music has no sound" or no sound itself reverberates into silence which gives it shape. There are many such instances in the film. Cuiqiao's ritual of drawing water, for example, or Gu Qing's growing intimacy with the family through wordlessly sharing the work: sweeping the courtyard, drawing water, sewing, ploughing. But the explicit human focus of this silence is Hanhan. Initially, he will not answer Gu Qing's questions and Cuiqiao explains that he does not like to talk. Gradually, he absorbs Gu Qing's words, smiles when Gu Qing caresses his head and, finally, sings for him and learns a revolutionary song. But, most importantly, his silent knowledge and acknowledgment of Cuiqiao's life give her an audience within the film; her songs echo in his silence. Her death is followed by his attempt to run, silently again, towards Gu Qing who appears like a mirage during the Rain Ceremony. Brother and sister both yearn for the liberation offered by the Party, Cuiqiao in song and explained action, Hanhan in silence and visualized action.

The human silences are reflected in the larger lack of response by both the Party (Cuiqiao's plight) and the natural world (the Dragon King's refusal to answer the peasants' prayers). The natural world, river, earth and sun, are pitilessly regardless of human plight, and placating rituals or Party rhetoric are powerless against these forces.

A Daoist reading of *Yellow Earth* gives a meaning that is seen and felt directly, a meaning beyond the images and words. The complexity and depth of the human lives are rendered in stark images against the vast backdrop of the natural world. Minimalized tone, color and composition are reminiscent of the restraint of classical Chinese painting. Songs and silence overlay the imagery and evoke the lyricism and elusiveness of traditional Chinese poetry. The relationships are not overt or explicit; Chen Kaige stated that the manipulation of the plot was to be concealed: like "reaching the opposite bank under water" (1984, 2). The full quote from the *Dao de jing* emphasizes the ambiguity and ephemeral nature of things, including the *Dao* which is "hidden and nameless, yet . . . supports all things and brings them to fulfillment" (Waley 1988, 193). In *Yellow Earth* the principles of *yin* and *yang* and, therefore, the very cosmos are out of harmony. These principles are not rigidly fixed to any human gender although Cuiqiao's story and representation are clearly aligned to the characteristics of *yin*. *Yang* symbols are articulated and explicit in the human world but *yin*, the feminine principle, is repressed and ignored. It is the "hidden" gender.

Conclusion

It was apparently trendy to use Daoist allusions in the mid-eighties when *Yellow Earth* was made.[7] But an analysis of the film suggests that Chen Kaige and Zhang Yimou, the cinematographer, took the possibilities of Daoist aesthetics seriously in this film. Indeed, by resuscitating and creatively applying traditional Daoism to Chinese cinema they produced a film which is stunningly "different" from the usual Communist product and unusually rich in its layers of meanings. Indeed, their very success was a challenge to the Marxist aesthetics represented by Gu Qing in the text which have ruled all Chinese artistic production, including cinema, since the early forties. This is not to say that a Daoist reading of *Yellow Earth* is the only valid reading but an approach that offers interpretations outside the usual western and Chinese commentaries.

Notes

This article was first published in *Screen* 33.2 (1992): 154–64. Copyright © 1992 by *Screen*. Reprinted by permission of Oxford University Press.

1. Yau 1987–88, 24 and 32. Quoted in Chen Kaige 1984, 2. The quote is from Chapter 42 of the *Dao de jing* and the first line should read "Great music has the faintest *(xi)* sound." See Carus 1898, 73, 119, 308.

2. Ni Zhen, "*Huang tudi* zhihou" (After *Yellow Earth*) in SWC (Shanghai wenyi chubanshe) 1987, 196.

3. See the synopsis of the story from Ronin Film.

4. "*Huang tudi* (Dianying wancheng taiben)" henceforth referred to as Film Script, in SWC (Shanghai wenyi chubanshe) 1987, 189.

5. Film Script, 179. Chen Kaige's notes.

6. Film Script, 147–48; translated in G. Barmé and J. Minford 1986, 256–57.

7. Told to me by Geremie Barmé, coauthor of *Seeds of Fire*; see also Kam Louie 1989, 76–90.

Twelve
Old Well
(*Lao jing,* dir. Wu Tianming, 1987)

Screenplay Zheng Yi
Cinematography Chen Wancai, Zhang Yimou
Producer Xi'an
Cast Zhang Yimou, as Wangquan
Liang Yujin, as Qiaoying
Lü Liping, as Xifeng

I n 1987, while the younger Fifth Generation directors were about to capture international attention, their "sponsor," the Fourth Generation filmmaker Wu Tianming, produced an equally innovative film that joined the breakthroughs not only in filmmaking but also in the cultural scene of the time. The film, *Old Well,* won top prizes at the 1987 Tokyo Film Festival and at China's eighth Golden Rooster Awards.

Since he had become the head of Xi'an Film Studio in 1983, Wu Tianming had been known for his crucial role in promoting a special genre in China's post-Mao new cinema, that is, the Chinese Western. *Old Well* furthered his earlier exploration in this genre in *Life,* a rather emotive tale about a young man's love and hate for his village roots and his land. *Old Well,* also set in a remote mountain village, is a communal saga of fighting for survival. It has a broader national-culture implication with symbolism functioning on all levels of its narration. Adapted from roots-searcher Zheng Yi's novel of the same title, the film illustrates how the Chinese Western participated in the contemporary roots-searching and cultural retrospection *(wenhua fansi)*. Stylistically, even with its strong reliance on symbolism, the film became the emblem of the 1980s' documentary aesthetics, a realistic antidote to the revolutionary hyperbole and artificiality that had once, especially during the Cultural Revolution era, dominated Chinese filmmaking.

Just as he had been good at encouraging young directors to try out their innovations, Wu also discovered Zhang Yimou's acting potential before the latter embarked on a successful career as the by now best-known Fifth Generation director. When the camera was about to roll on *Old Well,* Wu was still not satisfied with the candidate for the male lead, deciding that he shouldn't be so radiant but rather should look as thin and undernourished as his cameraman, Zhang Yimou. Upon this random comment, Zhang was asked to give the role a try, and Wu decided that he had finally found the right man. Zhang won the Best Actor award at 1987 Tokyo Film Festival for his acting in this film.

Suggested readings for *Old Well* are as follows:

Eugene Yuejin Wang 1988
Silbergeld 1999, 53–95

Director's Notes

I believe it's easier, after a film is shown, to win the viewers' applause than to keep them seat-bound, not knowing what to say about the film. We didn't want to make *Old Well* a tearjerker but wanted it to stimulate viewers' thinking. . . .

Honestly, I am not sure what the central theme of *Old Well* is. . . . The central theme of a film should contain multiple meanings; that is, it should represent different values, should allow these values to clash with each other, and should let viewers think and make their own decision—they can accept whatever they like from their perspective and criticize whatever they reject. . . .

Old Well is intended to demonstrate, culturally and historically, the development, current changes, and future prospects of the psychological composition of the Chinese. [The film is set against three such compositions.] (1) *Ethics:* China has long been a country of high ethics, which, since ancient times, have been higher than anything else. This is reflected in such sayings as "To keep the heavenly ways and to destroy human desires." If someone damages her reputation, she doesn't need to live anymore. . . . (2) *Land-use problems:* The old saying goes, "Food is the essence of human life." Since 1949, the prevailing value is that if one sticks to the farm land, she is a good person; if one desires to leave the land in search of a new horizon, she is a traitor. . . . (3) *The values of the individual and the collective:* The Chinese tradition has always been in favor of the collective. It's only natural that an individual should be sacrificed and such sacrifice be praised. . . .

We once thought of shooting *Old Well* in black and white to indicate the place's aridity and poverty, and to express the tenacity and strength [of the people living there]. Traveling to the countryside, however, we found that the harsher the life was in a place, the more striking were the colors used by its residents; the girls basically were dressed in three primary colors. . . . This sharp contrast of colors is the reality of life in the Chinese countryside. . . . We thus decided upon the color scheme of the film: to use striking colors and sharp contrasts of colors, to imitate the style of peasant painting, to be elegantly plain, and to appear both ancient and modern. (Wu Tianming 1987, 5–6, 9)

From "Digging an Old Well: The Labor of Social Fantasy"
Rey Chow

The Futurity . . . the Futility of the Nation

Old Well is a village located far into the Taiheng Mountains. There are endless stony mountains, but no water. Over the generations, the Old Well villagers have dug 127 wells, but they have all been dry. The deepest was over fifty meters. The greatest hope of all the villagers is that they will find water on their own land. The protagonist is an educated youth called Sun Wangquan ("Sun," his family name, also means "grandson," and "Wangquan" means "auspicious for flowing stream"). When the film begins, Wangquan has returned to his village and is determined to use his knowledge to find water. His own family is very poor. To reach his goal and to help his brothers get married, he marries Duan Xifeng, a young widow with a daughter, and gives up his love relationship with another woman, Zhao Qiaoying. After many failed attempts, including one in which Wangquan and Qiaoying are trapped at the bottom of a well, where Wangcai, Wangquan's younger brother, is killed, Wangquan finally succeeds in digging a well by applying his newly acquired hydraulic knowledge. For the first time in many generations, Old Well village has water.

Old Well can, of course, be read as a "national allegory." According to this type of reading, everything in the film would be assigned a national—that is, Chinese—significance. The struggle of the protagonist and the village would then be microscopic versions of the "nation" and its people struggling to consolidate their identity.[1] It would be a story with a positive ending. But what if the supposedly "national" sign "Chinese" itself is more than the "third world nation" that is conferred upon it by modernity? Once we stop using the "nation" to unify the elements of the film text, other questions begin to surface. A careful *allegorical* reading of *Old Well* would demonstrate that the allegory of the "nation" is, paradoxically, the nation's otherness and nonpresence.

The "nation" reading is impossible because a national *enemy* is absent. Instead, the space of an enemy, which is crucial for the unification of a community, is occupied by two "others"—the dry well and the romantic woman. Why would a "Chinese" film of the 1980s concentrate on enemies other than "national" enemies?

In the readings of recent world events, it is commonly recognized that the breakdown of communism in Eastern Europe since 1989 has not led to democratic prosperity in accordance with anticommunist beliefs but has instead caused the resurgence of old ethnic conflicts that were neutralized and covered up under communism. The prominence of nationalistic sentiments in the states previously dominated by the USSR indicates that nationalism was actually the repressed side of communism, a repressed side that boils over once the lid of communism is removed.[2]

In China, where ethnic differences are relatively undisruptive (except in Tibet) and where the centrality of the Han culture remains relatively uncontested by other ethnic groups, many of whom have been assimilated for generations,[3] nationalism functions in the past forty years to fuel communism rather than as communism's repressed side. As communism gradually loses its hold on the populace (even though it is still the official policy), what surface as the "social disorders" that are repressed under communism?—Two related things: sexual difference, which communism neutralizes, and "the West," which is communism's adversary but also its founding source. The surfacing of these disorders means the relative indifference not only to communism but also to communism's ally in China—nationalism itself.

Female Sexuality and the Nation

The eruption of romantic love in contemporary Chinese cinema continues the modernist interest in the controversies of love and sexuality among Chinese intellectuals since the beginning of the twentieth century. Why is romantic love such an issue? In the early twentieth century, the interest in love among popular literature writers (those of the Mandarin Duck and Butterfly School) was partly a result of the ideological rather than actual disintegration of the Chinese kinship family. The ongoing protest against the oppression of women and junior members of *jia*, the traditional family, meant that alternative spaces for human relationships had to be sought. During that period, when China's participation in anti-imperialism meant that resistance against Western and Japanese aggression had to be conceived in the form of nationalism, the "internal" battle against the family became allied with the promotion of Chinese culture as the "nation," which was literally conceived of as the state-family, *guojia,* the large organizational unit that would give China a place among the nations of the world.

If the conception of "woman" was in the past mediated by women's well-defined roles within the Chinese family, the modern promotion of the nation throws into instability all those traditional roles. How are women's sexuality, social function, economic function, contribution to cultural production, and biological reproduction to be conceived of outside the family and in terms of the nation?[4] This is the historical juncture when, in what appeared to be a sudden "liberation" of the traditional constraints on Chinese women's identity, romantic love became a leading social issue. For what is "romantic" about romantic love is not sex but the apparent freedom in which men and women could choose their sexual partners, in a way that differed from arranged marriage. And since the traditional family system was paternalistic—that is, resting on the sexual stability, chastity, and fidelity of women while men were openly promiscuous or polygamous—the new freedom meant first and foremost the production of a new female sexuality. In other words, because the conception of the nation sought to unify the culture regardless of sexual and class difference, it left open many questions as to how women's sexual identities, which were carefully differentiated and monitored within the kinship system, should be reformulated. This is why, one could say, in the discourse of modernity, the Chinese woman suddenly became a newly discovered "primitive"—a body adrift between the stagnant waters of the family, whose oppressiveness it seeks to escape, and the open sea of the nation, whose attention to "woman" is only such that her sexual difference and history become primarily its support (i.e., become erased).

The emotional as well as economic forms of the family, on the other hand, die a slow and drawn-out death. Especially because the modern discourse of the nation has not really provided real alternatives other than an apparently emancipated "body" with no constraints, the tenacious bonds of the family live on. And this is ironically even more so under the communist revolution. When Mao Zedong upheld women as "equal" to men in the public spheres of work and economic production for the nation, and when Western feminists were delighted to see Chinese women being honored without discrimination with the same tasks as men, the family continued to thrive in the ideological vacuum left by the creation of the communist nation, simply because women's labor in the home, unlike their kinship roles and positions, which could be taxonomically classified, remained real and material but traditionally unclassified and unpaid, and hence much more difficult to reclassify in the new system. The consequence is that the oppressiveness resulting from such labor is left intact to this day, leaving their imprints on cultural productions even when such productions are not overtly about gender, sexuality, or women.

In *Old Well*, the kinship-bound and modernized female sexualities are represented by Wangquan's different relationships with Xifeng and Qiaoying. From the beginning, the two women are portrayed stereotypically, in accordance with the literary and historiographic conventions of understanding Chinese modernity. While Qiaoying is, like Wangquan, coming back to the village after having been in the outside world, Xifeng is the woman who remains at home. Qiaoying's attractiveness is associated with her "novelty": she brings back with her such modern items as a television set. Xifeng, although widowed, is clearly more "stable": her stability is represented by the support she has from the multiple roles she plays within the kinship system, in which the women are as strongly functional as the men.

Xifeng has a mother, who supervises her sexual life, and is herself a mother. All she needs is a husband who would make her female social identity complete. Qiaoying, on the other hand, is an unknown entity: one of the reasons Wangquan's grandfather disapproves of her is that he thinks she would not stay put in the village. Even though, in terms of social progress, Qiaoying is much closer to man himself than to the woman at home, in the rural village her avant-garde ontological proximity to masculinity is eyed with suspicion and distrust. The modernized, educated woman signifies romantic freedom—that is, "choice" over her own body—and thus social instability. Qiaoying is represented as without family relations. Like a mysterious signifier unleashed from centuries of anchorage to kinship, she does not know where she is heading.

What is most remarkable, however, is the way this convention of understanding modernity—the convention of exorcizing the romantic woman and romantic love from traditional society—surfaces in post–Cultural Revolution cultural production. What does this convention do here?

First, it helps consolidate the traditional female sexuality represented by Xifeng and her relation to Wangquan, whose genealogical as well as career stability is guaranteed through marriage. In Chinese "digging an old well" conjures up idioms and expressions that carry sexual connotations. *Gujing qingbo* (the stirring of ripples in an old well) and *taogujing* (dredging an old well), for instance, are expressions that allude to the renewed sexual activities in a woman who has been without them for a long time. The man who has sex with such a woman is then an old-well-digger, which is the role played by Wangquan, who "receives" not only food, cigarettes, and money from Xifeng but finally, though reluctantly, her body. Toward the end of the film, Xifeng is pregnant. By contrast, the romantic woman is turned into an outcast. Qiaoying is the "enemy" to the economic basis of the village community, who must be exiled.

Second, in the aftermath of the Cultural Revolution, the affirmation of traditional family values comes as an attempt to mask the lack created by the bankruptcy of communism *and* nationalism, even though nationalism may persist by reinscribing itself in traditional forms. The main point is that the central roles played by the family and village community are here signs of the *dismantling* of the modernist revolution from "family" to "nation." "Woman" is now caught between the bankruptcy of nationalism and communism, in which the sexes are "equal" and women's problems do not exist, *and* the resurgence of older patriarchal forms of community, in which female sexuality is strictly managed for purposes of kinship reproduction.

A film such as *Old Well* demonstrates that the "Chinese nation" itself does not have to exist in order for the social and sexual issues to be circulated—and negotiated. Like the female body emancipated from traditional kinship bonds, the "nation"—that imaginary anchorage for primitive passions—is *nowhere* except in the politics that uses it to fight the past (be that past primitive, ethnic, feudalist, or colonized). Like the female body thrown into "romantic love," the nation is theoretically capable of all kinds of dangerous libidinal possibilities. Because it is fundamentally empty, the "nation" must be controlled by a more locally grounded production and reproduction. In their relative silence on the subject of the nation, contemporary Chinese films seem to say: "It is the 'nation' with all its extravagant promises that has led to the internal catastrophes in modern China. But—still, we must continue to seek such extravagant promises elsewhere!"

The Barrenness of Romantic Love

If the decline of the "nation" is as elusive as its rise, this elusiveness finds a convention of staging itself in the romantic woman.

In spite of Wangquan's marriage to another woman, Qiaoying loves him, and we feel, through his silence and guilty expressions, that he still loves her. After Wangquan is married, Qiaoying has been going out with Wangcai, who earlier had a quarrel with Wangquan about his own lack of everything, in particular his lack of experience with women. Qiaoying's association with Wangcai is clearly presented as futile and futureless: Wangcai is an example of the "decadent" younger generation of contemporary China, who, unlike his brother, has neither the stamina nor the altruism to persist in a quest for the communal good. Instead of digging for water, he is more interested in stealing women's underwear and ridiculing women performers in ways that are clearly sadistic and misogynistic. A hilarious scene shows Wangcai leading a group of young people dancing wildly to the noisy tunes of Western rock and roll music played over a transistor radio at the site of an attempted well drill. In Wangcai, the "dangers" of Westernization threaten to become destructive. Here is a youth with no long-term plan and no concern for society's future. During a well-digging accident, Wangcai is killed by rubble falling into the well.

Because of the accident, however, Qiaoying is finally able to "consummate" her love for Wangquan. In this love scene, we have perhaps one of the most romantic portrayals of romantic love in contemporary Chinese cinema. Its romanticism lies in an excessiveness that can only belong to film.

From under the well, the image of the two lovers kissing in passion is superimposed with the cosmic landscape—the sky, the mountains, the trees—in a series of shots that are, like the accompanying music, in motion rather than still. The lovers' entrapment inside the well thus becomes, in a dreamlike fashion, the freedom one can find in "nature" outside the confines of human wants and desires. If this moment captures romantic fulfillment, it is also, I suggest, a capturing of the uncapturable through the juxtaposition of what is temporally and geographically specific—romantic love—with what is timeless and placeless—the cosmos. As that which is here and now, love does not and cannot reproduce itself outside the circuit of the two lovers. The sacrifice it requires, as well as the meaning of its intense presence, is that of an unrecuperable death. Romantic love is thus literally experienced as death, at a moment when the lovers have lost hope of getting out alive. It is in death that they can dream of being at one with each other and with the cosmos, in a way that—thanks to the imaginary possibilities of cinema—transcends the constraint of the specific here and now. This transcendence is fantastical and antisocial. Romantic love becomes the signifier of emptiness—the emptiness and emptying of the social.

After this death, society goes on. The fantasy of romantic love is from now on remembered with nostalgia, as what happened at a different time in a different place. Importantly, it is the woman, Qiaoying, who carries death with her. She eventually leaves the community and donates her dowry to the cause of continual well digging. Wangquan, who found himself a mistress in the depths of his failed social labor, reemerges as a cultural hero who is aided not only by his mistress but also by his wife, who calls upon the entire village to give what they can to help his cause. While one woman gets nothing and the other retains her husband, Wangquan keeps his family, the memory of love,[5] and leaves himself a name.

The futility of the nation is thus signified by the barrenness of romantic love, the consummation of which takes place in the depths of a dry well at the moment of a collapsed effort at drilling. Romantic love is barren not because it is impoverished but because it is surplus: its excessiveness threatens economic productiveness because it prevents that productiveness from being stabilized. Another way of putting this is to say that the sacrifice of romantic love is pure: unlike the attempt to drill a well, it cannot be rewarded or "completed" in the way that the "In Memoriam" plaque, as I will go on to argue, completes and rewards the sacrifices of men's lives down the centuries. If well digging generates the "value" that compensates for the loss of lives, the barrenness of romantic love lures modernity against itself and back toward the long-disputed family.

The Labor of Social Fantasy

Ethnicity *can* mobilize the vast majority of its community provided its appeal remains sufficiently vague or irrelevant.
—E. J. Hobsbawm, *Nations and Nationalism since 1780:*
Programme, Myth, Reality

How is one to interpret the fact that large numbers of people collectively hold beliefs that are false?
—Partha Chatterjee, *Nationalist Thought and*
the Colonial World: A Derivative Discourse?

If one "foreign enemy" to the community is the romantic woman, who must be cut off, the other "foreign enemy" is the lack that is inside Old Well village—the dry wells themselves. This lack awaits being filled and, once filled, will give meaning to the community.

The theme of dry wells repeats the obsession that has characterized "Chinese modernity" since the nineteenth century: the power of technology. Although we are familiar with the many technological inventions that owe their origins to the Chinese—the compass, paper, printing, fireworks, gunpowder, deep drilling,[6] to name just a few—in the modern period, notably after Western imperialism became unavoidable, one might argue that "technology" situates the Chinese culture vis-à-vis the West in the form of a lack. Political trends in the twentieth century vacillate between the desire to fill this lack and the pretense that China needs nothing. In the post–Cultural Revolution period, following Deng Xiaoping's modernization campaigns, we see once again the openness to technology, from the most mundane items for household use to computers. Contemporary Chinese films necessarily reflect these developments.[7] One of the narratives that has sustained China's relationship with Western modernity can thus be described as a quest for technology—a quest for that "power" without which China cannot become strong.

At the same time, in this film, the quest for technology is legitimated not so much in terms of the elusive "nation" as in terms of a post–Cultural Revolution *humanism* that tries to preserve the traditional in modernization. As such, the film also repeats one of the basic fantasies that have run throughout the course of Chinese modernization since the nineteenth century, which is expressed in the phrase "Chinese learning for fundamental structure, Western learning for practical use." The fantasy is that the Chinese can have part of the West—technology—without changing its own social structure. Today, this fantasy continues in the evident split between official Chinese rhetoric, which still remains loyal to the classical themes of Marxism, Leninism, and Maoism, and Chinese social practice, which now includes all kinds of Western and capitalistic ventures and enterprises. Such fantasy is crucial to the narcissistic value-writing that I suggest as the alternative way of understanding "third world" cultures.

This narcissistic value-writing is, moreover, masculinist. *Old Well* begins with shots of part of a naked male body against a dark background hammering away in sweat. We read "determination" into these signifiers. The ending of the film *completes* these opening signifiers with an "In Memoriam" plaque indicating the lives (presumably all male) that have been lost in the centuries of failed attempts at well digging. The completion is the completion of the sacrificial process: finally, the film seems to say, the sacrifices pay off.

From the perspective of Wangquan, technology is strictly a means to an end. Technology is instrumental in fulfilling the mandate that is loaded on him and that he cannot resist. He cannot protest against that mandate because in it lies a communal meaning of responsibility; he cannot decline it because in it lies the very personal identity he receives from society as a reward. The mandate not only takes from him his life energy; it also gives him his life and his immortality.

What is interesting is not the simple affirmation of humanistic values and a process of identity production through stamina, effort, and willingness to self-sacrifice but how such an affirmation is at the same time part of that cultural narcissism that exoticizes its own alterity, its own otherness. The fact that the affirmation of humanistic values takes place not in metropolitan centers such as Shanghai and Beijing[8] but in backward villages in remote mountains suggests that the reinvestment in humanism in contemporary Chinese cultural production is at the same time an uncanny *ethnographic* attempt to narrate a "noble savagery" that is believed to have preserved the older and more authentic treasures of the culture, in ways as yet uncorrupted by modernity.

At the center of the treasures to be preserved is a system of production in which the will to work will be duly rewarded—if not in the form of an immediate gratification to the individual, then definitely in the form of the reproduction and continuance of the life of a community. The fascination not only with technological production or genealogical reproduction alone but with the welding of the two in the successful perpetuation of a culture is probably the most important fascination of the post–Cultural Revolution period, in which the diversion from the mindless destructiveness of the previous two decades needs to graft itself onto something substantial and concrete. These two kinds of production together make up the economy of the third kind—the production of value/ideology, a production that is at the same time a series of translations, decodings, and recodings between "contemporary" and "rural" China, between communism (with its emphasis on loyalty to the party) and humanism (with its emphasis on loyalty to the clan and the family, and on individual effort), between China's status as other to the West and the status of the "other" cultures of China's past and unknown places to China's "present self." In *Old Well*, the "lack" of China (in terms of technology) is projected onto the "lack" of China's rural area, which is further projected onto an actual lack, the lack of water. In this series of projections and substitutions, the "lack," always at once frustrating and empowering, finally gives way to a filling that stabilizes signification for survival.

At this point, we need to say, But wait, it's not only the "filling" and the production of water that enable the survival of the community. The *failure* to produce water is what has already sustained the culture of Old Well village for generations!

What indeed is the old well?

In terms of narrative structure, the old well is, of course, nothing: it is the lack that makes narrative possible. The old well is the obsession that, precisely because it remains unfulfilled, perpetuates itself in the village as a kind of collective memory, collective responsibility, and collective desire. Do the men in Old Well village know what they really want? Or do they continue digging simply because their ancestors have formed that habit—simply because it has become a *tribal ritual?* The sense of absurdity that figures in what looks like a revered tradition is clearest in the scene where villagers from a neighboring village attempt to close up a well that the Old Well villagers claim to be theirs. This competition over the rights to the well leads to the question as to the whereabouts of the plaque indicating the well's "ownership." Finally, it is the women who produce the "original" plaque, which has, it turns out, long become a latrine stone.

But the absurdity of this discovery does not change the powerful impact that the obsession has on the village. And such is the power of social fantasy: even when the "original" plaque has been turned into a latrine stone and is thus shown to be, after all, *no more than a (shitty) stone,* the belief that it is *more* persists. In a discussion of Eastern Europe after the collapse of communism, Slavoj Žižek writes about the fantastical nature of what he calls the "nation-Thing" in a way that is equally applicable to the old well:

> The Thing is not directly a collection of these features [composing a specific way of life]; there is "something more" in it, something that *is present* in these features, that *appears* through them. Members of a community who partake in a given "way of life" *believe in their Thing,* where this belief has a reflexive structure proper to the intersubjective space: "I believe in the (national) Thing" is equal to "I believe that others (members of my community) believe in the Thing." The tautological character of the Thing—its semantic void, the fact that all we can say about it is that it is "the real Thing"—is founded precisely in this paradoxical reflexive structure.[9]

This fantasy turns all accidents—events that are real but somehow cannot be accounted for coherently—into *mere* accidents, mere errors, which have no place in the actual functioning or *labor* of the fantasy. Similarly, all the lives that have been sacrificed in the course of searching for water are simply meaningless until the first well is successfully dug. Until then, we can say that the lost lives do not *matter*: they remain chance components waiting to be materialized into the full-blown fantasy peopled with real bodies. Instead of describing the history of Old Well village as one in which the villagers are united by a hope for the future (when water will be found), therefore, we should describe it this way: the discovery of water validates the sacrifices *retroactively* as parts of a concerted communal effort at well digging. This is the paradox of the ending, at which we are shown a close-up of the plaque "In Memoriam" of all the well-digging martyrs with the dates of their failed efforts and their deaths. Superimposed upon the rolling image of this plaque is the author's/director's inscription documenting Sun Wangquan's accomplishment: "January 9, 1983: Water was found, and fifty tons of water were produced every hour from the first mechanized deep well." The current success proves by its chance occurrence that "it" is what all the previous generations have been slaving for and that, moreover, their deaths were finally *worthwhile*.[10]

The act of discovering water, in other words, is like a signifier that enigmatically constitutes the identity of the past by its very *contingent presence* or *randomness*. If, because of its success, this act becomes endowed with the value of a "primary" act, then "primary" value itself must be described not as an absolute origin but instead as a supplementary relation: like all previous attempts of well digging, the latest attempt is a random event; at the same time, this latest attempt is marked by an *additional* randomness—the discovery of water, the accident of "success." This additional randomness, this accident that is more accidental than all the other accidents, marks the latest attempt of well digging apart from the others, thereby constituting in the same moment the "necessary" structure that coheres the entire series of events in a meaningful signifying chain, a signifying chain that I have been referring to as social fantasy. The labor of social fantasy, then, comprises not only the random physical efforts at well digging and their failures but also the process of retroactive, supplementary transformation in which the random and physical becomes the primary, the necessary, and the virtuous, and henceforth functions and reproduces itself ideologically as such.

Crucial to this social fantasy is the danger represented by the romantic woman and the recurrent dry well, both of which are "taken care of" at the end. The fantasy is that the village can have the technology of the running well without the technology of the new (running) woman, that the village can turn into a self-sufficient community with only as much outside help as *it wants*—precisely at a time when Chinese countryside self-sufficiency, like that of other "third world" rural areas, has been irredeemably eroded by modernized production and distribution, and the permeation of global capitalist economics.

A film such as this, which demonstrates the fundamental nothingness of the labor of social fantasy, inevitably lends itself to a reading that is exactly the opposite. Attesting to that is *Old Well*'s warm reception by Chinese audiences at home and overseas, and its success at the Second Tokyo International Film Festival of 1987,[11] in contrast to the regular official censorship of films by the Fifth Generation directors that are consciously critical of Chinese culture. The intense appeal of a film that celebrates the rewarding of a communal, collective effort makes little sense unless we understand the magnitude of the fantasy of collectivity on the largest scale—the Cultural Revolution—and its collapse. The emotional vacuum left behind by the latter awaits the legitimating work of some other thing. This other thing is increasingly being sought in China's old and remote areas, where social fantasy, whose creation of a present identity is always through a nostalgic imagining of a permanent other time and other place, can flourish most uninhibitedly. And so, beyond the futility of the nation and the barrenness of love, the labor of social fantasy, like the muscular, masculine arms at the film's beginning, hammers on.

Notes

This article was first published in *Primitive Passions: Visuality, Sexuality, Ethnography, and Contemporary Chinese Cinema* (New York: Columbia University Press, 1995), pp. 65–78. Copyright © 1995 by Columbia University Press. Reprinted with permission of the publisher.

1. Such a reading informs, for instance, the discussions collected in Jiao Xiongping 1990.

2. "Hence, as we can now see in melancholy retrospect, it was the great achievement of the communist regimes in multinational countries to limit the disastrous effects of nationalism within them. . . . Indeed, it may be argued that the current wave of ethnic or mini-ethnic agitations is a response to the overwhelmingly non-national and non-nationalist principles of state formation in the greater part of the twentieth-century world." Hobsbawm 1992, 173.

3. For a discussion of the construction of the "Chinese" ethnic identity, see David Yen-ho Wu 1991. For a discussion, of related interest, of the traditional ethnic conflict between the Hans (who make up 94 percent of the Chinese population) and the Huis (Chinese-speaking Muslims), see Jonathan N. Lipman 1990, 65–86.

4. The common view among some feminist China scholars is that issues of female sexuality have been subsumed under either the traditional kinship family or the modernist discourse of the nation. In the early twentieth century, when nationalism was replacing familial pieties as the valid self-strengthening discourse in the "third world," the family and the nation could indeed be looked upon as equally "major" historical forces that dwarf and erase women in different but comparable ways. However, the major shortcoming of this view lies in that, after pointing out the masculinism of nationalism, it cannot explain why nationalism has such a great appeal to women as well as men. The analysis of the relation between "woman" and "the nation" I offer here is quite different from this common view.

5. The story ends with these lines: "Below, on the flowery banks of a the Qinglong River, in the little village half hidden by the morning smoke, lie his dry land, his small son, his virtuous wife, his dearest elders and brothers, and memories of the love that he will never forget." Zheng, *Lao jing*; my translation.

6. For a recent discussion of how the Chinese extracted brine for making salt by drilling the deepest well (one kilometer) in the world over a century and a half ago, see Hans Ulrich Vogel, "The Great Well of China," *Scientific American,* June 1993, pp. 116–21. According to Vogel, the Xinhai well, which is located in Sichuan Province, "was the culmination of an 800-year-old technology." The epigraphs by Hobsbawm and Chatterjee at the beginning of the present section are taken respectively from *Nations and Nationalism Since 1780,* p. 169 (emphasis in the original), and from *Nationalist Thought and the Colonial World—A Derivative Discourse?* (United Nations University, Tokyo: Zed Books, 1986), p. 11.

7. The "technological" interest is evident even in films that are not explicitly about technology. For instance, in Zheng Dongtian's *Yuanyang lou* (Young couples, 1987), we find the stories of six couples living in the same apartment complex that are cinematically narrated against a background of new common household objects, from the vacuum cleaner to the cassette tape player. Even as mere silent background, technology in the home effectively demonstrates the changes in cultural value.

8. The films that are set in big cities are, by contrast, always about the loss of such humanistic values. Recent examples include Zhou Xiaowen's *Fengkuang de daijia* (Obsession, 1989), and Xie Fei's *Ben ming nian* (Black snow, 1990).

9. Slavoj Žižek, "Eastern Europe's Republics of Gilead," *New Left Review* 183 (Sept.–Oct. 1990): 53; emphases in the original. As he argues in another context, social fantasy is "precisely the way the antagonistic fissure is masked." Fantasy is a means for an ideology to takes its own failure into account in advance. See [Zh]I[zh]ek 1989, 126.

10. If we substitute the word *communal* for *national,* the following quotation would apply well to our present discussion: "Where national memories are concerned, griefs are of more value than triumphs, for they impose duties, and require a common effort." Ernest Renan, "What Is a Nation?" trans. and annotated by Martin Thom, in Bhabha 1990, 19.

11. *Old Well* won four of the thirteen awards given by the festival, including the "special affirmation award by international film critics."

Thirteen
Red Sorghum
(*Hong gaoliang,* dir. Zhang Yimou, 1987)

Screenplay Mo Yan et al.
Cinematography Gu Changwei
Producer Xi'an
Cast Gong Li, as Jiu'er
Jiang Wen, as head sedan carrier

At the Berlin Film Festival in 1988, *Red Sorghum* won the Golden Bear
Award; in China, this honor thrust popular attention on its director,
Zhang Yimou. A cinematographer by training, Zhang had made a diversified contribution to the Chinese new cinema: he had been the cameraman for
the visually impressive *One and Eight* and *Yellow Earth;* he had performed the
leading role in *Old Well;* and now he had directed his own prize-winning film.
His popularity, however, was also accompanied by heated criticism that he had
degraded images of the Chinese on-screen and that he had violated socialist
realism.

The film's subversion was inspired by its literary base, a novel of the same
title by an important and prolific contemporary fiction writer, Mo Yan. One
obvious deviation of the book from convention is that it glorifies the family
saga of a bandit, a subject that no writer would have dared to touch years earlier. Stylistically, the book mixes a mischievous narrative with brutal images.
One critic referred to the brutality of the novel as "a chorus of the ferocity of
folk livelihood" and an illustration of "the uprightness of national spirit" (Li
Qingquan 1986). As to the mischief of its narration, this critic used as his
metaphor a miracle from the novel—a few jars of wine purposefully spoiled by
urine turn out to be the best ever made in the distillery: "I read the story heartily
as if drinking the wine in the same story, knowing some urine had been mischievously mixed in it" (Li Qingquan 1986). With this book, Mo Yan illustrated the fondness of the roots-searching literature for depicting a remote place
either in time or in political geography so that the contemporary political dis-

course might be canceled out and a spectrum of primordial, folkloric, and down-to-earth elements might guide the residents of this remote place and lend them a subversive inspiration.

The film *Red Sorghum* joins the roots-searching literature in projecting an imaginative folk life of wine-god worshiping. The color red ties together its important sequences: a red sedan chair occupies the foreground in the pre-wedding procession; the woman's red dress and the red tone of the sunshine emphasize adulterous love in the sorghum field; although it is actually colorless, the sorghum wine becomes red in the film as it is passed from hand to hand during the ritual of worshiping the wine god. Fire and blood mark Japanese cruelty; the boy's constant looking at the dazzling sun lends intensity to the wait to ambush the Japanese trucks, and it leads to the final dominance of the red on the screen when the blood and wine merge in the fire of the war that temporarily darkens the sun (a solar eclipse much emphasized in the concluding sequence of the film). Deviating from the usual rational critique, Zhang presents a landscape in which the real is manipulated in such a way that it recedes in favor of a free play of desires for individuality, strength, and vitality. Even though they must be interrupted on-screen by foreign invaders, these desires reflect all the more the urgency of a cultural anxiety over Chinese human and national conditions and a call for cultural and national resurrection.

The representation of male desire and its underlying narcissism is an important issue for properly understanding this film. Here, we have to be reminded of gender representation in the spirit of "socialist feminism" in the 1950s and 1960s and its later development during the Cultural Revolution decade, which featured an array of political super-women. The subversion of this tradition unavoidably assumed a sexist orientation, as shown in *Red Sorghum,* in its amorous shots of muscular male bodies and in its dramatization of male vigor. Here the sexist orientation also has a nationalist tint, reflecting a yearning for cultural masculinity (known in Chinese as *gangyang zhi qi*).

Folk songs, ballads, and ritualistic music portray the exalted and elaborate moments of the woman protagonist's life and death. Jiu'er, the object of male desires, is given a mythical status: born on the ninth day of the ninth month and given a name that means "nine," Jiu'er is blessed by her lover's song encouraging her to travel bravely along a road of 9,999 miles; her distillery has double nine (that is, eighteen) in its name; and the wine-god-worshiping song repeats the numeral nine. The emphasis on this culturally mythical number relates the importance of Jiu'er to that of the wine god.

In casting Jiu'er, the film introduced actress Gong Li, who later played most

of the female leads in Zhang's major films. The different cross-cultural perception of this best-known Chinese actress in the West is an interesting issue for discussion. Gong's popularity in the West, Berenice Reynaud believes, is based "not
so much [on] her poise or versatility, but her ability to signify Chineseness, femininity and mystery outside her own culture" (1993, 15). In other words, Gong
has become an exoticized icon that often helps sustain an allegorical perception
of China. Most Chinese viewers, as observed by Sheldon Lu, are "not as enam-
ored of the self-exoticization" of Gong Li in such internationally better-known
films as *Red Sorghum, Ju Dou,* and *Raise the Red Lantern.* Instead, they "love
The Story of Qiu Ju and *To Live.* The stories of the ordinary characters in these
films re-enact for Chinese spectators a shared, collective past and present, a life
and history with which they are shockingly familiar and they can easily identify" (1997, 126–27).

Suggested readings for *Red Sorghum* are as follows:

Yau 1989a
H. C. Li 1989
Yingjin Zhang 1990
Rey Chow 1995, 142–72
Tam and Dissanayake 1998, 23–34
Silbergeld 1999, 53–95

Director's Notes

To praise life is my major concern [in directing *Red Sorghum*]. Mo Yan makes
two comments in his story that I want to share here. First: "As I feel the progress
of human beings, I also feel the degeneration of the species." Second:
"Compared with people like my grandpa [head sedan carrier in the film], I look
like an emaciated bug that has been starved for three years." In China, long-time
repression and closure to the outside world have distorted people physically
and spiritually. If this [distortion] continues, how can the nation be resurrected?

I depicted this group of peasants from a new perspective. The Chinese artistic explorations of the national essence, be they critical or laudatory, share a
weakness for retrogressive thinking. *Red Sorghum* looks forward: it represents
the future personality or the ideals of personality. The representation transcends
social class and national affiliation to reach the height of human nature.

I would like to talk about creating *mise-en-scènes* and the ritualization of
action. I feel that the arts and rituals are close relatives. I tried to create, recre-

ate, and enrich this kind of *mise-en-scène* and actions to express myself, my feelings that life is always great, holy, and mysterious. (Qtd. in Zhou Youzhao 1988, 12–13)

Red Sorghum: Mixing Memory and Desire
Eugene Yuejin Wang

For some Chinese, watching *Red Sorghum* could almost be a traumatic experience. Strikingly rough, forthright, rugged, bold and unrestrained both stylistically and morally to Chinese tastes, the film is a shocking affront to many cherished and received formulae of Chinese cultural praxis; to the deep-rooted Confucian ethical and moral codes of sobriety and decorum; to the ingrained artistic codes favoring strategies of concealment and restraint; and to the aesthetic taste which prioritizes emotional delicacy and refinement. Never before has the medium of Chinese cinema been so unquestionably given over to the countenancing containment of an unbridled and abandoned manner of life and visual wantonness and crudity.

Hence its controversial Chinese reception that amounted to a "*Red Sorghum* Phenomenon." Over-shooting itself, a film originally meant as a modest stylistic and aesthetic exercise has been taken as seriously as any other product that addresses certain cultural images in the socialist ideological scaffolding. The film has been forced to transcend itself and grow into a nationwide cultural phenomenon. Everyone could not care more. But how is it that the film scandalizes and offends the public's not-too-delicate taste? How come so many people find it so hard to swallow, absorb and "buy"? By measuring the negative critical response against what the film shows, we will not only come to a better understanding of the true power of the film, but also lay bare the way in which regressive ideology masquerades as a self-righteous rhetoric that represses desire and against which desire seeks to find itself.

The film is based on Mo Yan's already controversial novella of the same title. A voice-over narrator tells the legend of his grandparents. Set in northern China, the narrative begins with the arranged marriage of Jiu'er, a young girl, also known as "my grandma," to a leper thirty years her senior, a winery boss, in exchange for a mule. The marriage procession breaks into a "tossing-the-sedan dance," where the crude sedan-bearers want to have fun with the pathetic bride whose sobs, however, silence the revelers. The procession is unsuccessfully waylaid by a masked bandit who is killed by the sedan-bearers, led by "my grandpa-to-be." It is elliptically suggested that the wedding night does not end with consummation, as the bride defends herself with a threatening pair of scissors. She spends three subsequent days at her parents' home, according to local custom. On her journey back to her husband, she is kidnapped by "my grandpa" and carried off into the depths of the sorghum field, where she happily acquiesces and they make love. Her return to the leper's winery is greeted by the news that the leper has been mysteriously killed. She recovers from the shock and persuades the workers to stay and help her run the winery. The narrator's "grandpa" returns, drunk, to claim Jiu'er. His tipsy manner wins him a beating instead, and he is thrown into a vat where he stays groaning for three days. Meanwhile, the real local bandit has kidnapped Jiu'er, who is ransomed for 3,000 pieces of silver. Grandpa awakens and goes to seek revenge for the disgracing kidnap, only to be disgraced himself. The winery is now in full swing. Grandpa reappears, and defies the ensemble there by pissing into the wine vat, and with a powerful demonstration of strength. He claims Jiu'er and nine years pass. The Japanese come, rounding up the local people to trample down the sorghum field, and to witness the flaying of an anti-Japanese bandit and Luohan, once a helper at Jiu'er's winery. After the event, the furious group at the winery resolve to seek revenge for Luohan by ambushing a Japanese truck. They succeed at the cost of almost all their lives except those of the narrator's grandfather and father. The latter appears on-screen as a small child whose chant for his dead mother ends the film.

Red Sorghum's detractors in China dismiss the film as mindless sensationalism, a libidinal impulse for "the ugly," a regressive effort at "the uncivilised and the savage," and a stylistic horror indulging in moral and visual "crudities."[1] For a Chinese film, a narrative blatantly addressing issues of desire, sexuality and transgression is itself already a transgression, even in an age of radical transformation of values. The film transgresses a lot of boundaries and codes, moral and cinematic, in a Chinese context where the two are traditionally yoked intimately together. The charges brought against the film cluster round its indulgence in boorishness, forthrightness and a savage lifestyle in defiance of refinement, inwardness and civility, all traditional Chinese virtues. Surprisingly, the central antithesis around which sound and fury erupt simply implicates a sexual difference: favouring femininity over masculinity. The pejorative epithets attached to the film are almost exclusively masculine, while the attributes detractors find lacking are mostly feminine restraint, introversion, refinement and so forth. This critique betrays a cultural priority given to femininity, a priority embedded in the deep structure of an ideology that seems contradictory to itself. In the feudally informed hierarchy of the Chinese ideological superstructure, women have traditionally been scaled down to the lowest stratum, so how is it that this traditional subordination is reversed? By examining this paradoxical contradiction, we will see how the masculine send-up of *Red Sorghum* confronts, challenges and transgresses ideological boundaries.

In Search of Man: The Politics and Aesthetics of Masculinity

In the Chinese cultural context, gender is a rich node couched in a panoramic intertextuality produced out of the entire historical intellectual canon. In the ancient Chinese metaphysical framework, the two fundamental metaphysical entities *yin* and *yang* create, define, perpetuate and perfect the cosmic mode of existence or essence of the world (referred to as *"taiji"* in the *Yi zhuan* or *"Yuan"* by Dong Zhongshu). Provided they are coordinated and in equilibrium, as with any of the other semantically undefined notions in the intuitive system of Chinese thought, this dichotomy is amorphously polysemic to the extent that its ultimate meaning seems to reside in a structure of shifting dialectic relationships that project themselves on to diverse categories and spheres. Hence the unanimously accepted reluctance to pin these two words to specific English equivalents in any context. Here, however, for a working clarity, some simplification is licensed. Among the commonly accepted connotations attached to *yang* are light, warmth, summer, daylight, masculinity, ascent and action; while attributes clustered around *yin* include the opposites: darkness, cold, winter, night, femininity, descent and inaction (Li Zehou 1985, 161–62). "The *yang* and strong becomes the male, the *yin* and smooth becomes the female" (Zhang Dainian 1982, 34). In Dong Zhongshu's interpretative text, probably the most comprehensive after the *Yi zhuan*, *yin* and *yang* are rendered mutually exclusive in that the presence of one means the absence of the other, as seen for example in seasonal change and temperature alternation. Moreover, the dichotomy enters the moral spectrum in his explication: "The *yang* is benign while the *yin* is malign, the *yang* means birth while the *yin* means death. Therefore, *yang* is mostly present and prominent; *yin* is constantly absent and marginal."[2] From this isolated text alone, it would be too far-fetched to press for a consciously misogynistic vision. Yet considering that Dong is one of the most significant interpreters and disseminators of Confucian ethics, and in view of the Confucian ethical dictum "the noble male and base female," it is easy to see how the very structure of the phrases allows an easy equation with the "noble male and base female."[3]

Dong is known for disclaiming plurality of thought in favour of Confucian ethics, which has been officially privileged, hermeneutically tamed and politically congealed to form the canonical bedrock of Chinese feudal ideology ever since. The "noble male and base female" became not only a feudal moral value, but was also displaced into the feudal social structure. The dichotomy of, and tension between, masculinity and femininity was no longer only a matter of sexual difference; it began to figure class difference, too. The hierarchical feudal order sought to structure itself around the figure of gender, with the ruler as the dominant male and the ruled as the submissive female.

Moreover, despite the diversity of undercurrents that may provide alternatives to dominant Confucian ethics, for example Taoism and Buddhism, there is one thing almost universally embraced by the Chinese mentality: the belief in internal stillness and passivity as a positive way to appropriate external reality. This has been affirmatively rhetoricised in various ways, and the ruling classes have been only too happy to appropriate it into ideology to consolidate the existing class structure. As the aspired-to stillness and passivity have touches of femininity, femininity itself becomes a condition highly aspired to. Instead of being afflicted by castration anxiety, the problematic of the lack is quite reversed in the Chinese cultural context. It is the man who lacks. If anything, a femininity complex would be a more appropriate form of the unconscious in the Chinese psyche. All those historical figures which, once filtered through ideological refracture, are mythicised into cultural archetypes that partake in masculinity, are also shown to be born with fatal flaws usually associated with braggarts and bigots. Even though they may be basically humane, they are always objects of ridicule, such as Li Kui and Lu Zhishen from *Water Margin*.[4] Well-known dynastic struggles for the throne always end up with overblown masculine warriors outwitted by feminine quasi-warlords (their femininity hardly earning them the name of a warlord at all).

"The fair beauty and the fragrant plant" *(meiren xiangcao)* is a clichéd classical poetic figure that ancient poets, mostly male, identify with to embody their yearning for spiritual purity and loyalty:

> And I thought how the trees and flowers were fading, and falling,
> And feared that my fairest's beauty would fade, too.
> Gather the flower of youth and cast out the impure! . . .
> All your ladies were jealous of my delicate beauty;
> They chattered spitefully, saying I lived wantonness.
>
> (Hawks 1962, 22–25)

It does not follow, however, that the femininity complex relieves women of their inferiority, nor is the curse of the "lack" lifted from woman as her place is elevated. What happens is that men usurp women's proper space so that women are pushed aside, marginalised, expelled, suspended, bracketed, and exiled into the realm of the imaginary to become icons and absences. It is interesting to note how persistent is the Chinese poetic convention of a male poet figured in his own poems as a sentimental woman who waits and longs for her/his lover's overdue arrival or return from a long journey. In "Song of Yan" *(Yan ge xing),* allegedly the first complete poem in the seven characters per line format, the emperor-poet Cao Pi assumes the role of a neglected woman pining away in her lonely chamber:

> Autumn winds whistle sadly, the air grows chill,
> Plants wither, leaves fall, dew turns to frost,
> Swallows fly homeward, geese wing south;
> I think of your distant wandering and am filled with love.
> Longingly you think of returning to your old home,
> Why linger on in remote places?
> Forlorn, your wife keeps to the deserted room;
> Misery cannot make me forget my love.
> Unaware of the tears that moisten my gown,
> I play zither tunes in the *ch'ing shang* mode,
> The songs are brief, the breath, weak—nothing lasts. . . .
>
> (Wu-chi Liu and Lo 1975, 46)

Working in conspiracy with this practice is the enduring moral value that "for woman, ignorance is a virtue." Thus men not so much speak for women as stand in their place to speak, thereby replacing women's linguistic space, usurping their world of consciousness, and depriving women of their right to speak. According to Barthes, the denial of speech is the ultimate deprivation of existence, as speech is the final mode of proving one's existence.[5] Female subjectivity is out of the question. Women have no way of articulating "I." Worse still, they live in a limbo: they cannot even inhabit the place of "thou" as the "thou" addressed in poems, since that place is male when the speaker is a textual female.

Femininity is seen by Lin Yutang as an overriding descriptive figure that brings together a set of otherwise loosely associated characteristics of the Chinese, including the priority given to intuition and a commonsensical way of thinking, and the tendency towards stability and nonaggression.[6] Temperamentally, it may have its positive side, but the loss of masculinity necessarily creates a blank in the cultural body. Even from the perspective of the ancient dialectic of *yin* and *yang,* balance between the two is a prerequisite for a wholeness of the cosmic order. The "sick man of Asia," a curse that haunted China during the semi-colonial era, suggests the diseased cultural body then at its worst. Spiritual feebleness, moral spinelessness, silent suffering and absorbing passivity certainly betray a loss of spiritual masculinity.

This loss is even reflected in Griffith's *Broken Blossoms,* a Hollywood narrative about a feminised "chink" and a "chinkised" woman—an equation implicitly drawn by the Western colonial ideology that informed Hollywood cinematic discourse. Cheng, an idealistic young Chinese, comes to London with the hope of teaching "the Western white man of the peace and inner tranquillity of the Buddha" (Martin Williams 1980, 109). The values Cheng embodies are already categories of *yin*/femininity according to the classical Chinese taxonomy of *yin* and *yang.* *Broken Blossoms* is blatantly critical of the abusive and sadistic *yang*/masculinity, and sympathetic to the oppressed *yin*/feminine side, physically figured by Lucy (the Lillian Gish character), and metaphorically figured by Cheng, the "chink." Both are immature, fragile victims of male dominance and power. Battling Burrows, the masculine paradigm, is strong, militant, overpowering, menacing, and tall; the girl and the "chink" are fragile and vulnerable. Instead of facing up to Battling with an equal amount of masculine strength, Cheng is seen to be as femininely vulnerable as the girl. The "chink" and Lucy become mirror-images of each other. Hence his inadequacy as her potential lover, as if he has been castrated. By appropriating him into the female side, the film politicises sexual difference, a metaphorical site onto which are collapsed class difference and racial difference.

Feminisation of men as a form of the cultural collective unconscious is manifested in traditional models of Chinese artistic representation. The exchange of sexual identity is a conventional theatrical licence. In Beijing opera, men play women by seriously masquerading as women in every way. In Shaoxing opera, an extremely popular variant among people in Shanghai, Zhejiang and Jiangsu provinces, male characters are played by women because of generic imperative: the stock-in-trade of Shaoxing opera is a love story between a young woman and a "tender" male scholar or potential scholar good at poetry and painting. The tenderness is required to the extent that only women seem able to portray it. Yet by having women impersonate men, the convention creates a theatrical illusion that stands in for an illusion of reality: desirable male prototypes fit for such romantic slots should be, and are, feminised men. These cultural praxes have created an ingrained aesthetic taste in Chinese audiences for feminine male icons onstage, and consequently on-screen.

In the early 1980s, the speculation on the past, on our cultural history, and on the structure of the Chinese mentality, led to a radical change in taste. The intelligentsia were awakening to the ideological implications of feminisation, while average theatregoers became fascinated by the charisma of "tough guys" in Japanese and Western movies. Suddenly there was an excruciating realisation of the fundamental "lack." There was a "masculinity" anxiety which culminated in a stage play, *In Search of Man*. Once popular delicate, "cream-puff" male stars lost audience favour, and even became despised.

Before *Red Sorghum*, the Chinese "dream factory" had already been diligent about churning out new masculine icons to meet the new appetite for masculinity. These were usually rough-featured, lip-biting, brow-knitting types. However, the overtly self-conscious cinematic evocation of masculinisation betrayed the essential lack and the anxiety of that lack all the more. The clumsiness also came from the awkward imitation of Japanese or Western tough types that appeared preposterous in Chinese diegetic milieux, and hence unconvincing.

Red Sorghum is a cinematic milestone that proposes a powerful Chinese version of masculinity as a means of cultural critique. The film creates a masculine world rather unself-consciously and cavalierly. It is unmistakably a male world (though itself problematic, as we shall see), with its boisterous swing and with only a minimum female screen presence (there is only one full-fledged female character). The intimidation, the subversive potential, and the sense of a cultural relevance in the creation of masculinity derive from its harking back to the under-represented genealogy of historical male archetypes and mythical prototypes, with a perennially historicised undesirability dogging their presence/absence in historical textuality. The pre–*Red Sorghum* self-conscious concoction of "perfect male icons," given their lack of credibility, posed no threat. The audience's consciousness of their imitative "foreignness" and fictional status rendered their presence on the Chinese screen harmless. Any immediate political consequences and cultural implications they may have had were comfortably suspended and bracketed. Yet once an unaffected earthier version of masculinity took shape, the audience was frightened. For them, the experience of watching Japanese tough guys could safely lock them in an enclosure of distanced aesthetic pleasure. They were screened off from a culturally irrelevant world. *Red Sorghum* screens them in. Their fear of some particular version of native masculinity is the unease with, if not fear of, the return of the collectively repressed and the recuperation of historically exiled outlaws: the masculinity in *Red Sorghum* is a reiteration of the outlaws, drunkards and rebels who were historically marginalised and expelled from official historical documents, and survived only in folk tales, romances, myths and historicised fictional narratives. These characters could be enjoyed for their beauty of characterisation from the safe distance of another age without the need to fall into moral speculation, though the moral overtones are already congealed into them.

Red Sorghum is therefore a return of the collectively repressed, an evocation of the cultural unconscious, a remembrance of the forgotten, and a tapping of intertextual memories.

One historical/fictional narrative readily collapses into the film: the well-known *Water Margin*, a sixteenth-century novel about outlaws and rebels based upon a real historical event, a peasant uprising in the Northern Song dynasty. This fictional world is inhabited by a galaxy of 108 idiosyncratic outlaw-warriors. Mostly male, they shape a spectrum of masculinity with one end bordering on femininity (for example, Yanqing the Dandy) and at the other end, macho (Li Kui, Lu Zhishen, and others). This spectrum is also a moral taxonomy. The group inhabiting the more feminine end are talented and clever, whereas the motley crew clustered around the more masculine end share a certain lack: represented as boorish, crude in manner and speech and rash in action, as bare-bellied, shaven-headed and swaggering. They are boozers, most daring when drunk. It is this end of the spectrum that *Red Sorghum* sub- or unconsciously evokes. "Grandpa" is a continuation of the masculine outlaw type. He kidnaps a woman, drinks heavily, is dauntless in defying everything, and given to occasional mischief such as pissing into the wine vat.

The problematic of drinking, along with its reiteration of historical narrative implications, is foregrounded in *Red Sorghum*. The red sorghum, the central image, connotes both the awe-inspiring landscape of the wild sorghum field and the raw material used to brew wine. In the Chinese historical memory, heavy drinking can be a transgression of decorum, an act of defying convention, a route to visionary intensity for transcendental possibilities and poetic ecstasy, or a way of achieving autonomy. It also bears the burden of moral condemnation for spiritual degradation, over-indulgence, moral corruption and social irresponsibility. Dialectically, the former derives its strength from the moral overtone of the latter. The most memorable feats of the masculine heroes in *Water Margin* are all one way or another the aftermath of drinking. The celebrated narrative about Wu Song single-handedly killing a tiger persistently emphasises the effect on him of the strong local liquor. Lu Zhishen's dramatic defeat of Zhen Guanxi, a bullying butcher, and his later mischievous and fearless defiance and blasphemy in a Buddhist temple are also shown to be the side-effects of a drop too much.

It is interesting to note how in Chinese texts, past and present, drinking is a way to attain masculinity. This betrays ideology: it presupposes a sober state of mind which is other than masculinity. It is as though masculine courage and defiance were impossible while in one's "right mind." Therefore, masculinity is a self-deluded state. *Red Sorghum* is both parasitical and critical of this historical tradition.

The sorghum wine, named by Jiu'er as *"Shibali Hong"* ("Eighteen Mile Red"), is the central constituent of the film's symbolic color scheme. The film is ritualistically motivated, with the power of wine as a central dynamic. The drinking of the red wine derives its meaning from a network of red motifs: the red wine, red marriage dress and decor, the blood, the sun, etc. They combine to evoke a world of visualised passion, a topology of fertility, a cinematically articulated life force, an iconographic presence of creativity and destruction, and death and rebirth. Placed within this system, the ritualistic celebration of the red wine radically transcends the traditional moral dichotomy of defiance and debauchery attached to heavy drinking. In a way, the film appropriates Western values such as the Nietzschean celebration of the Dionysian spirit, and indeed the 1980s in China saw the revival of a Nietzschean wave.

The chant that accompanies the sacrificial offering to the wine god, however, narrows down the meaning and returns to a familiar historical echo, politicising and defining the wine-drinking as an externalisation of masculinity: a way of coming into one's own and the bold defiance of authority. "Drink our wine, the *yin* and *yang* will be strengthened"; "one dares to walk through the Black Death Gorge . . . one does not kowtow even at the sight of the emperor." This echoes the historical motif of drinking as a way of challenging authority.

The equation of drinking with masculinity in the film points to an ideological taxonomy: masculinity means transgression, which presupposes femininity as propriety and decorum in the Chinese political unconscious. Masculinity is defined therefore as what Bakhtin calls "carnival," which is "sensuous," "life turned itself out," suspension of "hierarchical structure, and all the forms of terror, reverence, piety and etiquette connected with it"; "profanation: carnivalistic blasphemies, a whole system of carnivalistic debasings and bringings down to earth, carnivalistic obscenities linked with the reproductive power of the earth and the body"; shifts and changes in the "joyful relativity of all structure and order," crowning and uncrowning, birth and death, blessing and cursing, praise and abuse, face and backside, stupidity and wisdom, negation and affirmation (1984, 122–37).

Red Sorghum is a cinematic carnival enacting almost every aspect of Bakhtin's scenario. As Bakhtin says of the carnival, it "absolutises nothing."

The potentially pathetic opening exposition about the heroine's miserable marriage to a leper immediately careens into the hilarious tossing-the-bridal-sedan dance. The solemn ritual of sacrificial offering to the wine god is yoked to the comic scene of "my grandpa," the intruder, pissing into the wine vat. The climactic moment of the tragic death of the heroine is matched on the soundtrack by a celebratory wedding tune. A more sustained carnival moment is an earlier sequence in the winery yard. The heroine, having recovered from the shock of her husband's mysterious death, persuades the workers to stay on. Disclaiming the title "Mistress," she suspends the social hierarchy. But the moment she gives orders, she is "crowned," while simultaneously "uncrowning" the dead boss and his patriarchal order. At her wildly imaginative suggestion, which borders on perversion, the winery men gleefully splatter the wine on the ground "three times" and then set the wine on fire to purge the curse on the winery. This is immediately followed by the drunken intrusion of "grandpa" whose obscene account of the ravishment in the sorghum field disrupts the temporary reign of matriarchal order. Jiu'er is thus as easily "uncrowned" as she was casually "crowned" a moment ago. Under the rapid alternation between "crowning" and "uncrowning" lies "the core of the carnival sense of the world—the pathos of shifts and changes." As Bakhtin puts it:

> Crowning/uncrowning is a dualistic ambivalent ritual, expressing the inevitability and at the same time the creative power of the shift-and-renewal, the joyful relativity of all structure and order, of all order, of all authority and all (hierarchical) position. Crowning already contains the idea of immanent uncrowning: it is ambivalent from the very start. And he who is crowned is the antipode of a real king, a slave or a jester. . . . (1984, 124)

Soon grandpa is "uncrowned": at the embarrassed Jiu'er's order, the newly "crowned" is, as in Bakhtin's scenario, "ridiculed and beaten" while giving out a cry of joy and pain (itself a carnivalistic gesture), and is then thrown into a big vat (1984, 125). The hero who once bravely took the lead against the kidnapper and later became a kidnapper himself (another carnivalistic shift of crowning/uncrowning)—fulfilling what the first kidnapper failed to do, carrying away and ravishing the woman—is now rolling in the dust, his face masked with mud just as he masked it with cloth to capture the woman. The film "introduces the logic of misalliances and profanatory debasings" of the hero in order to renew him (Bakhtin 1984, 124). Nothing is absolute in the film, either negation or affirmation, in accordance with the imperative of carnival.

The uncrowning of "grandpa," future boss of the winery, is replaced by the sudden menacing descent of a mob of local bandits. What ensues is "a striking combination of what would seem to be absolutely heterogeneous and incompatible elements," the yoking together of generic narrative elements (Bakhtin 1984, 134). The accelerated montage of the gangster head descending from the roof to surprise Jiu'er clearly establishes a gangster-genre strand of suspense. Yet it is soon relativised and temporarily/partially negated by juxtaposition between gangster narrative and comic narrative: in the midground is the drunk, obliviously and ridiculously groaning and grumbling; in the background, high on the surrounding hills, is a line of gangsters menacingly hemming in the winery. As described by Bakhtin:

> Carnivalisation constantly assisted in the destruction of all barriers between genres, between self-enclosed systems of thought, between various styles, etc.; it destroyed any attempt on the part of genres and styles to isolate themselves or ignore one another; it brought closer what was distant and united what had been sundered. (1984, 134–35)

The comic undermines the threat posed by the gangsters; the gangster presence negates the comic element. Out of the dialectic interplay characterised by carnival levity and rapid change emerges the fundamental impulse of defiance and transgression that underlies or figures the film's vision of masculinity.

A discourse about masculinity in the Chinese context is in a way some version of what Mary Ann Doane would call the "medical discourse," as it is pitched against disease. *Red Sorghum* echoes certain motifs recurrent in the literary "search for roots" that surged in China in the early and middle 1980s. Set in an imagined faraway, long ago world where naked human existence is every bit as crude as it is unpretentious, this new literary genre has as one of its leitmotifs the poetic celebration of masculine potency. D. H. Lawrence was a great source of inspiration. Masculine potency is often defined not so much around physiology as it is dialectically posited against the aging, disabled and diseased, for example the master well-digger in Jia Ping'ao's "Heaven Dog" (*Tiangou*, 1985), who has to pull a wall down onto himself to give his wife away to his apprentice and son-figure.[7] Masculine potency becomes therefore a figure of coming into one's own being, of spiritual independence of authorial power. As an antithesis to "disease," masculinity is an ideologically charged critique of a past cultural psyche afflicted with moral and spiritual disease.

Red Sorghum also sets up its masculinity as an antithesis to disease. The diegetic set-up is the potential victimisation of the heroine by Big Head Li, whose only boast is wealth. He "generously" pays in the form of a big mule to acquire a beautiful young girl. Big Head Li is, both fortunately and unfortunately, a leper. He is figured on-screen as a lean, old and haggard sulk whose sole action consists of smoking a water pipe (itself a culturally loaded signifier of addiction). The wedding does not appear to be consummated. Instead of approaching his bride with menacing desire, the misfit bridegroom is seen yards away wrapped up in the screen of his own smoke. One feels a lack, an impotence implied. Later we learn from the voice-over that the heroine kept her virginity with a pair of scissors, which again suggests the man's cowardice. He is also ridiculed in the sedan-bearers' song when they toss the bride by dancing along.

The medical discourse is also conducted at a deeper level. The masculinity posited as an antithesis to disease constitutes a critique of some essential lacks in the cultural body. Insensitivity to suffering, in a Western scenario of sexual difference, would mostly be categorised as a pretentious gesture towards masculinity. In Chinese historical and cultural codes, however, insensitivity to others' suffering in the form of passivity, indifference and evasion would have been considered an "unmanly" attitude. In a classical narrative about outlaws or a martial arts legend, "real men" would "pull out the knife at the mere sight of injustice on the road." Yet that masculine spirit seems to have disappeared, remaining only in the realm of the imaginary, in narrative utopias, whereas in the recent historical period of semi-colonisation there developed a "national disease" of insensitivity and numbness which points to an inner cowardice and weakness.

Red Sorghum recuperates this issue. Yet the very recuperation through a melodramatic scene, while putting the presupposed spectatorial attitude under critique and proposing a *cause* of masculinity, at the same time creates a critique of itself.

A Japanese officer orders the butcher to flay two anti-Japanese heroes, one of whom happens to be the butcher's own gang leader. To do or not to do becomes a highly suspenseful narrative dynamic that is prolonged, deferred and twisted. The butcher kills the gang leader to relieve him of pain and is killed immediately. The suspense resumes when a kid, his apprentice, is ordered to do what is left undone. The torturing sequence ends with a prolonged shot of the boy approaching the hanging Luohan, once the foreman in the winery, reaction shots of the anxious spectators and a brief shot of the boy slicing Luo's eyelids.

This action may be meant as a visual stoicism to test the limit of human tolerance, to justify the inevitable masculinity as a Darwinist imperative and an ultimate survival strategy, and to buttress the cinematic representation of the masculine mood. The sadistic reification of the cruelty of reality may shatter any illusions about a feminine utopia of receptiveness, positive passivity, tenderness and harmony. The scene, however melodramatic it may seem, does have its cultural grounds: under the cultural surface of feminine tenderness and modesty, the satanic dark side of sadistic praxes such as flaying, branding, fragmenting and frying alive living humans—probably the cruelest on earth—was once a realised nightmare. The positive shock value of the scene may lie in its potential to jolt the audience out of their self-delusion about a tranquil feminine utopia, and out of their collective and private insensitivity to all kinds of massive social horror—a deep-rooted collective stupor characterised by Lu Xun, our most relentless and scathing cultural critic of the century, as one of the "rotten diseases" of the Chinese cultural psyche.

Lu Xun is worthy of some attention here not only as an intertextual index on cultural attitudes towards the reality of violence and as a cultural frame of reference, but also because his work is generically significant. A number of his crucial narrative moments involve the problematic of spectatorship. The pivot in Lu Xun's physician-turned-writer career was a singular experience of movie-watching. On the screen were Japanese soldiers slaying a Chinese charged with spying for the Russians. The intradiegetic spectators—mostly Chinese—witnessed the scene in absorbing numbness and disinterested interest. Outraged and deeply hurt, Lu Xun walked out of the theatre with the painful documentary footage that was to surface and resurface in his literary imagination inscribed in his memory (Lu Xun 1956, 2). He resolved to cure the nation of its cultural disease with his scalpel-like pen. Lu Xun's most famous fictional character is Ah Q. He has become a prototype in the taxonomy of cultural archetypes, and an embodiment of all stupidities and insensitivity. When Ah Q is sent for public execution, we have the most ironic narrative in Chinese fiction. Ah Q's last visual impression is of "the crowds of spectators thronging both sides of the street" to witness a breathtaking spectacle. Their eyes seem to merge into a mass that starts to sink its teeth into his soul, and his last auditory memory is the spectators' "Bravo!" that "sounded like wolves howling" (Lu Xun 1956, 89). In *Medicine,* one of his short stories, the spectators watch a revolutionary's head being chopped off, their necks stretched "as if they were a flock of ducks being gripped by an invisible hand and lifted upward" (Lu Xun 1956, 20). What Lu Xun deplores is not only the inhuman torpor attending such occasions and the selfish, unsympathetic coldness, but also the tragic mechanism implicating all the insensitive spectators: the victim of their visual pleasure may actually be a mirror, a flash-forward to their own future fates.

What we infer from these cultural narratives is the dichotomy of public moral insensitivity and private visual pleasure that lies at the heart of spectacle-watching as a deplorable cultural practice motivated by a diseased imagination. If we take this to be a cultural and historical given, we begin to feel an implicit critique of the contemporary Chinese mentality by Zhang Yimou's cinematic treatment of the spectacle of flaying in *Red Sorghum*. The sequence is almost a cinematic transcription of the Japanese soldiers slaying a Chinese in Lu Xun's memory. There is, however, a radical difference: the intradiegetic spectators are not those numb creatures that outraged Lu Xun. They are shown to be angry, only they have to suppress their helpless silent rage and defer its outburst to the narrative denouement. But for this sequence the locus is not in the intradiegetic spectators, though the main protagonists are among those who are given a few sporadic reaction shots. The vested cinematic interest here is in *showing* the spectacle for us, the spectators outside the screen world.

Zhang has publicly announced his interest in trying to steer a middle way between art cinema and the commercial blockbuster (Li Xing 1988). He does not want to lose audiences. Therefore *Red Sorghum* is motivated not only by cultural urgency, historical imperative and aesthetic vision, but also by a desire to act out the audience's spectatorial desire. This double aim could only be achieved through a bond dependent on tapping the depths of the audience's unconscious. Zhang's generous attention to the prolonged and profuse cinematic elaboration of the flaying as a privileged narrative moment betrays his awareness of the audience's private interest in violence. If violence is a universal, perennial stimulus that feeds on the audience's fantasy, then Zhang Yimou, while partly in complicity with that masochistic desire, politicises and historicises the violence so it cannot be taken comfortably as a mere visual thrill by a Chinese audience with a collective World War II trauma in their memory. The violence is pushed to extremes to jolt the audience out of their cowardice and insensitivity. This *presupposes* the continued existence of the pervasive insensitivity and torpor lampooned by Lu Xun half a century ago. Zhang therefore both acquiesces in and challenges the spectators' private desire.

On the other hand, there is always a danger that the audience will temporarily bracket the political, racial and historical significance of the scene for vicarious sado-masochistic pleasure. Even if the jolting effect exists, its cinematic elaboration may work in conspiracy with the audience's secret visual pleasure. In this way, the film encourages an insensitivity as well as discouraging it. And in so far as insensitivity has the potential to fall into an equation with passivity—as with the "chink" in *Broken Blossoms*—which could be problematically attributed to femininity, it may subvert Zhang's project. In other words, the mass-culture motivations behind the film—the search for the melodramatic, for the visual stimulus—may deconstruct the texture motivated by a consciousness of high culture.

Autonomous Ecstasy: A New Version of Female Sexuality

One central dynamic in the cinematic narrative of *Red Sorghum* is men's kidnapping and ravishing of women, whether successful or not. Jiu'er is carried off by men four times in the film: first, as an unwilling bride carried by a group of lusty sedan-bearers to the leprous bridegroom; second, as a potential rape victim in the sorghum field; third, as a willing mate on her second trip through the sorghum field; and last, as a kidnapped victim to be ransomed by the local bandit. Even when "grandpa" returns to assert his identity as her one-time love, he does it by the ritualistic act of carrying her off under his arm. As a regression and reversion to ancient myth, like the Western myth about carrying off Sabine women, described by Barthes as a masculine act in opposition to modern man's motionlessness which implies femininity (1978, 188), this diegetic impulse towards masculinity is unmistakable.

Should we then dismiss the film as a blatant discourse privileging patriarchal order? Is female subjectivity jeopardized in this ostensibly masculine universe? A Barthesian dialectic is more than illuminating here. The subject/object paradigm in the problematic of the ravishment could well be reversed: "It is the *object* of capture that becomes the *subject* of love; and the *subject* of the conquest moves into the class of loved *object*" (Barthes 1978, 188). The traditional scenario of subjective/active/aggressive male versus the objective/receptive/passive female is appropriated into the diegetic body, yet highly problematised, transfigured, challenged and subverted in the film. Jiu'er has to *wait* for men to initiate her. Yet passive waiting, the traditional fate of women in the Chinese narrative and scenario, attains a dialectic reversal in the film.

Red Sorghum transgresses the conventional Chinese melodramatic narrative pattern of the vulnerable woman intimidated by bullying men. As "surprise" constitutes the heart of what Barthes calls the "ancestral formality" of capture, the film subverts that by positing the woman as anything but panic-stricken or surprised prey to male desire. Jiu'er's first encounter with the masked kidnapper, or actually with a man, is one of the most transgressive and ambiguous moments in Chinese cinema. The shot–reverse shot structure establishes the woman's defiant confrontation with an unknown intimidating male presence, a diabolic male power. The filmic constraint of her explicit outward response signals her inner stability. The conqueror becomes the conquered. The frontal shot of Jiu'er is held still, correlating to the stupefied daze/gaze of the spiritually daunted and overwhelmed kidnapper. The reverse shot of the man, from Jiu'er's point of view, allows the camera the leisure and ease of tilting down from the mask to his body. The camera, as suggested by Christian Metz, can caress by tilting down the body, thus fetishising it. The camera that holds the bride could have conformed to Metz's formula, and it would be diegetically appropriate though symbolically different. Instead, we have the reverse. It is the woman's point-of-view shot "fetishising," or rather exploring and sizing up, the man which is highly unexpected in such a situation. The bride's break into a smirk is even less expected. Her giggle neutralises the moral implication of the situation. The kidnapper's identity is temporarily bracketed; he is just an uncertain man desiring a woman who has an equal undiscovered and unchannelled desire.

A frontal treatment of female sexuality is almost a taboo in Chinese moral codes on representation. Female sexuality is traditionally split between moral denunciation and stylistic enunciation in Chinese texts. Women have been morally denounced as vamps and scapegoats bearing the historical burden of being roots of corruption and curses on imperial solidarity. Daji and Yang Guifei are just two examples.[8] At the same time, they have been stylistically enunciated as objects of desire with their subjectivity at stake. This duality itself bespeaks the inner workings of Chinese ideology: the mechanism of putting desire under erasure through which desire peeps.

Red Sorghum not only deletes that erasure, thereby unleashing the repressed desire, but also attempts to articulate an autonomous female sexuality/subjectivity. This is very rare in Chinese cinema. The film opens with a close-up of the bride. The ensuing shots put her among an undifferentiated male group, vaguely establishing an "I-thou" relationship with the woman as "I."

The celebrated tossing-the-bridal-sedan sequence could superficially be taken as a scene of vulnerable woman at the mercy of lusty men. Yet the womb-like interior of the sedan, the condition of the Freudian "oceanic self" where she floats as an effect of being tossed about, is symbolically self-sufficient and self-creative. The frontal close-up of her against a shrouding interior darkness not only frees her from the menacing male world, but also simulates the topology of interiority, an inner world. Its relationship with the outside world becomes tenuous. Her anxiety is indeed a response to the frightening picture of the feudal marriage awaiting her, sung out loud by the sedan-bearers. Yet by frequently registering the ballad as an off-screen auditory presence, and in view of the situation where she is the enunciated character—the "I" amidst an undifferentiated male ensemble—it is easy to see that it is through her consciousness that the song enters.

But this is not an enclosure of narcissism. In this sequence, we are offered both the interior view of the sedan and the exterior view outside. A reiterated point-of-view shot by the bride looks out through the slightly open curtain on to a sweating, half-naked and muscular male body swaying in the dust. The following shot is the heroine's faintly dazed and desiring look. We may accept that the female gaze in classical cinema is often undermined, deflected, framed, erased by the male gaze catching the act of the female gazing, through *mise-en-scène* or editing, "a strategy which is a negation of her gaze, of her subjectivity in relation to vision" (Doane 1987, 100). However, the bride's gaze here is undistracted and subjectively autonomous. The interior is almost a figurative extension or externalisation of her subjectivity. Imprisoning as it is, it nevertheless resembles Kaspar's cave corresponding to Freud's "oceanic self" or what Lacan calls "l'hommelette."[9] The slightly raised curtain offering the female heroine a keyhole-like or telescopic glimpse of the male body is almost a reversal of the classical formula for a male voyeuristic experience.

The group of sedan-bearers tossing a bride, while singing a lurid song or their own sexual fantasies out loud, is a displacement of sexual energy. The tossed woman panting and gasping is easily read as a sign of physical nausea, her emotional discomposure a mixture of fright and thrill. Yet the prolonged and repeated shots, cinematically rhetoricised here, are not so much sadistically motivated as a way of articulating a hitherto undiscovered female sexuality, both in the film and in historical textuality. The ruffled and confused look, heavy breathing and distractedness all suggest an overtone of sexual ecstasy, if not orgasm.

The establishment of autonomous female ecstasy, though a cinematic illusion, is highly subversive politically. In the context of Western Lacanian algebra, this might be yet another proof of female narcissism that impedes woman's stepping into subjectivity. In the Chinese scenario, however, posited against the deeply ingrained myth of female passivity and incompleteness, the twist in *Red Sorghum* is certainly a welcome cinematic gesture with its ideological effect, and it is not brought about by man's contact/act. Rather, we see the woman working herself into an ecstatic state through the agency of the structure of shot–reverse shot editing. Rather than falling into the conventional scenario of female sexual dependence on male initiation, the film maps out an autonomous space to foreground the world of her subjective consciousness. Female sexuality is represented not through the frank sexual scenes, which are kept off-screen, thus denying male spectators' voyeuristic impulses, but rather by focusing on the female presence as the locus of discourse. Gong Li, who plays Jiu'er, has a look of rapture and ecstasy that is always there. This assumes its most expressive form in the sequence where "grandpa" shovels the distiller's grain out of the boiler. The grain falls on Jiu'er, who remains where she is, doused by the grains as if under a shower. She looks raptured and dazed. The shot carries a strong sexual overtone, as sexual intercourse is euphemistically alluded to as "clouds and rain" in traditional Chinese texts. This allusion is visually recuperated here. What is important is that the shot concentrates on her while marginalising the male character, now an agent, who pours that shower off-screen.

The sequence where Jiu'er is shot unawares by a machine-gun from the approaching Japanese truck and her struggling on the verge of death is also highly stylistically transfigured and displaced into a nondiegetic moment of agony and dance. The slow motion plus the unexpected wedding music transform the scene into a moment of death and transfiguration, of death as a form of ecstasy (as if unconsciously echoing the Elizabethan equation of death with sexual ecstasy). In this way, the film could again be seen as a narrative return of the historically and culturally repressed. The idea of female sexual autonomy, probably derivative of the primitive matriarchal imagination, has survived more as a fantasised construct of desire and defiance against feudal patriarchy, in myths, legends, romances, folk tales, and various (sub)cultural Chinese texts.

These mythological narratives about autonomous female sexuality are diversely contained and reiterated in various historical/mythical narratives, such as *Huai nan zi, Shan hai jing, San guo zhi,* and *Hou Han shu.*[10] Though imaginatively perverse, they fall into two basic categories: the myth of autonomous maternity, and the myth of a female utopia. In these female utopias, women become pregnant through immediate contact with the elements and forces of nature, for example through naked exposure to the "South Wind"[11] or by dipping into the "Yellow pool,"[12] or by dreaming of the white elephant.[13] These fantastic constructs project utopian visions of imagined realities in which even mere male existence is not to be tolerated; the female sex, self-reproductive, reigns all by itself.

One may argue that these narratives are the products of underlying Chinese feudal ideology privileging the homogeneity of femininity as a figure for class identity and a model for submissive consciousness. Yet considering the formal imaginative perversity of these fantasies that transgress the decorous mode of feudal discourse, the repressed desire sublimating into creative displacement is almost unmistakable.

These narratives also establish a scenario in which female sexuality and maternity are fused together. *Red Sorghum,* despite its predominant male presence, articulates an all-embracing female subjectivity which, in the same mythic fashion, destroys the distinguishing line between female sexuality and maternity, a line that is usually drawn in classical cinematic narrative, for example King Vidor's *Stella Dallas* (1937).

The film, ostensibly about the uninhibited manners of masculinity, is, however, ironically and structurally contained or cocooned in a discourse about the maternal, narrated by a first-person voice-over: "Let me tell you a story about my grandpa and grandma. Where I come from, they still talk about it to this day. It has been a long time, so some believe it, some don't." This opening dissolves into a medium close-up of a beautiful young woman and we hear the voice-over: "This is my grandma." The discrepancy between the connotations of the grandma and the actual iconographic figuration establishes a version of pre-Oedipal attachment. The very first frontal shot of "my grandma" could thus be seen as a mirror structure, the pre-Lacanian mirror-phase mirroring, inviting the unseen "I"—whose very absent gaze towards the scene of his dreamscape also implicates us, the spectators in the dark theatre—towards a primary identification. "Knowledge of the maternal is constituted as immediacy (one has only to look and see) (Doane 1987, 70). In the cinema, according to Gaylyn Studlar, we all regress to the infantile, pre-Oedipal phase, submitting ourselves to and identifying (fusing) with the overwhelming presence of the screen and the woman on it (1985, 616). The device in *Red Sorghum* only accentuates that state of mind.

The voice-over frequently punctuates the cinematic narrative and reminds us that the screen presences, the young man and the young woman, are my "grandpa" and "grandma." The first-person narrator, however, is absent throughout; at best he is figured on-screen by a small boy spoken of as "my father."

The maternal discourse is, as it were, a framing structure and a strategy of containment: the film begins with the shot of "grandma"/beautiful young woman, a fantasised image envisioned in the mind's eye/"I" of the voice-over narrator, and ends with a child's incantation and evocation of the maternal soul. The whole narrative is thus enclosed by this maternal discourse. One may even argue that this narrative strategy can be seen as a cinematic variant on the "fort/da" game played by Freud's grandson, in an auditory form, experiencing the pain of the loss of his mother and the evocation of her recovery. The very beginning frontal shot of "my grandma," a fiercely beautiful young woman— a frontal shot that resembles a still picture (and still pictures have an inherent pastness)—can thus be seen as recuperated from the historical/cultural memory, evoked by the child's incantation towards the end of the film.

Hence the film is a cinematic utopia, a dream narrative in which the speculative male "I" of the narrative projects his desire and wishfulness onto a female/maternal world and ends up being contained by the final silent maternity: the voice-over narrator becomes absent towards the end of the film, replaced, or figured, by his father, iconographically represented on the screen as an infant who longingly chants after his dead mother. This narrative strategy holds the absent past in the cinematic present, while at the same time punctuating the illusion of presentness with a sense of the historical past. What is most interesting is that it is through "my grandma"/young heroine's point of view that the past is mediated, reconstructed and totalised. In other words, it is through a feminine vision of totality that the masculine past is reconstructed and obtains coherence and meaning.

It follows that the death of Jiu'er, the "grandma"/young heroine, in the diegetic space means the loss of perception, consciousness and meaning, since she has hitherto been the pivot around which the cinematic universe evolves. That traumatic blackout is cinematically enacted: "grandpa"/young sedan-bearer, the survivor, turns into a stone as if without the female character's gaze he is one of the living dead.

The climactic denouement is actually an externalisation of Jiu'er's subjective consciousness on the verge of extinction. The shrieking *suona* (Chinese horn), playing the wedding song, projects her inner flashback of the moments of her past life. The agonised ecstasy and the ecstatic agony, the sexuality and death, are all (con)fused together. The death of the female's subjective consciousness means therefore a nondifferentiation of everything, symbolised by the sweeping wash of red that dominates the screen—the dispersion of her entire being. Redness bespeaks desire, passion, blood (itself signifying birth and death), beauty and cruelty, and destruction and construction (in that the homogeneous color scheme destroys the previous world of color and re-orders a new world). The eclipse of the sun and moon defies any verbal formulation here, yet it is at least an emblem of Jiu'er's blackout, of a state of nondifferentiation into which are collapsed the *yin* and *yang*, masculinity and femininity, day and night, self and other, warmth and coldness, war and peace. The haunting incantation praying for the soul of the mother is at once the echoes heard by the dying and echoes that reverberate in the corridor of historical memory, resounding Qu Yuan's poetic evocation for lost ancestral souls.[14]

The ending of the film is therefore the moment of cinematic *jouissance* in which we experience the loss of meaning as well as the birth of an infinite myriad of meaning. It is an orgastic and maternal synthesis, a maternal enclosure and mastery of narrative that proposes to construct a masculine identity.

Maternity is closely related to the natural, the unquestionable. "Paternity and its interrogation, on the other hand, are articulated within the context of issue of identity, legality, inheritance—in short, social legitimacy. To generate questions about the existence of one's father is, therefore, to produce an insult of the highest order" (Doane 1987, 70). The maternity of "my grandma"/Jiu'er is an absolute given in the narrative while the paternity of "my grandpa"/sedan-bearer is narratively "mediated . . . it allows for gaps and invisibilities, of doubts in short" (Doane 1987, 70). "My grandpa" is often an intruder onto the scene, which posits him outside of the maternal discourse and to be recuperated. The primal scene with "my grandma," which admits the sedan-bearer into the narrative as "my grandpa," is suggested but is only present as a narrative ellipsis. Ravished and sexually fulfilled, "grandma"/young bride resumes her journey on a donkey, and "my grandpa's" song, a barbarous yelp, is heard, designating his screen absence and off-screen presence. The sexual encounter is thus internalised into the heroine's consciousness and becomes a blank in the memory of the first-person narrator who has been denied the complete primal scene, a blank that may question its actuality and credibility in a later sequence when he appears from nowhere, drunk, and retells in a fragmented and crude manner what has taken place between him and Jiu'er. The narrative blank consequently puts the identity of the voice-over narrator at stake. Paternity in *Red Sorghum* is therefore frequently represented as absence, as the questionable, as the other. The irreverent attitude implied in the way the cinematic narrative comically contains him betrays not only an Oedipal complex with which the narrator tries to evince the paternal, but also the anti-patriarchal mastery of the narrative by maternity.

Red Sorghum also rewrites the maternal discourses of Chinese textuality. Identified with the mother earth, the motherland and the mother Party,[15] mother as a figure of identification in socialist ideology is traditionally evoked to elicit absolute unthinking allegiance, as maternity is related to the natural, the unquestionable. By positing the spectator vis-à-vis the sexuality of the maternal, the film not only pulls down all that is on the pedestal, but also revisions history as embodied in the dead grandma by setting free the repressed, figured as sexuality.

It is consequently tempting to fix *Red Sorghum* in a Freudian algebra as a narrative about the return of the repressed; or to water down the film into a Lacanian phraseology as the liberation of desire. Even director Zhang Yimou's own confessional statement seems to favour that formulation: "My personality is quite the contrary to the mood of the film. I have long been repressed, restrained, enclosed and introspective. Once I had a chance to make a film on my own, I wanted to make it liberated, abandoned" (Li Xing 1988). But there is also a difference. *Red Sorghum* is fundamentally a liberation of repressed collective desire. A lot of psychoanalytic categories, when placed in the Chinese context, cannot be embraced without some reorientation. The patterns of masculinity and femininity, dominance and submission, repression and desire are bound up with other cultural praxes in the Chinese context, and acquire new dimensions. In this way, *Red Sorghum* can be said to teeter on the borderline of the Western psychoanalytic scenario. And from this, we can come to feel the relevance of Fredric Jameson's critique of Western psychoanalysis in cultural criticism:

> The object of commentary is effectively transformed into an allegory whose master narrative is the story of desire itself, as it struggles against a repressive reality, convulsively breaking through the grids that were designed to hold it in place or, on the contrary, succumbing to repression and leaving the dreary wasteland of aphanasis behind it. At this level it is to be wondered whether we have to do with a mere interpretation any longer, whether it is not a question here of the production of a whole new aesthetic object, a whole new mythic narrative. (1981, 67)

Western allegories of desire and wish-fulfillment, according to Jameson, are "locked into the category of the individual subject" (69) and are therefore in need of expansion by transcending individual categories and tapping the political unconscious in terms of the collective and associative. This strategy remains comparable to a psychoanalytic one only in the persistence of just such a valorisation of desire. Also, the Western psychoanalytic scenario of the male/female problematic, given its social implications and collective relevance, is equally motivated towards individual existence and finalised in the private realm.

One essential distinction that marks the contemporary Chinese New Wave cinema is its propelling sense of cultural urgency couched in the collective consciousness, and the impossibility of private isolation in a critical moment of historical transformation that will eventually implicate every individual. Issues of masculinity and femininity acquire more social symbolic resonance than the consequences they may have in the West. The problematic of sexual difference is politically more displaced, more often figured as signifiers of social and ideological entities than the immediate reality it denotes. Therefore Fredric Jameson's critique of the individualistic psychoanalytic critical paradigm seems especially relevant to the current cultural scenario of which Chinese cinema is a ramification. The strong repercussions *Red Sorghum* invoked confirm the public insistence on the wider collective implications of the cinematic narrative and the denial of any individual categories.

It is here, however, that Jameson's effective critique also becomes problematic. The very denial of the individual categories, given its cultural and historical imperative, has been shown to be regressive and repressive in the Chinese cultural context. In this way, the very placement of private categories, psychoanalytic or other, given their displacement in an urgently collective cultural landscape, can be seen as politically positive, affirming values that are nevertheless absent. In this sense, the culturally irrelevant psychoanalytic formula can be politically relevant.

In the ideological circumstances and cultural context of China, the narrative of psychoanalysis itself needs rewriting. In the case of *Red Sorghum*, repression and revolt—two fundamental events of psychoanalytic narrative—meet each other only through a tension across the threshold of the screen. The cinematic absence of repression renders the revolt undirected and dispersed into the ideological space outside the screen. The perennial off-screen reality as an antithesis to the screen world is *presupposed* and the cinematic world is an alternative to the off-screen world we inhabit. We see the importance of presupposition—the presupposition of a cultural presence registered on the screen as absence. Here we come to a critique of the simple-minded mimetic assumptions that sometimes go unquestioned in the rhetoric of cross-cultural studies (e.g., a culturally specific film is an iconographic representation of that culture). *Red Sorghum* and many other culturally specific texts do not reflect the *appearances* of a culture; they mirror what the actual cultural landscape *lacks*. They reflect fantasies and imagined memories—that which society expels. Any attempt to picture the Chinese cultural scene from this film requires an imaginative approach—in the same way one infers an image from a film negative.

Notes

This article was first published in *Perspectives on Chinese Cinema,* edited by Chris Berry (London: British Film Institute), pp. 80–103. Copyright © 1994 by BFI. Reprinted with permission.

1. For an example of negative critical response, see Zhu Shoutong, "The Increasingly Ugly 'Savage' Sensationalism" ("Yuyi choulou de 'man' ciji"), and Zhong Youxun, "They Lack Emotion," ("Tamen queshao 'qing'"), in *Film Art (Dianying yishu)* no. 192, Beijing, July 1988, 35–40.

2. Dong Zhongshu, "The Noble Yang and the Base Yin ('Nanzun nübei')", quoted from Zhang Dainian 1982, 31. Dong Zhongshu (179–104 B.C.) founded the orthodox Confucian school of the Han dynasty (206 B.C.–A.D. 220). A civil servant in the reign of Emperor Wu, he was also an influential scholar who politicised, secularised and canonised Confucianism, turning it into a dominant feudal ideology. The *Yi zhuan* is a compilation of Confucian texts. Once attributed to Confucius himself, it is now thought to have been written by a group of scholars over a period from the beginning of the Warring States period (475 B.C.) to the end of the Han dynasty (A.D. 220).

3. This common saying may have its origins in the *Liezi,* a classical work of philosophy. See Zhang Zhan, ed., *Liezi; zhuzi jicheng III* (Shanghai: Shanghai shudian, 1986), 6.

4. *Water Margin (Shuihu zhuan)* is an extremely popular classical novel about a peasant uprising during the Northern Song dynasty (960–1127). Li Kui and Lu Zhishen are exemplary macho characters familiar to all Chinese.

5. Roland Barthes writes: "I am wiped out more completely if I am rejected not only as the one who demands but also as the speaking subject (as such, I have at least the mastery of the formulas); it is my language, the last resort of my existence, which is denied" (1978, 149).

6. Lin Yutang 1978, 97–101. Lin Yutang (1895–1947) was a Chinese scholar who, with others, fashioned a Chinese equivalent of the English genre of familiar essays, with an emphasis on wit and brevity, which earned him a wide readership.

7. Jia Ping'ao, "Heaven Dog" *(Tiangou), October (Shiyue)* 2 (1985): 6–29.

8. Captured and taken as a favourite concubine by the last emperor of the Shang dynasty (1600–1100 B.C.), Daji is portrayed in various classical works as a vicious *femme fatale,* responsible for innumerable cruelties, perversities and corruptions. Named Royal Concubine in 745, Yang Guifei's elevation brought various of her brothers and sisters powers which they abused. This provoked an insurgency in which the emperor had to let Yang commit suicide to appease his own soldiers. The story forms the basis for Mizoguchi's 1955 film, *Princess Yang Kwei-fei.*

9. Kaja Silverman, "Herzog's *Kaspar Hauser,*" *New German Critique* (Summer 1982): 74.

10. Also known as *Huainan honglie, Huai nan zi* is a philosophical work compiled by Liu An (179–122 B.C.) and typical of a school known as the Eclectics, which flourished at the end of the Warring States period (475–221 B.C.) and the beginning of the Han dynasty (206 B.C.–A.D. 220). The *Shan hai jing* is an ancient fantastic geography of China and its sur-

rounding lands. It remains a major source of Chinese mythology. The *San guo zhi* is a 65-volume chronicle of the Three Kingdoms period (220–265), compiled by Chen Shou (233–297) of the Western Jin dynasty (265–316). The *Hou Han shu* is a chronicle of the Eastern Han dynasty (25–220), compiled by Fan Ye (398–445). The latter two works are canonical examples of classical Chinese historiography.

11. "The Female Kingdom", *Yi yu zhi* (The exotic places), quoted from Yuan Ke, *Zhongguo shenhua cidan* (Encyclopedia of Chinese mythology) (Shang: Cishu Press, 1985), 45.

12. Guo Pu, *Shan hai jing,* in *Jingyin wenyuange siku quanshu,* ed. Ji Yun et al. (Taibei: Taiwan Shangwu Yinshu Guan, 1986), vol. 1042, p. 47.

13. Ji Yun, *op. cit.,* vol. 254, p. 542.

14. Qu Yuan, *"Guo shang"* and *"Zhao Hun,"* in David Hawks 1962, 43–44, 103–9.

15. "Sing a folk song to the Party," a popular song widely circulated in the 1960s in China, explicitly equates Mother with the Party: "Sing a folk song to the Party, I liken the Party to Mother." This identification has been wholeheartedly embraced by the Chinese since 1949, and has become almost a clichéd figure in various kinds of emotional rhetoric.

Part Five

New City Films
Beyond-Yellow-Earth Experiences of Postsocialism

Conference scene in *Black Cannon Incident (Heipao shijian)*, directed by Huang Jianxin, 1985.
Courtesy of China Film Archive, Beijing.

In late 1988, Zhang Wei, a Chinese film critic, made a perceptive remark about "the Fifth Generation film directors' return to the city" (1988, 3). His observation has a double connotation. The People's Republic of China's by-then youngest generation of film directors had returned to the cities after an involuntary sojourn in the countryside during the Cultural Revolution. And these directors had finally turned to shooting city films, a shift away from the Chinese Westerns set in the countryside. The phrase "return to," interestingly enough, coincides with a term that Michel Foucault uses in his study of "discursive practices": "The phrase, 'return to,' designates a movement with its proper specificity, which characterizes the initiation of discursive practices. If we return, it is because of a basic and constructive omission, an omission that is not the result of accident or incomprehension. [This return] is an effective and necessary means of transforming discursive practice" (1977, 134–35).

Can the young film directors' return to the city also reflect a discursive practice? That is, does their return bring forth a new language of art in films? To answer this question, the city films should be contrasted with the "roots-searching films" represented by such titles as *Yellow Earth* and *Red Sorghum*. Following Foucault, additional questions can be raised. What differences does this return to the city make? What omission does this return try to resolve? What is the "space" that the city has cleared out for the young film directors to return to, and what are the issues that urge this return?

The new city films first emerged in the mid-1980s (most noticeably in 1986), and their producers were not confined to Fifth Generation directors; some Fourth Generation directors such as Huang Jianzhong, Xie Fei, and Zhang Nuanxin also made significant contributions to the genre. Early titles include Huang Jianxin's *Black Cannon Incident* (*Heipao shijian*, 1985) and *Dislocation* (*Cuowei*, 1986), Huang Jianzhong's *Questions for the Living* (*Yige sizhe dui shengshe de fangwen*, 1986), and Song Jiangbo's *Masquerade* (*Chengshi jiamian wuhui*, 1986). The major body of the new city films, however, was produced between 1988 and 1990: Zhang Zeming's *Sunshine and Showers*, 1988, Sun Zhou's *Add Some Sugar to Your Coffee* (*Gei kafei jia dian tang*, 1988), Tian Zhuangzhuang's *Rock Kids* (*Yaogun qingnian*, 1989), Zhang Junzhao's *Arc Light* (*Huguang*, 1989), Zhou Xiaowen's *Price of Madness* (*Fongkuang de daijia*, 1988), Huang Jianxin's *Samsara* (*Lunhui*, 1988), Mi Jiashan's *Masters of Mischief* (*Wanzhu*, 1988), Xie Fei's *Black Snow* (*Benming nian*, 1989), Zhang Liang's *A Woman's Street* (*Nüren jie*, 1989), Hu Bingliu's *Commercial Circles* (*Shangjie*, 1989), and Zhang Nuanxin's *Good Morning, Beijing*, among others.

The "return" of the younger film directors helped the PRC's film critics focus on the contrast between city and countryside. For a few years after 1988, this focus maintained a fairly central position in film criticism and greatly enriched its language by contributing to a definition of an otherwise not-so-interesting term: "city film." It is in contrast to the previous cinematic wave, to the figurative "yellow earth" of the Chinese countryside, that the term "city film" gains its new meanings. In PRC film criticism, "city" is frequently contrasted with "countryside" *(xiangtu)* to suggest social and cultural metamorphosis in China. In this schema, "city" is paired with modernity and "countryside" with tradition; "city" is seen as embodying Spengler's Faustian cultural model (representing conflicts and the human conquering of such conflicts) and "countryside" as Apollonian (representing the order and the human acceptance of such order).

The city becomes Faustian because it is informed by an emerging cultural discourse that speaks of the separation of individual beings *(geti ren)* from collective beings *(qiunti ren)*, and economic beings *(jingji ren)* from political beings *(zhengzhi ren)*. Viewed from this perspective, the new city films differ from earlier city films—those of the late 1970s and early 1980s, which presented the countryside as a close-knit community, as one title suggests, *A Village in the Metropolis (Dushi lide cunzhuan,* 1982). These earlier films emphasized community problems rather than the problems of individuals. For example, in *Sunset Alley (Xizhao jie,* 1983), community-centered moral standards were offered to solve the problems of delinquent city youth. The new city films tend to avoid moral judgment and take the existential conditions of contemporary urban youth as a social and cultural given. As the socialist discourse faded away, the city of the new "city films" was endowed with the special concerns and anxieties of a period of transition.

The new city films also configured a new type of anti-hero, the dislocated young urbanite, and they greatly divided the critics: some asserted that the new configuration was a testimony to the difficulties and anxieties experienced by the PRC's first generation of urban economic beings; others, reminded of the Western "Beat Generation," abhorred the rebellious psyche and countercultural behavior those young urbanites embodied. Heated dispute focused mostly on the new configuration's moral and ideological implications. While some believed that it was disgraceful, decadent, in bad taste, and a catalyst to the rise of "ruffian films" *(pizi dianying),* others justified it, holding that the new configuration embodied "new social messages, mentality, ideology and ethics" that were worth looking into (Wei Xiaolin 1990a, 70).

The disruption caused by this marginal configuration, in a way, reflected a different cultural revolution—not the ten years of Chinese chaos (1966–76) in the name of the proletariat but what Fredric Jameson defined as "a moment in which the coexistence of various modes of production becomes visibly antagonistic, their contradictions moving to the very center of political, social, and historical life" (1981, 95). Ironically, the Chinese proletarian Cultural Revolution fragmented the PRC's socialist mode of production and paved the way for something very close to what Jameson describes as a bourgeois cultural revolution, "in which the values and the discourses, the habits and the daily space, of the ancien régime were systematically dismantled so that in their place could be set the new conceptualities, habits and life forms, and value systems of a capitalist market society" (1981, 96).

The Chinese had postponed this bourgeois cultural revolution until the postsocialist era. From this perspective, marginal young urbanites are no longer the once politically simplified characters now rehumanized and given complexity and ambiguity; rather, they are anti-heroes who question the possibility of being human within the confines of the older mode of production (material and representational). They are not what the new human beings should be but what the older human beings experience while trying to be the newer kind. The rising anxiety in this special kind of cultural revolution has made the new city films significant.

The younger film directors' "return to the city" changed the perspective and the tone of cinematic cultural investigation. The film language of yellow earth and red sorghum suggests a contemplation, in collective terms, of Chinese history, legend, and national ethos. This cultural totality of a nation, though often denying sacrifice (as in *Yellow Earth*) or demanding it (as in *Old Well*), also endorses a certain fantasy. For example, in *Red Sorghum,* a sorghum liquor is shared by a group of people who pass it hand to hand, a filmic narrative of how community solidarity is achieved. Similarly, in *Old Well,* a whole village persists, even after repeated failure, in digging a community well, until the water gushes out. This kind of investigation of the totality is reflected in the serious question asked in a popular TV series, *Elegy for the Yellow River* (1988): Can the Chinese afford to lose one more game (since the Opium War) in a competitive world?

Returning to the city by filming their immediate present, these young directors confronted fragmentation, a special kind of Chinese modernity that has emerged with the bankruptcy of the old-fashioned socialist ideological totality, the rapid commercialization of urban—as well as rural—life, and the emergence of a sense of the individualized self. The city *mise-en-scène* is not in the traditional sense a totality that characters can either identify with or rebel against; it functions more as the projection of the characters' fragmented feelings of anxiety, annoyance, and loss. In a certain sense, one can surely diagnose these symptoms as the "beyond-yellow-earth" syndrome, with yellow earth representing an irretrievable social and cultural totality.

Given its strong political implications, the beyond-yellow-earth syndrome should also be considered a postsocialist one. In discussing films by Fifth Generation director Huang Jianxin, Paul Pickowicz questions the appropriateness of using the modernist framework to appraise these films (and, by extension, those of most other young film directors). Pickowicz believes that the modernist framework "is incapable of accounting for what is most distinctive about post-Mao cultural and political conditions in the decidedly socialist People's Republic" (1994, 59). In his view, a postsocialist framework is more explanatory of "the type of popular cultural diversity, cultural ambiguity, and cultural confusion that became so pronounced in China in the 1980s" (61).

The postsocialist framework is not, it should be pointed out, incompatible with the modernist framework, for the latter was already widely employed in the discourse on cultural change in other former socialist countries. It indicates the Western presence there, and it may serve as an indispensable point of reference, often with political implications. After all, it is the Western presence rather than the presence of the former socialist partners that is strongly felt in postsocialist culture today. The postsocialist framework, nevertheless, helps historicize Chinese modernity and helps explain the differences underlying its superficial similarities to Western modernity. For instance, the loss of cultural totality and the emphasis on individual choice in existential fragmentation can easily be considered a shared feature of Western and Chinese modernities. In the West, this cultural feeling and the diverse individual cultural choices are most succinctly pronounced in Nietzsche's saying, through the mouth of a madman, that "God is dead." It is also reflected in the rise of the philosophy of existentialism, which, in its various versions, centers on the individual and the individual's relationship to the universe or to God. Chinese modernity also pronounces that "God is dead" and emphasizes the emergence of individual beings in a process of difficult and painful separation from the collective. This Chinese "God," however, is not as metaphysical and religious as it is in the Western context; it is mostly ideological and connotatively identical to a political icon, that is, Mao. China's post-Mao modernity is clearly related to the poor track record of a political system that has failed to reproduce traditional Maoist ideology, that has alienated the people living in it, and that has produced a strongly "rebellious social psyche." What Pickowicz defines as "cultural diversity, cultural ambiguity, and cultural confusion," one Chinese critic would describe as the "gray ideological syndrome of *fin de siècle*" *(yishixingtai shijimo huise zonghezheng):* "With the understanding that 'God is dead,' the ethical model—which emphasized the other and which was pushed to its extreme by political totalitarianism in the Cultural Revolution—was collapsing; the new ethical model that emphasizes the self, however, is still to be established—all conventions are lost in a value vacuum" (Huang Shixian 1989, 41). The new city films are "new" precisely because they project this "God-is-dead world" on the screen. Their importance as "new" lies in this adjective's relation to its close cultural synonyms of "beyond" (yellow earth) and "post" (socialism).

Fourteen
Black Cannon Incident
(*Heipao shijian,* dir. Huang Jianxin, 1985)

Screenplay Li Wei
Cinematography Feng Wei, Wang Xinsheng
Producer Xi'an
Cast Liu Zifeng, as Zhao Shuxin

If a narrow meaning of "Fifth Generation"—the first post-Mao graduating class from Beijing Film Academy—is adhered to strictly, then director Huang Jianxin does not really belong to it. His résumé shows six years of army service, one year as a cameraman for the Medical Education Bureau at Xi'an, and one year of college training in journalism before he became a script editor at Xi'an Film Studio in 1978. From 1981 to 1983, he apprenticed in film directing by assisting various directors at the studio where he got his talent recognized. He was then sent by the studio to the Fifth Generation's cradle, Beijing Film Academy, for two years of training as a special student.

In 1985, Huang returned to Xi'an Film Studio and, at age thirty-one, was appointed the youngest director there. By 1985, the Fifth Generation had already started their cinematic new wave from other provincial studios, and they would soon be invited by the head of Xi'an Film Studio, Wu Tianming, to continue the wave featuring films set in the remote countryside or in minority regions. Huang, somehow, set off on a different route and, with his *Black Cannon Incident, Dislocation,* and *Samsara,* pioneered another wave of city films in the PRC's post-Mao new cinema.

Although Huang has trod a different path by persisting in urban subjects, the cultural spirit and the critical edge detected in his urbanism are not too far from those roots-searching films set in the remote and imaginative rural landscape. What dominates Huang's urbanism is his strong interest in PRC political culture. Here I would suggest that themes of enclosure and inertia are found in most of Huang's earlier films. These themes help Huang showcase how the

283

PRC's political culture confines people's perspectives and how this culture renders people (in his favorite imagery) into machine parts—doing things mechanically, without much thought, as if driven by the force of inertia. Using these themes as points of comparison, we may find similar enclosure and inertia themes in many of the roots-searching films. Take Zhang Yimou's *Raise the Red Lantern,* for example. In this allegorical denouncement of patriarchy, which illustrates how women are victimized in a polygamous culture, enclosure is shown by the interlocking courtyards, the circular motion of seasons, and the repeated performance of the same ritual of getting the women ready for their almost "faceless" master (no close-up shot is used to give a clear view of him); inertia is shown by how the master's wives are helplessly engaged in dehumanized competition for the favor of the master.

Huang's difference lies in his persistence in representing a present China. For Huang, "cultural roots are found in the present time, and within every one of us. People's behavior and psyche spell out a culture" (Chai 1994, 37). His urbanism showcases an array of anti-heroic characters in various cultural microcosms. Often it is the urban setting that helps highlight various allegorical undertones of these characters who, in their turns, typify their cosmos with their behavior. Huang's only detour from depicting the present China is found in a legendary landscape in *The Wooden Man's Bride* (*Wu kui,* 1993)—he directed the film as if wanting to show that he could be as spectacular as other directors of the roots-searching genre.

Black Cannon Incident is Huang's first film and is an interesting mixture of the two kinds of city films that he directed later. In an interview, Huang contrasted the differences between Chinese cities and the cities of the industrialist West: "According to the post-modernist concept, China has no genuine cities. The Chinese cities are the more commercialized places within an agricultural culture and they embody mostly the agricultural structure of thinking. The basic characteristics of a [genuine] city should be about industrialization, about how the highly developed industries will speed up the rhythm of life, about how people are alienated by such a society. China is not there yet" (Chai 1994, 38). Throughout this interview, Huang indicates his changed perception of "city" and a progression of his city films after *Black Cannon Incident:* his earlier films about alienation, such as *Dislocation* and *Samsara,* pursue an outward resemblance with the Western (individualistic, fragmented, and isolated) cities; his later films, such as *Stand Up, Don't Grovel* (*Zhan zhi le, bie paxia,* 1992) and

Back to Back, Face to Face (*Bei kao bei, lian dui lian,* 1994), focus more on using the behaviors of the urbanites to depict Chinese (communal, agricultural, and inter-human) cities.

Black Cannon Incident was an adaptation of Zhang Xianliang's story "Romantic Black Cannon." Working with a crew whose average age was twenty-eight, Huang was given free rein to try new things. The visual and artistic impact of the finished product was comparable to other Fifth Generation pioneering films. It won Huang quite a few awards, including Best Picture and Best Director at the 1986 Golden Rooster Awards. Liu Zifeng, who played Zhao Shuxin, also won the Best Actor award; critics praised him, saying that he had portrayed an unforgettable image of the typical Chinese intellectual of the 1980s.

Suggested readings for *Black Cannon Incident* are as follows:

H. C. Li 1989
Pickowicz 1994
Silbergeld 1999, 234–304

Director's Notes

[*Black Cannon Incident*] tells an almost absurd story seriously. It purposefully disrupts the distinction between tragedy, comedy, and serious drama. By trespassing genres, it becomes an "unconventional" mixture with multiple structures, and it displays a sense of humor—a cold humor.

The depth of *Black Cannon Incident* is achieved by its ideas. [Vertically,] the film deals with a short span of time and has to seek symbols horizontally in various spaces, in a method known to us as "dispersed symbolism." Differing from independent symbols, these dispersed symbols are arranged in a "relay" manner; they accumulate to create the whole meaning. Like moods, they symbolically cut into the plot, leaving it fragmented. Scenes such as the dance performance, the conference, the soccer field, the church, and the concluding scene of bricks, all complement the plot to assure a psychological reality.

On the surface, *Black Cannon Incident* tells the story of an intellectual and how others [mis]treat him. Deep down, it shows that a particular mentality and an inert way of thinking restrain us. This frame of mind is not all due to politics but also to the spirit of the traditional culture. (Huang Jianxin 1996, 401, 407–8)

From "Post-Socialist Strategies:
An Analysis of *Yellow Earth* and *Black Cannon Incident*"
Chris Berry and Mary Ann Farquhar

Rodin said: "A real artist always expresses his own thoughts and is not afraid to break the existing rules."

—Huang Jianxin, *Heipao shijian: Cong xiaoshuo dao dianying*

Introduction

In 1982, the first class of cinematographers, directors, and art directors since the start of the "Cultural Revolution" in 1966 graduated from China's only film school, the Beijing Film Academy. Previous graduates might have had to work for twenty years in subsidiary, apprentice-like jobs before they had the opportunity to make their own films, but an unusual combination of circumstances enabled these young newcomers to make their first films within two years of graduation.[1] The films shocked the Chinese film world and the filmmakers became known as the Fifth Generation.

There is no question that the Fifth Generation were doing something different, and nearly all interviews with them attest to the fact that their effort to mark themselves out from their predecessors was self-conscious and deliberate.[2] This differentiation occurs across all aspects of the films, from character types to plot structure, theses, and locations. In this article, we will consider what was new about the Fifth Generation by comparing the painting traditions they draw upon with those used by their predecessors.

This task is made complicated by the remarkable variety of Fifth Generation films. To take but a few brief examples, Tian Zhuangzhuang's film about life in Mongolia, *On the Hunting Ground* (*Liechan zhasa*, 1984), adopts an almost cinema-verité style of ethnographic filmmaking, although it is a fiction film; Hu Mei's investigation of the personal sacrifices Chinese women make in exchange for participation in the public sphere, *Army Nurse* (*Nü'er lou*, 1985), adopts stream-of-consciousness techniques with meandering voice-over and melancholic memories; and Chen Kaige's *Yellow Earth* (*Huang tudi*, 1984) is frequently related to Chinese landscape painting techniques. However, although they have adopted a great range of different techniques, all these filmmakers are united in their effort to move away from what we will call here the socialist-realist model of Chinese filmmaking.[3]

In China this socialist-realist model was dominant from the fifties through the late seventies, and still exists today. Unlike the Fifth Generation films, it was relatively unified and constant. It was adapted from the classical Hollywood cinema and the Soviet socialist-realist cinema. (The latter was itself derived from the Hollywood model, prompting Jean-Luc Godard to refer to it as the "Hollywood-Mosfilm style.") The aesthetics of these two cinemas are founded on post-Renaissance realist painting techniques and, in the case of the Soviet films, agitprop poster art. Perspectival space is, of course, established, and illusionist editing techniques collaborate with this to ensure that a clear position is maintained for the viewer in relation to what is depicted. Mimesis is carefully constructed with close attention to authenticity of sets, costumes, acting, and so forth, and the humanist tradition operates in composition focusing on well-centered figures carefully displayed, full face and well lit, for inspection by the audience.[4] Narrative characteristics draw upon the nineteenth-century European novel, which complements the realist painting tradition with a linear structure whose absence of disjuncture helps to suture the viewer/reader into an illusion of reality, and a primary focus on human relations.[5]

After the break with the Soviet Union at the end of the 1950s, which occurred because the Chinese Communist Party was unwilling to join in the repudiation of Stalin, the socialist-realist tradition in the cinema was renamed as a combination of "socialist realism and revolutionary romanticism" and Chinese filmmakers were called upon to sinicize their films. Revolutionary romanticism was interpreted to mean the integration of an element of idealization, or "typicalization," whereby the revolutionary potential inherent in contemporary reality was supposed to be stressed.[6] For example, both heroes and villains were constructed as larger-than-life class types rather than psychologized individuals, a tendency which reached its apogee with the theory of the "Three Prominences" during the Cultural Revolution.[7] This technique might be referred back to Soviet poster art, but was also explicitly claimed as sinicized by reference to characteristics of traditional opera, but with proletarian figures replacing the emperors, generals, and courtesans of old.[8]

Sinicization was also applied to the image, with a certain aesthetic decorative style, where the basic socialist-realist style was stuccoed over with Chinese motifs. Catherine Yi-yu Cho Woo has noted the appearance of symbols derived from ancient poetry and painting, and the construction of isolated shots to resemble classical painting, for example, by framing a shot with branches of blossoms in the "bird and flower" style or using natural metaphors such as flocks of geese to represent the character far from home or a pair of fish to imply sexual desire (1991, 21–29). Other similarly isolated examples of a decorative sinicization might include the tendency to start a scene or a film with a lengthy pan of the landscape in which the story is set, referring to landscape scroll paintings, as in the opening of the 1963 film about Tibet, *Serfs (Nongnu)*. However, these flourishes hardly formed part of an integrated style, as in the use of landscape painting traditions in *Yellow Earth*.

The socialist-realist model we have described both adopted and adapted elements from Hollywood, Soviet socialist realism, and traditional opera, as well as from certain ancient painting and poetry traditions, but it did not do this simply to reproduce these elements. Rather, they were actively deployed to didactic ends. Similarly, the Fifth Generation directors have not drawn upon a wide range of different styles simply to distance themselves from the socialist-realist model. We could briefly gloss references to non-socialist-realist styles in a large number of films, but we do not wish to represent Fifth Generation films as sites where other styles are simply reproduced. Instead, we would emphasize the purposeful deployment of these styles as part of a larger project by way of extended discussion of two very different tendencies. One is a return to classical traditions not used extensively in the socialist-realist film, as represented by *Yellow Earth*. The other is the adoption of a style carrying connotations of Western modern art in Huang Jianxin's political satire, *Black Cannon Incident*.

Before we enter this extended discussion, one further issue remains to be discussed: the nature of the shift away from the socialist realist style. As indicated by the sheer variety of Fifth Generation work, it cannot be argued that their work constitutes a unified paradigm. In this sense, it seems that either Marxist or modernist theories of historical change—which speak in terms of the completely new and different, the revolutionary, the radical rupture, and the paradigm shift—may be inappropriate. Even though Huang Jianxin's *Black Cannon Incident* draws upon Western modernist art traditions and examines the Chinese discourse of modernization in the eighties, placed in reference to the Fifth Generation as a whole, it is only one instance in a network of different references which are drawn upon, pastiched together, played with, and transformed. Therefore, we would venture to suggest the term "post-socialist" to refer to the style and strategies of Fifth Generation films as worthy of further consideration.

This term, originated by Arif Dirlik in his discussion of Chinese politics, has already been adopted by Paul Pickowicz in his discussion of Huang Jianxin's films (1994). Pickowicz's decision to use this term is highly suggestive, but he uses it mainly in reference to the plots of Huang's films to suggest that they mark the death of socialism and the emergence of something different. What remains to be fully explored is the homology between this term and "postmodernist," from which it is clearly derived. Can postsocialism be seen as a complement to postmodernism? Is its pastiche of other styles, its ambiguity and play, part of an aesthetic parallel to postmodernism? And is its move away from socialist realism without establishing a new orthodoxy a "mutation" rather than a revolutionary break (to adopt Foucault's borrowing from Nietzsche)?[9] We hope that the discussion that follows can provide some ground for the elaboration of these questions.

Black Cannon Incident

Picasso said: "An artist must know how to make people believe the true in the false."

—Huang Jianxin, *Heipao shijian: Cong xiaoshuo dao dianying*

Among the films that emerged in the wake of *Yellow Earth* was *Black Cannon Incident*, completed one year later in 1985. When *Black Cannon Incident* first appeared, Chinese critics discussed the two films in the same breath as "stylized" films. This critical construction contrasted them to the "on-the-spot" *(dangchang)* trend toward documentary-style naturalism, which had dominated the early eighties following the publication of translations of works by Siegfried Kracauer and André Bazin lauding the realist possibilities of film.[10] These "on-the-spot" films included *Neighbors (Linjü, 1981), Yamaha Fish Stall (Yamaha yudang, 1984), A Corner in the City (Dushi de cunzhuang, 1982), Sunset Street (Xizhao jie, 1982),* and others back to *The Drive to Win (Sha'ou)* in 1981.[11] Like the "stylized" films, the "on-the-spot" films saw themselves as moving away from the socialist-realist model, but their main drive was against what they saw as the theatrical and "false" elements of the socialist-realist model in favor of a truer and more naturalistic realism.

The stylized elements that bind *Black Cannon Incident* and *Yellow Earth* together include distanced, static camerawork in which the long shot is heavily favored; a limited palette of the same colors (red, white, yellow, and black predominate in each film); and a narrative structure distended with empty shots. Each of these features has been discussed in the preceding analysis of *Yellow Earth* [not reproduced in this volume] under the respective rubrics of brushwork, ink, and composition. However, none of the writings on *Black Cannon Incident* surveyed for this piece consider the film in terms of classical painting.[12] This is perhaps unsurprising, because whereas *Yellow Earth* looks back to explore the roots of China's present dilemmas in its ancient cultural traditions, *Black Cannon Incident* resolutely situates itself within a problematic of the modern. In this context, these stylized elements take on the connotations of Western modern (and modernist) art rather than classical painting, and can be considered under the headings of alienation, expressionism/abstractionism, and distanciation rather than brushwork, ink, and composition.[13]

The Modern

To understand how and with what effects these stylized elements take on connotations of Western modern art in *Black Cannon Incident*, it is necessary to examine what is meant by the "problematic of the modern" and "Western modern (and modernist) art" in the Chinese context in which the film was produced. It could be argued that since defeat in the Opium Wars of the nineteenth century, China has understood its relationship with the outside world in terms of a need to modernize. However, what "modern" means has been revised many times, and along with it the appropriate aesthetic of the modern. The socialist-realist aesthetic and its variations discussed in the introduction to this piece form one example.[14]

Black Cannon Incident, on the other hand, situates itself firmly with reference to the ideas constituting the modern established by Deng Xiaoping in the 1980s. This is marked quite clearly by the narrative of the film, which invokes all the main constituents of that particular drive to modernization. The basic premise involves a Chinese company which hosts a West German engineer on two visits to help with the installation of some imported equipment mysteriously called the "WD." This premise refers to the Open Door policy (toward the West); the emphasis is on up-to-date (Western) technology and trade (with the West). This renewal of interest in the West is made visually explicit (if ironic) in the flashback to the preparations for translator-engineer Zhao Shuxin's meeting with the German guest, Hans. Here, his bosses persuade Zhao into what they are convinced is an appropriate Western suit and tie they have borrowed from a song-and-dance troupe, although Hans himself never appears in such clothes throughout the film.[15]

In taking up all sorts of things with Western connotations as signifiers of the modern, *Black Cannon Incident* is no different from any number of other films made around this time. However, what does differentiate it is its construction of the modern not as an imminent utopia, but as dystopic. The conflict that develops out of the premise concerns the debilitating effects of disagreements within the Chinese company between the Party vice-secretary in charge of ideology and the manager of the company regarding the translator assigned to the German "expert." This conflict refers to obstacles to structural reform within Chinese work units designed to downgrade the role of the Party and encourage initiative and self-reliance; and unlike most other films that acknowledge these obstacles, *Black Cannon Incident* does not show them to be successfully overcome.

In fact, as those familiar with the plot of the film will know, it is this conflict that motivates the almost farcical (but certainly tragic) string of misunderstandings that make up the film. After Hans's second visit to China, Zhao discovers he has lost a Chinese chess piece called a "black cannon" in a hotel room and sends a telegram for it. His message is misunderstood as code, and the Party vice-secretary is convinced he is engaged in industrial espionage. She and her colleagues investigate the past in a search for clues, and keep Zhao away from the German expert, even though there is no other suitable translator available. The manager protests, but ineffectually, and by the time Zhao's innocence is proved to the vice-secretary, who is still incredulous that anyone would pay for a telegram to chase something as inexpensive as a chess piece, the damage has been done, and the "WD" has been incorrectly installed.

It is this unusual combination of dystopic and Western connotations around the modern that could be said to be the "idea that precedes the brushwork" of *Black Cannon Incident,* and which the film shares with certain tendencies in Western modern art. This combination therefore overdetermines the association of the film's aesthetic with Western modern art. The quotes from Rodin and Picasso that begin both the introduction and this section of this essay, although heroic in tone rather than dystopic, are clear instances of this invocation of Western modern art in relation to *Black Cannon Incident.*

The very use of a term like "Western modern art" to cover everything from Cubism through abstractionism would be grossly reductionistic in a Western context. However, in a Chinese context, what appears, to the Western eye, as a historically and stylistically differentiated series of nonrealist movements and tendencies is more like one object. All these anti- and nonrealist movements were excluded from Chinese painting and art teaching during the period in which the socialist-realist cinema was dominant, and condemned as "bourgeois" and "decadent." It was only when China opened its fabled door to the world again after Deng Xiaoping's ascent to power in late 1978 that these foreign tendencies arrived in China through books, art journals, and exhibitions. As such, they arrived all at the same time, and as one multifaceted fine art tendency, contemporaneous with Deng's reform movement. Articles in art journals on modernism, modern art, impressionism, surrealism, and Klimt appeared in 1980, and on German expressionism, Matisse, Millet, Picasso, and Munch in 1981, when an exhibition including abstract expressionist art was held in Beijing. German expressionist oil paintings were shown in 1982, as were works by Picasso and contemporary French painters. The following year, Shao Dazhen's *Traditional Art and Modernism (Chuantong meishu yu xiandaipai)*, an influential book which treated modern art precisely as one multifaceted phenomenon, appeared.[16]

Given this history, it is not surprising that *Black Cannon Incident* builds associations with Western modern art in a much looser, more indiscriminate and less explicitly identified fashion than the way *Yellow Earth* draws upon the Chinese classical painting tradition. Nonetheless, those associations are easily drawn and contribute heavily to the highly original aesthetic of the film. To give a nonvisual but parallel example, the film uses various forms of music, all of which carry connotations of being Western and modern. The film opens with clashing, discordant music played on Western wind instruments over the title "Black Cannon Incident." In other places, "jazzy" saxophone music is used to suggest thoughtfulness and slight unease, for example in the Western food restaurant.[17] At lighter moments, Muzak-like synthesizer music is preferred. These three types of music, which might seem to have quite distinct and different connotations to many Westerners, are apparently considered sufficiently close and coherent in China today to be used together in this one film as an integrated set, all simultaneously signifying modernity, dystopia, and the West.

Alienation

Also contributing to the modern, Western, and dystopic aesthetic of *Black Cannon Incident* is a visually constructed double-alienation effect, whereby the viewer is refused an identification with the characters in the diegesis (the world of the film), while at the same time being given the sense that the characters have no control over their modern world. This corresponds to modern art techniques that have sought to draw attention to the subjugation of the individual in large-scale capitalism by refusing to employ the sovereign subject effect of traditional realism discussed in the introduction to this essay. Be it the abstractionist paintings of Jasper Johns or Picasso's cubism or the expressionist protest of the alienated soul, much antirealist modern art experiments with, and works to undermine or even reject, this subject position for the spectator, either refusing to provide any figure with which an identification might be possible, or else constructing such a figure as in extremis.

One of the most obvious ways in which this effect is achieved in *Black Cannon Incident* is through the manipulation of the supermodern setting of the film to dwarf the characters. This is quite different from both the warm, maternal dwarfing by nature described in *Yellow Earth*, and from the optimistic relationship to technology represented in various tendencies, including socialist-realist boy-loves-tractor optimism, the "Four Modernizations" proclaimed by Premier Zhou Enlai in 1974 and upheld ever since, Western popular culture science fiction as exemplified by *Superman* and *Star Trek,* and by early twentieth-century futurism. In these latter instances, the modern appears mainly as a prosthesis for the human subject, empowering him (and it is usually him). Almost the only example of this relation to the modern in the entire film occurs after the industrial accident that results from the suspicious interference of the Party vice-secretary. In this scene, Zhao is called in to determine the cause of the accident, and is shown heroically riding to the scene on a huge, speeding earthmover—head up, face forward, and hair swept back in the wind.[18]

However, the more common relationship in *Black Cannon Incident* (as in, for example, German expressionist films, Neue Sachlichkeit paintings, and the cartoons of Georg Grosz) is the opposite: the modern is an exaggerated and distorted environment that dwarfs and threatens the human individual. Right at the very beginning of the film, when Zhao rushes into a post office, he bumps into two giants, and is thus both dwarfed and obstructed.[19] Huang Jianxin discusses the appearance of these giants at the beginning of the film in fairly generalized terms as markers of the "absurd" *(huangdan)* and "stylized" *(fenggehua)* character of the film, provoking the audience into conscious analysis and thought (1988, 217–18). However, they also have a more specific function as the first example of dwarfing, a tendency generally taken on for the rest of the film by the huge machines and buildings that make up the plant where most of the film is set.

The best example of this dwarfing occurs where the Party vice-secretary and the manager are having yet another unproductive discussion of the translator problem. As they walk along, set against a towering heap of rocks, one of the enormous earthmovers that Zhao will later ride to the scene of the accident rushes past them. Its tires alone are twice the height of the men. Its engine noise drowns out their speech, and it kicks up a tremendous cloud of dust that obscures them almost completely.[20] Other examples in the film include the huge modern clock that dominates the two Party meeting scenes, ticking away relentlessly as the interminable discussions fail to resolve anything.[21]

These meeting scenes, and especially the first meeting scene, typify another set of devices which adds to the dwarfing and "absurd" stylization to produce the double-alienation effect. This is a repeated combination of camera position and *mise-en-scène* which refuses the viewer an identification with the characters at the same time that it makes those characters appear trapped, squeezed between the set and the camera. In the first shot of the first Party meeting scene, the camera is set up at the end of a long, narrow table, down two sides of which are ranked the Party members, and at the head of which is Party Secretary Wu. The manager and the vice-secretary are on either side of him, and the clock towers over all of them. Because the walls and the clothes the characters are wearing are white, they appear suspended against a borderless expanse of white, which the camera confronts head-on. The effect of this is quite the opposite of the long shots of the landscape in *Yellow Earth*, where the characters appear out of and disappear back into the depths of the landscape itself. Rather, the limitless expanse of the pristine white wall and the head-on, confrontational angle of the camera refuse depth, and leave the characters with nowhere to go. This constricted effect is enhanced at the very end of the scene, when the meeting closes and the participants have to exit, moving in the small space between chairs and wall, and then squeezing past the camera on their way out.

Furthermore, the viewer is held at a distance from the scene by the use of the long shot. In the first Party meeting scene, the opening shot lasts several minutes, and although an argument breaks out between the various participants, we are not drawn in by use of shot/reverse-shot techniques, but kept outside by the interminable long shot. Even when this shot is abandoned and replaced by an exchange of shots between the manager and the vice-secretary, the characters are filmed from the side, and the viewer is still not afforded the full position of identification that shot/reverse-shot structures provide. To some extent, our position might be said to be similar to that of Zhao, who is also sidelined from the conflicts over the major decisions which affect his life throughout the film. However, whereas Zhao is not allowed in the Party meeting room and continues to trust his superiors, we are privy to the shenanigans that go on. As a result of being forcibly sidelined by the camera, we are more likely to be filled with anger and frustration than Zhao is, although we may tend to feel that Zhao should be angry, as many Chinese critics pointed out at the time.

This combination of devices producing a double-alienation effect is used repeatedly through the film. In one of the earliest scenes of fruitless discussion between the Party vice-secretary and the manager, they ride an enormous piece of orange red machinery as they argue. The camera is placed perpendicular to the machinery, which moves relentlessly ever closer to the camera, filling the frame, cutting the depth, and squeezing the characters between it and the camera. A long take is maintained throughout, and there is no shot/reverse-shot sequence to draw the viewer into an involvement with the argument, which, once again, gets nowhere.[22]

Another scene which foreshadows the Party meeting scenes occurs in a Western food restaurant, where Zhao has an argument with Hans. Here, the dominant color is an orange red, and Hans and Zhao sit across from each other at a red table, against a boundless orange red wall. As in the Party meeting scenes, the camera is placed at the other end of the table, head-on to the wall. No shot/reverse shot takes place during the exchange, and instead a long take is used, until Zhao smashes a bottle of beer on the floor. At this point, Hans stands up (dwarfing Zhao), and the film cuts between the two of them; but as in the Party meeting scene, the camera is side-on to them, not taking their positions. Maybe this time we want to stop the argument, but once again we are held at a distance, and certainly not in a position to release our emotions by being positioned to identify with one or the other of the warring parties.[23]

Expressionism/Abstractionism

The strong presence of certain colors has been mentioned a number of times in the preceding discussion. The palette of yellow, red, white, and black in *Black Cannon Incident* is the same as *Yellow Earth*, but although both films use these colors in stylized ways toward expressive ends, in *Black Cannon Incident* they do not call to mind classical painting so much as Western modern art, or Chinese modern art based on the Western model. Whereas in *Yellow Earth* these colors are used to characterize the natural landscapes of northern Shanxi, in *Black Cannon Incident* they are part of an aesthetic that excludes nature.

Cinematographers Wang Xinsheng and Feng Wei have explained how they worked to establish the range of colors used in the film in an article entitled "Emphasizing the Expressive Function of Form," a title itself cognate with many of the slogans of Western modern art. Red, yellow, white, and black were taken as the main colors, and much work was done to exclude green and blue from most scenes by avoiding shots with sky in them and cutting down offensive vegetation.[24] Unlike *Yellow Earth*, in the context of *Black Cannon Incident* this amounts to the equation of modernization and industrialization with the exclusion of nature, and associates red, yellow, white, and black with the manmade (and dystopic) setting in which most of the film occurs. Yellow overalls, red plastic table tops, white walls, and black machinery are characteristic of the film.

These colors occur all across the film: even the furniture and the characters' clothes are usually confined to a palette that excludes blue and green. However, they also occur in forms that draw attention to themselves by being abstract rather than naturalized and integrated. Most obviously, there is the scene at the football field, where Zhao and the football coach talk as, behind them, a man paints an enormous billboard a bright primary red, like that of an abstract painting.[25] When Zhao and his girlfriend go to a rock concert, the singer appears against a background of black and white concentric rectangles, and when the manager speaks with a girl in red, they both appear against an abstract black-and-white pattern on the wall behind them.[26] Even the montage of shots of the sun that comes just before the closing scene of the film is highly abstract, with the sun rendered in yellow against a red ground, crossed by a few electricity wires, chimneys, cranes, or other elements of the industrial world.[27]

Not only is abstractionism invoked in this use of colors, but as indicated by the title of Wang Xinsheng and Feng Wei's article "Emphasizing the Expressive Function of Form," so is their potential expressive function. As in *Yellow Earth*, it would be difficult to tie any single connotation to any of the four colors dominating the film, and indeed none of the essays by either the director or the two cinematographers tries to do so. Certainly, red does not simply mean communism (as it might have done in many socialist-realist films), or happiness (as in many traditional customs), nor does white mean death.

However, the colors are often primary and distinct, especially in the abstractionist uses mentioned above, making them powerfully attractive to the eye. They are used so extensively and exclusively within individual shots that it is almost impossible to avoid thinking about what their function might be in a particular scene. Overall, it can be noted that the use of red increases throughout the film as the situation grows more urgent and gets more out of hand. At first there is just a red umbrella Zhao trips over in the post office scene, but the film ends in a montage of red suns where, after the industrial accident, the entire screen is saturated with red. The director has mentioned to Berry on various occasions a fondness for the films of Antonioni, and so a reference to *Red Desert* (*Deserto Rosso*, 1964) seems plausible. In this sense, it may be that red connotes urgency in the film, although it may also be that the primary function of a highly controlled and stylized palette is simply to promote conscious thought on the part of the audience.

Distanciation

In promoting conscious thought, colors, like the alienation effect, play a part in the final characteristic also associated with modern art to be discussed here: distanciation. This section will concentrate less on devices that share something in common with modern Western painting, however, than on modern drama and novels (and, as discussed in reference to empty shots in *Yellow Earth*, Chinese classical painting). This is because we will be detailing devices that promote narrative distension, functioning like the unresolved, often meandering plots of the modernist novel (*Ulysses,* for example), or the voids in the slowly unrolled Chinese scroll painting, both of which call upon and make space for the audience to engage in critical thought.[28]

Among the devices that promote this effect throughout *Black Cannon Incident* are empty shots like those found in *Yellow Earth.* Throughout Huang Jianxin's film, there are montages of scenes from the worksite and sunsets which suspend development of the narrative in the film. In addition to the series of suns at the end of the film, scenes 24 and 5, for example, show various long shots of the worksite, and one shot of the sun, and there are also single shots of a yellow sun suspended in a red sky punctuating the film between other scenes.[29]

However, narrative distension in *Black Cannon Incident* bleeds beyond empty shots like those described above. Sometimes, there are whole scenes in which characters do appear and perform actions, but in which there is no dialogue and which appear to serve little narrative function other than to provide a space to think. For example, scenes 44 through 47 show Zhao doing some inspections in the plant at night while his girlfriend and her daughter prepare food at home.[30]

Even within scenes that serve very clear narrative functions, there is a tendency to append long tails in which the characters are often seen to be pondering the situation. For example, the scene at the football field where the wall is painted red ends with a long tail after the players have begun fighting, in which Zhao is seen wandering out of screen, his head presumably full of worries. At the end of the first Party meeting scene, after everyone except the manager of the plant has left, the manager is seen deep in thought as we cut to various remnants of the inconclusive meeting, such as cigarette butts in ashtrays. Then Zhao enters, and there is a silent shot/reverse-shot exchange between them, with no easily identifiable expression on either's face.

Another device that promotes distanciation besides emptiness is ambiguity, and there are whole scenes in the film which appear to be in some way part of the narrative (unlike, for example, the montages of the suns), but whose signification is very obscure. For example, there is the scene in the old Christian church. This scene is placed in the film after Zhao has found out why he has really been prevented from working with the German expert on the latter's second visit to help install the WD equipment, and we presume these scenes are consecutive. It draws attention to itself and suggests it must be important in some way by its clear difference from the industrial milieu that dominates the rest of the film, its exotic status in a Chinese context, and the presence of clear blues and greens in a film that otherwise works to exclude these colors. Zhao, who was brought up as a Christian, is shown on the threshold of the church observing worshipers, but does not go in. The signification of this scene is unclear, but it certainly calls upon the audience to consider the possible implications of the situation.[31] The same is true of the scene at the very end of the film, after the montage of suns, where Zhao watches a pair of little boys set up bricks like dominoes, knock them down, and then begin to set them up again. The green field is an unusual color in the film, and the epilogue-like position seems to suggest that the scene may be meant as a symbolic comment, but no precise signification is apparent.[32]

In addition to these delaying functions that distend the narrative and open up space in which the viewer is called upon to analyze ambiguous meanings, one final effect also found in many modern novels promotes distanciation. This is a certain confusion over time. We know there are two visits by the German to the plant, and that the film begins from a point where the industrial accident has already occurred and the manager is recounting the "black cannon incident." Beyond that, however, things become difficult to figure out, as the film slips back and forth between different visits by the German and different intervening moments, without using any of the standard cinematic devices to signal flashback, such as a zoom-in to a close-up on a character's face accompanied by a dissolve, or even a voice-over explaining what is happening. This makes the film quite disorienting at times, and the viewer is again distanced and encouraged into conscious analysis.

Toward a Post-Socialist Aesthetic

Black Cannon Incident is probably less well known outside China than *Yellow Earth,* but inside China it is just as famous, having been one of the most successful Fifth Generation films at the box office.[33] Its look was also just as original, setting a trend for contemporary urban films, although most used it in a fairly superficial manner. For example, a Changchun Film Studio film about a group of single modern women all living together called *Strange Circle (Guai quan)* returned repeatedly to an image of a white taxi against a red shipping container. The camera is head-on, the red of the container takes up the whole frame, and then women in black enter, get in the taxi, and drive off. Huang Jianxin further developed the aesthetic himself in his sequel to *Black Cannon Incident, Dislocation (Cuowei,* 1986).

In different ways, then, both *Black Cannon Incident* and *Yellow Earth* were highly influential films, and both worked to break the aesthetic stranglehold of socialist realism on the cinema and, in so doing, suggested many broader social criticisms. However, they also represent two extremes in a wide range of Fifth Generation and other films that appeared in the eighties and marked themselves out strongly from the socialist-realist tradition. As such, they did not constitute a new paradigm or formula so much as a nonformulaic formula. In the opening up of this postsocialist space, traditions within the fine arts, including painting, functioned not as set forms to be recreated in the cinema but as possibilities to be drawn upon. In turning to classical painting, *Yellow Earth* does not attempt to return to the past, but revives past traditions for very contemporary purposes. And in invoking Western modern art, *Black Cannon Incident* does not signify worshiping the West, but rather draws upon certain Western devices for very Chinese purposes.

Notes

This article was first published in *Cinematic Landscapes: Observations on the Visual Arts and Cinema of China and Japan*, edited by Linda C. Ehrlich and David Desser. Copyright © 1994. By permission of the University of Texas Press.

1. For a full discussion of the institutional background to the Fifth Generation, see Tony Rayns 1991; and Chris Berry, "Market Forces: China's Fifth Generation Faces the Bottom Line," in Berry 1991, 114–24.

2. See, for example, Chen Kaige 1988; Huang Jianxin 1988; Tian Zhuangzhuang 1989; Chris Berry 1989; and Pei Kairui, "Zhang Yimou: Film Maker with the Golden Touch," *China Reconstructs* 37.5 (May 1988), among others.

3. This model is also frequently referred to as the "classical mainland Chinese cinema." See, for example, Chris Berry, "Sexual Difference and the Viewing Subject in *Li Shuangshuang* and *The In-Laws*" in Berry 1991, 30–39. However, because we are also going to talk about classical Chinese painting in this article, we have avoided using the term "classical" in reference to film to avoid confusion.

4. One of the better-known examples of the construction of this sovereign-like subject position for the spectator/owner of post-Renaissance Western art is the nude, as discussed by John Berger in *Ways of Seeing* (London: Pelican Books, 1983). Here Berger points out that the female nude is physically positioned in such a way that she is displayed for the viewer, often looking in a direction that implies acknowledgment of (what is presumably) his gaze. In this way, the viewer is constructed by the painting as the owner of the nude woman. Foucault's famous discussion of the Velázquez painting *Las Meninas* (1656), at the opening of *The Order of Things* (New York: Vintage, 1973), makes a similar point about the function of perspective in Western realist painting in the construction of the sovereign subject.

5. See Berry, "Sexual Difference and the Viewing Subject" (1991, 30–39), for an extended

discussion of how the socialist-realist cinema draws upon the Hollywood model. Gina Marchetti also discusses the integration of Soviet and Hollywood styles with Chinese traditions in her article, "*Two Stage Sisters:* The Blossoming of a Revolutionary Aesthetic" (in this book).

6. Paul Clark gives more details on the supposed indigenous qualities of this formula as opposed to the Soviet import, socialist realism, in his discussion of its introduction; Clark 1987b, 63–64.

7. "Give prominence to positive characters among all the characters, to heroes among the positive characters, to the principal hero among the heroes. Create special environment, character and personality and use all kinds of artistic media to make the proletarian heroes stand out. Reveal the heroes' inherent communist spirit" (qtd. in David Laing 1978, 79).

8. Discussed in Mary Ann Farquhar, "Children's Literature in China" (Ph.D. diss., Australian National University, 1983), 242.

9. See Foucault 1977, 139–64.

10. See, for example, Chen Kaiyan 1988 (330–40). Kracauer's *Theory of Film: The Redemption of Physical Reality* was published in Chinese around this time under the tile *Dianying de benxing: Wuzhi xianshi de fuyuan* (Beijing: Zhongguo dianying chubanshe, 1981). In 1982 the famous translator, critic, and theorist Shao Mujun published his *Xifan dianyingshi gailun* with the China film press, which also includes discussion of both theorists. A translation of a discussion of Bazin by Dudley Andrew appears in *Shijie dianying,* no. 6 (1981), a journal largely devoted to the publication of translations in which a number of Bazin's essays have appeared over the years.

11. For a contrast between the almost hyper-real naturalism of *Yamaha Fish Stall* and the stylization of *Black Cannon Incident,* see Berry 1988d.

12. For a sampling of writings on this film, see Chen Kaiyan 1988; Zhang Ziliang and Zhu Zi 1989.

13. That such similar elements can be understood in reference to classical Chinese painting for one film and Western modern art for another should not come as any surprise; it is well known that many modern artists looked to a variety of nonrealist traditions for ways of differentiating themselves from the realist tradition, including the dramatist Bertolt Brecht, whose alienation effect was at least partly inspired by a performance of Beijing Opera.

14. It is clearly beyond the scope of this essay to consider the complete range of different paradigms for the "modern" that China has considered during the past 150 years; but it should be noted that even though it only became dominant in 1949, the socialist, and more specifically the Soviet model, held wide currency in China well before that: Jiang Jieshi (Chiang Kai-shek) was trained in Moscow and built his Guomindang (Kuomintang) Nationalist party on Bolshevik principles of democratic centralism.

15. Huang Jianxin, "*Heipao shijian*—Fenjingtou juben," scene 16, in Chen Kaiyan 1988, 109–10.

16. For these and further details of the exposure of non-Chinese modern art in the People's Republic, see John Clark 1991.

17. Huang Jianxin, "*Heipao shijian*—Fenjingtou juben," scene 20, in Chen Kaiyan 1988, 114.

18. Ibid., scene 83, 177.

19. Ibid., scene 4, 102.

20. Ibid., scene 56, 146–47.

21. Ibid., scenes 32, 34 and 67; 124–29, 163–69. Huang Jianxin specifies that this clock is four meters wide by three meters tall. This is the same width as the meeting room itself and only eighty centimeters short of the ceiling, which means that the clock takes up almost an entire wall in the room; Huang Jianxin 1988, 215.

22. Huang Jianxin, "*Heipao shijian*—Fenjingtou juben," scene 23, in Chen Kaiyan 1988, 117.

23. Ibid., scene 20, 114. Other examples of this construction include: the rock concert scene (scene 26, 118–19), where the singer performs between a backdrop of concentric black and white, alternating rectangles and the camera; the scene between Hans and the incompetent alternative translator, Feng, after an argument (scene 31, 123–24), where they sit on part of the huge WD installation, one on each side of the screen, with the camera confronting machinery head-on; the scene during the "bullet incident" episode where the laborers climb a stairway outside a wall to ask for some bullets (scene 51, 141) and where the wall again forms a boundless plane confronted by the camera; and the scene in the hotel where the manager discovers that the woman in red on his staff speaks little German (scene 63, shot 259, 155) and where the two characters are squeezed between the camera and a wall with a black-and-white abstract pattern.

24. In Chen Kaiyan 1988, 232–34.

25. Huang Jianxin, "*Heipao shijian*—Fenjingtou juben," scene 43, in Chen Kaiyan 1988, 136–37.

26. Ibid., scene 26 and 63, 118–19, 155.

27. Ibid., scenes 88–95, 182–83.

28. Although Huang Jianxin has not discussed either of these possible antecedents, he is quite explicit that his efforts at "stylization" and "absurd" are intended to promote distanciation and therefore thought on the part of the audience: see Huang Jianxin 1988.

29. Huang Jianxin, "*Heipao shijian*—Fenjingtou juben," scenes 24 and 25, 117–18. The series of suns at the end of the film appears in scenes 88–95, 182–83. Examples of single suns include scene 35, 129, and shot 183, 138.

30. Ibid., 137–38.

31. Ibid., scene 77, 173.

32. Ibid., scene 96, 183–84.

33. In an interview on February 15, 1988, Wu Xiaojin, deputy director of planning and research for the China Film Corporation in Beijing, told Berry that *Yellow Earth* sold only thirty prints within China. Two hundred would be a more typical figure for a film. *Black Cannon Incident* sold ninety-nine prints, making it the most popular Fifth Generation film apart from *Secret Decree* at that date.

Fifteen
Good Morning, Beijing
(*Beijing, nizao,* dir. Zhang Nuanxin, 1990)

Screenplay Tang Danian

Cinematography Zhang Xigui

Producer Qingnian

Cast Ma Xiaoqing, as Ai Hong (bus conductor)

Jia Hongsheng, as Keke (fake foreign student)

Wang Quan'an, as Zou Yongqiang (bus driver)

Jin Tiefeng, as Wang Lang (Ai Hong's fellow bus conductor)

Between *The Drive to Win* and *Good Morning, Beijing,* Zhang Nuanxin had lost some of her earlier idealism; this was typical among Fourth Generation directors. In answer to a question about this at a Harvard screening of *Good Morning, Beijing* in the early 1990s, Zhang said she believed that she had been as true to life as always and that it was life itself that had changed. As an advocate of prose films as opposed to conventional melodrama, Zhang's aloofness from ideological idealism created an excellent film about the changed lives of people in the contemporary metropolis of Beijing. Here is a slice of life showing the Western influence on the younger generation, the budding desire for material well-being, the emerging private entrepreneurship that challenges state-run business, and the coexistence of the old and the new in the culture.

Compared with other contemporary female directors—Huang Shuqin of *Woman, Demon, Human,* for example—Zhang Nuanxin shows less of a feminist consciousness: she doesn't seem to care about gender specificity and has claimed that artistic pursuits are more important than gender concerns. Critics also talk less about feminism in her films and more about how her women characters are used in allegories. Concerning *Good Morning, Beijing,* and Ai Hong's allegorical role of moving from one man to the other, a Chinese critic noticed "a historical change" in this kind of allegory about women's affiliation, or about who possesses women (Zhang Wei, 1990). Conventionally, the logic for this kind of allegory is that the central woman will be happy if she sticks to the "nonmaterialist" good guy and will be lost if she goes with the "materialist" bad guy. In this film, the historical change invokes the viewers' difficulty in deciding who is the good guy: the bus driver, Zou, or the fake foreign student, Keke. This difficulty reflects ongoing changes in the values that the film depicts.

Suggested reading for *Good Morning, Beijing* is as follows:

Kuoshu 1999b, 121–52

Director's Notes

The best script I've ever come across is Tang Danian's *Good Morning, Beijing.* I, in fact, made some revisions of it but kept its basic character relationships and the vivid dialogues that were so typical of the time.

At the time when I shot *Good Morning, Beijing,* I had already started to pay more attention to audience reception and believed that the *auteur* expression of a director might be coalesced with it. The film kept my personal style and favorite themes but also told a story that concerned everyone. (Qtd. in Wu Guanping 1995, 64)

I named the film *Good Morning, Beijing* because it represents a segment of life of thousands of its residents, that is, those underrepresented ordinary working people.

This film seeks a style that is close to the flow of life: it is a prose-like [with no dramatic intensity] film with a lyrical touch, a documentary feature, some sense of humor, and some of the elements of a light comedy. (Zhang Nuanxin 1990, 53)

In Search of the Real City:
Cinematic Representations of Beijing and the Politics of Vision
Xiaobing Tang

> Potentially, the city is in itself the powerful symbol of a complex society. If visually well set forth, it can also have strong expressive meaning.
> —Kevin Lynch, *The Image of the City*

That the city of Beijing presents a perfect spatial embodiment of a traditional culture caught in the maelstrom of rapid and condensed modernization is readily observable, even to a passing tourist. "Beijing is a microcosm of China," so an up-to-date pocket travel book informs its readers and potential travelers. "It combines village and metropolis, Western-style modernization and Chinese tradition, new-fashioned pomp with old-fashioned modesty. It is a showcase of China's policy for reform and opening up to the West" (Cohn 1992, 12). Another contemporary guidebook (from the "Travel Survival Kit" series) gives more in-depth information: "All cities in China are equal, but some are more equal than others. Beijing has the best of everything in China bar the weather: the best food, the best hotels, the best transport, the best temples. But its vast squares and boulevards, its cavernous monoliths and its huge numbers of tourists are likely to leave you cold. It is a weird city—traces of its former character may be found down the back alleys where things are a bit more to human scale" (Cummings et al. 1991, 485).

Indeed, probably no visitor to Beijing in the 1990s would fail to notice the weird, sometimes mind-boggling character of this sprawling urban center that is becoming increasingly similar to Los Angeles. It is one of the oldest cities in the world, and yet compressed sites or islands of its imperial past are now barely visible under the veil of brownish smog and against the ragged backdrop of masses of prefabricated, international-style apartment buildings or more recent all-glass high-rises. Its broad and often dishearteningly straight, but increasingly jammed and billboarded boulevards, while still stridently reminding you of the scale and aspiration of a recent collective project and central planning, are continually humanized and made lively by an unstoppable flow of millions of bicyclists. If you decide to move across the city, either on foot or by any means of transportation, you will soon find yourself experiencing starkly different sections and neighborhoods (in terms of the appearance of their residents, architectural style, spatial arrangement, and noise level), which, as in almost any other large city in the world, exist side-by-side and form silent commentary on one another. This "synchronicity of the nonsynchronous," as Ernst Bloch's useful phrase describes it, finds its expression in another space-related human experience, namely, the multiple means of transportation on Beijing's streets, from pedicabs, to overcrowded buses, to the latest Lexus.

Of this uneven but changing cityscape, we find timely and fascinating representations in Chinese cinema since the late 1980s, for which the dynamics and social, if also libidinal, energy of the modern city have become a much-explored theme and created a new film genre. The one particular sequence of images and soundtrack I have in mind is the opening collage in *Wanzhu* (*Troubleshooters*, dir. Mi Jiashan, 1988). The film's location is emphatically contemporary Beijing. Two enormous characters for the title of the film are pro-jected onto three re-created primitive masks; they are accompanied by a sound-track that captures a vocal fragment from some traditional opera or storytelling, shifts to a shrill siren that drowns out the narrating voice, and then records some boisterous marketplace where voices shouting out the names of popular magazines can be distinguished. But this brief temporalized sequence of sound effects is only the preface to an explosive juxtaposition of often fragmented but nonetheless spectacular images of the city. Through a zoom lens, the spectacle of traffic congestion is brought much closer, and minimal depth of field under-scores a compressed urban spatiotemporal regime; unsteady and fast-moving shots of glass buildings (unmistakable signs of contemporaneity), with twisted reflections of other high-rises and construction cranes, suggest the spatial frag-mentation with which an awestruck observer is forced to become reconciled. Then, quickly, the camera is directed back at the hustling and bustling streets where it presents a series of incomplete, unrelated snapshots of crawling vehi-cles, expressionless old women, hordes of bicyclists, country girls gathering at a labor market, a frowning youth with a punk haircut—all horizontal images of an expanding metropolis from the perspective of an apparently disoriented subject. Over this collage of urban spectacles, contemporary Chinese rock and roll (clearly reminiscent of early Bruce Springsteen) is introduced to make direct commentary:

> I once dreamed about life in a modern city,
> But I don't know how to express my present feeling;
> Buildings here are getting taller and taller every day,
> But my days here are not that great.[1]

In fact, 1988 saw the production of a series of films on the subject of con-temporary city life, at least four of them based on novels or novellas by the popular Beijing writer Wang Shuo. Hence, 1988 has been dubbed "the year of Wang Shuo" in Chinese cinema.[2] These films about the city, mostly directed by members of the Fifth Generation,[3] form a distinct genre and indicate a differ-ent intellectual concern and cultural criticism than in earlier Fifth Generation experiments or, indeed, in the tradition of New China cinema. By New China cinema, I mean the state-supported film industry that came into being with the founding of the People's Republic in 1949. Its brief and frequently interrupted course of development notwithstanding, New China cinema is mass-oriented and generally identified with a formulaic socialist realist aesthetic, "a didactic fusion," as one critic puts it, "of classic Hollywood filmmaking and Soviet Stalinist style."[4] The preferred subject matter for this determinedly revolutionary popular cinema is collective heroism and socialist construction, while its audience is often imagined to be a politically engaged nation instead of sentimental urban dwellers. Consequently, the experiential city fades as a pertinent cinematic theme or field, and the well-lit imagery of contemporary life found in New China cinema invariably comes from either an industrial construction site or the countryside undergoing profound transformations. Even the revolutionary past, when it is projected in New China cinema, is systematically romanticized and made to adhere to the current representational hierarchies. Against this staid tradition of "revolutionary realism combined with revolutionary romanticism," the Fifth Generation of filmmakers introduced a fresh cinematic language and vision in the mid-1980s by bringing into focus a remote and obscure location, temporal as well as spatial, that bespeaks a different and yet concrete reality of depth. What enabled their breakthrough was clearly a modernist aesthetics and avant-gardist challenge against didactic mass cinema.[5] Hence, the initial defamiliarizing impact of *Huang tudi* (*Yellow Earth,* dir. Chen Kaige, 1984), *Daoma zei* (*Horse Thief,* dir. Tian Zhuangzhuang, 1986), and *Hong gaoliang* (*Red Sorghum,* dir. Zhang Yimou, 1987), all now considered classics of Fifth Generation filmmaking.

In the new genre of city films that attracted members of the self-consciously innovative Fifth Generation, a central symbiosis is suggested between the experience of discontented youth and a vast, disorienting urban space that invariably provides a symbolic replication of the complexity of contemporary sociopolitical life caught in the maelstrom of modernization. Against the spatial complexity of the city, youth, while celebrated as a concentrated expression of the cultural dynamics of modernity, is nonetheless frequently depicted on the screen as a disillusioning experience of foreclosed mobility, repressed libidinal energy, and entrenched filial obligation and duties. For instance, in *Troubleshooters,* we see how three young men struggle without much success to run their own service company, whose daily operation and customers bring to the surface the frustrations and crises deeply embedded in contemporary society. A significant development in the film is that once the story line begins and we are witnessing the nitty-gritty of the company's business, the city no longer appears as a spectacle to marvel at. Instead, the urban landscape recedes, as it were, into the distance and turns simultaneously into an untranscendable historical condition and an experiential immediacy that together smother any coherent perception. Put differently, the city becomes both an all-encompassing cultural construct and an inescapable natural environment, one reinforcing the other. By the end of the film, it is clear that the filmmaker has persistently refused to present the city as promising a possible perceptual totalization; contrary to the opening collage, the final, slow-rolling shot of people lining up to seek help at the revamped service company conveys a reconciliation, on the part of a besieged and reflective subject, with ordinariness as well as situatedness. The city by now irretrievably recedes into the distance and becomes a grandiose myth no longer relevant to the daily lives of its inhabitants. It is now a labyrinthine complex without a coherent pattern, or what Kevin Lynch once promoted as the "legibility" and "imageability" of the cityscape.

However, this film genre, with its critical message about "the estranging city and a paralyzed subject" (Peng 1990, 41), did not reach its thematic and cinematic perfection until 1989, when Xie Fei completed *Benming nian* (Black snow), a sober portrayal of ordinary life in Beijing executed with a film-noir sensibility. It may appear coincidental that an outstanding member of the Fourth Generation (here the term refers to the group of Chinese filmmakers who were systematically trained from the late 1950s to early 1960s and reached their professional maturity only in the late 1970s because of the disruption of the Cultural Revolution) had to come in to realize the potential of the new genre, for the directors in this transitional generation of directors are often viewed by critics as forever negotiating for their own artistic identity. Compared to the more cosmopolitan Fifth Generation, they appear as "reluctant, awkward pursuers of the novel and embarrassing believers in cheap humanism and historicism" (Xudong Zhang 1997, 223). As the proud, however abused, offspring of New China cinema, they now find themselves, by default, inheriting a battered establishment, and yet they cannot afford to dissociate themselves either emotionally or intellectually from what shapes and defines them. This character profile of the Fourth Generation is closely borne out by another intriguing city film, *Beijing, nizao* (Good morning, Beijing, 1990), directed by Zhang Nuanxin (*Sha'ou*, 1981; *Qingchun ji* [Sacrificed youth], 1986). Given their professional training and familiarity with socialist realism, Fourth Generation directors have a strong sense of social responsibility and usually feel more at home dealing with the rural landscape or the contrast between the city and the countryside. Indeed, members of this generation are the ones who made some of the most successful and realistic films about rural China in the 1980s, such as *Rensheng* (Life, 1984) and *Laojing* (Old well, 1987) by Wu Tianming, and *Yeshan* (In the wild mountains, 1985) by Yan Xueshu.

Fully accepting his identity as a Fourth Generation director, Xie Fei never-

theless from the beginning exhibited a spiritual affinity with the younger generation. From his earlier, emotionally charged *Women de tianye* (Our wide
fields, 1983) to *Xiangnü Xiaoxiao* (The girl from Hunan, 1986), which echoed
the ethos of critical cultural root-seeking, Xie Fei established himself as the most
sensitive filmmaker of his generation. In *Black Snow,* he not only redirects his
own philosophical thinking, but also introduces a new intellectual tension into
the city-film genre. As the film critic Peng Wen observes, while city films by the
Fifth Generation express a hidden desire to identify with and belong to the new
urban culture, "in *Black Snow,* 'the city' is obviously presented as an estranging and hostile space, to cope with which the filmmaker recommends resistance
and disengagement" (1990, 42). Still, there is enough continuity to read Xie
Fei's intervention as an extension of the general interest in the city. It is mostly
a thematic continuity, an increasingly critical examination of an emergent urban
culture. "From *Troubleshooters* to *Black Snow,*" as another film critic remarks,
"Chinese cinema has reached a universal subject matter in world cinema,
namely, the experience of anomie and disorientation in a commodity society,
also known as the age of market economy" (Wei Xiaolin 1990b, 51). In this
light, *Black Snow* deserves a closer look, especially from the perspective of how
the city now figures in the everyday experience of unfulfilled youth.[6]

Depth and Social Criticism

While reviewing films about Rome by Vittorio De Sica in postwar Italy, Pierre
Sorlin sees the filmmaker as someone who experimented with two different
groups of images of the city. In the neorealist cinema of the 1950s, filmmakers
"were aware of the blossoming of urban areas and tried to express, cinematically, the complex relationships between old town centers and new outskirts.
After 1965 or so, other cinematographers were no longer able to tell, or see,
what towns were, and [they] created a blurred image of cities" (Sorlin 1991,
135). This blurred vision, according to Sorlin, was first articulated in De Sica's
The Roof (1956), in which "the strong system which associated the center and
outskirts, presented as complementary entities, vanished, and the picture of
towns began to lose focus" (Sorlin, 126–27). Subsequently, images of open and
formless shantytowns came in to diffuse the neorealist effort that, through cinematic projection, had sought to make sense of an expanding urban landscape
and the intricate human lives embedded in it. One classic moment of such neorealist clarity can be found in De Sica's *The Bicycle Thief* (1948), where
"extreme depth of field shots accentuate Ricci's isolation: when he searches the
thief's home for traces of his stolen bicycle, for example, we see in the back-

ground most clearly a neighbor closing her window, as if to cut off all possibility of communication between Ricci and the thief's neighbors."[7]

The loss of such all-encompassing visual clarity in the wake of neorealist cinema, suggests Sorlin, registered a new perception of the European city, a historical moment in which "filmmakers ceased to view cities as potential works of art" (Sorlin, 136). Thus, the gradual disappearance of neorealism may point to a general disavowal of allegorical totalization on the one hand and of active social engagement on the other. It may even signal the arrival of a postmodern urban life, for which the source of excitement is no longer the visionary modern city or a neorealist "aspiration to change the world."[8] If this fundamentally moral commitment underlies all forms of the realist ideology, one crucial difference between neorealism and socialist realism may be no other than the former's fascination with, and critical exploration of, the anonymous and multidimensional modernizing city. Socialist realist cinema, at least its Chinese variant, is identifiable insofar as the city on a human scale is disallowed. "The Chinese version of what the Italians called 'neorealism' had been a feature of the 'golden age' of Chinese cinema in the late 1940s," remarks Paul Clark, but it was superseded by socialist realism in the 1950s (1991, 40–61). As a result, "the urban tragicomedies and social melodramas of the late 1940s were replaced by socialist melodramas set in either urban workplaces or the countryside." In the 1980s, with socialist realism falling into disrepute, the city and its cinematic possibilities returned to the Chinese screen with considerable vengeance.

What I wish to accomplish through a close reading of *Black Snow* and *Good Morning, Beijing* is to show that the return of the city in late twentieth-century Chinese cinema once again highlights questions of realism and social engagement. These two starkly different cinematic representations of the city of Beijing articulate separate visions of reality and politics. While in *Black Snow* our view is constantly immobilized by closeups and focal lighting, *Good Morning, Beijing* moves us with a gratifying story and fluid cinematography. The city in *Good Morning, Beijing*, which may be provisionally described as "neorealist" in style, is amply narratable and eventually comes together as an allegorical social space. In *Black Snow*, however, through the prevalent use of limited field-depth cinematography, Xie Fei focuses our gaze on an embattled individual by keeping his surroundings in a shadowy blur that effectively blocks the city from ever emerging as a graspable totality.

The dramatic tracking shot at the beginning of *Black Snow* immediately sets the chromatic tone and visual structure of the film and establishes itself as an exemplary moment in a conceivable Beijing noir. Hearing first a passing train

and then solitary but heavy footsteps, we realize that we are in a dimly lit subway station and following someone, presumably toward the exit. Then the credits begin to roll, and the hand-held camera films to the rhythm of someone
walking. Soon we see stairways leading to the ground and a street scene. The
person in front of us and at the center of the screen, in the light of the exit,
shoulders a stuffed knapsack and wears a bulky coat. Yet the looming, open
space is hardly inspiring because the narrow strip of a wintry sky is an impen-
etrable gray, and a few ghostly bystanders all appear to be uniformly blue or of
a nondescript monochrome. As the man (we can assume that by now, judging
from his build and the gender-specific hat he is wearing) is about to fully emerge
from the subway, the camera quickly shifts, and we see him again, from a
slightly downward angle, in some narrow and tortuous lane, which is hopelessly cut short by another train hissing by at the top of the screen. It is a virtual shantytown, void of any human presence at the moment. Then the man
walks through a gate, and the camera is noticeably lowered so that the lane
becomes even more oppressive and suffocating. There are still no human beings
in sight, and the overcrowded space is dominated by an official radio voice
announcing first some prohibitive policy and then a train disaster. The impersonal voice fades away as we turn a corner, and an old man's sickly cough,
together with a baby's impatient cry, becomes more irrepressible, punctuated
only by the sound of flowing tap water. After yet another unexpected turn, we
hear a fragment of softened pop rock that seems to float listlessly, and when
we are sufficiently lost in this directionless space, the man is suddenly stopped
by a fence, and at the same time the camera comes to a standstill.

But the man quickly pushes open the fence and walks up to a shanty that
shows no signs of life. While he struggles with his key in the lock and eventually has to break through the door, a compassionate female voice, probably
from a radio next door, gradually replaces the news broadcast and, in the elegant style of the traditional art of storytelling *(pingshu)*, either narrates a distant event or proffers a reflective commentary. In fact, this formulaic but
mysteriously soothing voice will remain as the predominant background sound,
as if supplying a slightly sorrowful historical commentary on present conditions, during the sequence in which the man enters the room, bumps into a few
ill-placed objects, examines the disorderly surroundings, and finally takes off his
hat and gloves. Only at this moment do we get our first frontal view of him, a
sturdy young man in his mid-twenties. Apparently he knows this place, for very
soon he finds himself a cigarette buried in a drawer and, while searching for
matches, catches sight of a framed picture. He picks up the frame, gazes into it,

and blows hard at the dust gathered on it. At this moment, the alarmed voice of an old woman comes from off the screen: "Who is it? Is it Quanzi?"

Li Huiquan is the name of the young man, the hero of the film. He has just returned home after spending about a year in prison, during which time his mother has died. Now he finds himself back in a desolate room, all alone, job-less, and facing the task of starting his life anew. Based on a psychological novel by Liu Heng, the plot of the film is about how hard, and eventually impossible, it is for Li Huiquan the ex-convict to assimilate himself back into society and lead a normal life. Unable to get a job at the factory where his mother used to work, which is now officially declared bankrupt, Li Huiquan decides to rely on himself and sets up a stall at a street market to sell shoes and clothes. After a slow start, his business grows steadily; in the meanwhile, he gets to know Zhao Yaqiu, an aspiring singer performing part-time in a bar. At the bar, he also meets Cui Yongli, a shrewd, self-made broker who profits from clandestine and appar-ently illegal business deals. While Cui Yongli supplies quantities of popular fash-ion goods (mostly lingerie), Li Huiquan occasionally escorts Zhao Yaqiu home after her work. With her charming innocence she seems to restore in him a sense of being respected and even needed. Subsequently, she becomes the object of his libidinal desire. Yet he cannot bring himself to express his tender feelings toward the trusting young girl; instead, he resorts to masturbation at night. At the same time, partly thanks to Cui Yongli's brokering, Zhao Yaqiu becomes rel-atively successful and grows increasingly indifferent to the young man whom she once obviously admired. Then Li Huiquan's former accomplice and prison mate, Chazi, descends one night from the skylight window, hungry as a wolf after being on the run from the law for about two weeks. Chazi's sudden return devastatingly reminds Huiquan of his own solitary existence, which makes his advice that Chazi turn himself in ring hollow. Finally, the fact that Chazi, ruth-lessly disowned by his own family, has to run away from him and for his life, together with the knowledge that Zhao Yaqiu has become her agent's mistress, crushes Li Huiquan's fragile world. He badly beats up Cui Yongli, and, in a des-perate last effort, he presents the now glamorous Zhao Yaqiu with a gold neck-lace. His offer is politely turned down, and after aimlessly roaming into a park at night Li Huiquan is robbed and then fatally stabbed by two teenagers. In the film's last shot, we are given a prolonged look downward at his bent body lying among waste paper and garbage on the floor of a deserted open-air theater, which, according to director Xie Fei, constitutes his authorial comment on the vacuity of a purposeless existence (1990b, 23–24).

The senseless death at the end certainly appears to attach an anticlimactic conclusion to the narrative. Yet it symbolically brings to completion the film's critical reflection on the limits and anxieties of city life. A full circle of hermeneutical meaning is thus achieved in terms of both narrative and cinematography. As Peng Wen remarks, the unfolding of the story adopts the pattern of a classical linear narrative, and from Li Huiquan's return (new life) to his death there is a "complete closure" (1990, 43). This narrative closure is reinforced by a visual as well as auditory imagery that at the very end recalls the film's beginning. Here is again a prolonged and uninterrupted tracking shot of the young man, his back turned to us and his footsteps echoing hollowly. The movement of the camera suggests unsteady steps, while the muffled and unreal background noise and laughter of a dispersing theater crowd do not divert our attention from the dying hero. The image of the public and the public space itself both fall out of focus and become a grotesque blur. Li Huiquan finally collapses in the empty theater. Through such structural symmetry, this last moment of arriving at his death and his return in the film's beginning powerfully complement each other, the result being a disturbing transgression of given categories and myths about city life. If, at the beginning, Li Huiquan's coming home can be viewed as returning to an interior hopelessly under surveillance (suggested by the harsh radio voice), the ending represents a final disconnection between the public and the private, the environment and its perception by the individual. Only at the moment of his random death, in a deserted public space, does Li Huiquan voicelessly and yet in vain express his individuality and with desperation expose the underlying current of loneliness.

Both critics and the filmmaker himself have remarked on the strong tendency of intellectualizing, obviously in the humanist tradition, throughout *Black Snow*.[9] The whole style of the film, from its predominant melancholy, grayish-blue tone to the virtual absence of external music, reflects the meditative commentary of a sympathetic intellectual. I wish to argue, however, that it is this philosophical interest in the existential condition of an individual in the modern city that leads to the blurring of the city itself, which has the cinematographic effect of keeping the viewer and, by extension, the subject on the screen from gaining a commanding perspective on the urban environment and its relationships. The concerned gaze that the film directs upon the subject and his immediate surroundings is so intense that the rest of the city has to be kept at a distance and as an incomprehensible background. In other words, for the anxiety of the individual subject to be experienced as such, the connection between him and the city must be revealed as nonexistent, and his anguish shown as that of one incapable of identifying himself with the environment from which he nonetheless cannot escape. "But let the mishap of disorientation once occur," Kevin Lynch writes when emphasizing the importance of keeping the city an imageable environment, "and the sense of anxiety and even terror that accompanies it reveals to us how closely it is linked to our sense of balance and well-being" (1960, 4).

At this point, we may identify a modernist aesthetics of depth in the film *Black Snow*. Such an aesthetics is usually articulated with a self-conscious, if not ideological, exploration of favorite high modernist themes of interiority, anxiety, experiential authenticity, and frustrated desire. This "inward turn" that we will discuss in relation to Li Huiquan's experience, however, does not carry the same "politicality" or utopian desire that Fredric Jameson sees underlying the alleged subjectivism in the classics of Western modernism. "Modernism's introspective probing of the deeper impulses of consciousness, and even of the unconscious itself," proposes Jameson, "was always accompanied by a Utopian sense of the impending transformation or transfiguration of the 'self' in question" (1991, 312). The anxiety that Xie Fei portrays in his film, while clearly echoing a modernist introspective probing, is generated less by a blocked utopian excitement about transforming the self or society than by a profound uncertainty over the very content of such a transformation. It is a postutopian anxiety, in that the interiority explored here resides not so much in some meaningful transitional linkage between tradition and modernity as in a nonspace rejected by, and excluded from, both the past and the future. In the interior space encircling Li Huiquan, while memory or nostalgia offers hardly any comfort, the future is disclaimed with equal dismay. It is the grim reality of a cagelike present that renders anxiety as the experience of inescapability and claustrophobia.

Let us return again to the opening shot to further examine the aesthetics of depth in the film as a whole. One reading of that seemingly endless walk along a tortuous lane in a shantytown is that it suggests the difficult path through which one arrives at the present. It is a metaphor of living through twisted history itself. "If the gray experience of walking belongs to history," the literary critic Chen Xiaoming comments, "then the shabby house as the 'present tense' of the narrative is joined with the 'now' of the character. This small house therefore becomes the starting point for Li Huiquan's self-renewal; it also indicates the end of past history. As a closed space of existence for an individual and a 'present' that must separate itself from its own history, this house has to resist the outside world as much as society" (1990, 103). Indeed, what Li Huiquan does here is walk away from the city, from any form of collectivity, and into his own interior space. As he moves into the depths of the shantytown, the camera

begins to descend from an encompassing view of the site down to a close tracking shot of the hero. Very soon, we are brought so close to the person walking
in front of us that we can no longer have the initial, although momentary, coherent perception of the environs. Our understanding of the situation becomes
firmly meshed with Li Huiquan's vision, which quickly turns out to be partial
and unmediated.[10] While the sorry images of an overcrowded shantytown evoke
poverty as the poignant critique of a failed social project, the failure of the current situation is ultimately presented—by means of camera angles and an evoca-
tive soundtrack—as a dead-end entrapment. The only escape seems to be Li
Huiquan's home or his private room, but this much-needed interior holds for
the young man a memory both too painful and too broken to be of any redemp-
tive value for the present.

This spatial tension, in which depth is embraced out of despair, gives rise
to an existential anxiety and at the same time endows that anxiety with social
criticism. It also generates two related kinds of visual imagery. The city, when
it appears at all, is reduced to fleeting images of empty streets, noisy traffic,
dimly lit back alleys, and pale, cold streetlights. All of these images irrepressibly suggest Li Huiquan's unease with the public dimension of the city and even
his fear of it. In contrast, the interior into which the individual subject now
retreats is continually interrupted and revealed to be vulnerable. Within this
second group of images, we can further distinguish two distinct clusters. One
consists of those midrange shots of Li Huiquan in his home. Here, the camera
always remains at the hero's eye level, and, through a zoom lens, as the director Xie Fei later reminds us, the character is shown in much sharper focus than
his surroundings so as to intensify his psychological isolation (1990b, 26). Also,
invariably, a top light intrudes, which, like the neighbor's loud radio and TV,
reinforces a sense of both antisociality and voyeuristic surveillance.[11]

The other cluster of representations of the interior occurs in the bar
(another favorite symbol of modern city life that I comment on below) where
close-ups of a pensive Li Huiquan, usually in the dark but sometimes under a
direct top light, are frequently crosscut with luminous and intensely colorful
images of the singer Zhao Yaqiu. The interiority experienced in this situation
is of a more emotional nature and is contrasted to the fluidity and vacuity of
popular music as a pliable form. The visual proximity of a desiring subject to
the object of desire actually underlines the unbridgeable gap between them and
forms a disturbing imagery of an emotional and communicational blockage.
The profound irony is that commodified art now supplies the expression and
appropriates the content of the subject's inmost memory and desire.

If Li Huiquan's ultimate despair is partly attributable to his inability or unwillingness to accept the cruel fact that Zhao Yaqiu is, after all, a popular performer who has to prostitute style for marketability, truthfulness for a universally appropriable external form, his own political identity—or, rather, a blatant lack thereof—constitutes his tragic character. An ex-convict for the crime of aggravated assault, and now the owner of a fashion stall, Li Huiquan finds himself an automatic misfit in a society where a highly moralistic political culture still dominates, while economic activity outside the public sector inevitably smacks of (or rather thrives on) amorality and even illegality (as embodied by the broker Cui Yongli). One defining feature of the dominant political culture is its refusal to recognize the complexity of everyday life, in particular its quotidian ordinariness and mundane needs and passions. Because the crime he committed and the punishment he consequently received appear to be so utterly "petty" in the sense that neither can be explained away by some political misfortune or injustice and thereby rehabilitated and turned into a source of honor, Li Huiquan is at once identified as a dismissable outsider and an invisible member of society. His explosive anger at Chazi's parents, who disown their criminal son so as to be accepted by society at large, directly articulates his frustrated protest against a tightly knit and dehumanizing social fabric. A stunning representation of Li Huiquan's social invisibility comes at the end, when, in that fateful evening in the park, he drags his wounded body through a complacently indifferent crowd. By now a thematic connection is established between Li Huiquan's ambiguous political identity, or the difficulty of narrating his life story, and the blurring or perceived illegibility of the city on which I commented. The unapproachable city, from which Li Huiquan wishes desperately to disengage himself, becomes the gigantic symbol of a social failure.

Urban Relationships Reconnected

The historical significance of *Black Snow* in contemporary Chinese cinema lies in the fact that, better and more focally than other films of the same genre, it presents the city as a social issue and makes visible the deep anxiety it simultaneously generates and suppresses. Private interior space is masterfully shown to be both a necessary shelter and an inescapable entrapment, while realistic images of stark poverty and disrepair quietly depict a demoralized collective imagination. The psychological depth, together with the libidinal frustration, of the individual is sympathetically explored and turned into a metaphor for the anxious, embattled subject of a peculiar historical moment—before a repressive political order ceases to demand homogeneity from members of society, a vibrant market economy sets in to instill anonymity and indifference. If the political reality is embodied in the gloomy urban landscape (predominantly the oppressive shantytown), new and rampant commercialism finds its perfect figuration in the attractive but heartless singer Zhao Yaqiu. The final death of the hero, therefore, while suggesting a strong social criticism, also drives home the impossibility of dissipating individual anxiety through any overarching myth or rationalization, which in recent Chinese history has shifted from an egalitarian vision of socialist paradise to the ideology of economic development and prosperity.

To further understand the politics of such a postutopian anxiety, we should turn to *Good Morning, Beijing,* a noticeably different filmic representation of contemporary life in that city. Here, in contrast to a blurred image of the city, we see a continual mapping of the sprawling cityscape; instead of an aesthetics of depth as social criticism, we find a persistent temporalization of space, linking different parts of the city through narratable, individual experiences. In her preproduction exposition of the film's theme, director Zhang Nuanxin made it clear that *Good Morning, Beijing* would pursue an "expressive, documentary" style to truthfully reflect the flow of daily life, with a sense of humor and light comedy. The soundtrack would be mostly live recording, and the color a shade of pleasantly harmonious gray. Set in a contemporary Beijing awash in the "great wave of the market economy," this film would follow everyday events in the life of a group of young people, but in reality mirror the contemporary social theme of "reform and opening up." It should also convey a refreshing broad-mindedness—"everyone's pursuit has its rationality and every attitude to life should be given its due understanding." The director decided to use the title *Good Morning, Beijing* "because this film will present a snapshot of millions of Beijing citizens, depicting the life of those ordinary people quietly working in the most basic strata of our society" (Zhang Nuanxin 1990, 53–54). Consciously or not, Zhang Nuanxin envisioned her movie largely in terms of a neorealist style of filmmaking, central to which are semidocumentary techniques and social concerns.[12]

This preproduction statement, however, should not limit our reading of the film too much because it was a document intended to secure the film its official approval and funding (in post-1989 China). Still it does strike the keynote for this public-oriented representation of life in Beijing. The plot of *Good Morning, Beijing* may appear complex at first glance. It centers on a young woman, Ai Hong, who works as a bus conductor, and it follows her successive relationships with three young men: first, her co-worker Wang Lang, then the bus driver

Zou Yongqiang, and finally the currently unemployed but new-fashioned and imaginative Keke. She eventually marries Keke and with him starts a private business. Because Wang Lang has no definable character of his own, Ai Hong's departure from him is relatively easy to explain, but her break with Zou Yongqiang, a caring, honest young man who somehow lacks the courage to imagine a different life for them, causes her much soul-searching. Her liaisons with and movement among these three very different young people have an obviously allegorical importance. They repeat, as one critic suggests, a classic narrative format in which the female character, by her departure, either symbolizes negation of an outmoded or objectionable way of life, or, through her acquiescence or eventual return, represents affirmation of a certain value system or accepted ideology.[13] In such a narrative tradition, women are made to express rather than create value. The value system to which Ai Hong subscribes in the end is therefore an emergent one associated with the market, which specifically calls for desirable character qualities such as energy, independence, and adventurousness. In the film, Keke, who at first pretends to be an overseas Chinese and wears a Harvard T-shirt, personifies such a new spirit, and his enthusiasm and modern lifestyle will help him win Ai Hong away from a reticent and much-inhibited Zou Yongqiang.

Indeed, the economy of passion in *Good Morning, Beijing* makes it a narrative that explicitly participates in an ongoing and large-scale cultural revolution through which habits, mentalities, and social structures will all be systematically transformed so as to legitimate the market as an important organizing principle of society. It is also a narrative about social discontent and its mitigation through the introduction of desire.[14] Desire becomes a positive social value in the film, not only in that it expresses a putatively collective vision of a different Lebenswelt, but also, perhaps more crucially, because it sets free the energies and imaginations of individuals. The engendering of this emancipatory desire is narrated and at the same time explained in Ai Hong's departure from Zou Yongqiang and her subsequent fascination with Keke, who appears to move in a more mobile space with unmistakable signs of modernity (taxis, nightclubs, Western-style grocery stores, and general sociability). (The social content of such a desire can be gauged from the fact that, although this can be read as a conventional triangular love story, "love" is never pronounced as of major significance in the plot's unfolding. On the contrary, Ai Hong's affair and eventual marriage with Keke, an odd twist, are auxiliary means for her to discover and assert her own new identity.) As a direct opposite to Keke, Zou Yongqiang belongs to a conformist world in which filial duty and respect for his superior combine to demand from him gratitude and, at the same time, provide him with a sense of security. He lives with his parents in an overcrowded Beijing courtyard where his mother has to continually cut short his only expression of individuality (playing the traditional Chinese violin and later the guitar) out of consideration for the neighbors. Unlike Keke, he shops in a featureless department store, and he expresses his affection for Ai Hong by buying her a practical skirt, whereas Keke enchants her with a Walkman and a tape of American rock and roll.

Thus, these two rivals for Ai Hong's affection are highly symbolic figures, each representing a separate social reality and cultural logic. Yet the residual and the emergent conditions of existence, if we wish to so understand the symbolism here, are engaged in a rhetoric of compromise and tolerance. The ideological emphasis placed on compromise renders untenable a facile dichotomy of tradition versus modernity that seems to suggest itself here as an interpretative framework. On the contrary, this rhetoric of compromise enables the film to sympathetically portray Zou Yongqiang's frustration, the grave social-historical (dis)content of which is now effectively displaced as momentary personal misfortune. As director Zhang Nuanxin puts it, even though he cannot, primarily emotionally, identify with the dominant Zeitgeist of the market, Zou Yongqiang maintains his decency and worthiness and continues to work and contribute to society (1990, 54). At the same time, Keke is transformed in the process from a conspicuous consumer of urban culture back into a productive member of society. The film's concluding sequence brings together all the major characters in a dramatic moment when Ai Hong, now an apparently successful self-employed businesswoman, and her husband get onto the bus that Zou Yongqiang still drives and on which Wang Lang still works as a conductor. After a brief and polite exchange of greetings, Zou Yongqiang turns around and starts the bus. Slowly, the camera pulls back to show all four very different young people aboard the same bus peacefully moving along a sunny street in Beijing.

This comforting moment of rapprochement, we are told by a subtitle on the screen, arrives one year after the main action of the film. In this rich final image, the element of time is as important as the central message about the ineluctable coexistence of different modes of production. Time here signifies change, progress, and a healing process as well. Time also becomes identified with the future, or rather with some utopian projections from the present. Actually, even at the beginning of the film, where we are shown Ai Hong still in bed one early morning, time as a major factor is introduced emphatically when the ticking alarm clock goes off. It is time for the young bus conductor to go to work, and the whole interior space is thus redefined and forced open by a universal clock time. Unlike *Black Snow,* where time is subjectivized and locked into a depressing present, *Good Morning, Beijing* is a film about the multiple and contradictory temporal flows in the space of the enormous city. Spatial structures, locations, and relations now acquire a temporal, historical significance to the extent that we can speak of a socially produced "spatiality" which, according to Edward Soja, "like society itself, exists in both substantial forms (concrete spatialities) and as a set of relations between individuals and groups, an 'embodiment' and medium of social life itself" (1989, 120). Through the narrative of the film, the uneven and multidimensional spatial relations are mapped and reconnected, and the city of Beijing is brought together as an imaginable totality, as a fascinating collection of images of various social realities that simultaneously exist and interact.

So a central plot in *Good Morning, Beijing* is the movement from the initial spatiotemporal structure of a confining domestic interior (underlined by the close-up shot of a cage with an impatient bird chirping in it) to an open cityscape that is emphatically contemporary and modernizing. Of particular interest in the opening sequence is a stark "crudeness" of the interior space—crude surfaces as well as crude conditions of existence. In this cramped room we realize that life has to be reduced to its bare necessities; it is an enclosed space kept flat and public by the absence of any refinement or the possibility of privacy. It becomes a most efficient extension of the workplace because "home" now stands less for separation from work than for a direct reproduction of labor. When at home, Ai Hong, as we see later, also has the task of taking care of her invalid grandpa. She readies coal for heating, fixes the exhaust pipe with the help of Zou Yongqiang, and, in the same room where her grandpa lies in bed year round, she prepares porridge for him and washes her hands in a basin next to the window. The same embarrassing experience of scarcity is even more pointedly represented at Zou Yongqiang's home, where, in his parents' makeshift bedroom, the whole family eats supper and watches TV while the father soaks his feet in a basin of warm water. At the end of dinner the son's duty is to take the basin, walk through a dark hallway, and drain the water into a public sink located in the courtyard.

In isolation, such images of impoverishment and severely constrained conditions of existence would not necessarily mean social criticism or cultural commentary. On the contrary, scarce and overcrowded domestic space would only appear "natural" or "realistic" enough, since some public places to which the camera brings us (such as the bus company headquarters, the police station, and the hospital) have surfaces and structures no less shabby and perfunctory. A Third World condition—here the term is used strictly to refer to generalized inadequate living conditions and a preindustrial, underdeveloped socioeconomic infrastructure—can hardly be grasped as such unless defamiliarized by images of, or references to, a different, more advanced stage of modernization. In *Good Morning, Beijing,* as we will see momentarily, the Third Worldness of the city is candidly acknowledged, together with its explicitly anticipated changeover. It is extremely significant, however, that the Third World condition presented by the film carries with it not so much mere self-loathing (would that be politically incorrect?) or self-glorification (would that be politically correct?) as an almost restless utopian desire for self-transformation. In this sense, the film as a Third World production is also conscientiously for a Third World audience, insofar as an undesirable present condition of existence is both represented as an immediate collective reality and historicized as some fast-vanishing remnant of a better future.[15]

Consequently, the series of images that reveals an impoverished everyday life acquires its historical content when it is juxtaposed with a different sequence, a different set of spatiotemporal structures. We may even argue that history, or a historical understanding of contemporary Beijing, becomes accessible precisely when this juxtaposition of different spatial realities and relationships is employed as a strategy of characterizing an incomplete, in-progress present condition. One way to describe this spatial coexistence or simultaneity could be the architectural notion of "a collage city," where "disparate objects (are) held together by various means" to form a composite presence.[16] In the film, the city of Beijing does become fragmented into a collage of various sites, rhythms, and intensities, but the movements through the city of the characters, in particular Ai Hong, reconnect all these obviously discontinuous moments. Thus, there is still the possibility of narrating one's story in the city, of presenting a spatial experience in temporal terms. As an apt symbol of collective practice, the moving bus, where much of the movie's action takes place, provides an ideal vehicle for linking up different parts and functions of Beijing. From here we see images of Beijing as a political center (Tiananmen Square), a rapidly modernizing metropolis (all-glass high-rises), and an overpopulated Third World city (business districts and shopping streets). In a sense, the moving bus serves as a clever self-reflection on the rolling camera and our viewing experience.

It is, however, Ai Hong's experiences as an individual subject who strives to change her own historical situation that endow the city with a humanizing narratability and a spatiotemporal coherence. We first see her get up early in the morning, run through the empty lane of the neighborhood, and hop onto Wang Lang's bicycle to go to work. Working on the bus is a demanding job, but she gets to meet and observe people. (Here, the bus is also a substitute for modern city streets, bound to be occupied by what Walter Benjamin once called an "amorphous crowd of passersby" [1969, 165].) One day her friend Ziyun comes onto the bus and proudly tells her that she now works as a typist for a joint-venture company. At her invitation, Ai Hong decides to pay her friend a visit and subsequently finds herself inside a business office on the sixteenth floor of a guarded building. This is one of those standardized, new international-style offices (polyester carpet, air-conditioning, and low ceilings), equipped with word processors, contemporary furniture, and a coffeemaker. The most astonishing feature of this claustrophobic office, when we recall Ai Hong's home as well as her workplace, are the smooth white walls and shiny objects. The glass coffee table quietly reflects, the sofa extends a comfortably curvaceous line, and the steel sink gives forth a hygienic silver glare. This interior space is totally alien to Ai Hong, and at first she appears intimidated. The polished surface not only out-lines a new form of labor no longer associated with bodily discomfort or endurance, but it also suggests a simplification of social relationships to those of an impersonal "cash nexus." Rather fittingly, in this seemingly depthless space, Ziyun, with her own experience, calmly illustrates to her awestruck friend some fundamental aspects of modern urban life: contingency and mobility.[17]

This modern office space can also be taken as an instance of the post-modern "relief" that a world of smooth objects may promote (Jameson 1991, 313–15). If it has a shattering effect on Ai Hong because it exposes as "pre-modern" or "yet-to-be-modernized" the shabbiness of her own world, it also initiates a readjustment of her relation to the city. Her eyes are suddenly opened, as it were, and she is able to experience and perceive the city as an enormous spatiotemporal structure that energetically produces a wide range of social real-ities and personal identities. In the following sequences, we see Ai Hong enjoy Korean food at a fancy restaurant with Zou Yongqiang and a friend of his; we see her wander into an upper-grade grocery store and find herself followed by an admirer who introduces himself as Keke. Soon, she and Keke go to a night-club where he performs with passionate emotion and dedicates a song to her. At the end of that evening, he takes her home in a taxi. Finally, as a high point of their romantic affair, and also to divert Ai Hong from her work, Keke sug-gests that they leave the city and go on a vacation. This series of concrete and very often discontinuous spatialities demands that Ai Hong constantly map and re-map the city in order to achieve a coherent perception of both herself and her environment. Indeed, instead of being incapacitated by this new spatial multi-plication, Ai Hong insists on keeping the city a legible human space by hero-ically redesigning herself and rewriting her own story. Her narrative therefore presupposes the possibility of becoming, and it is this conviction that supports a profound optimism about social change and self-transformation, personal as well as collective. In this light, the brief trip that Ai Hong and Keke make to some historical site (now a popular tourist attraction) away from Beijing becomes a significant move. It reintroduces historical time as the untranscend-able horizon of experience, and it localizes—albeit in its absence—the city as a reality with reachable limits.

Our reading therefore suggests that the spatiotemporal structure underlying the narrative of *Good Morning, Beijing* remains resolutely accessible to repre-sentation, in spite of all apparent conflicts and disjunctures. Ai Hong's story can be read as a narrative of the birth of urban individualism and self-consciousness, and her spatial movement in the city at once reveals and reconnects the com-plexity of social structures and relations, whether public or private, emergent or residual. Not surprisingly, the cinematic images we witness here are eventually controlled and organized by the subject, rather than the other way around. Unlike in postmodern cinema, where representation, according to David Harvey's persuasive analysis, runs into crisis because of a pervasive "time-space compression" engendered by a late capitalism of flexible accumulation, (1989, 322), *Good Morning, Beijing,* as a visual representation, is still fascinated by the seemingly infinite possibilities and frontiers promised by a modernizing metrop-olis. If one dominant theme of postmodern cinema, as Harvey shows through his readings of *Blade Runner* and *Wings of Desire* (respectively about Los Angeles and Berlin), is an impossible conflict "between people living on differ-ent time scales, and seeing and experiencing the world very differently as a result (1989, 313), what we find in this particular Chinese film is rather a "neorealist" arranging of urban relations and a utopian resolution of conflicts arising from city life. By continually moving its characters across the uneven urban landscape, *Good Morning, Beijing* evokes the city itself as an intimate participant that qui-etly justifies their endeavors and aspirations. It is a film that refuses to let close-up images of the city blur its organizational logic and multiple functions, or to allow the city to disappear as a mappable totality. Its general visual clarity, enhanced by continual shots with great depth of field, mirrors the filmmaker's effort to influence and shape our understanding of the changing city.

By way of conclusion, I wish to bring together and compare the different political visions in *Black Snow* and *Good Morning, Beijing.* Both films feature a pivotal scene in a lively nightclub. In *Black Snow,* Li Huiquan as a member of the audience is painstakingly separated from the solo singer, both visually and emotionally. But when Ai Hong and Keke in *Good Morning, Beijing* go to a bar with live music, Keke joins the band and asks to participate. He sings and dedicates to Ai Hong a popular song by rock star Cui Jian, which Ai Hong will also learn to sing, even though she appears to be at a loss when hearing the song for the first time. The interpretation that I would propose, if only too schematically, is that these two different moments express two approaches to the city that are at odds with each other. If we characterize the politics of *Black Snow* as a refusal and contemplation by means of a modernist aesthetics of depth, the rhetoric of compromise in *Good Morning, Beijing* necessarily valorizes cultural and political participation, which in turn articulates the legitimating ideology of a growing market economy. Whereas the market economy arrives to present an open city to Ai Hong and her contemporaries, some deep (well-nigh instinctive) suspicion of the market triggers Li Huiquan's anxious, and to a large extent forced, retreat to interiority. In one case, neorealist techniques are used to rationalize the modernization project, while in the other a hypertrophy of modernist subjectivity emits uncompromising social criticism. Herein lies the cognitive value of *Black Snow,* which may be realized only with critical reflection on the part of the viewer.

These two significantly contradistinct political visions and cinematic languages hardly escaped the notice of the Chinese audience when *Black Snow* and *Good Morning, Beijing* were released in 1989 and 1990, respectively. They were quickly recognized as representative works of the rising city cinema. While *Black Snow* enjoyed the rare distinction of winning both domestic and international honors (Best Picture at the Thirteenth National Hundred Flowers Awards and the Silver Bear Prize at the Berlin Film Festival), *Good Morning, Beijing* was a remarkable box-office success. Quoting Cesare Zavattini, the theorist of Italian neorealist cinema, an enthusiastic commentator commended the second film for truthfully capturing contemporary everyday life in the ancient capital city and in the process revealing a deeper historical meaning.[18] At the same time, the critical recognition of *Black Snow* caused considerable uneasiness among mainstream critics and media. A brief essay in *Popular Cinema,* appearing next to Lei Da's endorsement of *Good Morning, Beijing,* sought to explain why the Hundred Flowers Award won by *Black Snow* did not mean that the film is flawless. In fact, the essayist denounced the film as deeply flawed because, in spite of its artistic achievements, "it does not find (or does not want to find) a new worldview and a new character that new social forces, who represent a new mode of social production, ought to possess."[19] It would be an involved task to unpack the loaded discourse and ideological stances here. Suffice it to say that at stake are some profoundly unresolved questions about artistic and social forms, about representation and engagement, all of which these two films succeed in bringing to the fore by evoking separate intellectual and aesthetic traditions. If our analysis of their indebtedness to either modernism or neorealism shows both films to be an ideological intervention, it should also be clear that we cannot dismiss one on the account of the other. Rather, these two films should be viewed together, and perhaps between them we will begin to approach the impossible urban reality signified by Beijing.

Notes

This article is reprinted from *Chinese Modern: The Heroic and the Quotidian* (Duke University Press, 2000): 245–72; first published as "Configuring the Modern Space: Cinematic Representation of Beijing and Its Politics," *East-West Film Journal* 8.2 (1994): 47–69. Copyright © 2002 by Xiaobing Tang. Reprinted by permission of the author.

1. The lyrics go on like this: With a friend I always kill some time in a bar, / While the tape player repeats all the hit songs. / You think one way and you talk one way, / Because everyone wears a toy-like mask. / What should I say?

2. These four films are *Wanzhu, Lunhui* (dir. Huang Jianxin), *Da chuanqi* (dir. Ye Daying), and *Tiban shi haishui, yiban shi huoyan* (dir. Xia Gang).

3. Two other city films that came out in 1988 are *Yaogun qingnian* and *Fengkuang de daijia*, directed, respectively, by Tian Zhuangzhuang (*Daoma zei*, 1986) and Zhou Xiaowen (*Zuihou de fengkuang*, 1987), two well-established Fifth Generation filmmakers. In 1987, at least two films by directors of the Fifth Generation were also about the contemporary cityscape: *Gei kafei jiadian tang* (dir. Sun Zhou) and *Taiyangyu* (dir. Zhang Zeming).

4. For analyses of some representative film texts from the New China cinema tradition, see Chris Berry, "Sexual Difference and the Viewing Subject in *Li Shuangshuang* and *The In-Laws*," in Berry 1991, 30–39; Ma Junxiang, "*Shanghai guniang*: Geming nüxing ji 'guankan' wenti" (*The girl from Shanghai*: Revolutionary women and the question of "viewing"), in Tang Xiaobing 1993, 127–46.

5. For a genealogical account of the origin of the Fifth Generation and its modernist politics, see Xudong Zhang 1997, 215–31. See also, for instance, the statement by one of the leading members of the Fifth Generation in the interview "A Director Who Is Trying to Change the Audience: A Chat with Young Director Tian Zhuangzhuang," conducted by Yang Ping, in Berry 1991, 127–30.

6. In a 1984 essay, Xie Fei emphasized the importance of representing daily life. Commenting on Raizman's *A Personal Life* (1983), Xie Fei wrote: "No significant events, heated dramatic conflicts, and unusual techniques arc used. On the contrary, it vividly depicts

a variety of characters, touches profound social problems and philosophies, and is obviously a contemporary product." See Xie Fei, "My View of the Concept of Film," in George S. Semsel et al. 1990, 79.

7. Peter E. Bondanella, *Italian Cinema from Neorealism to the Present* (New York: Unger, 1983), 60.

8. After making clear the relationship between the classical realist ideology of the nineteenth century and neorealism, Millicent Marcus, in his *Italian Film in the Light of Neorealism* (Princeton, N.J.: Princeton University Press, 1986), observes that neorealism in Italian cinema expressed an "immediate postwar optimism about the attempt to shape political reality according to a moral idea" (28).

9. See, for instance, Chen Xiaoming, "Daode zijiu: Lishi zhouxin de duanlie" (Moral self-salvation: The breaking of a historical axis), *Film Art*, no. 215 (1990): 105. While describing the difference between *Black Snow* and his earlier films, Xie Fei emphasizes his philosophical beliefs. "Surely there was some change in my conception, but in my artistic creation, I as always held dear my ideals, and stayed with my value judgment as far as the true, the good, and the beautiful versus the false, the evil, and the ugly in our life experiences are concerned." See Xie Fei 1990b, 20.

10. The "inward turn" or psychologization of experience that I relate here with the aesthetics of depth can also be observed in the original novel, which opens with Li Huiquan's return to his home and a wintry present. Here is Howard Goldblatt's translation of the first sentences: "A fat white guy was squatting in the yard. Li Huiquan, his knapsack slung over his shoulder, noticed the frosty grin as soon as he walked through the gate, so he walked over and wiped it off. Chunks of coal for eyes, a chili-pepper nose, a wastebasket hat—the same stuff he used as a kid." Liu Heng, *Black Snow,* trans. Howard Goldblatt (New York: Atlantic Monthly Press, 1993), 3.

11. See Liu Shuyong, "Zaoxing zuowei yuyan: Qianlun *Benming nian* de yongguang chuli" (Imaging as language: On the lighting technique in *Black Snow*), *Dangdai dianying* (Contemporary cinema), no. 35 (April 1990): 87–91.

12. Acknowledging the formidable difficulty in generalizing about neorealism, Millicent Marcus nonetheless offers a useful description of what constitutes its basic style and techniques. "The rules governing neorealist practice would include location shooting, lengthy takes, unobtrusive editing, natural lighting, a predominance of medium and long shots, respect for the continuity of time and space, use of contemporary, true-to-life subjects, an uncontrived, open-ended plot, working-class protagonists, a non-professional cast, dialogue in the vernacular, active viewer involvement, and implied social criticism" (Marcus, *Italian Cinema,* 22).

13. Zhang Wei 1990, 55–56. One needs to note here that this reading is heavily influenced by Laura Mulvey's critical analysis of classic Hollywood narrative cinema.

14. It is interesting to note that in its subtitled English-language version, the film is given a much more suggestive title, *Budding Desires*.

15. There is another group of films in contemporary Chinese cinema whose cultural "Third Worldness" is marketed primarily to First World film audiences. Films by Zhang Yimou (*Ju Dou,* 1990; *Raise the Red Lantern,* 1992) seem to be favorite samples of this group.

16. Colin Rowe and Fred Koetter, *Collage City* (Cambridge, Mass.: MIT Press, 1978), 139–40. I would like to point out that Rowe and Koetter's vision of a "collage city" expresses a typical postmodernist sensibility and ideology. "Collage city" is offered as a solution to the anxiety generated by both utopia and tradition: "because collage is a method deriving its virtue from its irony, because it seems to be a technique for using things and simultaneously disbelieving in them, it is also a strategy which can allow utopia to be dealt with as image, to be dealt with in *fragments* without our having to accept it in *toto,* which is further to suggest that collage could even be a strategy which, by supporting the utopian illusion of change-lessness and finality, might even fuel a reality of change, motion, action and history" (149).

17. While putting on makeup in the office lavatory, Ziyun tells Ai Hong that even though her salary is handsome, she has no job security; then, when asked about her boyfriend, she replies that they split up because "it was too demanding for both of us."

18. See Lei Da, "Dangda dushi fengjing xian: Tan yingpian *Beijing nizao*" (Contemporary urban landscape: About the film *Good morning, Beijing*), *Dazbong dianying* (Popular cinema), no. 450 (December 1990): 4–5.

19. See Zheng Shu, "Xie zai *Benming nian* huojiang zhihou" (Afterthoughts on *Black Snow* winning the award), *Popular Cinema,* no. 450 (December 1990): 5.

Appendixes
Bibliography
Index

Appendix 1 Discussion Questions

1. *Two Stage Sisters* (Xie Jin, 1965)

1. Are you familiar with any Hollywood backstage melodramas? How is *Two Stage Sisters* comparable to these films? What are the elements that make *Two Stage Sisters* melodramatic?

2. Please find out what the "alienation effects" are that Brecht argued for in relationship to Chinese opera acting. Do you detect any alienation effects in the acting of the two actresses, either in their film roles or opera roles?

3. Why would the film present a Chunhua replica (a girl of the same name and the similar experience of being purchased by a family to be used as a maid)? Focus on the sequences where the actress Chunhua is being humiliated at the marketplace and the maid Chunhua is feeding her water and where the actress Chunhua is leaving the town and the maid Chunhua is seeing her off by the river. How are these two characterized in relationship to each other, and what is the purpose of this relationship?

4. When Manager Tang pays the two actresses for the first time, a photo of the former Queen of Yue opera, Shuihua, is revealed in his drawer. What messages are delivered in this brief moment of the film? How do other episodes of the film reinforce these messages?

5. When Chunhua and Yuehong quarrel backstage, their former stage friends arrive on a visit from the countryside. Why does the visit occur at this time?

6. Have you detected a feminist spirit in this film? How does it help define what is a good woman or a fallen woman? How are the two actresses portrayed according to the values of this feminism?

7. Why would Chunhua want to change what she and her fellow actresses perform on-stage? Is there any ironic contrast between the life of female characters they perform and their actual lives as actresses? Please use incidents from the film to illustrate this contrast.

8. Find out what the stories of *Xianglin's Wife* and *White-Haired Girl* are about. How do Chunhua's performances of these two plays help illustrate the kind of feminism that she stands for?

9. In a way, *Xianglin's Wife* and *White-Haired Girl* represent the influences of Shanghai (the cultural discourses and leftist filmmaking) and Yan'an (the class struggle ideology) on *Two Stage Sisters*. Can you identify the major features of these influences, respectively, with the help of the two plays?

2. *Hibiscus Town* (Xie Jin, 1986)

1. What is a melodrama? Is *Hibiscus Town* melodramatic? How does it illustrate the following features of a melodrama?

a. the schematization of good and evil
b. emotional effects
c. theatricality and spectacle
d. the individual as victim
e. the individual-social relationship represented as a matter of justice

2. Would you agree with the argument that Chinese political life is itself a melodramatic performance? Can you give examples from this film to support this argument?

3. How do Western and Chinese cultures conceptualize differently such ideas as "person," "self," and "individual"? How does *Hibiscus Town* inform you about this issue? In turn, how does this issue inform the basic *mise-en-scène* of the film? Consider here the problem of self and social space: how do these two basic concepts function in a melodramatic film?

4. How do the sound track and the color scheme of the film contribute to the tensions within the film? Is there a general pattern of contrast here?

5. What does the camera speak to in this film (i.e., how does the camera, representing an ideology, direct our ways of viewing this film)? In what ways does the camera manipulate our responses to the film and our identification with the characters?

6. How are the female characters represented in this film? What is the topological opposition of the two (or more) central women?

7. Is Comrade Li a villain? Explain your answer.

8. Reflect on Crazy Chin's humor in life. What is the effect of his humor on our understanding of the film?

9. What cinematic means are used to create the contrasting impressions of the small town: a town of beauty, happiness, and harmony versus a town of ugliness, terror, and chaos?

3. *Farewell My Concubine* (Chen Kaige, 1993)

1. How does the performance of the same opera by Duan Xiaolou and Cheng Dieyi at different times of their lives comment on their lives and the times? Consider here the interplay of text (the opera) and context and how it produces different meanings for each performance. Can you contrast at least two such moments of performance?

2. Consider the performance within the performance. How do the lives of Duan Xiaolou and Cheng Dieyi and their performances correspond with each other emotionally to produce a deeper meaning in the drama? Is there a difference between the two

stars' attitudes toward their performances? If you have seen *Woman, Demon, Human*, how are the two stars' relationship to their performance comparable to the female ghost performer in that film?

3. Consider the value of loyalty and the additional question of the objects of loyalty (loyal to what?). How many "kings" are there who demand loyalty in this film? How do the various demands of loyalty complicate the lives of the two stars? Are these demands reconcilable?

4. What is the role played by "the little one" in this film? Is he a foil for the two stars? Does he represent a different kind of loyalty contradicting the loyalties held by the two stars?

5. Chen Kaige, the director, suggests that the central theme of the film is betrayal. How is that so? Who betrays whom? How and why? Does the betrayal narrated in the film contrast with the idea of loyalty shown in the opera performances?

6. Although homosexuality is in the foreground in the original novel, it has been significantly downplayed in the film. Its representation has become less melodramatic and more psychologically real. According to the film, can one be assured that Dieyi (the player of the concubine role) is homosexual? Is this consideration important to our understanding of the film? Why or why not?

7. Consider Dieyi's fixation on role and art. Dieyi embodies Chen Kaige's nostalgia for sincerity and a pure love for art. What are the emotional effects of this fixation and embodiment throughout the film? What is the film trying to say by showing this fixation and embodiment?

4. *Street Angel* (Yuan Muzhi, 1937)

1. Let's have a closer look at the opening sequence. With the help of Ma Ning's essay, can you detect and explain:

   a. How the camera is (dis)placed so that a clashing effect is achieved? What general rules of editing is this sequence violating?
   b. What is an open POV structure and what is a closed POV structure? How are these two structures mixed in this sequence and to what effect?
   c. What elements make the two different marching processions appear different?

2. In which sequences is Xiao Hong's role pushed closer to allegory? How many kinds of allegory does her role (and body) sustain?

3. While Xiao Hong has received the most attention, what do you think is the function of Xiao Yun? Would the allegorical gender representation be complete without the roles played by Xiao Yun?

4. How would you describe Zhao Huishen's acting style in portraying Xiao Yun?

How do *mise-en-scène,* lighting, and the use of shadows help contrast Xiao Yun from Xiao Hong?

5. What are the vertical and horizontal dimensions of the allegory that Ma Ning mentions? How do they apply to this film?

6. What is the effect of Wang's constant reference to newspapers? Do you see a contrast between journalistic discourse and popular discourse here? (Note: Remember the close resemblance of official discourse and journalistic discourse in China during this time.)

7. The film's editing style often achieves a bizarre effect. For example, when Xiao Yun is ordered to take off her clothes, a "misleading" shot of Gu's valet taking *his* clothes off is cut in. Can you list some other junctures where editing suggests certain associations that force the audience to think? Can you explain one or more of the various effects of these junctures?

8. While the Hollywood influence is strong in this film, do you detect anything similar to Russian montage? How do the two different styles interact in this film?

9. For a "lower-depth" subject matter, are the comic touches used throughout the film suitable? What are the elements in the narrative that check these comic effects?

5. *Three Women* (Chen Liting, 1949)

1. How does the characterization of Ruoying illustrate the bourgeois nature of her "new woman" ideal? What are the elements in the narrative that are designed to show that her "new woman" ideal is impractical?

2. When Ruoying finds out that another woman has stolen her husband and she rushes to a bookstore to find her and fight, what stops her? Is this moment typical of the film? What is the general implication of this moment? Take a closer look at the following sequences: Ruoying returns to the house, is on her way to the bookstore in the cab, encounters the demonstration, and understands her husband's political affiliation through reading a leaflet. What are the stylistic features (such as *mise-en-scène* and camera placement) in which these sequences are executed?

3. How does the film represent the issue of the ways women appear? Does this relate to the "male gaze" and the female social status of the time? Start by considering the following details:

   a. Why is Ruoying constantly concerned about her looks, even while she is in prison? What is the film trying to make the audience feel about her concerns?

   b. When Jinmei becomes a prostitute, she changes her look, causing family tension. Is Jinmei's change in looks comparable to Ruoying's concerns about her looks?

4. At the beginning of the film, why are the assault of the Japanese soldiers on Jinmei and Ruoying's quarrel with her husband presented as parallels?

5. This film, typical of many made in the black-and-white era, is very good at using shadows to express certain feelings. Can you locate and explain some sequences in which the shadows play a role?

6. One feature of social or critical realism is that characters typify social forces. What social forces are represented by the three women in this film?

6. *Woman, Demon, Human* (Huang Shuqin, 1988)

1. How is the film comparable to other films you know in which the lives of actors and actresses embody an important motif? What motif? Can you give some examples? Consider how the leading actor either lives out the drama in his/her real life or transforms his/her life experience into drama, or both.

2. The legend of Zhong Kui in this film has two implications: (1) A capable warrior is wronged in the human world but is given a ghost-busting job in the underworld. (2) He journeys as a loving brother in search of his sister so that he can see that she is properly married. Consider the following in relation to the legend:

   a. Where in the film do we find the manifestation of these two implications?
   b. Which characters in the film are like Zhong Kui in the sense that they are wronged and pushed into a ghostly form?
   c. Which characters are like Zhong Kui in trying to fulfill their brotherly duties?
   d. How many "brother-and-sister" relations are there in the film?
   e. Who actually desired brotherly love in the film? Did this person get it?

3. Zhong Kui appears ten times in the film. What are the stylistic features of most of Zhong Kui's appearances? How do these appearances correspond differently with various intense moments of the drama of the film? Analyze a few such junctures.

4. Consider Qiuyun's identification with Zhong Kui, through the male role she plays.

   a. Analyze *his* ostracism (fears) as a ghost versus his desire to do good for his sister and other human beings.
   b. Analyze *her* ostracism (insults and injuries) as the daughter of a tainted woman, the daughter of a loving but sometimes monopolizing father, the female disciple of a male mentor whom she cannot love, and the wife of a degenerate husband versus her desire to be fulfilled and loved.
   c. What might be the feelings of a ghost who has to be in the shadows to help those living in the light?

    d. What might be the feelings of Qiuyun about performing behind the mask
       of a male ghost on the stage to balance out her inadequacy (what she is
       lacking in her offstage life)?

    5. Why does the encounter of Qiuyun with her mother having sex with a man and
her later encounter with Master Zhang share the same *mise-en-scènes?*
    6. On quite a few occasions, an idiot is used as an important element of the *mise-
en-scène;* for example, he walks by Master Zhang at the train station when the latter is
forced to leave the theater troupe. What do the various appearances of the idiot imply?
Is there a unified implication that accounts for all these appearances?
    7. Why is Qiuyun's real father only viewed from the back? Is this way of hiding his
identity in any way related to the invisibility of Qiuyun's husband?
    8. Would you consider this film feminist? Analyze, for example, this sequence: An
exhausted Qiuyun lies on the ground after a training session when a little boy comes
into the frame, asking if she is dead. Qiuyun is so irritated that she tells the boy to go
elsewhere to play with his own balls. The boy's upper body is not shown, only his tiny
genitals. The director herself said that she didn't know much about Western feminism
but was happy with the execution of this sequence in that her character could say some
rough words to release her woman's anger.

7. *Ju Dou* (Zhang Yimou, 1990)

    1. Since the film is about a mill that produces colors, first consider how colors are
employed in the different sequences to complement the drama. Find examples. Does the
film use any color symbolism consistently?
    2. What is the significance of the enclosed space in various sequences? How does
the film convey the sense of enclosure?
    3. Bell, bell, ding dong,
       We walk to the Wang village.
       The Wang village has a crowd of dogs,
       They bite us and we have nowhere to run.
       Nowhere to run, we go back home,
       Go back home to blow our little trumpets.

    Consider the circular use of this children's chorus, which we hear when Tianqing
and Ju Dou meet outside of the house and which is sung by Tianqing when he happily
reigns in the house. It also becomes the old man's song when he forces Tianqing to refer
to his son as "brother" and is the concluding song of the film. How does this song suggest a structuring motif for the film? What is this motif?
    4. Still considering the song above, can you determine what message it conveys at
the end of the film? Please compare and discuss your answer with the two possible read-

ings offered by Sheldon Lu: "To read the ending negatively, the words of the song may also reinforce the impression that the children are inescapably haunted by the dogs in an impending doom. Thus, the burning of the mill and the children's song may be read as an indication of hopeless destruction. Or, as one may also willfully read in the opposite way, the ending is an intimation of the myth of a new beginning, an allegory of the rebirth of a nation out of the ashes of the old" (1997, 116).

5. What kind of character is Tianbai? Why does his first utterance of the term "father" draw so much dramatic tension? Is it significant that he kills both the old man and Tianqing? At what moments in the film does Tianbai seem to function as a "reincarnated father"?

6. Do you agree with the argument that this film's resemblance to Western Oedipal narrative is only superficial and that, in a cultural sense, the film is about the denying of sons rather than the slaying of fathers? Please argue for or against this observation.

7. If you believe that Tianqing often behaves rather pathetically, do you think that this suggests a certain cultural status of Chinese men? In her essay, Ann Kaplan argues: "Given the prior phallic order, and given classical Oedipal rivalry with the Father, they [Chinese males] may be harmed even more than women. State communism, in demanding male submission to the Law of the Father with little possibility for obtaining at least some parity with the Father position (as in free-enterprise capitalism), may produce men psychically damaged in deeper ways even than women" (1991, 153). Although *Ju Dou* is set in an earlier time, does it also illustrate this gender situation?

8. In *Ways of Seeing* (1977), John Berger categorizes women's to-be-looked-at-ness into "nude" and "naked": the former denoting a woman as an object of the male voyeur, and the latter indicating that a woman has her own identity separate from the viewer. Does this distinction help describe the relationship between Ju Dou and Tianqing? Here, consider especially the sequence in which Tianqing peeps at the half-naked Ju Dou who, knowing what's happening, turns around to show the bruise on her body (see also W. A. Callahan, 1993).

8. *Girl from Hunan* (Xie Fei, Wu Lan, 1986)

1. Shen Congwen's text reflects the influence of the Southern romantic tradition, which leads our attention away from today's contrasts with the ethnic minorities to the ancient contrast of Northern Confucian conventions and Southern romantic imagination shown by Qu Yuan's *Songs of the South*. How is today's contrast comparable to the ancient one? Are there any "Southern" elements, in the broadest sense, in this film? Do they help comment on mainstream culture?

2. Is "pastoral" a suitable description for Shen's text? What theme and imagery dominate its narration? What is the function of dream here? What are the narrative roles played by the girl students?

3. What is the effect of positioning the "unnatural" marriage in a narration filled with the imagery of nature? Is this contrast true to both the literary text and the film?

4. Is there any symbolism in the literary text? Can literary symbols always be successfully transferred to the screen? Here, start by considering the symbolic implications of the caterpillar. Has this been translated to the screen? How?

5. Have you noticed the film's additions to the literary text, such as the story of the widow, the intimidation of the heads of the families, and Chunguan's exposure to modern education? What are the effects created by these additions? How is the widow related to Xiaoxiao? Is she Xiaoxiao's alter ego? How does the addition of the grown-up Chunguan comment on the Xiaoxiao story?

6. Is the style of the film, on the whole, melodramatic? What emotional effect related to a certain critique does the melodrama try to create? Consider the following detail: During Xiaoxiao's wedding, since baby Chunguan is not cooperating, a rooster is used in his place. Why is this practice not emotionally exploited?

7. Why is the film punctuated by a frame showing the monotonous movement of the water-operated punching device? How does this frame comment on the drama of the film? Does this frame help express a certain theme (e.g., circulation), symbolism (e.g., nature), or tone (e.g., the rhythm of life in the countryside)?

8. What are the roles played by the images and sounds of nature, such as rippling water and the changing of seasons, shown in the foliage? Can you give some examples to illustrate how the grand force of nature both contrasts and absorbs the intensity of the human drama? Why is the human drama juxtaposed with nature?

9. Is what happened to Xiaoxiao at the mill house a rape? How is this rather "sexist" scene represented cinematically? What other cultural codes could be used to explain the execution of this scene, especially concerning the loosening of the bonds on Xiaoxiao and the close-up shots of water gushing through the mill?

10. Chris Berry observes that viewers are often distanced from Xiaoxiao rather than called to identify with her (1994, 98). Do you agree? Why is this so? If Xiaoxiao is not the narrative agent in the film, who or what else is?

11. What is the implication of Xiaoxiao turning into a mother-in-law herself and enforcing the same abnormal marriage that was once imposed on her? Is this an example of woman's patriarchal positioning? How do the themes of circularity in nature and culture comment on each other here?

12. Hoare noticed a reduced presence of male characters or the lack of masculinity in the film, especially in contrast to its literary base. Why would the filmmaker do this when the film is about the oppression and exploitation of women?

9. *Sacrificed Youth* (Zhang Nuanxin, 1985)

1. How is the human desire for beauty depicted? How is this desire contrasted between the Dai and the Han? Why is the desire for beauty an issue of interest for an understanding of this film?

2. Consider the sequence in which Li Chun watches young Dai women lining up to

see themselves in a full-length mirror, a clever idea of some Han "entrepreneurs" to make quick money during a market gathering. What is the director trying to say with this sequence? How does this sequence comment on the Han-Dai contrast?

3. How is the love triangle exploited—is it for sentimentality or to explore a cross-cultural dilemma? Why does Li Chun refuse Dage—is it to deny him as a person or to reject the social position of a Dai woman that marriage to him would impose on her?

4. What conveys Li Chun's allegorical search for a loving mother? How does her relationship with Ya, or Granny, fit into this search?

5. Consider the sequence of harvest dancing. What kind of atmosphere is created by the cinematography and the music? See if you agree with this observation: Although the dancing is surely a happy time, with a hearty fire, strong liquor, shadows of the dancers cast by the fire, plus the music with its exotic touch, all seem to create an ominous intensity. Why does this sequence produce this effect?

6. What is the effect of the music that first ushers Li Chun into the Dai world—warmly comforting or strangely disturbing?

7. How well has the director used colors? In which sequences do colors play important roles? Here, consider especially the four sequences that conclude the film. The dominant colors of these sequences change from white to red to gray and then to golden orange. What is the significance of this pattern?

10. *Horse Thief* (Tian Zhuangzhuang, 1986)

1. Tian Zhuangzhuang claims that *Horse Thief* was shot for the audience of the next century. We've now stepped into Tian's "next century." Do you still find this film avant-garde? How does a film like this require a different viewing? Can you compare your viewing of this film with other films and see what you would ignore in other films but tend to notice more here?

2. Is the film devoid of any narrative line? If not, can you sketch out this narrative line?

3. What is the specific time during which the plot of this film occurs? Is it important to know this to understand the film?

4. Is the style of this film documentary? Since "documentary" often denotes "realistic," does the film appear realistic to you? If not, what are the elements that make this film unrealistic?

5. Consider such elements as life, death, humanity, nature, religion, etc., and see how the film relates these elements. Has the film developed a certain allegory with the help of these elements?

6. Do you detect certain paradoxes such as the beauty and cruelty of nature, the rebellion and submission of humans, or the inspiration and repression of religion? Support your description of these paradoxes with details from the film.

7. What "oriental orientalism" or "internal othering" is found in the PRC? How

would *Horse Thief* illustrate these strategies? Whose point of view controls this film? Does this film tilt more toward silencing the Han voice, shunning the majority perspective, and giving the Tibetan minority a better representation?

11. *Yellow Earth* (Chen Kaige, 1984)

1. Why does the film choose "concealment" as its general style? What is concealed? Start by considering such contrasts as image over plot, symbolism over realism, song over dialogue, ambiguity over didacticism, and the like.

2. What is the function of the homological structures or parallelism that we detect in this film—e.g., two weddings, two mass performances of certain "rituals," two different images of yellow earth, and Cuiqiao's parallel relationship to both the soldier and her father?

3. Consider the representation of some of these parallel sequences.

a. Why are the two weddings identical and why are they shot with long takes rather than dramatized with close-ups?

b. What constitutes the sharp contrast between the two rituals, the one in Yan'an and the one in Cuiqiao's home village? Will dust versus water imagery describe this contrast? How?

4. Still in terms of parallelism, in what ways can we think of Cuiqiao's father as identical to the land he lives on, the Loess Plateau?

5. Cuiqiao's roles include the on-screen viewer, the hidden singer, and a young woman hoping to be saved. Can we think of her as an allegorical character? What is the allegory about?

6. Why does Cuiqiao's brother, Hanhan, always have a blank look (i.e., lacking any trace of emotion)?

7. Do the father, daughter, and son all characterize concealment? From the Taoist perspective, concealment is mostly about nature and how the human should be attentive to nature. Do these characters direct our attention to nature?

8. Do you understand Farquhar's argument about "hidden" gender? Can you illustrate the *yin/yang* scheme with the imagery from this film? Start with yellow earth versus Yellow River, or earth versus water.

9. Does Chen Kaige's film of concealment contain a cultural critique? If so, what is he critiquing?

10. Shift perspectives from Taoism to Confucianism, from heeding the music of nature to heeding human voices. The film is about collecting and rewriting songs. Can the songs here be considered, in accordance with the Confucian belief that names create social reality, as a cultural creating force? What kinds of songs are presented and how do they relate to each other?

12. *Old Well* (Wu Tianming, 1987)

1. In representing the various values found in this mountain village, which values does the film endorse? Does the film exemplify the ambiguity in value judgment of roots-searching? What or who decides the values in this village?

2. If the village is a specific culture in contrast with the outside world, can this be an allegory of Chinese national culture versus that of the international community? What in the film makes you feel that such an allegory is valid?

3. What is the film's message in contrasting a romantic woman and a family woman? Can you think of a few pairs of contrasting *mise-en-scènes* that imply the same differences as between these two women? Has the film shown a preference or an ambivalence in dealing with this contrast? Start by analyzing these two sequences:

a. Morning at Wangquan and Xifeng's house. Wangquan watches his wife feeding the pigs and chicken.
b. Wangquan meets with Qiaoying by a failed well.

Do the *mise-en-scènes* here convey a message, such as fertility versus barrenness, which comment on the two women? Or is this contrast only temporary since the well, which contains the second woman's contribution, will eventually gush with water?

4. The contrast of the romantic woman and the family woman is only one of many in this film. Can you give examples of other parallelism (not confined to characterization) in this film? Start by thinking of the contrast between the flock of sheep struggling for water and the crowds of villagers fighting for the ownership of the dried-up well.

5. How do the costumes contribute to the characterizations? Consider Wangquan's costumes: a red sweater in the first half, a buttoned-up blue jacket at the wedding, a black jacket toward the end of the film. What are the added meanings that these costumes offer to his characterization at different times? Also consider Qiaoying's costume: a white modern-style dress and a glowing red down jacket.

6. Broaden the scope of contrast to the four major characters: Wangquan versus Wangcai, Qiaoying versus Xifeng. Can you complete the following lists and comment on the contrasts of these characters?

Wangquan: disciplined, confused . . .
Wangcai: erotic, wild (disco) . . .
Qiaoying: novel, romantic, outcast . . .
Xifeng: stable, family-oriented . . .

7. How does the film depict Wangquan's dilemma? Can you think of some frames or sequences in which this dilemma is either visually (*mise-en-scènes*, etc.) or cinematographically (visual and sound-track editing, lighting, movement, etc.) expressed?

Examples: (1) the frames showing Wangquan carrying a huge sheet of stone walking on the mountain road, (2) the sequence depicting Wangquan and Xifeng in bed on their wedding night.

8. What is the role played by the insane uncle? Is his insanity a metaphor in the film?

9. What kind of symbolism is associated with the use of echoes in the mountains? Can you give examples of other similar use of symbolism in this film? The film is filled with all kinds of culturally and cinematically cued metaphors. See how many of them you can list.

13. *Red Sorghum* (Zhang Yimou, 1987)

1. Consider the carnival sense of the film, that is, a mischievous, joyful, profane, drunken, and destructive challenge to a certain cultural decorum. Do you know what the Chinese sense of decorum is in everyday life and representation? Can you give some examples of what you believe to be your cultural decorum so that your instructor can contrast them with those of the Chinese? How has *Red Sorghum* violated this decorum? Can you give examples of violence, vulgarity, indecency, and abusive language used in the film? What kind of cultural critique does the film offer in its carnival transgression? What kind of cultural desire does it reflect?

2. How does the carnival sense lend a unique feature to the film's *mise-en-scène* and narrative? How does the film stylistically reflect a certain subversive marginality and transgression? What is the artistic and historical context of China in the mid-1980s that produced this carnival sense?

3. Consider the ritual quality of the film. What sequences reflect this quality most? Does it change or broaden the meaning of the sequence (here, start by looking at the sequence of the lovemaking scene in the sorghum field)?

4. The sorghum wine in the film is given some magic properties. Here, think of the influence of the Garcia Marquez kind of magic realism in contemporary literature. What narrative role does the wine play? Culturally, how is it comparable with the Dionysian spirit of the West? What is liquor's role in creating ecstasy in Chinese culture?

5. There have been different approaches to the gender issue in this film. Consider the following two examples:

a. Esther Yau, in "Cultural and Economic Dislocations: Filmic Phantasies of Chinese Women in the 1980s," argues that the film showcases a narcissistic pleasure for men at the expense of women. It rejects the conventional meek, conformist male, especially those represented under the influence of socialist feminism. It empowers the male as a subversion to the socialist feminist castration of all forms of male power except those conforming to the Party's power. Can you use examples from this film and other Chinese

films you have seen to illustrate this argument? Is the female representation in this film damaged by this subversion?
   b. Wang, in his essay in this chapter, argues that the film's celebration of
   masculinity is contained in a framework of "maternal discourse." "It is
   through a feminine vision of totality that the masculine past is reconstructed and obtains coherence and meaning." If the "maternal discourse"
   designates a sense of totality, does it involve a rewriting of the conventional totality (keeping in mind the film's subversive nature)?

   6. Is the Japanese presence important to the general artistic style and the message
of the film?

14. *Black Cannon Incident* (Huang Jianxin, 1985)

   1. What kind of color scheme is used in this film? Can you make a list of images that
fall into the following four categories of colors? (One example is given for each color to
get you started.)

Red: company cars . . .
White: conferences . . .
Black: the missing chess piece . . .
Yellow: construction machinery . . .

   2. With the help of your list of colors, can you give some examples of how these colors interplay in certain scenes to provide some underlying meanings? For example, consider the scene when the major accident occurs for the project: the heavy yellow trucks
are on their way for a rescue while the red company cars carrying Party bosses zigzag
around them all the way. In another example, the scene of investigation: while the others are wearing white shirts, only Zhao is wearing black.
   3. Look at the sequence in which Zhao watches the performance ("Ali Baba . . .").
What is the dominant color (stage, costume, lighting, etc.) here? How does this color
relate to other sequences? How does this sequence contribute to the meaning of the film?
In what way is the use of color here comparable to the sequence of the quarrel between
Zhao and Hans at the restaurant?
   4. Look at the sequence showing Zhao watching a soccer game when he is not
allowed to work with Hans. What is the shooting style here? Why at one point does the
camera not follow the action on the playground but rather allows it to move out of the
frame? Why in the background does a worker paint a wall red?
   5. The concept of circularity and enclosure are important, and they function on various levels of the plot, *mise-en-scène,* and characterization. Consider the following examples and then discuss how these two concepts provide the film with a deeper meaning.

What is this deeper meaning?

> *Circularity:* of the chess piece, of the clock, of the bricks falling on one
> another, etc.
> *Enclosure:* the empty tin box that has been used by Zhao as the substitute
> for the missing chess piece and which puzzles the German engineer about
> the fuzz it may cause (is this box a metaphor?), etc.

6. What is the overall significance of the machine imagery? Does it imply that the Party functions as a machine, or does it imply an industrial and scientific technology that restrains the Party's political interference, or both?

7. How do you like the characterization of Zhao? Do you agree with Pickowicz (1994) that he is an Ah Q, that is, a Chinese Everyman? Is this character an object or a vehicle—or both—of the cultural critique contained in this film?

8. Zhao's characterization seems to be foiled by images of children. How is it related to these images? What is the implication of this relationship? Does it contrast sophistication and simplicity? If so, what kind of sophistication and simplicity are they? If not, what else might they represent?

9. How is the political world of the film comparable with that in George Orwell's writing? What is the logic of Huang's world on-screen? What produces the effect of absurdity here?

15. *Good Morning, Beijing* (Zhang Nuanxin, 1990)

1. Did you notice a bird cage in the opening sequence? Is it a metaphor here? How is it related to cinematography (e.g., range of shots) and other images to express a certain theme of the film? In addition, what is the impact of sound effects in this opening sequence (e.g., the constant coughing of Ai Hong's grandpa)?

2. Can you think of some related sequences where tones of colors, keys of lighting, and features of *mise-en-scène* contrast each other? An example is Ai Hong at a bar with Keke versus Ai Hong back home. Analyze this contrast and give examples of similar contrasts from the film.

3. Make closer analysis of the following sequence:

> Returning home for dinner, Zou, the bus driver, is urged by his mother to date
> a girl the mother likes and is asked to work well by the father—whose job Zou
> has succeeded to. He is also ordered by his mother to empty his father's foot-
> washer. Then he returns to his curtained-up space to play *erhu* (a Chinese string
> instrument) but is stopped by his mother for the sake of the neighbors.

What kind of generation relationship and culture does the sequence reflect, and what responses does it expect from the Chinese audience? How does this sequence relate to other sequences to express certain themes of the film? Consider here if the foot-washer also appears in other sequences. Take a closer look at the *mise-en-scène* of Zou's curtained-up space. What kind of paintings does he have on the wall? Note: The poster is a picture of Cui Jian, China's most famous rock and roll star, whose songs Keke sings to Ai Hong at the bar.

4. How is the foreign presence felt in this film? How has it influenced these characters' lives? Does the title of the film, *Good Morning, Beijing,* reflect the influence of this presence? What is dawn to Beijing? For what does it serve as a backdrop?

5. Consider Keke, the fake foreign student—is he a traditional negative character, for example, one found in a melodrama? How is he related to the foreign influences? If you are familiar with Lu Xun's Fake Foreign Devil from "The True Story of Ah Q," do you think the two characters are comparable in any way?

6. What is the difference between Zou and Keke? Does the film make you like one and hate the other? How?

7. What kinds of discourse constitute the language of the young urbanites? As the older political discourse of the Party fades out, what is stepping in to inform those characters?

8. Do you agree that the bus in this film not only relates the characters in narration but also helps express the idea of compromise and coexistence in an era of cultural ambiguity? Give examples.

Appendix 2 Pronouncing Romanized Chinese

Among different systems used in this country to romanize Chinese, *pinyin* and *Wade-Giles* are most widely used. Pinyin, meaning to spell phonetically, is a newer system, is the only one used in the People's Republic of China today, and is used more and more often in American publications about China. Wade-Giles, an older system, is now among a few systems used in Taiwan and was standard in American sinological publications before the 1970s. For the Chinese collections in American libraries, while Wade-Giles was initially used, pinyin has recently been added. For the sake of clarity and consistency, the pinyin system is used throughout this book, except for some cases of reference in which a different system, usually the Wade-Giles, was used originally in author names and titles.

The following is a list of the Chinese phonetic alphabet of the two romanized systems (Wade-Giles in parentheses): it provides English approximation of pronunciation and examples (Wade-Giles still in parentheses) illustrating the differences between the two systems.

b (p)	consonant as in *be* ex., Bai Yang (Pai Yang)
p (p')	as in *par*, strongly aspirated ex., putong hua (p'u-t'ung hua)
m (m)	as in *me* ex., Mei Lanfang (Mei Lan-fang)
f (f)	as in *foot* ex., Fuxi (Fu-hsi)
d (t)	consonant as in *do* ex., Dao (Tao)
t (t')	as in *top*, strongly aspirated ex., Taiwan (T'ai-wan)
n (n)	as in *no* ex., Nie Er (Nieh Erh)
l (l)	as in *land* ex., Lu Xun (Lu Hsün)
g (k)	consonant as in *go* ex., Guomindang (Kuo-min tang)
k (k')	as in *kind*, strongly aspirated ex., Kunlun (K'un-lun)

h (h)	as in *her,* strongly aspirated ex., hong (hung)
j (ch)	consonant as in *jeep* ex., Juxian (Chü-hsien)
q (ch')	as in *cheek* ex., Qu Yuan (Ch'ü Yüen)
x (hs)	as in *she* ex., Xie Jin (Hsieh Chin)
zh (ch)	consonant as in *jump* ex., Zhang Yimou (Chang Yi-mou)
ch (ch')	as in *church,* strongly aspirated ex., Chen Kaige (Ch'ên K'ai-kê)
sh (sh)	as in *shore,* strongly aspirated ex., Shanghai (Shang-hai)
r (j)	as in *right* ex., Ruan Lingyu (Juan Ling-yü)
z (ts)	consonant as in *zero* ex., zao (tsao)
c (ts')	as in *its* ex., Cao Yu (Ts'ao Yü)
s (s, ss, sz)	as in *sister* ex., *San'ge modeng nüxing (San-kê mo-têng nü-hsing)*
ng (ng)	as the ending sound of *being* ex., Zhang Nuanxin (Chang Nuan-hsin)
y (y)	semi-vowel in syllable beginning with *i* or *u* when not preceded by consonants, as in *yet* ex., Yuan Muzhi (Yüen Mu-chih)
w (w)	semi-vowel in syllable beginning with *u* when not preceded by consonants, as in *want* ex., Wu Tianming (Wu T'ien-ming)
a (a)	vowel as in *far* ex., A Cheng (A Ch'êng)
o (o)	vowel as in *law* ex., Bo Yang (Po Yang)
e (ê)	vowel as in *her* ex., Ge You (Kê Yu)
i (i)	vowel as in *eat* ex., Li An (Li An)
u (u)	vowel as in *too* ex., Gu Hua (Ku Hua)
ü (ü)	as in the French *tu* ex., Nüwa (Nü-wa)

Rules of Phonetic Spelling

1. When a syllable beginning with *a, o,* or *e* follows another syllable in a phrase, an apostrophe is added to mark the division.
   ex., Yan'an, Xi'an

2. At the beginning of a syllable, *i* is written as *y*. When used by itself in a syllable, *i* is written as *yi*.
   ex., iao—yao, i—yi

3. At the beginning of a syllable, *u* is written as *w*. When used by itself in a syllable, *u* is written as *wu*.
   ex., uo—wo, u—wu

4. When appearing after *j, q,* or *x, ü* is written as *u*, with the umlaut omitted.
   ex., Ju Dou

Appendix 3
Video Purchase and Film Rental Information

Purchase. What follows is a list of distributors who sell the videotapes of the titles used in this book (and many other related titles). For a list of more distributors, see Diane Carson, "Chinese Film: Sources and Resources," *Cinema Journal* 34.4 (Summer 1995): 83–88. It is important to check the latest directories as addresses and phone numbers of distributors may change.

Cheng and Tsui Co.
25 West St.
Boston, MA 02111
tel. 617-426-6074, fax 617-426-3669

China Books and Periodicals
2929 Twenty-fourth St.
San Francisco, CA 94110
tel. 415-282-2994, fax 415-282-0994

Nan Hai Co.
510 Broadway
Suite 3000
Milbrae, CA 94030
tel. 415-259-2100, fax 212-222-8952

Rental. Some of the titles used in this anthology may be rented in 35mm or 16mm formats from

China Film Import and Export (L.A.), Inc.
2500 Wilshire Blvd., Suite 1028
Los Angeles, CA 90057
tel. 213-3380-7520, fax 213-487-2089

The following is a list of films they have. Contact them for an updated list.

Black Cannon Incident (16mm, 35mm)
Hibiscus Town (16mm, 35mm)
Horse Thief (35mm)
Old Well (16mm, 35mm)
Sacrificed Youth (16mm, 35mm)
Woman, Demon, Human (16mm, 35mm)
Yellow Earth (16mm, 35mm)

Bibliography

Titles of suggested further readings are marked with an asterisk.

When an institution is the editor of a book, its name is often abbreviated in textual citations. In the bibliography, the name is kept in full but is preceded by its abbreviation in parentheses. For example, ZDZ is the abbreviation for Zhongguo dianying ziliaoguan. In text, one will find this abbreviation, year of publication, and page number, e.g., (ZDZ 1981, 36), and in the bibliography, one will find a full reference, e.g.,

(ZDZ) Zhongguo dianying ziliaoguan and Zhongguo yishu yanjuyuan dianying yanjusuo, eds. 1981. *Zhongguo yishu yingpian bianmu: 1949–1979* (A catalogue of Chinese artistic films). 2 vols. Beijing: Wenhua yishu chubanshe.

Anderson, Benedict. 1991. *Imagined Communities: Reflections on the Origin and Spread of Nationalism.* 2nd ed. London: Verso Press.

Anderson, Nigel. 1994. "Film-Makers Baptized in Fire: An Interview with Chen Kaige." *Financial Times* (London), January 8.

Andrew, Dudley. 1976. *The Major Film Theories: An Introduction.* New York: Oxford University Press.

———. 1984. *Concepts in Film Theory.* New York: Oxford University Press.

Ansen, David. 1993. "The Real Cultural Revolution." *Newsweek,* November 1, 74.

Armstrong, Nancy, and Leonard Tennenhouse. 1992. *The Imaginary Puritan: Literature, Intellectual Labor, and the Origins of Personal Life.* Berkeley and Los Angeles: University of California Press.

Bai Xifeng. 1988. *Bai Xifeng juzuo xuan* (Selected plays of Bai Xifeng). Beijing: Zhongguo xiju chubanshe.

Bakhtin, Mikhail. 1981. *The Dialogic Imagination: Four Essays.* Edited by Michael Holquist and translated by Caryl Emerson and Michael Holquist. Austin: University of Texas Press.

———. 1984. *Problems of Dostoevsky's Poetics.* Translated by Caryl Emerson. Minneapolis: University of Minnesota Press.

Barlow, Tani E., ed. 1993. *Gender Politics in Modern China: Writing and Feminism.* Durham: Duke University Press.

Barmé, G., and John Minford. 1986. *Seeds of Fire: Chinese Voices of Conscience.* Hong Kong: Far Eastern Economic Review.

Barthes, Roland. 1972. *Mythology.* New York: Noonday Press.

———. 1978. *A Lover's Discourse: Fragments.* New York: Hill and Wang.

Baudrillard, Jean. 1981. *For a Critique of the Political Economy of the Sign.* Translated and with an introduction by Charles Levin. St. Louis, Mo.: Telos Press.

Baudry, Jean Louis. 1985. "The Ideological Effects of the Basic Cinematographic Apparatus." In *Movies and Methods,* vol. 2, edited by Bill Nichols, 531–42. Berkeley: University of California Press.

Bazin, Andre. 1967. *What Is Cinema?* Berkeley: University of California Press.

Benjamin, Walter. 1969. *Illuminations.* Translated by Harry Zohn. New York: Schocken Books.

Berger, John. 1977. *Ways of Seeing.* New York: Penguin.

Berry, Chris, ed. 1985. *Perspectives on Chinese Cinema.* East Asia Papers, no. 39. Ithaca, N.Y.: China-Japan Program, Cornell University.

* ———. 1986. "Han and Non-Han: China's Avant-Garde and the National Minorities Genre." *China Screen* 1: 34.

———. 1988a. "China's New 'Women's Cinema.'" *Camera Obscura* 18: 8–19.

* ———. 1988b. "Interview with Zhang Nuanxin." *Camera Obscura* 18: 20–25.

———. 1988c. "Interview with Hu Mei." *Camera Obscura* 18: 32–41.

———. 1988d. "Chinese Urban Cinema: Hyper-realism Versus Absurdism." *East-West Film Journal* 3.1: 76–88.

———. 1989. "Poisonous Weeds or National Treasures: Chinese Left Cinema in the 1930s." *Jump Cut* 34: 87–94.

———. 1990. "A Turn for the Better?—Genre and Gender in *Girl from Hunan* and Other Recent Mainland Chinese Films." Unpublished paper, presented at the Asian Cinema Studies Society Conference, Latrobe University, Melbourne, Australia, July 11.

* ———, ed. 1991. *Perspectives on Chinese Cinema.* London: BFI Publishing.

———. 1992. "'Race': Chinese Film and the Politics of Nationalism." *Cinema Journal* 31.2: 45–58.

———. 1993. "Farewell to My Concubine: At What Price Success?" *Cinemaya* 20: 20–22.

* ———. 1994. "Neither One Thing nor Another: Toward a Study of the Viewing Subject and Chinese Cinema in the 1980s." In *New Chinese Cinemas: Forms, Identities, Politics,* edited by Nick Browne et al., 88–115. Cambridge: Cambridge University Press.

———. 1998. "*East Palace, West Palace:* Staging Gay Life in China." *Jump Cut* 42: 84–89.

* Berry, Chris, and Mary Ann Farquhar. 1994. "Post-Socialist Strategies: An Analysis of *Yellow Earth* and *Black Cannon Incident.*" In *Cinematic Landscapes: Observations on the Visual Arts and Cinema of China and Japan,* edited by Linda C. Ehrlich and David Desser, 81–116. Austin: University of Texas Press.

Bhabha, Homi K., ed. 1990. *Nation and Narration.* New York: Routledge.

Bordwell, David. 1985a. *Narration in the Fiction Film.* Madison: University of Wisconsin Press.

————. 1985b. "The Classical Hollywood Style." In *The Classical Hollywood Cinema: Film Style and Mode of Production to 1960*, by David Bordwell, Janet Staiger, and Kristin Thompson. New York: Columbia University Press.

Bourdieu, Pierre. 1977. *Outline of a Theory of Practice*. Cambridge: Cambridge University Press.

Branigan, Edward. 1984. *Point of View in the Cinema: A Theory of Narration and Subjectivity in Classical Film*. New York, Berlin: Moutin Publishers.

Braudy, Leo. 1976. *The World in a Frame: What We See in Films*. New York: Anchor Press.

Brecht, Bertolt. 1964. *Brecht on Theatre: The Development of an Aesthetic*. Edited and translated by John Willet. New York: Hill and Wang.

Brooker, Peter. 1988. *Bertolt Brecht: Dialectics, Poetry, Politics*. London: Croom Helm.

Brooks, Peter. 1976. *The Melodramatic Imagination*. New Haven, Conn.: Yale University Press.

Brown, Carolyn T. 1984. "The Paradigm of the Iron House: Shouting and Silence in Lu Hsün's Short Stories." *Chinese Literature: Essays, Articles, Reviews* 6.1–2: 101–19.

Browne, Nick. 1994. "Society and Subjectivity: On the Political Economy of Chinese Melodrama." In *New Chinese Cinemas: Forms, Identities, Politics*, edited by Nick Browne et al., 40–56. Cambridge: Cambridge University Press.

* Browne, Nick, et al., eds. 1994. *New Chinese Cinemas: Forms, Identities, Politics*. Cambridge: Cambridge University Press.

Brugger, Bill, ed. 1985. *Chinese Marxism in Flux: 1978–84*. London: Croom Helm.

* Callahan, W. A. 1993. "Gender, Ideology, Nation: *Ju Dou* in the Cultural Politics of China." *East-West Film Journal* 7.1: 52–80.

Canby, Vincent. 1993. "Action, History, and Love Above All." *New York Times*, October 8: B1, B8.

————. 1994. "Top Prize at Cannes is Shared." *New York Times*, May 25: C13.

Cao Maotang and Wu Lun. 1987. *Shanghai yingtan huajiu* (The old days of the Shanghai film world). Shanghai: Shanghai wenyi chubanshe.

Carus, Paul. 1898. *Lao-Tze's Tao Teh King, Chinese-English*. Chicago: Open Court Publishing Company.

Chai Xiaofeng. 1994. "Huang Jianxin fangtanlu" (An interview with Huang Juanxin). *Dangdai dianying* 2: 37–45.

Chai Xiaofeng et al., eds. 1996. *Huang Jianxin: Nianqing de yanjing* (Huang Jianxin: Youthful eyes). Changsha: Hunan wenyi chubanshe.

Chan, Ching-kiu Stephen. 1993. "The Language of Despair: Ideological Representations of the 'New Woman' by May Fourth Writers." In *Gender Politics in Modern China: Writing and Feminism*, edited by Tani E. Barlow, 13–33. Durham: Duke University Press.

Chang, Arnold. 1980. *Painting in the People's Republic of China: The Politics of Style*. Boulder: Westview Press.

Chatterjee, Partha. 1986. *Nationalist Thought and the Colonial World—A Derivative Discourse?* United Nations University, Tokyo: Zed Books.

Chen Bo, ed. 1993. *Sanshi niandai Zhongguo dianying pinglun wenxuan* (Selected Chinese film criticism of the 1930s). Beijing: Zhongguo dianying chubanshe.

Chen Huangmei et al. 1988. *Xin shiqi dianying shinian* (A decade of films in the new era). Sichuan: Chongqing chubanshe.

Chen Kaige. 1984. "Xiwangpian" (Film of hope). In *Huang tudi* (Yellow earth), edited by Zhongguo dianying fanying gongsi. Beijing: Zhongguo dianying chubanshe.

———. 1988. "Interview." *Playboy,* Chinese edition, May.

Chen Kaiyan, ed. 1988. *Heipao shijian: Cong xiaoshuo dao dianying.* (*Black Cannon Incident:* From novella to film). Beijing: Zhongguo dianying chubanshe.

Chen Wu. 1935. "Guanyu *Xin nüxing* de yingpian, piping ji qita" (Regarding the film *The New Woman,* criticism and other matters). *Zhonghua ribao,* March 2.

Chen Xiaoming. 1990. "Moral Self-Salvation: The Break of Historical Axis." *Dianying yishu* 215: 102–7.

Ch'en Yüan. 1966. *Western and Central Asians in China under the Mongols: Their Transformation into Chinese.* Monumenta Serica Monograph XV. Los Angeles: Monumenta Serica at the University of California.

Cheng Jihua et al. 1963. *Zhongguo dianying fazhan shi* (The development of Chinese cinema). 2 vols. Beijing: Zhongguo dianying chubanshe.

Chow, Rey. 1986–87. "Rereading Mandarin Ducks and Butterflies: A Response to the 'Post-Modern' Condition." *Cultural Critique* 5: 69–93.

* ———. 1990. "Silent Is the Ancient Plain: Music, Filmmaking, and the Conception of Reform in China's New Cinema." *Discourse* 12.2: 82–109.

———. 1991. *Woman and Chinese Modernity: The Politics of Reading Between West and East.* Minneapolis: University of Minnesota Press.

* ———. 1995. *Primitive Passions: Visuality, Sexuality, Ethnography, and Contemporary Chinese Cinema.* New York: Columbia University Press.

Chow, Tse-tsung. 1960. *The May 4th Movement.* Cambridge and London: Harvard University Press.

Ch'ü, T'ung-tsu. 1961. *Law and Society in Traditional China.* Paris: Mouton.

Chu, Tung-tsu. 1972. *Han Social Structure.* Vol. 1 of *Han Dynasty China* series, edited by Jack L. Dull. Seattle and London: University of Washington Press.

Clark, John. 1991. "Recent Chinese Painting: Postmodernism and Expressionist Tendencies in Recent Chinese Oil Painting." *Asian Studies Review* (Australia) 15.2: 128–29.

* Clark, Paul. 1987a. "Ethnic Minorities in Chinese Films: Cinema and the Exotic." *East-West Film Journal* 1.2: 15–31.

* ———. 1987b. *Chinese Cinema: Culture and Politics since 1949.* Cambridge: Cambridge University Press.

———. 1989. "Reinventing China: The Fifth-Generation Filmmakers." *Modern Chinese Literature* 5.1: 121–36.

————. 1991. "Two Hundred Flowers on China's Screens." In *Perspectives on Chinese Cinema,* edited by Chris Berry, 40–61. London: BFI Publishing.

Cochran, Sherman, et al., eds. and trans. 1983. *One Day in China: May 21, 1936.* New Haven, Conn.: Yale University Press.

Cohn, Don J. 1992. *A Guide to Beijing.* Lincolnwood, Ill.: Passport Books.

Croll, Elisabeth. 1978. *Feminism and Socialism in China.* New York: Schocken.

* Cui, Shuqin. 1997. "Gendered Perspective: The Construction and Representation of Subjectivity and Sexuality in *Ju Dou.*" In *Transnational Chinese Cinemas: Identity, Nationhood, Gender,* edited by Sheldon H. Lu, 303–30. Honolulu: University of Hawaii Press.

Cummings, Joe, et al. 1991. *A Travel Survival Kit: China.* 3rd ed. Berkeley: Lonely Planet.

* Da Hou'er. 1989. "An Interview with Xie Jin." *Jump Cut* 34: 107–9.

Dai Jinhua. 1989. "Xieta: Chongdu disidai" (On the leaning tower: Rereading the Fourth Generation). *Dianying yishu* 4: 3–8.

————. 2001. "*Human, Woman, Demon:* A Woman's Predicament." In *Cinema and Desire: Feminist Marxism and Cultural Politics in the Work of Dai Jinhua,* edited by Jing Wang and Tani Barlow. London: Verso.

de Lauretis, Teresa. 1984. *Alice Doesn't: Feminism, Semiotics, Cinema.* Bloomington: Indiana University Press.

————. 1988. "Displacing Hegemonic Discourses: Reflections on Feminist Theory in the 1980s." *Inscriptions* 3.4: 127–44.

Deng Xiaoping. 1984. *Selected Works of Deng Xiaoping (1975–1982).* Beijing: Foreign Language Press.

Diamond, Norma. 1988. "The Miao and Poison: Interactions on China's Southwest Frontier." *Ethnology* 27 (1): 1–25.

Dirlik, Arif. 1978. *Revolution and History: Origins of Marxist Historiography in China, 1919–1937.* Berkeley: University of California Press.

————. 1989. "Post-socialism? Reflections on 'Socialism with Chinese Characteristics.'" In *Marxism and the Chinese Experience,* edited by Arif Dirlik and Maurice Meisner, 362–84. New York: Sharpe.

* Dissanayake, Wimal, ed. 1993. *Melodrama and Asian Cinema.* Cambridge: Cambridge University Press.

Doane, Mary Ann. 1987. *The Desire to Desire.* Bloomington: Indiana University Press.

Duke, Michael S. 1985. *Blooming and Contending: Chinese Literature in the Post-Mao Era.* Bloomington: Indiana University Press.

Eagleton, Terry. 1983. *Literary Theory: An Introduction.* Minneapolis: University of Minnesota Press.

Eberhard, Wolfram. 1976. *Guilt and Sin in Traditional China.* Berkeley: University of California Press.

————. 1982. *China's Minorities: Yesterday and Today.* Belmont, Calif.: Wadsworth.

* Ehrlich, Linda C., and David Desser, eds. 1994. *Cinematic Landscapes: Observations on the Visual Arts and Cinema of China and Japan.* Austin: University of Texas Press.

Eisenstein, Sergei. 1979. "The Cinematographic Principle and the Ideogram." In *Film Theory and Criticism,* 2nd ed., edited by G. Mast and M. Cohen. New York: Oxford University Press.

Ellis, John. 1982. "Electric Shadows in Italy." *Screen* 23.2: 79–83.

Elsaesser, Thomas. 1985. "Tales of Sound and Fury: Observations on the Family Melodrama." In *Movies and Methods,* vol. 2, edited by Bill Nichols, 165–89. Berkeley: University of California Press.

Fan Ruijuan. 1983. "An Actress' Life in Old China." In *When They Were Young,* edited by Women of China and New World Press, 156–64. Beijing: New World Press.

Farquhar, Mary Ann. 1992. "The 'Hidden' Gender in Yellow Earth." *Screen* 33.2: 154–64.

Foucault, Michel. 1970. *The Order of Things: An Archaeology of the Human Sciences.* New York: Random House.

———. 1977. *Language, Counter-memory, Practice.* Ithaca, N.Y.: Cornell University Press.

———. 1980. *Power/Knowledge.* New York: Pantheon Books.

Gabriel, Teshome H. 1989. "Towards a Critical Theory of Third World Films." In *Questions of Third Cinema,* edited by Jim Pines and Paul Willemen. London: BFI Publishing.

Gallop, Jane. 1985. *Reading Lacan.* Ithaca, N.Y.: Cornell University Press.

Gao Jun. 1991. "A Changed Director: Transcription of a Dialogue with Zhang Junzhao." In *Perspectives on Chinese Cinema,* edited by Chris Berry, 130–33. London: BFI Publishing.

Giannetti, Louis. 1990. *Understanding Movies.* Englewood Cliffs, N.J.: Prentice-Hall.

Gilbert, Sandra M., and Susan Gubar, eds. 1979. *The Madwoman in the Attic: The Woman Writer and the Nineteenth-Century Literary Imagination.* New Haven, Conn.: Yale University Press.

Gilmartin, Christian Kelley. 1995. *Engendering the Chinese Revolution: Radical Women, Communist Politics, and Mass Movements in the 1920s.* Berkeley: University of California Press.

Gladney, Dru C. 1991. *Muslim Chinese: Ethnic Nationalism in the People's Republic.* Cambridge: Harvard University Press.

* ———. 1994. "Representing Nationality in China: Refiguring Majority/Minority Identity." *Journal of Asian Studies* 53.1: 92–123.

———. 1995. "Tian Zhuangzhuang, the Fifth Generation, and Minorities Film in China." *Public Culture* 8.1 (Fall): 161–75.

———. 1996. "Bodily Positions and Social Dispositions: Sexuality, Nationality, and Tiananmen." In *Narratives of Agency: Self-making in Chinese, Indian, and Japanese*

Cultures, edited by Wimal Dissanayake. Minneapolis: University of Minnesota Press.

Gledhill, Christine. 1987. "The Melodramatic Field: An Introduction." In *Home Is Where the Heart Is: Studies in Melodrama and the Woman's Film,* edited by Christine Gledhill, 5–38. London: BFI Publishing.

Han Xiaolei. 1995. "Dui diwudai de wenhua tuwei: Hou wudai de geren dianying xianxiang" (Getting beyond the Fifth Generation culture: Post-Fifth-Generation individual filmmaking). *Dianying yishu* 241: 58–63.

* Harris, Kristine. 1997. "*The New Woman* Incident: Cinema, Scandal, and Spectacle in 1935 Shanghai." In *Transnational Chinese Cinemas: Identity, Nationhood, Gender,* edited by Sheldon H. Lu, 277–302. Honolulu: University of Hawaii Press.

Harvey, David. 1989. *The Condition of Postmodernity: An Enquiry into the Origins of Cultural Change.* Cambridge, Mass.: Blackwell.

Hawks, David, ed. and trans. 1962. *Ch'u Tz'u: The Song of the South—An Ancient Chinese Anthology.* Boston: Beacon Press.

Herberer, Thomas. 1989. *China and Its National Minorities: Autonomy or Assimilation?* Translated by Michel Vale. New York and London: M. E. Sharpe.

Hinsch, Bret. 1992. *Passions of the Cut Sleeve: The Male Homosexual Tradition in China.* Berkeley: University of California Press.

Hinton, William. 1990. *The Great Reversal.* New York: Monthly Review Press.

Hitchcock, Peter. 1992. "The Aesthetics of Alienation, or China's 'Fifth Generation.'" *Cultural Studies* 6.1: 116–41.

Hoare, Stephanie. 1991. "'The New Year's Sacrifice': Using Literary Adaptation in the Chinese Literature Classroom." *Asian Studies Review* 14.3: 88–92.

Hobsbawm, Eric. 1992. *Nations and Nationalism Since 1780.* Cambridge: Cambridge University Press.

Holtz, Geoffrey T. 1995. *Welcome to the Jungle: The Why Behind "Generation X."* New York: St. Martin's Press.

Hsia, C. T. 1961. *A History of Modern Chinese Fiction.* New Haven, Conn.: Yale University Press.

———. 1984. "Hsu Chen-ya's *Yü-li hun:* An Essay in Literary History and Criticism." In *Chinese Middlebrow Fiction from the Ch'ing and Early Republican Eras,* edited by Liu Ts'un-yan, 199–240. Hong Kong: Chinese University Press.

Hsu, Francis L. K. 1983. "Eros, Affect and *Pao.*" In *Rugged Individualism Reconsidered: Essays in Psychological Anthropology,* 263–300. Knoxville: University of Tennessee Press.

Hsu, Tao-ching. 1985. *The Chinese Conception of the Theatre.* Seattle: University of Washington Press.

Huang Jianxin. 1988. "*Heipao shijian* chuangzuo sikao." In *Heipao shijian: Cong xiaoshuo dao dianying,* edited by Chen Kaiyan, 211–24. Beijing: Zhongguo dianying chubanshe.

———. 1996. "Dianying de meili" (Attraction of films). In *Huang Jianxin: Nianqing de yanjing,* edited by Chai Xiaofeng et al., 397–423. Changsha: Hunan wenyi chubanshe.

Huang Shixian. 1989. "Yishixingtai zhenghou: Wang Shuo shi 'fanpan wenhua' de shi-maoxing yu huihuaixing" (Ideological symptom: On Wang Shuo's "anti-culture" style). *Dianying yishu* 6: 40–45.

Huang Shuqin. 1995. "Nü daoyan zibai: Nüxing, zai dianyingye de nanren shijie li" (A woman director's confession: Female in the male world of film industry). *Tangdai dianying* 5: 69–71.

Huang Zuolin. 1981. "Mei Lanfang, Stanislavsky, Brecht—A Study in Contrasts." In *Peking Opera and Mei Lanfang: A Guide to China's Traditional Theatre and the Art of Its Great Master,* 14–29. Beijing: New World Press.

* Huot, Marie-Claire. 1993. "Liu Heng's *Fuxi Fuxi:* What about Nüwa?" In *Gender and Sexuality in Twentieth-Century Chinese Literature and Society,* edited by Tonglin Lu, 85–105. Albany: State University of New York Press.

Jameson, Fredric. 1981. *The Political Unconscious: Narrative as a Socially Symbolic Act.* Ithaca, N.Y.: Cornell University Press.

———. 1986. "Third-World Literature in the Era of Multinational Capitalism." *Social Text* 15: 65–88.

———. 1991. *Postmodernism, Or, The Cultural Logic of Late Capitalism.* Durham: Duke University Press.

———. 1994. "Remapping Taipei." In *New Chinese Cinemas: Forms, Identities, Politics,* edited by Nick Browne et al., 117–50. Cambridge: Cambridge University Press.

Jia Ping'ao. 1985. *Tiangou* (Heaven dog). *Shiyue* 2: 6–29.

Jiao Xiongping, ed. 1990. *Lao jing.* Dianying/Zhongguo mingzuo xuan, no. 1. Taibei: Wanxiang tushu gufen youxian gongsi.

Kaplan, E. Ann. 1989. "Problematizing Cross-Cultural Analysis: The Case of Women in the Recent Chinese Cinema." *Wide Angle* 11.2: 40–50.

* ———. 1991. "Problematizing Cross-Cultural Analysis: The Case of Women in the Recent Chinese Cinema." In *Perspectives on Chinese Cinema,* edited by Chris Berry, 141–54. London: BFI Publishing.

———. 1993. "Melodrama/Subjectivity/Ideology: Western Melodrama Theories and Their Relevance to Recent Chinese Cinema." In *Melodrama and Asian Cinema,* edited by Wimal Dissanayake. 9–28. Cambridge: Cambridge University Press.

* ———. 1997. "Reading Formations and Chen Kaige's *Farewell My Concubine.*" In *Transnational Chinese Cinemas: Identity, Nationhood, Gender,* edited by Sheldon H. Lu, 265–76. Honolulu: University of Hawaii Press.

Kelman, Mark. 1987. *A Guide to Critical Legal Studies.* Cambridge: Harvard University Press.

Kleinhans, Chuck. 1978. "Notes on Melodrama and the Family under Capitalism." *Film Reader* 3: 40–47.

Kristeva, Julia. 1977. *About Chinese Women*. Translated by Marion Boyars Publishers. New York: Urizen Books.

Kuoshu, Harry. 1997. "Beyond the Yellow Earth: The Postsocialist City as a Cinematic Space of Anxiety." *American Journal of Chinese Studies* 4.1: 50–72.

———. 1999a. "*Beijing Bastard*, Sixth Generation Directors, and 'Generation X' in China." *Asian Cinema* 10.2: 18–28.

* ———. 1999b. *Lightness of Being in China: Adaptation and Discursive Figuration in Cinema and Theater*. New York: Peter Lang.

Laing, David. 1978. *The Marxist Theory of Art*. Sussex: Harvester Press.

Laing, Ellen Johnston. 1988. *The Winking Owl: Art in the People's Republic of China*. Berkeley: University of California Press.

Lal, Amrit. 1970. "Sinification of Ethnic Minorities in China." *Current Scene* 8.4: 1–25.

Larson, Wendy. 1995. "Zhang Yimou: Inter/National Aesthetics and Erotics." In *Cultural Encounters: China, Japan, and the West*, edited by Soren Clausen, Roy Starrs, and Anne Wedell-Wedellsborg, 215–26. Aarhus, Denmark: Aarhus University Press.

———. 1997. "The Concubine and the Figure of History: Chen Kaige's *Farewell My Concubine*." In *Transnational Chinese Cinemas: Identity, Nationhood, Gender*, edited by Sheldon H. Lu, 331–46. Honolulu: University of Hawaii Press.

Lau, Jenny Kwok Wah. 1989. "Towards a Cultural Understanding of Cinema." *Wide Angle* 11: 42–49.

———. 1991–92. "*Ju Dou*—A Hermeneutical Reading of Cross-Cultural Cinema." *Film Quarterly* 45.2: 2–10.

* ———. 1994. "*Ju Dou*: An Experiment in Color and Portraiture in Chinese Cinema." In *Cinematic Landscapes: Observations on the Visual Arts and Cinema of China and Japan*, edited by Linda C. Ehrlich and David Desser, 127–45. Austin: University of Texas Press.

* ———. 1995. "*Farewell My Concubine*: History, Melodrama, and Ideology in Contemporary Pan-Chinese Cinema." *Film Quarterly* 49.1: 16–27.

Lee, Leo Ou-fan. 1990. "In Search of Modernity: Some Reflections on a New Mode of Consciousness in Twentieth-Century Chinese History and Literature." In *Ideas Across Cultures: Essays on Chinese Thought in Honor of Benjamin I. Schwartz*, edited by Paul A. Cohen and Merle Goldman. Cambridge: Harvard University Press.

* ———. 1991. "The Tradition of Modern Chinese Cinema: Some Preliminary Exploration and Hypotheses." In *Perspectives on Chinese Cinema*, edited by Chris Berry, 6–20. London: BFI Publishing.

Lent, John A. 1990. *The Asian Film Industry*. London: Christopher Helm.

* Leyda, Jay. 1972. *Dianying: An Account of Films and the Film Audience in China*. Cambridge: MIT Press.

Leys, Simon. 1983. *The Burning Forest*. New York: Holt Rinehart and Winston.

Li, Cheuk-to, ed. 1986. *Cantonese Melodrama: 1950–1969.* 10th Hong Kong International Film Festival. Hong Kong: The Urban Council.

* Li, H. C. 1989. "Color, Character, and Culture: On *Yellow Earth, Black Cannon Incident,* and *Red Sorghum.*" *Modern Chinese Literature* 5.1: 91–119.

Li Qingquan. 1986. "Zanshang yu buzanshang doushuo: Guanya *Hong gaoliang* de hua" (Approval and disapproval: About *Red Sorghum*). *Wenyi bao* 499 (August 30): 2.

Li, Wai-yee. 1993. *Enchantment and Disenchantment: Love and Illusion in Chinese Literature.* Princeton: Princeton University Press.

Li Xing. 1988. "*Hong gaoliang:* Xi Xing Ji" (*Red Sorghum:* A journey to the west). *Renmin ribao* (overseas edition), March 14.

Li Yiming. 1996. "Shiji zhimo: Shehui de daode weiji yu diwudai dianying de shouzhong zhengqin" (*Fin de siècle:* Ethic crisis and the end of the Fifth Generation filmmaking). *Dianying yishu* 1 and 2: 9–13 and 24–28.

Li Zehou. 1985. *Zhongguo gudai sixiangshi lun* (A critique of Chinese intellectual history). Beijing: Renmin chubanshe.

Lin Yutang. 1978. *Wutu yu wumin* (My country and my people). Taibei: Lin Bai Press.

Link, Perry. 1981. *Mandarin Ducks and Butterflies: Popular Fiction in Early Twentieth-Century Chinese Cities.* Berkeley: University of California Press.

Link, Perry, et al., eds. 1989. *Unofficial China: Popular Culture and Thought in the People's Republic.* Boulder, Colo.: Westview Press.

Lipman, Jonathan N. 1990. "Ethnic Violence in Modern China: Hans and Huis in Gansu, 1781–1929." In *Violence in China: Essays in Culture and Counterculture,* edited by Jonathan N. Lipman and Stevan Harell, 65–86. Albany: State University of New York Press.

Liu Heng. 1988. "Fuxi Fuxi." In *Zhongguo xiaoshuo yi jiu ba ba* (Chinese fiction, 1988), edited by Wang Ziping and Li Tuo, 80–171. Hong Kong: Sanlian Shudian.

Liu Shusheng. 1992. *Zhongguo diwudai dianying* (Chinese Fifth Generation film directors). Beijing: Zhongguo guangbo dianshi chubanshe.

Liu, Wu-chi, and Irving Yucheng Lo, eds. 1975. *Sunflower Splendor: Three Thousand Years of Chinese Poetry.* New York: Anchor/Doubleday.

Long Haiqiu. 1989. "Paihuai dushi: Tan jinqi de chengshe ticai yingpian" (Wandering city: On recent city films). *Yishu guangjiao* 2: 56–61.

Louie, Kam. 1989. *Between Fact and Fiction: Essays on Post-Mao Chinese Literature and Society.* Sidney, Australia: Wild Peony Press.

Lovell, Alan. 1976. "The Western." In *Movies and Methods,* vol. 1, edited by Bill Nichols, 164–75. Berkeley: University of California Press.

———. 1982. "Epic Theater and Counter Cinema's Principles." *Jump Cut* 27: 64–68.

* Lu, Sheldon Hsiao-peng, ed. 1997a. *Transnational Chinese Cinemas: Identity, Nationhood, Gender.* Honolulu: University of Hawaii Press.

———. 1997b. "National Cinema, Cultural Critique, Transnational Capital: The Films of Zhang Yimou." In *Transnational Chinese Cinemas: Identity, Nationhood, Gender,* edited by Sheldon H. Lu, 105–36. Honolulu: University of Hawaii Press.

Lu, Tonglin. 1995. *Misogyny, Cultural Nihilism and Oppositional Politics: Contemporary Chinese Experimental Fiction.* Stanford: Stanford University Press.

Lu Xun. 1956. *Lu Xun Xuanji, I* (Selected works of Lu Xun, I). Beijing: Zhongguo qingnian chubanshe.

———. 1973. "What Happens after Nora Leaves Home?" In *Silent China: Selected Writings of Lu Xun,* translated by Gladys Yang. London: Oxford University Press.

———. 1980. *Selected Works.* Translated by Yang Xianyi and Gladys Yang. 3rd ed. 4 vols. Beijing: Foreign Language Press.

———. 1981. *Lu Xun quan ji* (Complete works of Lu Xun). Beijing: Remin wenxue chubanshe.

Lufkin, Felicity. 1990. *Images of Minorities in the Art of the People's Republic of China.* Master's thesis, University of California, Berkeley.

Lutz, Katherine, and Jane L. Collins. 1993. *Reading National Geographic.* Chicago: University of Chicago Press.

Lynch, Kevin. 1960. *The Image of the City.* Cambridge, Mass.: Technology Press.

Ma Ning. 1987. "Notes on the New Filmmakers." In *Chinese Film: The State of the Art in the People's Republic,* edited by George S. Semsel, 63–93. New York: Praeger.

———. 1989. "The Textual and Critical Difference of Being Radical: Reconstructing Chinese Leftist Films of the 1930s." *Wide Angle* 11.2: 22–31.

* ———. 1994. "Spatiality and Subjectivity in Xie Jin's Film Melodrama of the New Period." In *New Chinese Cinemas: Forms, Identities, Politics,* edited by Nick Browne et al., 15–39. Cambridge: Cambridge University Press.

Mackerras, Colin. 1975. *The Chinese Theatre in Modern Times: From 1840 to the Present Day.* London: Thames and Hudson.

———. 1994. *China's Minorities: Integration and Modernization in the Twentieth Century.* New York: Oxford University Press.

Madsen, Richard. 1984. *Morality and Power in a Chinese Village.* Berkeley: University of California Press.

Mao Zedong. 1967. *The Selected Works of Mao Zedong.* 4 vols. Beijing: Foreign Language Press.

———. 1971. "Talks at the Yenan Forum on Literature and Art." In *Selected Readings from the Works of Mao Zedong,* 250–86. Beijing: Foreign Language Press.

Marchetti, Gina. 1997. *"Two Stage Sisters:* The Blossoming of a Revolutionary Aesthetic." In *Transnational Chinese Cinemas: Identity, Nationhood, Gender,* edited by Sheldon H. Lu, 59–80. Honolulu: University of Hawaii Press.

Marcuse, Herbert. *The Aesthetic Dimension: Toward a Critique of Marxist Aesthetics.* Boston: Beacon Press, 1978.

McConnell, Frank D. 1975. *The Spoken Seen.* Baltimore: Johns Hopkins University Press.

McDougall, Bonnie S., ed. 1984. *Popular Chinese Literature and Performing Arts in the People's Republic of China, 1949–1979.* Berkeley: University of California Press.

Meng Yue. 1993. "Female Images and National Myth." In *Gender Politics in Modern China: Writing and Feminism,* edited by Tani E. Barlow, 118–36. Durham: Duke University Press.

Metz, Christian. 1974. *Language and Cinema.* The Hague: Mouton.

———. 1982. *The Imaginary Signifier: Psychoanalysis and the Cinema.* Bloomington: Indiana University Press.

Minford, John. 1985. "Picking Up the Pieces." *Far Eastern Economic Review* 8: 30.

Mohanty, Chandra Talpade. 1991. "Under Western Eyes: Feminist Scholarship and Colonial Discourses." In *Third World Women and the Politics of Feminism,* edited by Chandra Talpade Mohanty, Ann Russo, and Lourdes Torres. Bloomington: Indiana University Press.

Mulvey, Laura. 1985. "Visual Pleasure and Narrative Cinema." In *Movies and Methods,* edited by Bill Nichols, vol. 2, 303–15. Berkeley: University of California Press.

———. 1989. *Visual and Other Pleasures.* Bloomington: Indiana University Press.

Munro, Donald. 1985. *Individualism and Holism: Studies in Confucian and Taoist Values.* Ann Arbor: University of Michigan, Center for Chinese Studies.

Murray, Edward. 1972. *The Cinematic Imagination: Writers and the Motion Pictures.* New York: Frederick Ungar.

Ono, Kazuko. 1989. *Chinese Women in a Century of Revolution, 1850–1950.* Stanford: Stanford University Press.

Peng Wen. 1990. "*Black Snow*: Estranging City and Paralyzed Subject." *Dianying yishu* 212: 41–46.

Percheron, Daniel. 1980. "Sound in Cinema and Its Relationship to Image and Diegesis." *Yale French Studies* 60: 16–23.

Pickowicz, Paul G. 1974. "Cinema and Revolution in China: Some Interpretive Themes." *American Behavioral Scientist* 17.1–2: 332–35.

———. 1985. "The Limits of Cultural Thaw: Chinese Cinema in the Early 1960s." In *Perspectives on Chinese Cinema,* edited by Chris Berry, 97–148. Ithaca, N.Y.: China-Japan Program, Cornell University.

———. 1989. "Popular Cinema and Political Thought in Post-Mao China: Reflections on Official Pronouncements, Films, and the Film Audience." In *Unofficial China: Popular Culture and Thought in the People's Republic,* edited by Perry Link et al., 37–53. Boulder, Colo: Westview Press.

* ———. 1993. "Melodramatic Representation and the 'May Fourth' Tradition of Chinese Cinema." In *From May Fourth to June Fourth: Fiction and Film in Twentieth-Century China,* edited by Ellen Widmer and David Der-wei Wang, 313–26. Cambridge: Harvard University Press.

* ———. 1994. "Huang Jianxin and the Notion of Post-Socialism." In *New Chinese*

Cinemas: Forms, Identities, Politics, edited by Nick Browne et al., 57–87. Cambridge: Cambridge University Press.

Pines, Jim, and Paul Willemen, eds. 1989. *Questions of Third Cinema.* London: BFI Publishing.

Plaks, Andrew H. 1976. *Archetype and Allegory in "The Dream of the Red Chamber."* Princeton: Princeton University Press.

———. 1977. "Towards a Critical Theory of Chinese Narrative." In *Chinese Narrative: Critical and Theoretical Essays,* edited by Andrew H. Plaks, 309–52. Princeton: Princeton University Press.

Pollock, Griselda, Geoffrey Nowell-Smith, and Stephen Heath. 1977. "Dossier on Melodrama." *Screen* 18.2: 105–19.

Pye, Lucian. 1985. *Asian Power and Politics: The Cultural Dimensions of Authority.* Cambridge: Harvard University Press.

Rayns, Tony. 1980. "An Introduction to the Aesthetics and Politics of Chinese Cinema." In *Electric Shadows: 45 Years of Chinese Cinema,* edited by Scott Meek and Tony Rayns. London: BFI Publishing.

———. 1991. "Breakthroughs and Setbacks: The Origins of the New Chinese Cinema." In *Perspectives on Chinese Cinema,* edited by Chris Berry, 104–13. London: BFI Publishing.

———. 1994. "The Narrow Path: Chen Kaige in Conversation with Tony Rayns." In *Projections 3: Filmmakers on Filmmaking,* edited by John Boorman and Walter Donohue. London: Faber.

Renan, Ernest. 1990. "What Is a Nation?" Translated and annotated by Martin Thom. In *Nation and Narration,* edited by Homi K. Bhabha. New York: Routledge.

Reynaud, Berenice. 1993. "Gong Li and the Glamour of the Chinese Star." *Sight and Sound* 3.8: 12–15.

Ricoeur, Paul. 1970. *Freud and Philosophy: An Essay on Interpretation.* New Haven, Conn.: Yale University Press.

———. 1971. *The Conflict of Interpretations: Essays on Hermeneutics.* Evanston, Ill.: Northwestern University Press.

———. 1976. *Interpretation Theory: Discourse and the Surplus of Meaning.* Fort Worth: Texas Christian University Press.

Rodowick, David. 1987. "Madness, Authority and Ideology: The Domestic Melodrama of the 1950s." In *Home Is Where the Heart Is: Studies in Melodrama and the Woman's Film,* edited by Christine Gledhill, 268–80. London: BFI Publishing.

———. 1988. *The Crisis of Political Modernism: Criticism and Ideology in Contemporary Film Theory.* Urbana: University of Illinois Press.

Rosen, Philip, ed. 1986. *Narrative, Apparatus, Ideology: A Film Theory Reader.* New York: Columbia University Press.

Rowe, Colin, and Fred Koetter. 1978. *Collage City.* Cambridge: MIT Press.

Rushkoff, Douglas. 1994. *The GenX Reader*. New York: Ballantine Books.

Said, Edward W. 1978. *Orientalism*. New York: Random House, 1978.

———. 1983. *The World, the Text, and the Critic*. Cambridge: Harvard University Press.

Sang Zelan. 1994. "Cheng Dieyi—yige quanshi de qidian" (Cheng Dieyi—an explanatory starting point). *Dangdai* 4.1: 54–60.

Saso, Michael R. 1972. *Taoism and the Rite of Cosmic Renewal*. Pullman: Washington State University Press.

* Semsel, George S., ed. 1987. *Chinese Film: The State of the Art in the People's Republic*. New York: Praeger.

* Semsel, George S., et al., eds. 1990. *Chinese Film Theory: A Guide to the New Era*. New York: Praeger.

* ———. 1993. *Film in Contemporary China: Critical Debates, 1979–1989*. Westport: Praeger.

Shen Congwen. 1981. "Hsiao-hsiao." Translated by Eugene Eoyang. In *Modern Chinese Short Stories and Novellas, 1919–1949*, edited by Joseph Lau et al., 227–36. New York: Columbia University Press.

———. 1983. "Xiaoxiao." In *Shen Congwen wenji* (Collected writings of Shen Congwen), vol 6. Sichuan: Huacheng chubanshe.

* Silbergeld, Jerome. 1999. *China into Film: Frames of Reference in Contemporary Chinese Cinema*. London: Reaktion.

Silverman, Kaja. 1983. *The Subject of Semiotics*. New York: Oxford University Press.

———. 1992. *Male Subjectivity at the Margins*. New York: Routledge.

Sklar, Robert. 1993. "Becoming a Part of Life: An Interview with Zhang Yimou." *Cineaste* 20.1: 28–29.

———. 1994. "People and Politics, Simple and Direct: An Interview with Tian Zhuangzhuang." *Cineaste* 20.4: 36–38.

Soja, Edward W. 1989. *Postmodern Geographies: The Reassertion of Space in Critical Social Theory*. London: Verso.

Sontag, Susan. 1966. *Against Interpretation and Other Essays*. New York: Farrar, Strauss and Giroux.

Sorlin, Pierre. 1991. *European Cinemas, European Societies, 1939–1990*. London: Routledge.

Spence, Jonathan D. 1981. *The Gate of Heavenly Peace: The Chinese and Their Revolution—1895–1980*. Middlesex, England: Penguin Books.

Spivak, Gayatri Chakravorty. 1987. *In Other Worlds: Essays in Cultural Politics*. New York: Methuen.

Stacey, Judith. 1983. *Patriarchy and Socialist Revolution in China*. Berkeley: University of California Press.

Studlar, Gaylyn. 1985. "Masochism and the Perverse Pleasures of the Cinema." In *Movies and Methods*, vol. 2, edited by Bill Nichols. Berkeley: University of California Press.

Su Xiaokang and Wang Luxiang. 1989. *Heshang* (River elegy). Hong Kong: Sanlian shu-dian.

Sun Longji. 1983. *Zhongguo wenhua de shen ceng jiegou* (The deep structure of Chinese culture). Hong Kong: Yishen chubanshe.

(SWC) Shanghai wenyi chubanshe, eds. 1987. *Tansuo dianyingji* (A collection of exper-imental films). Shanghai: Shanghai wenyi chubanshe. (This collection contains the shooting scripts of seven films: *One and Eight, Yellow Earth, On the Hunting Ground, At Beach, The Good Women, Sacrificed Youth,* and *Black Cannon Incident.*)

Sypher, Wylie. 1965. "Aesthetic of Revolution: The Marxist Melodrama." In *Tragedy: Vision and Form,* edited by Robert Corrigan, 258–67. Scranton, Penn.: Chandler.

* Tam, Kwok-kan, and Wimal Dissanayake. 1998. *New Chinese Cinema.* Hong Kong: Oxford University Press (China) Ltd.

Tang, Tsou. 1986. *The Cultural Revolution and Post-Mao Reforms: A Historical Perspective.* Chicago: University of Chicago Press.

Tang, Xiaobing, ed. 1993. *Zai jiedu: Dazhong wenyi yu yishi xingtai* (Rereading: The people's literature and art movement and ideology). Hong Kong: Oxford University Press.

———. 1994. "Configuring the Modern Space: Cinematic Representation of Beijing and Its Politics." *East-West Film Journal* 8.2: 47–69.

———. 2000. *Chinese Modern: The Heroic and the Quotidian.* Durham and London: Duke University Press.

Tessier, Max. 1993. "*Farewell to My Concubine:* Art over Politics." *Cinemaya* 20: 16–18.

Thierry, François. 1989. "Empire and Minority in China." In *Minority Peoples in the Age of Nation-States,* edited by Gérard Chaliand, 76–99. London: Pluto Press.

Thurston, Anne F. 1987. *Enemies of the People.* New York: Knopf.

Tian Han. 1983. *Liren xing* (Three women). In *Tian Han wenji* (The collected works of Tian Han), vol. 6, 157–279. Beijing: Zhongguo dianying chubanshe.

Tian Zhuangzhuang. 1989. "Reflections." *Cinemaya* 5: 14–19.

* Tung, Timothy. 1987. "The Work of Xie Jin: A Personal Letter to the Editor." In *Film and Politics in the Third World,* edited by John D. H. Downing. New York: Praeger.

Valk, M. H. Van Der. 1956. *Conservatism in Modern Chinese Family Law.* Leiden, Holland: Brill.

Waley, Arthur. 1988. *The Way and Its Power.* New York: Grove Weidenfeld.

Wang Anyi. 1993. *Jishi yu xugou—Chuangzao shijie fangfa zhi yi zhong* (Documentation and fabrication: One way of creating the world). Beijing: Renmin wenxue chubanshe.

* Wang, Eugene Yuejin. 1988. "The Old Well: A Womb or Tomb? The Double Perspective in Wu Tianming's *Old Well.*" *Framework* 35: 73–82.

———. 1989. "The Cinematic Other and the Cultural Self?: Decentering the Cultural Identity of Cinema." *Wide Angle* 11.2: 32–39.

————. 1991. "*Red Sorghum*: Mixing Memory and Desire." In *Perspectives on Chinese Cinema*, edited by Chris Berry, 80–103. London: BFI Publishing.

Wang, Jing. 1996. *High Culture Fever: Politics, Aesthetics, and Ideology in Deng's China*. Berkeley: University of California Press.

Wang Ziping and Li Tuo, eds. 1989. *Zhongguo xiaoshuo—1988* (Chinese novel—1988). Hong Kong: Sanlian chubanshe.

Watson, James. 1992. "The Renegotiation of Chinese Cultural Identity in the Post-Mao Era: An Anthropological Perspective." In *Popular Protest and Political Culture in Modern China: Learning from 1989*, edited by J. N. Wasserstrom and E. J. Perry. Boulder, Colo.: Westview Press.

Wei Xiaolin. 1990a. "Bianyuan ren: Yizhong xinde yinmu zhurengong xingxiang" (Marginal hero: A new image of the screen protagonist). *Yishu guangjiao* 2: 70–75.

————. 1990b. "The Cognitive Value of *Black Snow*." *Dianying yishu* 212: 47–52.

Widmer, Ellen, and David Der-wei Wang, eds. 1993. *From May Fourth to June Fourth: Fiction and Film in Twentieth-Century China*. Cambridge: Harvard University Press.

Williams, Charles A. S. 1931. *Encyclopaedia of Chinese Symbolism and Art Motifs*. New York: Julian Press.

Williams, Martin. 1980. *Griffith: First Artist of the Movies*. New York and Oxford: Oxford University Press.

Wilson, George M. 1986. *Narration in Light: Studies in Cinematic Point of View*. Baltimore: Johns Hopkins University Press.

Woo, Catherine Yi-yu Cho. 1991. "The Chinese Montage: From Poetry and Painting to the Silver Screen." In *Perspectives on Chinese Cinema*, edited by Chris Berry, 21–29. London: BFI Publishing.

Wu, David Yen-ho. 1991. "The Construction of Chinese and Non-Chinese Identities." *Daedalus: Journal of the American Academy of Arts and Sciences* 120.2: 159–79.

Wu Guanping. 1995. "Gangshou shenghuo" (Experiencing life: An interview with Zhang Nuanxin). *Dianying yishu* 243: 60–67.

Wu Tianming. 1987. "Yuanyu shenghuo de chuangzuo chongdong" (Creative inspiration rooted in life). *Dianying yishu* 185: 3–9.

* Xia Hong. 1993. "The Debate over *Horse Thief*." In *Film in Contemporary China: Critical Debates, 1979–1989*, edited by George S. Semsel et al., 39–49. Westport: Praeger.

Xie Fei. 1990a. "My View of the Concept of Film." In *Chinese Film Theory: A Guide to the New Era*, edited by George S. Semsel et al., 76–84. New York: Praeger.

————. 1990b. "'Di sidai' de zhengming" (The proof of the "Fourth Generation"). *Dianying yishu* 212: 17–29.

Xie Fei and Wu Lan. 1986. "*Xiangnü Xiaoxiao* chuangzuo suixiang" (Random notes about directing *Girl from Hunan*). *Dianying xinzuo* 48: 85–88.

Xie Jin. 1982. "Daoyan chanshu" (Director's notes). In *Wutai Jiemei: Cong tigang dao yingpian* (*Two Stage Sisters:* From a draft to the film), 274–78. Shanghai: Shanghai wenyi chubanshe.

———. 1987. "Pashe *Furong zhen* de shexiang" (Plans and ideas for shooting *Hibiscus Town*). In *Dianying nianjian*, 3.1–3.7. Beijing: Zhongguo dianying chubanshe.

Yang, Mayfair. 1993. "Of Gender, State Censorship, and Overseas Capital: An Interview with Director Zhang Yimou." *Public Culture* 5.2: 297–316.

* Yang Ping. 1991. "A Director Who Is Trying to Change the Audience." In *Perspectives on Chinese Cinema*, edited by Chris Berry, 127–30. London: BFI Publishing.

* Yau, Esther C. M. 1987–88. "*Yellow Earth*: Western Analysis and a Non-Western Text." *Film Quarterly* 41.2: 22–33.

* ———. 1989a. "Cultural and Economic Dislocations: Filmic Phantasies of Chinese Women in the 1980s." *Wide Angle* 11.2: 6–21.

———. 1989b. "Is China the End of Hermeneutics? Or, Political and Cultural Usage of Non-Han Women in Mainland Chinese Films." *Discourse* 11.2: 114–36.

Yuan, Heh-hsiang. 1980. "East-West Comparative Literature: An Inquiry into Possibilities." In *Chinese-Western Comparative Literature: Theory and Strategy*, edited by John Deeney, 1–24. Hong Kong: Hong Kong University Press.

(ZDC) Zhongguo dianying chubanshe, eds. 1962–82. *Zhongguo dianying xuanji* (Selected scripts of Chinese films). 11 vols. Beijing: Zhongguo dianying chubanshe.

(ZDX) Zhongguo dianyingjia xiehui, eds. 1982. *Zhongguo dianyingjia liezhuan* (Biographies of Chinese filmmakers). Vols. 1 and 2. Beijing: Zhongguo dianying chubanshe.

(ZDZ) Zhongguo dianying ziliaoguan and Zhongguo yishu yanjuyuan dianying yanjuisuo, eds. 1981. *Zhongguo yishu yingpian bianmu: 1949–1979* (A catalogue of Chinese artistic films). 2 vols. Beijing: Wenhua yishu chubanshe.

* Zha, Jianying. 1995. *Chinese Pop: How Soap Operas, Tabloids, and Bestsellers are Transforming a Culture*. New York: New Press.

* Zhang, Benzi. 1999. "Figures of Violence and Tropes of Homophobia: Reading *Farewell My Concubine* Between East and West." *Journal of Popular Culture* (Fall): 101–9.

Zhang Dainian. 1982. *Zhongguo zhexue dagang* (An outline of Chinese philosophy). Beijing: Zhongguo shehui kexue chubanshe.

Zhang Manling. 1982. *You yige meilide difang* (There exists a beautiful place). *Dangdai* 3: 128–48.

Zhang Nuanxin. 1985. "*Qingchun ji* daoyan chanshu" (Director's notes of *Sacrificed Youth*). *Dangdai dianying* 4: 134–36.

———. 1990. "The Director's Thematic Exposition of *Good Morning, Beijing*." *Dangdai dianying* 39: 53–54.

Zhang Nuanxin and Li Tuo. 1990. "The Modernization of Film Language." In *Chinese Film Theory: A Guide to the New Era*, edited by George Semsel et al., 10–20. New York: Praeger.

Zhang Wei. 1988. "Guailun diwudai" (Weird commentaries on the Fifth Generation). *Zhongguo dianying bao*, Sept. 25, Oct. 15, Oct. 25, Nov. 15, Dec. 5, Dec. 25.

———. 1990. "Nüxing guishu yu lishi qianyi: *Beijing, ni zao* de yuyanxing chanshi" (The position of the woman and historical transformation: An allegorical interpretation of *Good Morning, Beijing*). *Dangdai dianying* 39: 55–60.

Zhang, Xudong. 1997. *Chinese Modernism in the Era of Reforms*. Durham and London: Duke University Press.

Zhang Yimou. 1996. "Wei zhongguo dianying zouxiang shijie pulu" (Pave a path for Chinese film to reach the world). In *Zhang Yimou: Wei yi mou, bu wei daoliang mou* (Zhang Yimou: For arts, not for profit), edited by Han Xiufeng and Xiao Hai, 385–412. Changsha: Hunan wenyi chubanshe.

* Zhang, Yingjin. 1990. "Ideology of the Body in *Red Sorghum*: National Allegory, National Roots, and Third Cinema." *East-West Film Journal* 4.2: 38–53.

* ———. 1996. *The City in Modern Chinese Literature and Film: Configuration of Space, Time, and Gender*. Stanford: Stanford University Press.

* ———. 1997. "From 'Minority Film' to 'Minority Discourse': Questions of Nationhood and Ethnicity in Chinese Cinema." In *Transnational Chinese Cinemas: Identity, Nationhood, Gender*, edited by Sheldon H. Lu, 81–104. Honolulu: University of Hawaii Press.

———, ed. 1999. *Cinema and Urban Culture in Shanghai, 1922–1943*. Stanford: Stanford University Press.

* Zhang, Yingjin, et al., eds. 1998. *Encyclopedia of Chinese Film*. London and New York: Routledge.

Zhang Ziliang and Zhu Zi, eds. 1989. *Huang Jianxin xin zuopinji* (New works by Huang Jianxin). Xi'an: Huayue wenyi chubanshe.

Zhao Liming. 1992. *Zhongguo nüshu jicheng: Yi zhong qite de nüxing wenzi ziliao zonghui* (Encyclopedia of Chinese women's writing: A compendium of materials on a unique form of women's writing). Beijing: Qinghua daxue chubanshe.

Zhao Yuan. 1985. "Zai lishi wenhua de shenceng" (In the deep stratum of history and culture). *Dangdai dianying* 5: 24–28.

Zheng Yi. 1988. *Lao jing* (Old well). Taipei: Haifeng chubanshe.

———. 1989. *Old Well*. Translated by David Kwan with an introduction by Anthony P. Kane. San Francisco: China Books and Periodicals.

Zhou Youzhao. 1988. "Zhang Yimou Tan *Hong gaoliang*" (An interview with Zhang Yimou on *Red Sorghum*). *Daxibei dianying* 4: 11–14.

Žižek, Slavoj. 1989. *The Sublime Object of Ideology*. London: Verso.

Index

Harry H. Kuoshu, a.k.a. Haixin Xu, is an assistant professor of cinema studies and modern languages at Northeastern University, where he teaches Chinese film, culture, and language. He received his Ph.D. from Cornell University. In addition to articles on cinema and Chinese studies in professional journals, he is the author of *Lightness of Being in China: Adaptation and Discursive Figuration in Cinema and Theater* (1999).